Religion and Law in Austria

Religion and Law in Austria

Second Edition

Richard Potz

Brigitte Schinkele

This book was originally published as a monograph in the International Encyclopaedia of Laws/Religion Law.

Founding Editor: Roger Blanpain
General Editor: Frank Hendrickx
Volume Editor: Wouter Druwé

Wolters Kluwer

Published by:
Kluwer Law International B.V.
PO Box 316
2400 AH Alphen aan den Rijn
The Netherlands
E-mail: lrs-sales@wolterskluwer.com
Website: www.wolterskluwer.com/en/solutions/kluwerlawinternational

Sold and distributed by:
Wolters Kluwer Legal & Regulatory U.S.
920 Links Avenue
Landisville, PA 17538
United States of America
E-mail: customer.service@wolterskluwer.com

ISBN 978-94-035-1299-0

e-Book: ISBN 978-94-035-1309-6
web-PDF: ISBN 978-94-035-1319-5

The Authors

Richard Potz is Professor Emeritus of Canon and Ecclesiastical Law at the Law Faculty of the University of Vienna and was head of the *Department of Legal Philosophy, Law of Religion and Culture* from 2005 to 2013. He held the post of lecturer at the *Theologische Hochschule Benedikt XVI* in Heiligenkreuz from 1978 to 2011 and at the *Islamic Pedagogical Academy* in Vienna from 2001 to 2014. From 2004 to 2022, he was head of the Postgraduate Course *Canon Law for Lawyers.*

From 1983 to 2006, he was Vice-President of the *International Society for the Law of the Eastern Churches* and its President from 2007 to 2011 and a member of the *Pontificia Commissio Codici Iuris Canonici Orientalis Recognoscendo.* From 1993 to 2008, he was a member of the steering committee of the *Vienna International Christian-Islamic Round Table* and a permanent participant at the *Iranic-Austrian Theology-Law Conference.* In addition, from 1998 to 2015, he was the Austrian member of the *European Consortium for State and Church Research* and a founding member of the interdisciplinary research platform of the University of Vienna on *Religion and Transformation in Contemporary European Society.* Presently, he serves on the executive board of the Research Centre for *Religion and Transformation in Contemporary Society.*

He is co-author of *Österreichisches Religionsrecht* (2003), *Muslime in Österreich* (2012), *Orthodoxes Kirchenrecht* (2nd edition 2014) and *Grundriss Religionsrecht* (2024); co-editor of the periodical *Österreichisches Archiv für Recht und Religion (oearr)* and – until 2016 – of *Kanon – Yearbook of the Society of the Law for the Eastern Churches.*

The Authors

Brigitte Schinkele is Honorary Professor of Law and Religion at the Law Faculty of the University of Vienna (Department of Legal Philosophy, formerly Department of Legal Philosophy and Law of Religion and Culture) and was a member of the teaching staff of the Postgraduate Course Canon Law for Lawyers. Her research focuses on Austrian, European and comparative law on religion, fundamental rights and interaction between State and Church legal order.

She is co-editor of the *Österreichisches Archiv für Recht und Religion; Kirche und Arbeitsrecht* (1996), and *Recht – Religion – Kultur, Festschrift für Richard Potz zum 70. Geburtstag* (2014), co-author of the handbook *Religionsrecht* (2003), *Das Kreuz in Klassenzimmer und Gerichtssaal* (1996), *Religionsgemeinschaftenrecht. Anerkennung und Eintragung* (1998), *Grundriss Religionsrecht*(2024), and author of many articles on Austrian, European and comparative law on religion, dealing extensively with anti-discrimination law and the case law of the European Court and the European Court of Human Rights.

Table of Contents

List of Abbreviations

AAS	*Acta Apostolicae Sedis* (Acts of the Apostolic See)
AB	*Ausschussbericht* (Report of the Committee of the National Council)
ABl	*Amtsblatt* (Official Gazette)
Appl.	Application
BAG	*Bundesarbeitsgericht* (German Federal Labour Court)
Beil StenProt	*Beilagen zu den Stenographischen Protokollen des Abgeordnetenhauses* (Supplements to the Stenographic Protocols of the House of Representatives)
BGBl.	*Bundesgesetzblatt* (Federal Law Gazette)
BlgNR	*Beilagen zu den Stenographischen Protokollen des Nationalrats* (Supplements to the Stenographic Protocols of the National Council)
BM	*Bundesministerium* (Federal Ministry)
BVerfG	*Bundesverfassungsgericht* (German Federal Constitutional Court)
BVerfGE	*Entscheidungen des Bundesverfassungsgerichts* (Decisions of the German Federal Constitutional Court)
Cf.	Confer
ECJ	European Court of Justice
ECR	Records of the European Court of Justice
ECtHR	European Court of Human Rights
GP	*Gesetzgebungsperiode* (Legislative Period)
Ibid.	Ibidem
Ktn	*Kärnten* (Carinthia)
LG	*Landesgericht* (Regional Court)
LGBl.	*Landesgesetzblatt* (Law Gazette of a *Bundesland*)
no.	Number
NÖ	*Niederösterreich* (Lower Austria)

List of Abbreviations

NR	*Nationalrat* (National Council)
ÖBK	*Österreichische Bischofskonferenz* (Austrian Bishops' Conference)
OGH	*Oberster Gerichtshof* (Supreme Court)
OÖ	*Oberösterreich* (Upper Austria)
RV	*Regierungsvorlage* (Government Bill)
Rz	*Randziffer* (Margin note)
StGBl.	*Staatsgesetzblatt* (State Law Gazette)
Stmk	*Steiermark* (Styria)
VfGH	*Verfassungsgerichtshof* (Constitutional Court)
VfSlg.	*Entscheidungssammlung des Verfassungsgerichtshofs* (Decisions of the Constitutional Court)
VGW	*Verwaltungsgericht Wien* (Administrative Court Vienna)
VVDStRL	*Veröffentlichungen der Vereinigung der Deutschen Staatsrechtslehrer*
VwGH	*Verwaltungsgerichtshof* (High Administrative Court)
VwSlg.	*Entscheidungssammlung des Verwaltungsgerichtshof* (Decisions of the High Administrative Court)
Zl	*Zahl* (number)

Preface

It is a characteristic of the law on religion that it seems predestined to discuss fundamental questions of the liberal democratic state ruled by law, such as neutrality, equality, pluralism and tolerance in a paradigmatic manner. The historically grown structures of the state-church relationship must be embedded into significantly changed circumstances. This requires a re-definition of relevant legal structures, without being thrown overboard. The comprehensive human right of freedom of religion and belief implies a modified systematic conception of the interaction between the state and the religious communities, including a new specification of the subject matter of the public law status of legally recognized churches and religious societies. This conception must be based primarily on the cultural and social functions of the modern state integrated into a substantive understanding of fundamental rights. Thus, traditional privileges of churches and religious societies must currently be legitimized on reasonable and objective grounds.

Such developments have taken place along with an essential change in the legal dogmatic approach to the interpretation of fundamental rights, as is clearly reflected in judicial practice and scientific doctrine, strongly influenced by European case law. Since the early 1980s, the Constitutional Court has departed from its general attitude of 'judicial self-restraint' in its decision-making process, replacing this with a more evolutionary and progressive approach and thus a certain degree of 'judicial self-activism'.

Viewed against this background, for approximately thirty years, the term *Religionsrecht* as opposed to *Staatskirchenrecht* has become more and more established in Austria. Without overestimating this aspect, the use of this term expresses a particular fundamental attitude. Therefore, it is of certain programmatic relevance, especially with regard to specific principles of interpretation and a corresponding legal dogmatic approach. Whenever political authorities refer to churches and religious societies in the context of their legislative and promoting functions, they should be aware that they are primarily referring to the religious interests of the individual adherents.

Altogether, our description of the Austrian law on religion has been based on the fundamental position as set out above, following the basic structure outlined by the editor.

General Introduction

§1. General Background of the Country

I. Basic Structures

1. The Austrian constitutional system is based on a number of basic constitutional principles. A substantial alteration of any of these would be considered a total revision (Gesamtänderung) of the Federal Constitution (B-VG). In this case, the constitutional amendment would have to be approved by a popular referendum according to Article 44 section 3 B-VG.

2. Three principles are explicitly mentioned in Articles 1 and 2 B-VG:

(a) The democratic principle: According to Article 1 B-VG, Austria is a democratic Republic in which the law emanates from the people. In principle, the whole system rests on indirect democracy, combined with the guarantee of a pluralistic system of political parties by constitutional law and completed by some procedures of direct democracy, such as popular initiative, public consultation and referendum.
(b) The republican principle: It has rather minor positive content in present-day Austria but should be understood in its historical context. It simply rejects the previous political system of a constitutional monarchy.
(c) The federal principle: According to Article 2 B-VG, Austria is a federal state consisting of nine federal member states (Bundesländer). Legislative and executive power is divided between the Federation and the Federal States, and the Federal States cooperate in the legislation of the Federation by means of an institution similar to a second house of Parliament, the Federal Council (Bundesrat).

3. According to the doctrine, another three principles are implicitly contained in the Constitution: (i) the rule of law, according to which all state actions must have a legal basis and the judiciary must be independent; (ii) the principle of separation of power; and (iii) the liberal principle guaranteeing a system of fundamental rights and freedom.

4. Furthermore, in federal constitutional law, a number of state objectives and constitutional mandates are included to obligate the legislation and other state institutions to a corresponding action. This comprises the maintenance of a differentiated school system and the compliance with the comprehensive educational goals of the Austrian school also involving the religious dimension (Article 14 Section 5a B-VG).

5. Although there is no explicit social state clause, standards of labour and social welfare law are de facto treated as fundamental laws in Austria. Further structural principles are implicitly contained in the constitution, such as religious neutrality and a commitment to the idea that the state must support culture, which is of special importance because Austria is often identified by its emphasis on its cultural traditions.

6. There is also a traditional system of 'social partnership' (*Sozialpartnerschaft*), which for many years has formed a 'side government' of employers' and employees' associations. In 2008, the role of the social partnership was acknowledged on a constitutional level (Article 120a B-VG). The system of social partnership is also mainly responsible for the dominating concept of social market economy.

II. General Legal System

7. Austrian constitutional law is exclusively written law, but it is not codified in a single document. After the fall of the Habsburg Monarchy, the Federal Constitution of the Austrian Republic of 1920 brought about a significant constitutional change. Due to the failure of an agreement on a new catalogue of fundamental rights, the Constitutional Act on the Fundamental Rights of Citizens 1867 (StGG) was incorporated in the B-VG. Some articles of the Treaty of St. Germain 1919 (StVStGermain)[1] were also adopted. They extended the right to free exercise of faith, religion or denomination of every kind in public as well as in private to every inhabitant in Austria, thus also to the adherents of non-recognized religious communities insofar as this exercise was not incompatible with public order or morality.

8. It is specific to Austrian law that any legislation may be designated as a constitutional provision by a two-thirds majority of the National Council. Therefore, one can find 'constitutional law' out with the Constitution in many places spread over the whole legal order.

9. Constitutional law takes precedence over all other national laws according to the theory of the hierarchy of norms (Stufenbau der Rechtsordnung). The general rules of international law are automatically part of Austrian law (Article 9 Section 1 B-VG). International treaties must be transformed in a general or specific way into Austrian legislation. The law of the European Union has precedence over the Austrian Constitution as long as it does not contradict the fundamental principles contained therein.

---

1. Chapter V, Part III (Protection of Minorities) of the Treaty of St. Germain has been incorporated into the Federal Constitution (Article 149 B-VG 1920).

§2. SOCIAL FACTS ABOUT RELIGION

I. Religious Affiliation

10. After the Second World War, the confessional structure of Austria changed significantly. The Catholic majority decreased continually (from 89% in 1951 to 73.7% in 2001). As a result of their expulsion and extermination in the Shoah, the important Jewish minority (2.8% before 1938) was reduced to 0.1% by 2001, recently increasing again due to immigration from some successor states of the former Soviet Union. The Protestant minority increased after 1945 with the stream of German refugees (from 4.3% to 6.5% after 1945) but decreased to 4.7% in 2001. Since the 1960s, the number of Muslims has increased (rising from 1% in 1971 to 4.3% in 2001). In 2001, the last census in the traditional form of a questionnaire including religious affiliation was held. It was replaced in 2006 by register censuses, which are based on a combination of existing statistics and do not contain questions about the religious affiliation of the population.

11. In 2021, Statistics Austria conducted a voluntary survey on behalf of the Federal Chancellery on the 'Religious Affiliation of the Population in Private Households' as part of the 'Microcensus Labour Force Survey':

> Question 1 – 'What religion do you belong to?' with the following response categories:
>
> (1) Buddhism 0.3 %
> (2) Christianity 68.2 %
> (3) Hinduism 0.1 %
> (4) Islam 8.3 %
> (5) Judaism 0.1 %
> (6) Other 0.6 %
> (7) No Religion 22.4 %
> Question 2 – 'Are you a member of any church or religious society listed here? If so, please state the number listed on the card.'

	Microcensus of 2021
Total	8,932,664[2]
Roman Catholic (%)	55.2
Old-Catholic (%)	0.1
Eastern-Orthodox (%)	4.9
Oriental-Orthodox (%)	0.15
Protestant (Lutheran and Reformed) (%)	3.8
Methodist (%)	>0.05

2. On 1 Jul. 2023, the Austrian population was 9,129,652.

	Microcensus of 2021
New-Apostolic (%)	>0.05
Mormons (%)	>0.05
Jehovah's Witnesses (%)	0.2
Free Churches in Austria (%)	0.4
Israelite Religious Society in Austria (%)	0.1
Islamic Religious Society in Austria (IGGÖ) (%)	6.5
Buddhist Religious Society in Austria (%)	0.1
(Islamic) Alevite Religious Society in Austria (ALEVI) (%)	0.2
No religious affiliation (%)	22.4

II. Religious Practice

12. In the last three decades, religiousness in Austria suffered a dramatic decrease. According to an annual self-assessment survey held in 1999, 75% still considered themselves 'religious', 18% 'not religious' and 2% 'atheist'. In 2008, 61% described themselves as 'religious', 30% declared they were 'not religious', 4% considered themselves 'convinced atheists' and 5% said they simply 'did not know'. In 2022, 35% regarded themselves as 'religious', 38% as 'non-religious', 13% as 'convinced atheists' and 9% as 'did not know'. The decline is primarily due to the erosion processes among younger Austrians (under 30 years), resulting in a decrease in the proportion of those assessing themselves as 'religious' from 66% (1999) to 29% (2022).[3]

§3. Historical Background

I. Impact of History

13. In every European country, we can find different historical preconditions which have determined the system of church and state until the present day.[4] In the case of Austria, the following conditions are of crucial significance: the dominance of Catholicism for centuries; its geopolitical position in the centre of Europe, which created a multi-confessional society in earlier times, and traditional relations to eastern and south-eastern Europe, and last but not least, the dramatic experience with a totalitarian regime in the twentieth century.

3. We would like to thank Regina Polak for providing the figures. For further details and European comparisons cf. 'Werte - Zoom (werteforschung.at)'.
4. Cf. M. Liebmann, P. Tropper, G. Scheibelreiter & R. Leeb, *Geschichte des Christentums in Österreich: Von der Spätantike bis zu Gegenwart* (Vienna: Ueberreuter, 2003); A. Lichtblau, B. Staudinger, C. Lind, M. Keil & E. Brugger, *Geschichte der Juden in Österreich* (Vienna: Ueberreuter, 2006). Both volumes contain extensive references to the literature.

14. Since the tenth century, Austria was part of the Holy Roman Empire of the German Nation and organized as a bulwark against invasions from the southeast. In 1156, Austria became a Duchy, which, in 1282, was handed over to the Habsburgs. After 1526, the Habsburgs added Bohemia and Hungary to their territories and established a monarchical union of the Eastern Alpine, Danubian and Carpathian regions which had, *inter alia*, the aim of defending Europe against the Ottoman Turks. From the fifteenth century, members of the Habsburg dynasty ruled the Holy Roman Empire with brief intermissions until its end in 1806.

15. Austria differed from other Western and Central European territories in that from the very beginning, the emancipation of religious minorities was not a question of a bi-denominational but a multi-denominational system. Apart from Protestants, there were considerable Orthodox and Jewish minorities. Until the end of the monarchy, Protestants ranked demographically only fifth among confessional denominations.

16. During the last decades of increasing religious pluralism, the existing legal basis dating back to the multi-confessional Habsburg Monarchy could be utilized in particular for Islam and Orthodoxy. In both cases, it was easier in Austria than in other states to provide adequate special legal forms for these religions with a dominating migratory background.

II. The Middle Ages

17. In the Middle Ages, Austria as a part of the Holy Roman Empire, and the Duke of Austria as prince of the Empire, respectively, were involved in the conflict between Pope and Emperor, which in the course of the thirteenth century finally resulted in the decline of both powers. As a consequence, the fourteenth century not only strengthened the regional territories of the Empire but also the position of the regional princes in relation to the Church. In Austria, a large and relatively uniform territory on the south-eastern border of the Holy Empire with some special privileges, the Duke – and later on Archduke – was in a particularly powerful position with respect to ecclesiastical matters. In the fourteenth century, Duke Rudolf IV (1358–1365) in particular exercised strong control over ecclesiastical affairs.

18. According to an account from Jewish merchants in a source dating from the beginning of the tenth century, the oldest Jewish settlements in Austria were found in the eleventh century and in Vienna in particular in the twelfth century. The Jewish communities were given the usual medieval privileges and subjected to taxes, but, in 1420, the situation came to a head with the expulsion of poor Jews, the confiscation of Jewish property, and finally, the mass execution of the remaining Jews in Vienna (Viennese Geserah), following the accusation of the 'secretion of consecrated wafers'.

III. Reformation and Counter-Reformation

19. Initially, the Reformation found organizational support from the estates of the nobility and from the urban bourgeoisie in most Austrian provinces. The nobility used their right to present candidates for the parishes by appointing Lutheran preachers. Consequently, the confession issue was linked to the conflict between the prince regnant and the provincial estates, which negotiated religious concessions for tax grants.

20. In the second half of the sixteenth century, the Catholic side was reorganized under the leadership of the Habsburg princes and Austria became a centre of the Counter-Reformation. Gradually the 'religious concessions' were eliminated and an era of violent re-Catholicization began. Protestantism was monitored and persecuted by means of the developing absolutist state and driven into the underground (Kryptoprotestantismus).

21. Even after the Peace of Westphalia in 1648, the unity of the Catholic faith was maintained in the Habsburg hereditary lands, with the exception of Silesia. Article V of the treaty was interpreted by the Habsburgs to mean that they could still practice their *ius reformandi* in an unlimited manner within their domain with the exception of Silesia where thc Protestant minority was tolerated. At the same time, the Habsburgs also used religious quarrels to expand their dominion over the Catholic Church. Religious commissions were appointed to track down secret Protestants with the help of 'heretics police'. Still during the reign of Maria Theresia, forced relocations to Hungarian territories (Transylvania, Banat) – so-called transmigration – in many cases resulted in ruthless family separations. An official Consistory, which stood at the beginning of the Protestant institutions in Austria, was only set up for the regionally tolerated Protestants in Silesia.

22. The institution of Hofbefreite Juden existed since 1571. These were wealthy Jewish families who were allowed to stay in Vienna on the basis of sovereign privileges. They had mainly been in the Thirty Years' War, had been donors or army suppliers and were in charge of the coinage. In 1624, the Vienna ghetto with a far-reaching autonomy was established in what today is Vienna's Second District. The history of the ghettos ended in 1670 with the expulsion of the Jews from Lower Austria and Vienna. During Maria Theresia's reign, tolerance provisions for Jews were adopted in some parts of the Monarchy for economic reasons. Although the Regulations for Jews (Judenordnungen) were connected with a number of discriminations in everyday life, the wave of absolutist legal codifications thereby also reached the Jewish communities.

23. In the wake of the expansion of the Habsburg Empire after the defeat of the Turks before Vienna in 1683, Leopold I issued a proclamation to the Christian population of the Balkans. As a result, approximately 100,000 people of predominantly Serb nationality emigrated to the Habsburg Empire in 1690/91. The Serbian Patriarch of Peć, Arsenije III, had succeeded in preliminary negotiations for guarantees regarding the self-administration of his people under spiritual leadership, as had been developed in the Ottoman Empire on the basis of Islamic law. The territory was called 'Military Border' (*Militärgrenze*, in Serbo-Croatian: *Vojna Krajina*) and was a separate Habsburg administrative unit, directly subordinated to the Hofkommission for Illyrian affairs in Vienna. In 1770, according to the concept of the enlightened absolutist state, the administration of the 'Illyrian nation' was the subject of special 'regulamenta' which brought about the partial abolishment of the old privileges and gradually involved the Orthodox population in the civil society. The Military Border was a separate administrative unit, until 1881.

24. In the peace of Passarowitz/Pozarevac in 1718, all Ottoman subjects were granted freedom of trade and the right to establish commercial offices and factories in the Habsburg territory. Thus, the domestic exercise of religion for Muslims was guaranteed.

IV. Enlightened Absolutism – Josephinism

25. Josephinism is the Austrian variety of enlightened absolutism, named after the reform programme of Emperor Joseph II (1780–1790). Unlike Maria Theresia, Joseph II carried out innovations with great political haste and without considering the conservative attitude of the majority of the population. In addition to social improvements, his reforms of the administrative and financial systems, private and criminal law as well as the school system contributed significantly to the modernization of the Habsburg monarchy.

26. In a strict sense, Josephinism is considered a concept of reforms of the Church. The roots of this Josephinism are manifold. They include European anticurial movements (Gallicanism, Jansenism, Febronianism), in combination with the concept of an absolutistic state church with a strong economic component. Therefore, measures were adopted to counter excessive forms of baroque piety (restriction of the pilgrimage system, abolition of fraternities, closure of contemplative monasteries, reduction of holidays etc.). Moreover, the implementation of parish and diocesan regulations was organized not at least because ecclesiastical institutions were used to further the information policies of the state.

27. Religious policy further included measures which benefitted other religious communities. Of particular importance here were the laws on tolerance (especially the Toleranzpatent of 1781), although the Catholic Church maintained a prime position as the 'dominant religion' with the exclusive right of public worship. Both Protestant Churches were given the right of private worship (Privatexerzitium) and permission to build – although architecturally limited – houses of prayer and schools, provided that at least 100 Protestant families lived in the neighbourhood. In 1782, the Consistory in Teschen was reorganized. Its members from then on were Protestants, only the chairman as the representative of the sovereign had to be Catholic. In 1784, the Lutheran Consistory of Teschen was transferred to Vienna and shortly afterwards a Consistory for the Helvetian Confession was founded. However, both Consistories had a common Catholic chairman.

28. Besides the Protestants, considerable Orthodox and Jewish minorities existed – until the end of the monarchy Protestants ranked demographically only fifth among the confessional denominations. For this reason, the Toleranzpatent of Joseph II was put into force not only regarding Protestants but also the Orthodox minority. At the same time, Patents for the Jewish communities (Judenpatente) and a special act (Handschreiben) for the Armenians and for other groups such as Mennonites and the Russian Raskolniki in Galicia and Bukovina were enacted. In the Josephinian Age, therefore, apart from the dominant Catholic Church, there existed various 'tolerated' communities, with different legal foundations.

29. The economic aspect played a significant role within the framework of the Josephinian tolerance policy toward the Jews. In 1784, Jews were placed under general jurisdiction. Thus, the time of the expulsions was principally over, and the process of inclusion of the 'Jewish nation' as having equal status in civil society began. Nevertheless, in 1792, the Judenamt (Jewish Office) was established and existed up to 1848. This Office continued to place the Austrian Jewry under a special law with private law and public legal restrictions.

V. Revolution, Restoration and Constitutionalism

30. The result of the Revolution of 1848 was the installation, step by step, of a new system of state and church relationship. Thus, on the basis of the formal break with the tradition of Josephinism and the Catholic Staatskirchentum, a new religious-political system was initiated.[5]

31. The Catholic Church was ambivalent to the revolutionary events. On the one hand, these were seen as an opportunity to overcome the Josephine ties to the state, but on the other hand, the Church was faced with increasing liberal anti-clerical criticism. The Episcopal Assembly in 1849 called for a reduction of state control and, in this, it was partly successful; some of its demands were met in Regulations of April 1850, for instance, freedom of correspondence between the Roman Curia and the bishops, clergy and laity as well as the cancellation of the placetum regium and the introduction of the canonical mission for religious teachers and professors of theology.

32. By a decree of 1849, the legal status of the Protestants was improved in some points compared with the Toleranzpatent of 1781. Among other things, it effected the removal of the discriminatory term 'Non-Catholics' and the introduction of an independent Protestant civil status register, kept by the pastors. In 1860, a Protestant department was established at the Ministry of Cultus. From that year on, the Protestant Church received government grants.

---

5. For the period from 1848 to 1918 cf. in particular *Die Habsburgermonarchie 1848-1918*, vol. 4, 2nd ed., eds. A. Wandruszka & P. Urbanitsch (Vienna: Verlag der Österreichischen Akademie der Wissenschaften, 1985), with extensive references to the literature.

33. In 1848, all discriminatory restrictions for Jews also ceased to apply, and the Israelite Religious Community joined the newly created status of public law corporations for churches and religious societies.

34. In 1851, the revolutionary period finally came to an end and the Austrian Concordat of 1855 must be seen as an attempt to promote the anti-revolutionary neo-absolutistic system with the help of an 'alliance between throne and altar'. After 1848, Catholicism, 'as a system of limited freedoms with a supranational pattern of identification', offered 'the appropriate ideological basis for a post- and anti-revolutionary new structuring of the Austrian Monarchy'.[6] In this Concordat, the Catholic Church secured far-reaching privileges in the fields of matrimonial law and schooling. Article 1 guaranteed for the 'Holy Roman Catholic religion' that all powers and privileges which she enjoys according to divine order and the provisions of the laws of the Church should be maintained forever.

35. According to Article V of the Concordat, the entire teaching of Catholic youth was subject to episcopal supervision, ensuring that nothing could be taught in any subject which was contrary to the Catholic faith and morals. Article XIII provided that all elementary school teachers were placed under ecclesiastical control. For Catholics, canon matrimonial law and ecclesiastical jurisdiction in matrimonial cases were reintroduced (Article X). Regarding the state's authority, the imperial right of nomination to bishoprics (Article XIX) and the oath of allegiance to the Emperor were confirmed (Article XX).

36. Austria's defeat in the war against Italy and France in 1859 and the economic plight of the state forced a transition to a constitutional system, which was initiated with the Oktober-Diplom of 1860 and the Februar-Patent of 1861.

37. With the Constitutional Act on the Fundamental Rights of Citizens (StGG), a part of the so-called Dezemberverfassung of 1867, an important initial step towards a denominationally neutral system in ecclesiastical matters was taken. Article 15 StGG conferred certain rights to all legally recognized churches and religious societies. Therefore, since 1867 the Austrian legal order has been characterized by a strict differentiation between the position of the legally recognized churches and religious societies on the one hand and those which do not enjoy public law status on the other hand. Likewise, as far as the individual element of religious freedom was concerned, the right to manifest one's religion in public was only conferred – indirectly – upon the members of the first-mentioned group, whereas the followers of other religious communities were restricted to domestic and private practice of their convictions, respectively.

6. H. Rumpler, *Österreichische Geschichte 1804-1914: Eine Chance für Mitteleuropa: Bürgerliche Emanzipation und Staatsverfall in der Habsburgermonarchie* (Vienna: Ueberreuter, 1997), 343.

38. With the re-establishment of parliamentarism in 1860, the political struggle of the liberals against the Concordat began. With the StGG 1867 and its concept of religious neutrality, some regulations of the Concordat had become unconstitutional.

39. With the emergence of political parties 'de-confessionalization' was overshadowed by a 're-confessionalization', which became an element in the programme of the Christian-social Party (Christlich-soziale Partei) from the second half of the nineteenth century, leading to a kind of 'second confessional age'. Catholicism remained a powerful factor represented in both Houses of the Imperial Parliament and in state administration. The Christian-social Party was able to draw on a personal reservoir, including not only the episcopate and clergy but also the wide range of Catholic associations. Only for a relatively short time did the Austrian legislation show elements of a 'cultural struggle' (*Kulturkampf*) by implementing the constitution of 1867. The first summit can be seen in the three so-called Maigesetze (May Laws) of 1868. A Marriage Act replaced the provisions of the Concordat and subjugated the marriage of Catholics again to the – denominationally aligned – civil law and state jurisdiction. The Act on School-Church-Affairs (Schule-Kirche-Gesetz) transferred the supreme supervision of teaching and education to the state and its organs. Only the supervision of religious instruction remained with the churches and religious societies. The Act on Inter-confessional Relations (InterkonfG) repealed all legal regulations that contradicted the principle of the equality of legally recognized religious communities. For the first time in Austria, a law provided in a general form for the withdrawal from the membership of a religious community with effect on the state sphere.

40. After the May laws of 1868, the Concordat – albeit eroded in the core – remained in force. As a result of the declaration of infallibility at the first Vatican Council, anti-papal resentment was strengthened. After the refusal of the Holy See to enter into negotiations for a revision of the Concordat, Austria declared the Concordat invalid in 1870 with reference to the clausula rebus sic stantibus. It was argued that the partner of the contract had changed with the declaration of papal infallibility. Even the Emperor agreed to the abolition of the Concordat due to his disappointment about the 'unfortunate' declaration of infallibility.

41. Four years later, the Act on External Relationships of the Catholic Church (KatholikenG) was enacted, which formally derogated the Concordat. This law imposed restrictions on the Catholic Church so that its legal position was more comparable to that of the other churches and religious societies according to their special laws. The occupation of church offices came under state control (§8), ecclesiastical decrees were subjected to state censorship (§16) and even the opportunity to intervene in matters of worship was created. A great part of the provisions dealt with the ecclesiastical property law (§§38–59), the administration of which was placed under state supervision. However, due to the rather conservative pro-Catholic administration, the KatholikenG was executed in a friendly manner. The projects planned for an amendment to matrimonial law allowing the remarriage of

Catholics who had left the Church and for a liberal law on the legal status of monastic communities were not realized because the House of Lords and the Emperor refused to agree.

42. The Protestants Patent (Protestantenpatent) of 1861, in accordance with the guarantees of fundamental rights, included the right to common public worship, to ordering and managing independently the internal affairs of the Church, the freedom to build churches and schools, and to rename the Consistory in the Evangelical Supreme Ecclesiastical Council (Evangelischer Oberkirchenrat). However, its members were appointed by the Emperor and the laws of the Church had still to be confirmed by the Emperor.

43. The term 'Non-Uniates' by which the tolerated Eastern-Orthodox Churches were distinguished from the fully recognized Catholic Eastern Churches was abandoned as discriminatory in 1849. Consequently, the Orthodox communities were included in the circle of recognized churches and several independent Orthodox Church organizations were established within the Habsburg monarchy. For the Austrian half of the Empire, this was the Metropolis of Bukovina and Dalmatia with its seat in Czernowitz, in which the Viennese Greco-Oriental Churches and the Serbian Greek-Oriental Church Community of St. Sava in Vienna established in 1893 were integrated.

44. Article 15 StGG does not contain any details concerning either the preconditions of recognition of religious communities or the rules of the procedure to be followed. Therefore, the Law on Legal Recognition of Religious Communities was enacted in 1874 (AnerkennungsG) and is still in force. According to §1 leg cit, adherents of a hitherto not legally recognized faith are granted recognition as a religious community provided that the following conditions are met: first, that their religious doctrine, forms of worship, constitution and chosen name contain nothing illegal or immoral; and second, that the establishment and the continuous existence of a religious community, fulfilling at least the requirements of this law, is ensured. At the time of the monarchy, the legal recognition of the Old-Catholic Church 1877 and the Moravian Church (Herrnhuter-Brüderkirche) 1880 took place according to the AnerkennungsG.

45. The AnerkennungsG came into force for new religious communities and was, in principle, not directly applicable to churches and religious societies already recognized. That is, the reason that the development of the ecclesiastical law concerning the churches and religious societies which were 'historically recognized' in 1874 was ensured by way of special legislation. However, the High Administrative Court declared that the standards of the AnerkennungsG were applicable to those historically recognized religious communities in an analogous way.[7]

---

7. VwGH 22 May 1964, 1111/63.

46. By the Act of 21 March 1890 on External Legal Relationships of the Israelite Religious Society (IsraelitenG), the legal status of the Jewish Religious Community in Austria was for the first time regulated in a comprehensive manner. According to its time of origin, this law was determined by a number of state supervision rights which had gradually become obsolete. It was in force up to 2012 when it was replaced by a total revision (cf. 330 et seq.).

47. With the occupation of Bosnia and Herzegovina in 1878, the Austro-Hungarian administration was confronted with a Muslim population. After considerable difficulties at the beginning and the exodus of those Muslims who did not want to live under non-Muslim rule, the Austro-Hungarian administration succeeded in a few decades in modernizing a rather conservative and backward part of the Ottoman Empire and in transforming it in the direction of an Islamic-European symbiosis. The annexation of Bosnia in 1908 and the 'definite and inseparable integration of Bosnia and Herzegovina' into the Habsburg monarchy (according to the report of the Special Commission on the drafting of the Act on Islam in 1910), resulted in the need to establish a legal status for Islam in Austria and Hungary which was equal to that of the traditional Churches.

48. The Act of 15 July 1912 concerning the Recognition of the Adherents of Islam[8] as a Religious Community (IslamG) is of principal interest. The institutional recognition of Islam by the procedure delineated by the AnerkennungsG was not possible, mainly because of the lack of a juridical organization comparable to that of the Christian Churches, a concept which was the basis of the AnerkennungsG. The IslamG gave the individual Muslim the position of an adherent of a recognized religious community, though there was no corresponding Islamic organization. In this way, the IslamG built a bridge between corporate and individual status. It was in force up to 2015 when it was replaced by a new law (cf. 347 et seq.).

49. In the second half of the nineteenth century, the Austrian Monarchy transferred the idea of 'Concordats' to other religious communities. After the occupation of Bosnia and Herzegovina in 1878, the administration of the Orthodox Church and the Islamic Community was regulated on the basis of a convention with the Ottoman Sultan[9] and the Ecumenical Patriarchate,[10] respectively. In both cases, the basis of the contract was international law, which since then has often been referred to on the part of Greece in order to support a position of the Ecumenical Patriarchate under international law.

8. Originally this law was enacted only for the adherents of the Hanafite law school for being the official law school of Bosnia.
9. Text in K. Strupp (ed.), *Ausgewählte diplomatische Aktenstücke zur Orientalischen Frage* (Perthes: Gotha, 1916).
10. Text in I. Silbernagl, *Verfassung und gegenwärtiger Bestand sämtlicher Kirchen des Orients*, 2nd ed. (Regensburg: C. G. Manz, 1904), 63 et seq.

VI. The First Austrian Republic and the Authoritarian Corporative State

50. After the fall of the Habsburg Monarchy, there was a significant constitutional change, but in principle, the system of state-church relations prevailed. The small republic was more Catholic than the great empire, but there were two important minorities, the Protestant and the Jewish. The Treaty of St. Germain 1919 finally extended the right to free exercise of faiths, religions or denominations of every kind in public as well as in private to every inhabitant in Austria.

51. The coalition pact of 17 October 1919 between the Social Democrats and Christian-social Party was intended to reform the relationship of church and state under the new constitution. The project could not be brought to an end because of the differing views of the two political parties – not least in regard to issues such as family and matrimonial law, school and education, and the status of religious communities, in particular with regard to the Catholic Church.

52. With the failure of an agreement on a new bill of rights, therefore, the Constitutional Act on the Fundamental Rights of Citizens of 1867 was adopted in the Federal Constitution of 1920 as a transitional solution (Article 149 B-VG).

53. A revision of the laws on religion of the new Austrian republic initially affected only the Catholic Church, a renewal which was not the consequence of changing constitutional conditions, but behind which lay chiefly political reasons. Negotiations with the Holy See had already started in 1929, and, in 1933, the Christian-authoritarian government brought the negotiations to an end. The government thought it possible to realize the 'Christian State', whereby the social concept as laid down in the papal Encyclical Quadragesimo anno served as an ideological basis. Evident expression of the unity of state and church should be – as during the neo-absolutist area of the Concordat of 1855 – the successful conclusion of the Concordat's negotiations. The Concordat and the Additional Protocol were signed on 5 June 1933 and entered into force together with the Christian-authoritarian constitution on 1 May 1934. The Preamble of the Constitution programmatically holds: 'In the Name of God, the Almighty, from whom all law emanates, the Austrian People receives this Constitution for its Christian, German Federal State on a corporate fundament (auf ständischer Grundlage)'.

54. After 1918, a revision of the legal status of the Protestant Church was the objective of long and unsuccessful negotiations. In the era of the authoritarian corporate state, religious and political mistrust regarding the Protestants overlapped. The Protestant Church protested against discriminatory measures and even characterized the system as a 'new Counter-reformation', whereas the state authorities suspected Protestants of working illegally for Nazi-Germany.

55. After the end of the Monarchy and the dissolution of the Metropolis of Bukovina and Dalmatia with its seat in Czernowitz, the existing Orthodox communities, according to their nationality, recognized the jurisdiction of the Patriarch of

Constantinople and the Patriarch of Belgrade, respectively, and the Romanian Orthodox Community, newly created in 1923, recognized the jurisdiction of the Patriarch of Bucharest.

VII. The NS-Rule

56. The so-called Anschluss to Nazi-Germany on 13 March 1938 established a system of strict separation of church and state for seven years.[11]

57. The attempts of the Austrian episcopate to reach a modus vivendi under this policy failed miserably. The bishops compiled a list of demands of thirty-two points containing all matters relevant to state-church law. On 7 September, the bishops broke off negotiations, since the Nazi authorities had ruthlessly continued their measures against religion and churches.

58. On 12 July 1938, the Austrian Concordat was declared extinct and the German Reichs-Konkordat was not extended to Austria, because it 'could not find any appropriate conditions for application in Austria'. According to the Nazi-administration, therefore, a 'non-concordatarian state' existed in Austria which presented the possibility of establishing an exemplary Nazi church policy in the Ostmark.

59. One of the first legislative measures was the final laicization of the Marriage Law by the 'Act on the Unification of the Law of Marriage and Divorce in the Country of Austria and the Rest of the Reich' (EheG 1938, cf. 696 et seq.).

60. Another major concern of the Nazis was the laicization of the school system. On 17 October 1938, denominational private schools were closed. On 19 November 1938, religious instruction was placed completely under state supervision, and finally abolished as a compulsory subject and turned into an optional subject.

61. While the theological faculty of Vienna and Graz were merged on 29 March 1939, the Salzburg faculty and the Innsbruck 'Jesuit faculty', which was the largest theological faculty in German-speaking countries at the time, were abolished and the professors dismissed.

62. Finally, church financing was placed on a new basis. It resulted in the secularization of church property and the end of state benefits to the Churches. Instead, a church-contribution was introduced (Act on Church-Contributions – KirchenbeitragsG 1939, cf. 589 et seq.). Because of the 'mentality of the local population' this measure promised to be a 'devastating blow to the church organization'. However,

11. Cf. R. Potz, 'Nationalsozialismus und Staatskirchenrecht', in *Nationalsozialismus und Recht. Rechtssetzung und Rechtswissenschaft in Österreich unter der Herrschaft des Nationalsozialismus*, eds. U. Davy et al. (Vienna: Orac, 1990), 266–284.

contrary to the expectations of the Nazis, the introduction of a church-contribution did not result in a wave of members leaving the Church.

63. Unlike in Germany, where the public law status of the Jewish communities was repealed in 1938, neither the formal repeal of the IsraelitenG 1890 nor the dissolution of the Jewish Community of Vienna was enacted in Austria. Initially, the Community was not only maintained as a holder of Jewish institutions (hospitals, retirement homes, youth centres, and schools) but also used as an organizer and promoter of Jewish emigration. It had to pay funds to the 'Central Office for Jewish Emigration', which had been raised mainly by foreign Jewish organizations. In October 1941, emigration of Jews from the German Reich was finally prohibited. While, until then, two-thirds of the Jewish population of Austria managed to escape, one-third of the Austrian Jews were murdered in concentration camps. On 11 January 1942, the Jewish Community of Vienna was dissolved.

VIII. The Second Republic

64. After the reconstitution of Austria in 1945, the development of Austrian law on religion was determined by the liquidation of Nazi legislation and overcoming the last remainders of a confessional state in Austria. As a transitional measure, the laws and statutory instruments adopted after 13 March 1938 remained in force insofar as their content did not contradict 'the existence of a free and independent Austrian state and the principles of true democracy, and were neither in conflict with the sense of justice of the Austrian people nor contained ideological traits of National-Socialism' (§1 section 1 Act on the Transition of Laws, R-ÜG 1945). A number of laws relevant to the state-church relationship (e.g., the EheG 1938 and the KirchenbeitragsG 1939), therefore, were transferred almost entirely to the legal system of the Republic.

65. After 1945, the Catholic Church as the most important religious community had to cope with its past because of its support for the authoritarian regime between 1934 and 1938. The 'Mariazeller Manifesto' of 1952 played a key role in this reorientation of the Austrian Catholic Church (cf. 453 et seq.).

66. Since 1950, the question of the continued validity of the Concordat of 1933 has resulted in conflict between the dominant political parties due to the Concordat's provision on marriage law, which now and then has reached the dimensions of a 'cultural struggle'.[12] The crucial issue in this question has been whether the so-called Anschluss of Austria to Germany in 1938 should be evaluated as annexation or occupation. In the case of an annexation, Austria would have lost its status as a subject of international law and all international treaties would have expired. In

12. R. Potz & B. Schinkele, 'Die kirchliche Trauung im staatlichen Recht Österreichs. Ein Beitrag zur Geschichte des Verhältnisses von Staat und Katholischer Kirche in den langen Fünfzigerjahren', in *Österreich und der Heilige Stuhl im 19. und 20. Jahrhundert*, eds. H. Paarhammer & A. Rinnerthaler (Frankurt am Main et al.: Peter Lang, 2001), 401–442.

the case of occupation, Austria would have become incapacitated in international law, but would not have lost its legal capacity. Accordingly, all international treaties would be revived after the recovery act in 1945. Since the view prevailed that Austria had been an occupied country between 1938 and 1945, the Federal Government expressly recognized the validity of the Concordat in 1957.

67. This decision provided the starting point for new state and church relations and corresponding legislation so that from the 1960s onward a period of consolidation and modernization began. Some special agreements with the Holy See were concluded and special laws for other religious communities were enacted, in 1961, for the Protestant Church, and, in 1967, for the Orthodox Church. In 1978, the first Islamic Community was recognized according to the IslamG 1912.

68. The most important new law was the Federal Act of 6 July 1961 on External Legal Relationships of the Protestant Church in Austria (ProtestantenG), which represents the conclusion of a process leading to equal treatment of the Protestant and the Catholic Church. In comparison with the Concordat, this more recent law guarantees even greater religious freedom.

69. For the Greek-Orthodox Church, the Federal Act of 23 June 1967 on the External Legal Relationships of the Greek-Oriental Church in Austria (OrthodoxenG) was enacted. For the first time, the OrthodoxenG recognized the Greek-Orthodox Church in Austria as such in addition to the communities already existing.[13] Since that time, Austria has had a two-fold membership in the Orthodox Church and it is possible to be an adherent of the Orthodox Church without being at the same time a member of a certain established community, a legal position comparable to the content of the IslamG mentioned above.

70. In 2003, a special law for the churches of the oriental-orthodox tradition was issued, including not only the already legally recognized churches (Armenian Apostolic Church since Joseph II and confirmed 1973, and the Syrian-Orthodox Church since 1988) but also the Coptic-Orthodox Church, which had been a registered religious denominational community, since 1998.

71. The amendment of the IsraelitenG 1890 is also an interesting example in our context. In a Constitutional Court decision from 1981, §2 IsraelitenG was partially declared unconstitutional owing to a violation of the principle of equality.[14] The Court states that it is incompatible with this principle to prevent a group of Jewish people from founding another legally recognized religious community besides the only one existing in a certain territory. In this decision, for the first time, one of the

---

13. After World War I the system of autocephalous/autonomous churches was changed according to the new political order, so that only three communities (*Kirchengemeinden*) – two Greek and one Serbian – remained within the borders of the Austrian republic. Since 1925 there was also a Romanian community.
14. VfSlg. 9185/1981.

High Courts argued in a significant way that the individual element of the fundamental right must not be violated by overvaluing the corporative one. Consequently, in the context concerned the individual component of religious freedom prevails in its corporative sphere. The IsraelitenG 1890 was completely revised in 2012 (cf. 330 et seq.).

72. A particularly problematic area is the restitution or reparation claims by the Jewish religious society and its institutions. The implementation of the respective laws went ahead very slowly, and the evidence required by the legal provisions was often difficult to produce. In 1960 a law was passed providing for annual compensation, *inter alia*, to the Jewish religious society in operationalization of the obligation for compensation according to Article 26 of the State Treaty of Vienna (StVWien) of 1955. Since numerous synagogues and other Jewish places of worship, cemeteries and ritual objects, especially Torah scrolls, had been victims of riots during the Nazi era or of war events, a one-time compensation was also paid to help bridge the consequences of the damage.

73. From the beginning of the 1970s, the Islamic Community rapidly increased in number and the question was raised as to whether an institutional establishment according to the IslamG 1912 would be possible. The institutional recognition of the Islamic Religious Community finally took place by way of an ordinance in 1988, which summarized in seven points the elements to be contained ‘in particular’ in the constitution of the Islamic Religious Community with respect to its external legal relationships.

74. Since 1951, another six churches and religious communities have been recognized by statutory instruments according to the AnerkennungsG, namely the Methodist Church, Church of Jesus Christ of the Latter-day Saints (Mormons), the Armenian Apostolic Church, the New-Apostolic Church, the Buddhist Community, the Syrian-Orthodox Church. The process of establishing more and more religious denominations was brought to an end with the emergence of so-called New Religious Movements. The conception according to which legal recognition is based here did not seem suitable to be applied to some of these groups owing to their different structures. Moreover, in several cases, the administrative body hesitated to confer public law status on some of these groups for reasons pertaining to sociopolitical considerations.

75. By the end of the 1950s, characterized by linking cultural conservatism to revolutionary changes in the technical and economic fields, the time was definitively over for the Catholic Church to be successful with such a strategy. The mid-1960s, somehow, finally saw a change in the attitude towards the churches as institutions in the sense of ‘believing without belonging’. This had many reasons; on the one hand, the Church was caught up in the identity crisis of all major institutions, and on the other hand, the Church was not able to use the Second Vatican Council in a decisive way as a chance for an onset. As elsewhere, the developments in Austria also took a rather contrary course, reflected particularly in the public debate on the papal encyclical Humanae Vitae.

76. Since the 1970s, the main emphasis of the relationship between the state and religious communities has shifted more and more to general socio-political issues. The churches, though their influence has declined, have been able to keep their position as important dialogue partners within civil society. This was for the first time evident in the controversy concerning the introduction of the legal possibility of a first-trimester abortion.

77. In the following years, discussions have also taken place on a number of new legislations, such as reforms to family law, monumental protection, data protection, registration law and the question of inclusion of religion in the national census.

78. Since the 1990s, there have been changes in public perception of the churches. In Austria, a crisis at the beginning of the 1990s led to the so-called Kirchenvolksbegehren ('Church Referendum') in 1995. In general, the role of the churches – due to the activities of the Catholic Caritas and the Protestant Diakonia – was primarily seen in terms of their engagement with social problems, asylum and immigration laws and development aid in particular. Moreover, the churches are involved in discussing ethical issues associated with new technologies, in particular in the field of bio-sciences, and, most recently, the anti-discrimination law.

79. In more traditional church circles, complaints are often voiced that in public the churches are mainly or even exclusively regarded positively by virtue of their commitment to charitable works.

80. This change in perception can be attributed to a steady increase in religious pluralization, stemming mainly from the rise of New Religious Movements and the increase in Islamic, Alevi and Orthodox immigrants. In 2011 the Act on Greek-Oriental Churches was amended (cf. 318 et seq.) and in 2015, the Act on Islam of 1912 was revised, placing the relationship with the Islamic communities on a new footing (cf. 347 et seq.).

Part I. Legal Framework and Sources

Chapter 1. The Constitutional Position of Religion

§1. The Federal Constitution

I. Secular Concept

81. The Austrian Federal Constitution (B-VG) of 1920 contains no preamble due to its underlying positivistic concept. The first Article reads: 'Austria is a democratic republic. Its law emanates from the people.' This formulation not only refers to the democratic and the republican principles but is also seen as a rejection of a transcendent legitimacy. From 2003 to 2005, on the occasion of the Österreich-Konvent [15] – a project for creating a revised version of the Constitution – the integration of a preamble and a reference to God or religion were also discussed. In this case, no consensus could be found, but at least the initiative steps towards revision of the Constitution were not brought to an end.

II. Fundamental Laws Relating to Religious Freedom

82. The Austrian constitution guarantees the right to religious freedom in a comprehensive way. The most important provisions are contained in the StGG of 1867 which was declared a constitutional law of the Federal State by Article 149 section 1 B-VG (cf. 54). Guarantees of individual religious rights are contained in Article 14 StGG and institutional guarantees in Article 15 StGG. The legal provisions on religion in the Treaty of St. Germain of 1919[16] and Article 9 of the European Convention on Human Rights (ECHR) also have constitutional status. The constitutional norm of Article 9 ECHR overlaps the older specific guarantees (freedom of belief, freedom of conscience, freedom of cult, freedom of confession) and summarises them in one 'aggregated law' on religious freedom in which the separate

15. *See* H. Kalb, R. Potz & B. Schinkele, 'Religions- und Weltanschauungsfreiheit im aktuellen österreichischen Verfassungsdiskurs', *Österreichisches Archiv für Recht und Religion* 52 (2005), 1–37.
16. Section V (Protection of Minorities) of Part III of the Treaty of St. Germain is to be regarded as constitutional law according to Article 149 B-VG 1920. Art. 63 section 2 (cf. Chapter 2, § 1) is of special importance.

guarantees are combined. This comprehensive idea of religious freedom also makes it clear once and for all that not only is religious confession protected by constitutional order, but a Weltanschauung (non-religious belief) is similarly protected.[17]

83. There are also further guarantees in constitutional law aimed at protecting religious freedom; these include general rules of non-discrimination, relating, among other things, to differences in denomination. The general principle of equality is guaranteed in Article 2 StGG and in Article 7 B-VG. The right to religious freedom is, furthermore, functionally and systematically linked with other fundamental rights, such as freedom of expression, freedom of association and the right of assembly.

III. Special Constitutional Provisions Regarding Religion

84. Apart from guarantees relating to religious freedom, only a few provisions explicitly refer to religion as such. According to Article 14 section 5a B-VG, it is the aim of Austrian schooling to cooperate in the development of the aptitudes of young people regarding religious values – among other things – by way of appropriate instruction. Article 17 StGG and Article 14 section 10 B-VG deal with the relationship between Church and school (cf. 615 et seq.). The Constitution also provides for the possible exercise of religious assertions in oaths of office.

§2. Constitutional Provisions of the Bundesländer

I. Competences of the Bundesländer in Matters of Law on Religion

85. According to Article 15 B-VG, matters that do not expressly lie within the competence of the federal government in legislation and execution belong within the autonomous realm of the Federal States. Although 'matters of cultus' are exclusively federal matters, some legal regulations with implications for law on religion can be found within the framework of the competences of the Federal States. This primarily applies to the laws on schools and kindergartens, regional planning and building regulations, cemetery and funeral law (for reasons of sanitary police and preservation of piety), and some aspects of social and youth welfare, mostly relating explicitly to church activities.[18]

---

17. *See* B. Schinkele, 'Zur Weltanschauungsfreiheit in Österreich', *Österreichisches Archiv für Kirchenrecht* 39 (1990), 50–80.
18. Cf. R. Potz, 'Le confessioni religiose e la concezione federale dello Stato. L'esperienza dell'Austria', in *Confessioni religiose e federalismo. Esperienze e prospettive*, ed. G Feliciani (Bologna: Il mulino, 2000), 193–203.

II. Religion in the Constitutions of the Bundesländer

86. Religious references are included in the Constitutional Laws of two Bundesländer. In the Tyrol, the preamble of the constitutional order states – among other things – that faithfulness to God provides a basis for the mental, social and political foundations of the country, protection of which should be regarded as a supreme commitment by state legislation and administration. In Vorarlberg, the Constitutional Law explicitly recognizes the significance of legally recognized religious communities for the preservation and strengthening of the religious and moral fundaments of human life. Moreover, the protection of life and human dignity, the accompanying care of the last phase of life and the importance of Sundays and public holidays as a rest from work are particularly emphasized.

Chapter 2. Other Legislation with Regard to Religion

87. Ordinary state law relevant to religion falls into four categories: (i) general laws on the status of religious communities; (ii) general provisions on religious affairs; (iii) provisions relating, *inter alia*, to the religious sphere; and (iv) special provisions for individual churches or religious societies. Moreover, Austria has signed in principle all international treaties with general relevance to freedom of religion and belief. According to their transformation into Austrian law, these are usually qualified as ordinary laws, with the exception of the ECHR which was transformed at the constitutional level (cf. 393).

§1. General Laws on the Status of Religious Communities

88. The first category deals with general questions of the law on religion as, for example, the Law on Legal Recognition of Religious Communities (AnerkennungsG) of 1874 and the Act on the Legal Status of Religious Denominational Communities (BekGG) of 1998.

§2. General Provisions on Religious Affairs

89. The Act of 25 May 1868 on Interconfessional Relations of Citizens (InterKonfG, [cf. 156 and 771]), the Act on Religious Education at School 1962 (RelUG, [cf. 632 et seq.]), the Act on the Religious Upbringing of Children (RelKErzG, [cf. 158 et seq.]), the Federal Act on the Establishment of an Institute for Documentation and Information on Sect-Issues (EDISG, [cf. 465 et seq.]) and the Act on Church-Contributions 1939 (KirchenbeitragsG [cf. 589 et seq.]) fall into this category.

§3. Law on Religion as a Cross-Sectional Issue

90. The third category comprises matters of law and religion as a cross-sectional issue extending throughout the whole legal system. With regard to the manifold religious and denominational manifestations, inferring also many points of intersection of state and church, law on religion has been extended in the course of time to cover the whole of the legal system and so forms a cross-section of the law held together by reference to religion or belief. Hence, a great number of laws now exist which contain rules relevant to our context.

§4. Special Laws Which Apply to Individual Religious Communities

91. The fourth category relates to the legal status of churches and religious communities recognized under a special law (for more cf. 289). The existence of these laws for those recognized churches and religious communities which are of historic and social significance is a characteristic of the Austrian law on religion. Since 1867, in the process of emancipation, more and more religious communities have been placed on the same level as the historically dominant Catholic Church.

92. Special laws concerning the 'external legal relationships' of individual legally recognized religious communities usually refer to the following issues:

- Repetitions and concretizations of fundamental law guarantees (e.g., Articles I and II Concordat 1933, §1 section 2 ProtestantenG).
- External matters include the determination of regulation in statutes, such as name, membership, establishment of institutions endowed with public law status, and appointment of bodies in religious communities authorized to represent it externally.
- So-called res mixtae, the regulation of which requires cooperation between the state and the legally recognized church or religious society on religious instruction in schools, theological faculties, and religious support in the armed forces and other institutions. These res mixtae, implementing the principle of substantive parity (cf. 267 et seq.), include provisions which take the specifics of each church or religious community into account.
- State supervisory rights extend primarily to compliance with the statutes, especially in the appointment of governing bodies. Such supervisory rights have recently been strengthened in regulations of the IsraelitenG as amended in 2012 and the IslamG 2015 in a manner reminiscent of the state-church system of the nineteenth century.

Chapter 3. Typology of the System

§1. Basic Principles

93. Freedom of religion is guaranteed in a comprehensive way, encompassing its individual, collective and corporate components. The enjoyment of political and civil rights is completely independent of individual religious creeds or personal beliefs. Equal treatment and the prohibition of discrimination on religious grounds are guaranteed.

94. There is no Established Church, and state and religious communities are institutionally separated. The diverse corporate activities of religious communities in the public sphere are guaranteed. For this purpose, a system of different – nowadays three – options for determining the legal status of religious communities is foreseen, two of them being reserved for religious communities (cf. 223 et seq.). The basic idea of this concept is to offer an adequate legal framework for the pluralistic inclusion of religious denominations into those public spheres in which the state does not exert its genuine sovereign power. The essential meaning of this concept is the consideration of the special features inherent to religious life and of cultural phenomena qualified as religious, restricted only according to the well-known limitations of standards of human rights.

§2. Neutrality

95. The neutrality of the state in matters of religion is a consequence of the guarantee of freedom of religion and is described as a constitutional principle.[19] Its use in recent decades is primarily related to the increasing religious pluralization of society and the way in which it is managed under the rule of law.

96. Although the term ‘neutrality’ is not positivized, it is derived in literature and case law from the secular-state conception of the Federal Constitution, the provisions on religious freedom, and the principle of equality.

97. Religious neutrality is applied on three levels. First, in direct implementation of the secularity of the state, it means the prohibition of identification with religion in general or with a particular religion. Second, it stipulates equal treatment of religions and religious communities in view of the religious pluralization of society. Therefore, the denominational neutrality of the state must guarantee that the state does not identify with any particular conviction. Third, the ECtHR’s jurisprudence in particular assigns the state a neutral and impartial role in dealing with internal conflicts within religious communities. The state may not favour any group or exert coercion to reach an agreement.

---

19. K. Schlaich, *Neutralität als verfassungsrechtliches Prinzip* (Tübingen: Mohr, 1972).

98. As a fundamental principle, denominational neutrality is applied in practice in different ways. Consequently, a clear distinction must be made between two different forms of religious neutrality: 'distancing' neutrality (*distanzierende Neutralität*) and 'inclusive' neutrality (*hereinnehmende Neutralität*).[20]

99. In as far as the state acts within its central sovereign sphere – i.e., where genuine non-exchangeable state tasks are concerned (for instance, jurisdiction) – religious neutrality must be realized in its 'distancing' form, with no reference to religious or philosophical beliefs.

100. Regarding other state activities, especially in education and social welfare, establishing and enabling the individual practice of religion (including non-religious beliefs) can be regarded as mandatory and the legal framework must be created for the pluralistic incorporation of religion into society in a context in which, as a matter of principle, the state does not exercise its genuine sovereignty.

101. A denominationally neutral state does not mean that the state is not allowed to promote religious communities as socially relevant factors. Thus, the denominational neutrality of the state must be carried out in a cooperative way that integrates aspects of religion and belief, and, of course, without discrimination or identification with any particular denomination on the part of the state.

102. On the one hand, the principle of denominational neutrality has gained growing importance in an increasingly religiously pluralistic society. On the other hand, in view of the challenges posed by the religious pluralization of society and the overlapping of other policies, such as integration and security, the principle of neutrality is increasingly being relativized or even questioned. Either 'diversity management' in religious policy is called for[21] or a restructuring towards a comprehensive separation of state and religion (cf. 452)

§3. The System of Legal Recognition

103. The successive recognition of religious communities since 1867, in a process of emancipation, has incorporated more and more religious communities into a system of legal recognition on the same level as the historically dominant Catholic Church. Corporate guarantees for these religious communities constitute a basis

20. E.-W. Böckenförde, 'Kreuze (Kruzifixe) in Gerichtssälen? Zum Verhältnis von staatlicher Selbstdarstellung und religiös weltanschaulicher Neutralität des Staates', *Zeitschrift für Evangelisches Kirchenrecht* 20 (1975), 119–147; H. Kalb, R. Potz & B. Schinkele, *Das Kreuz in Klassenzimmer und Gerichtssaal* (Freistadt: Plöchl, 1996), 36–55.
21. K.-H. Ladeur & I. Augsberg, *Toleranz – Religion – Recht. Die Herausforderung des 'neutralen' Staates durch neue Formen der Religiosität in der postmodernen Gesellschaft* (Tübingen: Mohr Siebeck, 2007), 91 et seq.

for characteristic institutionalism in the Austrian law on religion.[22] There is a system of different – nowadays three – options for the legal status of religious communities. Two of these forms of legal status – legal recognition and state registration – are connected with a certification of the religious character of the community concerned. Hence, in the case of state registration, we can also speak of recognition in a broader sense of the word (cf. 231 et seq.).

§4. TOLERANCE

104. The principle of tolerance, though rather weakly embedded in the positive legal order (as, for instance, in Article 14 section 5a B-VG in the context of the aims of the Austrian school system), should, in essence, be considered as a mainly unwritten constitutional element (cf. Article 13 ICESCR). Primarily, because the ECHR has enjoyed constitutional status in Austria since the middle 1980s, the case law has often referred to the formula of the ECtHR regarding Article 10 ECHR in particular. Accordingly, pluralism, tolerance and broadmindedness are essential features of a 'democratic society' within the meaning of the Convention. Precisely, a liberal constitutional state can be said to rely on a tolerant attitude of the citizens.

105. Although the principle of legally guaranteed freedom of religion definitively goes beyond religious tolerance, the principle of tolerance was not rendered superfluous and annulled by that of freedom of religion, but it is inherent therein. The state must no longer merely be a tolerant party. Tolerance in the relationships between citizens, however, must in future also still remain a fundamental principle in every democracy, whereas intolerance, on the other hand, endangers the 'vital foundations' of every democracy. Without tolerance as the fundamental attitude freedom of religion cannot be conceived and lived. In this sense, the importance of practical tolerance is not to be underestimated even today.[23] The principle of tolerance is an important regulative instrument within the process of balancing the legal merits in accordance with the principle of proportionality. Thereby, the specific significance of fundamental rights for individuals as well as for minorities must be taken into account.

---

22. H. Pree, 'Gibt es ein dogmatisches Prinzip des österreichischen Staatskirchenrechts?', in *Gedenkschrift für Carl Holböck*, eds. F. Pototschnig & A. Rinnerthaler (Vienna: Verlag des Verbandes der Wissenschaftlichen Gesellschaften Österreichs, 1985), 577–600.

23. G. Luf, 'Die religiöse Freiheit und der Rechtscharakter der Menschenrechte. Überlegungen zur normativen Genese und Struktur der Religionsfreiheit', in *Freiheit der Religion. Christentum und Islam unter dem Anspruch der Menschenrechte*, ed. J. Schwartländer (Mainz: Matthias-Grünewald-Verlag, 1993), 80 et seq.; H. Kalb, R. Potz & B. Schinkele, *Das Kreuz in Klassenzimmer und Gerichtssaal* (Freistadt: Plöchl, 1996), 72–76; E. Holzleithner, 'Menschenrechte und Toleranz', in *Recht – Religion – Kultur. Festschrift für Richard Potz*, eds. B. Schinkele et al. (Vienna: facultas.wuv, 2014), 205–228.

§5. An Open Society for Religion

106. The Austrian system is characterized by its openness to religion. It corresponds to several famous concepts underlining the importance of religion in the context of a pluralistic civil society. They include, for instance, the frequently cited 'Böckenförde-Theorem',[24] according to which the liberal state must rely on preconditions that it cannot guarantee itself without questioning its own liberal substance. Among these conditions, religion plays a special role, because it is assumed that religion is socially effective and is of great benefit to society and state as well. Therefore, the legal order must ensure that religion is not banned from the public space. The secularization process has brought about a functional differentiation in society also comprising religion, but religion must not be reduced to spiritual practice.

107. As in other European countries, however, there is a growing awareness of the dangers of 'going too far'[25] in guaranteeing religious freedom and the need to incorporate considerations of security into law on religion.

24. E.-W. Böckenförde, *Staat, Gesellschaft, Freiheit. Studien zur Staatstheorie und zum Verfassungsrecht* (Frankfurt: Suhrkamp, 1976), 60.
25. Cf. the papers by U. Sacksofsky and C. Möllers and the contributions to the discussion at the 2008 conference of the 'Vereinigung der deutschen Staatsrechtslehrer' on 'Religious Freedom as a Danger?', published in VVDStRL 68 (Berlin: De Gruyter, 2009).

Part II. Religious Freedom in General

Chapter 1. Individual, Collective and Corporate Spheres of Religious Freedom

108. The traditional and clear distinction between individual and corporative Staatskirchenrecht was maintained for a long time in Austrian legal literature. Since the 1990s, it has been increasingly emphasized that both spheres are closely linked (manifestations) forms of freedom of religion, which is necessarily a fundamental status in a democratic secular state. Nowadays, it is stressed that the primary task of the state is to promote religious communities in order to protect the religious interests of the individual adherents.

109. The 'catalogue' of Austrian fundamental rights is characterized by the fact that they are embodied in Constitutional Acts or Treaties under International Law (Articles 14 and 15 StGG, Article 63 StVStGermain and Article 9 ECHR) respectively, that date from several historical epochs with different state-church relationships and a different understanding of fundamental rights. The most comprehensive protection of religious freedom became part of the constitutional system in 1958 by means of the ECHR.

110. Before the ratification of the ECHR in 1958, the religious sphere was characterized by separate and isolated guarantees of fundamental rights. Nowadays, an extensive, teleological synopsis of all relevant guarantees is predominant. Since the mid-1980s, such an approach has also been reflected in the case law of the Constitutional Court. As a result of this gradual development, the single constitutional provisions overlap. To an increasing extent, the Court considers the single fundamental guarantees a unifying factor in the sense of an 'aggregated law on fundamental rights'[26] though without using this term.

111. The different legal reservations in Article 9 ECHR, Article 63 section 2 StVStGermain and Article 14 StGG present no hindrance to such a harmonizing approach. Though the wordings of the individual legal provisos are rather different, the subject matter seems quite similar. Essentially, the various constitutional requirements of a specific enactment seem to amount to the same limitations. That

26. Cf. W. Berka, 'Die Europäische Menschenrechtskonvention und die Österreichische Grundrechtstradition', *Österreichische Juristen-Zeitung* 34 (1979), 428; B. Schinkele, 'Zur Weltanschauungsfreiheit in Österreich', *Österreichisches Archiv für Kirchenrecht* 39 (1990), 50–80.

is the way to reach a genuine concordance, not only a conclusion free of contradictions as a consequence of the most favoured principle according to Article 54 ECHR.[27] Thus, there is no need to refer to it.

112. Moreover, the relationship between the different sections of Article 14 StGG must be deemed a hierarchical correlation of norms. Consequently, in case of doubt, religious freedom takes precedence over the obligations inherent in the second and third sections. In general, limitations to fundamental rights must be interpreted in a restrictive way.

27. According to this article nothing in this Convention shall be constructed as limiting or derogating any of the human rights and fundamental freedoms which may be ensured under the law of any contracting party or under any other agreement to which it is a party.

Chapter 2. Individual Religious Freedom

§1. Normative Structures

113. Article 14 StGG:

(1) Everyone is guaranteed complete freedom of conscience and creed.
(2) The enjoyment of civil and political rights is independent of religious belief. Nevertheless, duties incumbent on nationals may not be prejudiced by religious beliefs.
(3) No one can be forced to observe a ritual act or to participate in an ecclesiastical ceremony in so far as he is not subordinate to another who is by law invested with such authority.

114. Treaty of St. Germain (StVStGermain)

Article 63:

(2) All inhabitants of Austria have the right to exercise in public or private every kind of belief, religion or confession freely, insofar as their exercise is not incompatible with public order or good morals.

Article 66:

(2) Differences of religion, creed or confession shall not prejudice any Austrian national in matters relating to the enjoyment of civil or political rights, as for instance admission to public employments, functions and honours, or the exercise of professions and industries.

115. Article 9 ECHR:

[1] Everyone has the right to freedom of thought, conscience and religion; this right includes freedom to change his religion or belief, and freedom, either alone or in community with others and in public or private, to manifest his religion or belief, in worship, teaching, practice and observance.
[2] Freedom to manifest one's religion or beliefs shall be subject only to such limitations as are prescribed by law and are necessary in a democratic society in the interests of public safety, for the protection of public order, health or morals, or the protection of the rights and freedoms of others.

116. Article 14 StGG in connection with Article 63 StVStGermain and Article 9 ECHR guarantee the individual freedom of religion in a comprehensive way. According to the historical legislator, Article 14 StGG only refers to religious convictions. Article 63 section 2 StVStGermain – incorporated into the Federal Constitution in 1920 – refers to 'faiths, religions and denominations of any kind'. The most comprehensive guarantee of religion and belief is entailed in Article 9 ECHR. This guarantee ultimately makes clear that not only religious beliefs but also philosophies without religious components are protected by the system of human rights.

117. In these constitutional provisions, four components of the comprehensive fundamental right of religious freedom are traditionally distinguished: freedom of conscience (cf. 136 et seq.), freedom of faith, freedom of worship and freedom of confession (cf. 155 et seq.). Though their delineation is becoming increasingly difficult, in each individual case one or other aspect might be prevalent. Such a construction must be taken into account whenever one of its single elements is referred to.

§2. Definitions

118. No exact legal definition of religion can be said to exist. It can merely be described by means of typically characteristic elements such as the following:

- entire meaningful conception of life, of the world, and of man's position therein;
- reference to transcendence;
- equivalent commandments for behaviour.

119. These basic elements correspond with myths which attempt to explain the world, rites for visualizing the supernatural and ethos for communicating moral principles.

120. The Explanatory Notes of the BekGG 1998 attempt to give an outline for the purpose of delimiting 'religion' from 'belief' (*Weltanschauung*) which reads as follows:

> Religion is a historically developed concept of convictions explaining the provenance of mankind and the world with a transcendent reference, including specific rites and symbols giving precepts for acting in accordance with its fundamental doctrines and which is presentable regarding its contents.

121. The requirement of a historically developed concept seems to be quite problematic because the lack of historical background is a distinct characteristic of new religious movements. Moreover, it must be emphasized that drawing a dividing line between transcendence and immanence has increasingly become an almost impossible task, such as in the case of Bekenntnisgemeinschaften, (cf. the application for registration as a religious confessional community by the 'Atheist Religious Community' of Austria 242).

122. In a decision of 15 September 2003, the High Administrative Court stated that Vishwa Nirmala Dharma (Sahaja Yoga) does not fulfil the precondition for obtaining state registration according to §4 section 1 no. 2 BekGG. The reason was that neither its religious doctrines nor the activities of the founder 'Her Holiness Shri Mataji Nirmala Devi' were set forth clearly or sufficiently.[28]

---

28. VwSlg. 16161 A/2003; Cf. R. Potz, 'Eintragung als Bekenntnisgemeinschaft, Vishwa Nirmala Dharma. Kommentar zu VwGH 15. 9. 2003, 2001/10/0139', *Österreichisches Archiv für Recht und Religion* 51 (2004), 285–296.

123. The application for registration by the 'Church of the Flying Spaghetti Monster (KdFSM)' as a religious denominational community was rejected in the second instance. The BVwG assumed that the 'KdFSM' has some basic doctrines, and offers alternative actions for a successful life. However, the 'KdFSM' lacks any essentially predetermined order for the performance of ceremonial, especially religious and in particular liturgical acts and rites and a sufficiently organised community (BVwG 22.3.2018, W 170 2115136-1). In a decision by the VGW concerning the picture on a driving licence, the Court held that the 'Church of the Flying Spaghetti Monster' is neither a religion nor a religious community but rather a religious satire that uses artistic means 'to exaggerate and question intolerant and dogmatic views and actions in a manner typical of satire', i.e., 'a pure parody of religion that seeks to ridicule the customs and beliefs of legally recognized religious communities', following German case law (VGW 14.1.2019, VGW-131/036/9981/2018).

124. In the Equal Treatment Act of 2004, implementing the European Directive 2000/78/EC, there is no explicit definition of religion, but the Explanatory Notes exemplify belief as follows: 'The term belief serves as a collective name for all religious, ideological, political and other conceptions of life and of the world as a meaningful entirety, being the basis for constructing the personal and common position for the individual idea of life'.[29] Furthermore, the 'Explanatory Notes' refer to 'world views, conception of man, and attitudes to morality'. Neither the European Directive nor the Austrian Equal Treatment Law gives clear information as to whether or not political convictions are included in the protection against discrimination (cf. 169 et seq.).

§3. Personal Scope of the Individual Guarantee

125. As a human right, freedom of religion or belief does not depend on the nationality of individual persons.

126. Children also enjoy freedom of religion or belief. Full legal capacity is reached with the completion of the 18th year of life, while religious maturity is already reached at the age of 14. From the age of 12 years onwards, the religious confession of a child cannot be changed against his or her will (§5 Act on the Religious Upbringing of Children, cf. 158 et seq.).

§4. Functions

I. Status Positivus and Status Negativus of Fundamental Rights

127. Fundamental rights do not only comprise a right to defence against the state (status negativus) but they also impose positive obligations the state has to comply with in order to render possible an effective exercise of fundamental rights (status

29. RV 307 BlgNR 22. GP; AB 499 BlgNR 22. GP, 61.

positivus). Such deliberations are consistent with a modern substantial understanding of fundamental rights. In order to ensure full protection of human rights and thus the realization of the underlying values, this concept implies a state protective liability. Accordingly, primarily the legislator, but in some way also administrative and judicial practice must adopt certain state measures depending on the particular circumstances.

128. This change in legal dogmatic approach to the construction of fundamental rights is clearly reflected in the case law of the Constitutional Court. Since the early eighties of the last century, the Court's decision-making has changed in such a significant way as to qualify as a 'paradigm shift'. Until then, a quite static and positivistic attitude was characteristic of the Court's jurisdiction. Especially, in relation to the principle of equality, it began to transform the understanding of fundamental rights as rights with a merely defensive effect against the state (status negativus) and, thus, its basic attitude was compensated to a certain extent. Later on, the Court departed from its attitude of 'judicial self-restraint' in general, replacing it with a more evolutionary and progressive approach. Nowadays, a certain degree of 'judicial self-activism' is a distinctive sign of its jurisdiction.[30]

II. The Positive and Negative Side of Religious Freedom

129. The above-mentioned understanding of fundamental rights also bears relevance for both components of religious freedom – positive and negative. The latter represents – similarly in connection with other fundamental rights warranting a certain liberty of action – the necessary correlate to the positive element. Freedom from religion means that no individual can be forced to practice any kind of religion, participate in religious ceremonies, or disclose personal religious or philosophical convictions.

130. Both aspects are manifestations of this multi-dimensional fundamental right, which are of equal status and as such, principally subject to the same restrictions. Though the protection of minorities is a special function of fundamental rights, the negative aspect is not prevalent. This would otherwise prevent the effective exercise of religious activities. In such cases, the crucial point is to find a fair balance between the conflicting legal positions. It is essential to establish a form of 'practical concordance' by carefully balancing procedures with a view to guaranteeing effective protection of both components of the comprehensive fundamental right.[31]

30. *See* T. Öhlinger, 'Die Grundrechte in Österreich', *Europäische Grundrechte Zeitschrift* 9 (1982), 224 et seq.; K. Korinek, *Entwicklungstendenzen in der Grundrechtsjudikatur des Verfassungsgerichtshofes* (Vienna: Orac, 1992).
31. *See* B. Schinkele, 'Positive und negative Religionsfreiheit – zwei Seiten einer Medaille? Zugleich eine Besprechung des EGMR-Urteils Grzelak gegen Polen', *Österreichisches Archiv für Recht und Religion* 60 (2013), 24.

131. To give an example controversially discussed: Crosses must be displayed in classrooms of public schools or private schools which have been granted public status (§2b section 1 RelUG). This provision might be improved upon insofar as there should be a legal possibility for the school governors to make a decision deviating from the general regulation, taking into account all the facts and circumstances of individual cases. Crosses in courtrooms, however, have no pertinence to religious interests as such and cannot be understood as an invitation to practise religion. The latter must rather be regarded as a misuse of the religious dimension and should consequently be removed.[32]

III. Horizontal Application

132. The question of horizontal application of fundamental rights should be regarded in connection with the above-mentioned modified legal dogmatic approach and the 'judicial self-activism' of the Constitutional Court.[33] More and more, fundamental rights are also understood as objective principles and consequently, as such they might impose certain positive obligations the state must comply with, even in order to protect an individual's right against infringements by private parties (so-called third-party effect; Drittwirkung).

133. There exists a multi-dimensional relationship structure, whereby the conflicting positions of private persons must be balanced to give both of them as much effectiveness as possible. These changes have been influenced by the dynamic evolutionary concept of the ECHR as laid down in its preamble and represented in the case law of the European instances.

§5. Scope of Individual Religious Freedom

I. Freedom of Conscience

A. General Significance

134. During the course of development, the particular importance of freedom of conscience has become increasingly clear. In a liberal denominationally neutral state ruled by law, a new description of its subject matter has taken place. As part of this, the state not only guarantees the free development and existence of religious, ethical and philosophical convictions but also freedom of practice. Thus, the scope of protection goes far beyond the forum internum. More and more, freedom of conscience is now regarded as a basic law from which comprehensive fundamental guarantees are derived, including not only religious freedom but also the right to

32. *See* H. Kalb, R. Potz & B. Schinkele, *Das Kreuz in Klassenzimmer und Gerichtssaal* (Freistadt: Plöchl, 1996), 88–108.
33. Cf. K. Korinek, *Entwicklungstendenzen in der Grundrechtsjudikatur des Verfassungsgerichtshofes*, (Vienna: Orac, 1992).

freedom of expression and freedom of assembly and association. At the very least, with regard to this understanding, the delineation between the different forms of religious manifestations seems to be not only a complex but even a superfluous undertaking. The close connection between these various elements shows that respect for convictions of conscience lies at the heart of the concept of freedom of religion.

135. One important aspect of freedom of conscience is its 'preventive function'.[34] In certain legal fields, the legislator provides for exemptions or offers alternatives to facilitate actions in compliance with one's conscience (so-called conscience clauses, cf. 141 et seq.).

136. With regard to the increasing societal complexity, the predictability of potential conscientious conflicts becomes more difficult. In the case of missing conscience clauses, the question arises as to how to qualify actions taken for reasons of conscience, however, contravening compulsory law, or even (administrative) penal law.[35] Should the need arise, such questions of conscience can attain legal relevance on the basis of thorough consideration of the legal merits strongly bound to the principle of proportionality, as long as basic principles of the rule of law are not compromised.[36]

137. In this context, one has to distinguish between two types of conflicting situations: Acting according to one's moral requirement is not referred to explicitly. A conscience-saving solution can often be found by means of an interpretation in conformity with the constitution, primarily in connection with indeterminate legal terms or general clauses in need of completion.

138. The problems are much greater if behaviour in conformity with one's conscience – be it acting positively or refraining from action – fails to fulfil an explicitly existing legal provision. In such cases, freedom of conscience can mainly have legal effect at the level of imposing sanctions, which for instance should be discussed in the context of the so-called church asylum.[37] However, questions concerning the position of an offender by conviction are not thoroughly dealt with in Austrian literature or jurisdiction. Primarily, crimes by omission are focused on whereby the criterion of reasonableness provides for indications to take conscientious conflicts into account. Should the need arise, the legal relevance of such decisions of conscience within the realm of the state legal system could be deduced on

34. Cf. N. Luhmann, 'Die Gewissensfreiheit und das Gewissen', *Archiv des öffentlichen Rechts* 90 (1965), 279.
35. *See* B. Schinkele, 'Gewissensgebot und Normativität des positiven Rechts. Überlegungen unter besonderer Berücksichtigung des so genannten Kirchenasyls', *Österreichisches Archiv für Recht und Religion* 50 (2003), 448–480.
36. *See* E.-W. Böckenförde, *Staat, Gesellschaft, Freiheit. Studien zur Staatstheorie und zum Verfassungsrecht* (Frankfurt am Main: Suhrkamp, 1976), 287.
37. B. Schinkele, 'Gewissensgebot und Normativität des positiven Rechts. Überlegungen unter besonderer Berücksichtigung des so genannten Kirchenasyls', *Österreichisches Archiv für Recht und Religion* 50 (2003), 448–480.

the basis of a thorough evaluation of the legal merits strongly bound to the principle of proportionality, as long as basic principles of the rule of law are not compromised.[38]

B. Conscience Clauses

1. Non-military Service

139. Article 9a B-VG guarantees the right to render a form of non-military service in the case of conscientious objectors. It is specified in §2 section 1 Act Concerning Non-Military Service 1986 (ZDG), according to which a person liable for military service is obliged to declare expressly that he is objecting for reasons of conscience – except in cases of self-defence or defence of another from imminent attack – to using force of arms against other human beings and would be subject to moral conflict if forced to do military service (cf. §2 section 2 ZDG). In this case, the person is obliged to serve in alternative civil services.

140. This constitutional provision – as in almost all European countries, though very differently implemented – went far beyond the established case law of the European instances referring to §4 section 3 lit. b in conjunction with Article 9 ECHR, before a significant change took place in the jurisdiction of the ECtHR in 2011.[39]

141. For several years, the practice existed that Jehovah's Witnesses who also rejected civil service were neither called to arms nor to non-military civil service.[40] At the end of the 1990s, this practice was changed so that some young Jehovah's Witnesses who rejected military and civil service were sentenced to imprisonment. However, in the following years, Jehovah's Witnesses revised their doctrine insofar as the question of active non-military service is currently considered to be a matter for one's conscience to decide.

2. Healthcare Law

142. Of course, in the field of existential questions of life and death, religious and philosophical regards are of great intensity. Regulating these areas in a pluralistic system is one of the most difficult tasks of legislation.[41] Most churches and religious communities give their comments on respective law drafts. The Catholic Church usually takes extremely critical positions.

---

38. Ibid.
39. ECtHR (Grand Chamber), *Bayatyan v. Armenien*, 7 Jul. 2011, appl. no. 23459/03.
40. *See* R. Kohlhofer (ed.), *Gewissensfreiheit und Militärdienst* (Vienna: Verlag Österreich, 2000).
41. *See* J. Wallner, *Health Care zwischen Ethik und Recht* (Vienna: facultas.wuv, 2007).

143. With the Criminal Code of 1974 (StGB), the so-called Fristenlösung was introduced, which limited criminal liability for abortion. Termination of pregnancy is not punishable if it is undertaken by a physician during the first three months of pregnancy and preceded by a medical consultation (§97 section 1 number 1). No physician is obliged to perform or assist in a termination of pregnancy unless this is necessary to avert imminent risk of death of the pregnant woman.[42]

144. §97 sections 2 and 3 StGB provide for prohibition of discrimination on the grounds of a lawful termination of pregnancy or participation in any such termination or the refusal to undertake or to participate in any such termination. This also applies to nursing staff and other medical corps. According to §6 section 3 Act on Hospitals and Healthcare Institutions (KaKuG), the institution's rules must not contain any regulation which prohibits the performance of an unpunished abortion or provides its refusal with disadvantageous consequences.[43]

145. Section 6 Act on Reproductive Medicine 1992 (FMedG) includes an analogous regulation for providing medical care for reproduction, participation therein or refusal to participate. De lege lata medical care for reproduction is only allowed in a conjugal relationship or in a matrimonial-like partnership and in the case that according to the scientific standards and experience, all other possible and reasonable treatments for becoming pregnant by means of sexual intercourse have been unsuccessful or considered hopeless. At present, a draft amendment is under discussion providing a significant extension of admissibilities, especially with regard to the legality of egg and sperm donation, a slight expansion of pre-implantation-diagnostic and the inclusion of homosexual life partners.

146. The Dying Will Act also contains a comparable conscience clause concerning any form of cooperation in the preparation of or participation in a person's dying will (cf. 542).

3. Research Law

147. The University Act 2002 (UnivG) guarantees freedom of conscience – as did the previous regulations – insofar, as a member of a University must not be forced to cooperate in any scientific or artistic project contrary to his or her conscience. Refusal to participate in such a research project must not have unfavourable consequences (§105 UnivG).

4. Education Law

148. The Act on Religious Education at School provides for the possibility of withdrawal from religious education classes (§2 section 1 RelUG). According to the

42. VfSlg. 7400/1974 (the so-called *Fristenlösungsentscheidung*).
43. VfSlg. 7720/1975.

Private School Act (PrivSchG), the teacher's freedom of conscience finds expression in the right to refuse any assignment to a denominational private school (§20 PrivSchG).

5. Taking the (Religious) Oath

149. According to §1 Act on Oath 1868 (EidG), the legal standard form of oath must be taken as an *affirmatio religiosa*, including an invocation of God, irrespective of the denominational conviction of the person concerned, whether they are witnesses, parties, defendants or experts. An oath is provided in civil proceedings, non-procedural issues (Außerstreitverfahren) or administrative court procedures. With regard to criminal procedures, the taking of oaths has been eliminated with the penal proceeding reform of 2008.

150. The legal provision in §1 EidG is in contradiction not only with the fundamental right of religious freedom but also with the general principle of equality. Furthermore, it hardly seems compatible with the state's obligation to denominational neutrality. Therefore, the legislator should consider the reasonableness of this legal instrument, and whether its maintenance in the still remaining areas can be legitimated, particularly regarding that its significance for the administration of justice seems rather minor or even counterproductive.

151. In judicial practice, the actual problems are diminished insofar as the judiciary handles the administration of oaths in a very restrained and cautious manner. Depending on the conviction of the person taking the oath, the courts are satisfied with a handshake and an oath without recourse to God. A decision[44] made by the Supreme Court reflects the problematic character of this legal instrument. In this particular case, the crucial issue was whether Druses, a group with an Islamic tradition, should be obliged to swear the oath in the special religious form provided for Muslims. On the basis of contradictory views on the qualification of Druses as an Islamic or Pseudo-Islamic group respectively, the Court decided – in conflict with the self-understanding of the defendant – that the general form for taking the oath should be applied.

6. Labour Law

152. As far as convictions of employees are concerned, there are special protective legal rules regarding the sphere of various media (§2 Act on Media [MedienG]; §32 section 1 Federal Act on Austrian Broadcasting [ORF-G]; §11 Act on Legal

---

44. OGH 11 Nov. 1999, 6 Ob 195/99s; cf. R. Potz, 'Beeidigung eines Drusen nach der allgemeinen Eidesformel. Kommentar zu OGH 11. 11. 1999, 6 Ob 195/99s', *Österreichisches Archiv für Recht und Religion* 47 (2000), 424–428.

Positions of Journalists [JournalistenG]). Beyond that, under specific circumstances, conscientious reasons can be granted legal relevance with respect to conflicts which could by no means be predicted. In such cases, aspects of exemptions of obligations and adjustments or even cancellations of contracts need to be considered.

II. Special Forms of Manifestation

153. Freedom of worship entails the right to hold or take part in holy services, prayers and other sacral ceremonies. In the state legal system, such manifestations are specifically covered by laws regulating public holidays, protection of religious places, confidentiality or other official forms of secrecy. Freedom of confession also comprises the guarantee to exercise one's religion or belief outside of worship, in speech and writing, through artistic activities, communication and other manifestations. State legislation makes reference to such forms of practice, for instance, in regard to the religious upbringing of children, denominational private schools, religious education classes in public schools and private schools with public status, or media law. Freedom of confession also comprises the negative component of religious freedom, including the question of compulsory declaration of religious beliefs, already discussed with particular regard to personal status and residence registration.

A. *Church Membership and State Law*

154. According to §3 AnerkennungsG and §4 section 1 no. 4 BekGG, the acquisition of membership is a matter for the internal regulation of religious communities. The access to a newly chosen religious community must be personally declared to the competent authority of the legally recognized church or religious society (Article 6 section 2 InterkonfG). Owing to the fundamental right of religious freedom comprising the right to leave as well as change a religious community, the state law has to guarantee such acts. The declaration of withdrawal must be submitted to the state administrative body which is obliged to inform the respective religious community, however, without this being a pre-condition for its effectiveness.

B. *Parental Care*

1. Religious Maturity and Right of Custody

155. Children also enjoy freedom of religion or belief. Full legal capacity is reached with the completion of the eighteenth year of life, while religious maturity is already reached at the age of fourteen. Until minors have reached religious maturity, their parents or legal guardians have to act on their behalf in religious matters. At the same time, parents exercise their own individual rights to the upbringing and education of their children, primarily as part of the fundamental right of respect to private and family life (Article 8 ECHR). Moreover, in 1993, Austria ratified the Convention on the Rights of the Child, which provides in its Article 14 that state parties 'shall respect the right of the child to freedom of thought, conscience and religion' and 'shall respect the rights and duties of the parents and, when applicable, legal guardians, to provide direction to the child in the exercise of his or her right in a manner consistent with the evolving capacities of the child'.[45] As far as medical treatment is concerned cf. 544.

2. Federal Act on the Religious Upbringing of Children

156. The Act on the Religious Upbringing of Children of 1985[46] (RelKErzG) provides for a detailed structure of religious maturity. According to §6 RelKErzG, all these rules also apply to non-religious beliefs. In a free agreement, the parents decide on the religious upbringing of the child as far as they have the right to parental care and responsibility for raising the child. This agreement can be revoked at any time and is dissolved by the death of one of the spouses (§1 RelKErzG).

157. If such an agreement does not exist or has been revoked, the general rules of the General Civil Law Code (ABGB) on parental care also apply to the religious education of children (§2 RelKErzG). However, as long as the marriage exists no spouse may decide without the other's consent that a child should be raised in another confession than that which was the common confession at the time of marriage, or in another confession than previously, or that the child should be withdrawn from religious instruction at school. If consent is refused, an application for mediation or a decision by the family (guardianship) court may be lodged. The court should hear both sides and also, if necessary, relatives and teachers of the child – provided this seems reasonable. After the age of ten, the opinion of the child should be heard. If the father or mother and a legal guardian share the care of the child and there is a difference in opinion about which confession the child should be raised in, the father or mother's decision will prevail over the decision of the legal guardian, unless the father or the mother has lost the responsibility of the religious upbringing of the child according to civil law (§3 section 1 RelKErzG).

158. If the exclusive right of custody for the child lies with the legal guardian he or she must make decisions about his or her religious upbringing. The approval of the guardianship court is needed for this decision. Before a decision is made, however, the child's parents, relatives and teachers should be heard – provided this seems reasonable. After the age of 10, the opinion of the child should be heard. The legal guardian cannot change any decision once made regarding the religious confession of the child (§3 section 2 RelKErzG).

---

45. Cf. also the Federal Constitutional Law on the Rights of Children (BVG-Kinderrechte) 2011, BGBl. I 2011/4.
46. Re-enactment of the (German) Act on the Religious Upbringing of Children 1921/1939.

159. Treaties concerning the religious upbringing of a child have no effect under civil law (§4 RelKErzG).

160. After the age of 14, the child is free to decide about his or her religious confession. From the age of 12 years onwards, the child's religious confession may not be changed against his or her will (§5 RelKErzG).

C. Circumcision

161. The legal situation in Austria regarding this issue may be considered quite clear. §90 section 1 StGB stipulates that physical injury is not contrary to law if the injured or endangered person agrees to it in advance and the injury or danger as such does not contravene good morals. According to section 3, consent to genital mutilation or any other genital injury which causes a lasting impairment of sexual sensation is inadmissible. In medical and legal practice and doctrine, the predominant opinion is that a medically unnecessary male circumcision may not be subsumed under this prohibition. In the case of minors, especially before their faculties of apprehension and judgment have been fully formed, parents or other legal guardians with custody rights may give their consent to performing circumcision. Here, they are exercising their right to raise their children in conformity with their religious convictions. Weighing up all the pros and cons of the case and taking into account that circumcision is an irreversible invasion of bodily integrity, the circumcision of male minors for non-medical reasons is considered legal if consent has been given. It may be deemed consistent with the child's welfare, provided the circumcision is carried out lege artis.

162. The Explanatory Remarks of §11 section 4 IslamG 2015 explicitly point out that circumcision is covered by the rights of the Islamic religious societies and their members to guide their children and youth through all traditional Islamic customs and to educate them in accordance with religious doctrines (cf. 361).

D. Anti-discrimination Law

1. General Remarks

163. The equal treatment of women and men in matters of employment was established by the Act on Equal Treatment of 1979 (GlBG) and the Federal Act on Equal Treatment of 1993 (B-GlBG) and with regard to disability special Acts have been issued.[47] Religious discrimination, however, was considered almost exclusively as an issue of the so-called Tendenzschutz (cf. 472 et seq.).

47. Behinderteneinstellungsgesetz, BGBl. 1973/329 as amended, and Bundes-Behindertengleichstellungsgesetz, BGBl. I 2005/82 as amended, implementing the European Directive 2000/78/EC.

164. The new enactment of both Acts on Equal Treatment of 2004[48] was rendered on the basis of the corresponding European Directives, Directive 2000/43/EC of 29 June 2000 implementing the principle of equal treatment of persons irrespective of racial or ethnic origin and Directive 2000/78/EC of 27 November 2000 establishing a general framework for equal treatment in employment and occupation on the grounds of a person's ethnic origin,[49] religion or belief, age and sexual orientation. Since then, both Acts have been amended several times, among other reasons, to implement the European Directive 2004/113/EC of 13 December 2004.[50] In compliance with the Directives, the scope of protection differs depending on the ground for discrimination. As regards equal treatment irrespective of ethnic origin (implementing the Anti-racism Directive) and gender (implementing the Directive 2004/113/EC), the scope of the law's application extends beyond employment law to other areas, mainly comprising social and educational matters as well as the supply of goods and other services such as housing accommodation (§§30 et seq. GlBG).

165. The obligation to equal treatment according to the GlBG essentially includes all types of employment based on civil contracts, while the B-GlBG applies to employment in the public sector, such as the Federal Republic as a whole (Bund), both under public and private law. The B-GlBG includes analogous provisions to the GlBG modified with regard to the public character of the employment.

166. Pursuant to §41 section 1 B-GlBG, the law also applies to the members of a university as well as to applicants for employment within that university, to any other legal relationship with the university and to the registration of students. A rule governing both direct and indirect discrimination covers students and university applicants (Cf. 206).

2. Religion, Belief and Political Convictions

167. There is no explicit legal definition of religion, but the Explanatory Remarks describe belief as follows:[51]

---

48. New Act on Equal Treatment (GlBG 2004) and Amendment to B-GlBG 1993, BGBl. I 2004/65.
49. In the course of the parliamentary proceedings, the notion of 'race' was removed from the text and replaced by the term *ethnische Zugehörigkeit*, representing 'race' and 'ethnic origin' in the text of the Directives. This should not imply any limitation of scope; it is the result of sensitivity to the notion of 'race' in the German language (AB 499 BlgNR 22. GP).
50. Cf. M. Windisch-Graetz, 'Gleichbehandlung in der Arbeitswelt ohne Unterschied der ethnischen Zugehörigkeit, der Religion oder Weltanschauung, des Alters oder der sexuellen Orientierung (Antidiskriminierung)', in *Kommentar zum Gleichbehandlungsgesetz*, ed. R. Rebhahn (Vienna & New York: Springer, 2005), 414–490; H. Hopf, K. Mayr & J. Eichinger, *GlBG: Gleichbehandlung – Antidiskriminierung* (Vienna: Manz, 2009), 592–604; C. Brünner (ed.), *Diskriminierung aus religiösen Gründen* (Vienna: Verlag Österreich, 2009). Cf. papers given at the 'Fachtagung: Religionsrechtliche Fragen des neuen Gleichbehandlungsrechts in europäischer Perspektive', *Österreichisches Archiv für Recht und Religion* 55 (2008), 177 et seq.
51. RV 307 BlgNR 22. GP; AB 499 BlgNR 22. GP, 61.

> The term belief serves as a collective name for all religious, ideological, political and other conceptions of life and the world as a meaningful entirety, being the basis for constructing the personal and common position for the individual idea of life.

168. Furthermore, the Explanatory Notes refer to 'world views, the conception of man, and attitudes to morality'. Therefore, the question arises as to whether this description principally includes political opinions, which are not necessarily linked to religious conviction or 'beliefs' (*Weltanschauungen*), though there might be occasions when this is the case. This issue is viewed differently in scientific literature, though a certain tendency to include political opinions in the scope of application is noticeable. However, attention should be paid to the fact that such a broad understanding of the term 'belief' implies a certain risk of losing the distinctiveness of this fundamental right in substance.[52]

169. In 2009, the Supreme Court discussed this problem for the first time; however, due to the concrete facts, there was no need to make a fundamental decision. The Court merely stated that critical views on asylum legislation and the case law of the Austrian Asylum Senate are not covered by the term 'belief' (*Weltanschauung*).[53]

170. In another decision, the High Administrative Court (VwGH) made reference to the Explanatory Remarks to §13 B-GlBG according to which the term 'belief' (*Weltanschauung*) is described (among others) as a basic political conception of life and the world as a meaningful entirety the basis for creating personal and common positions for the individual philosophy of life. Thus, political convictions – provided they are not confined to single issues but are of a systematic nature – are considered beliefs (*Weltanschauungen*) according to the national understanding of the norm concerned. Based on this argumentation, the Court decided that this provision prohibits discrimination against individuals on the grounds of affiliation with the Social Democratic Party, or on the grounds of non-membership.[54]

171. Pursuant to §17 GlBG, any direct or indirect discrimination on the grounds of ethnic origin, religion or belief, age or sexual orientation in the context of employment and occupation is prohibited. The legal definitions of direct and indirect discrimination, the concept of discrimination (§19), the exemption clauses or the occupational requirements (§20) all strictly adhere to the European Council Directives in their essential parts.

172. For the purposes of this Act, direct discrimination shall be deemed to occur where one person is treated less favourably than another is, has been or would be

52. Cf. R. Potz & B. Schinkele, *Religionsrecht im Überblick*, 2nd ed. (Vienna: facultas.wuv, 2007), 95 et seq.
53. OGH 24 Feb. 2009, 9 ObA 122/07t. *See* A. Potz, 'Kommentar zu OGH 24. 2. 2009, 9 ObA 122/07t', *Österreichisches Archiv für Recht und Religion* 58 (2011), 210–223.
54. VwGH 15 May 2013, 2012/12/0013. Notwithstanding the Court's attitude concerning political convictions, the complaint was rejected.

treated in a comparable situation, on any grounds referred to in §17 section 1 GlBG; indirect discrimination shall be deemed to occur where an apparently neutral provision, criterion or practice could in particular have disadvantageous effects on persons of a certain religion or belief, age, or sexual orientation compared with other persons, unless that provision, criterion or practice is objectively justified by a legitimate aim and the means of achieving that aim are appropriate and necessary.

173. Discrimination against a particular person is covered by §19 section 3 of the GlBG. Moreover, protection against discrimination includes discriminatory behaviour towards a person because of a close relationship with another person based on ethnic origin, religion or belief, age or sexual orientation in the context of employment and is prohibited (§19 section 4). Discrimination shall also be considered to have occurred when a person is subject to harassment by an employer or any other person (§21).

3. Exceptions to the General Prohibition

174. All exemption clauses or occupational requirements strictly adhere to the European Council Directives in their essential parts. §20 section 1 GlBG reads as follows:

> A difference of treatment based on a characteristic related to ethnic origin, religion or belief, age or sexual orientation shall not constitute discrimination where, by reason of the nature of the particular occupational activity or of the context in which it is carried out, such a characteristic constitutes a genuine and determining occupational requirement, provided that the objective is legitimate and the requirement is proportionate.

175. It must be taken into consideration that it is particularly likely that a religious ground for discrimination might perhaps coincide with an ethnic ground (for example in the case of Jews, Muslims or Sikhs). A clear delimitation between ethnic and religious discrimination cannot always be drawn. For this reason, complex questions may arise if more than one criterion of discrimination in the facts of one single case coincide inseparably, so-called multiple or intersectional discrimination.

4. The Equal Treatment Commission

176. The Federal Act on the Equal Treatment Commission and the Ombudsman for Equal Treatment (GBK/GAW) has established the Equal Treatment Commission and the office of the Ombudsman for Equal Treatment. The Equal Treatment Commission in the Federal Chancellery consisting of three senates sits alongside the labour and the civil courts. Essentially, the proceedings are intended as mediation between employers and employees in advance of legal proceedings. The commission is also authorized to give expert opinions on questions concerning the violation of the principle of equal treatment. The main task of the Ombudsman is to advise and support persons who feel discriminated against in the sense of the equal treatment law. The office of the Ombudsman can carry out surveys on discrimination independently and publish reports and recommendations. The Federal Equal Treatment Commission in the Federal Chancellery is a special federal administrative facility. Any matter concerning discrimination in connection with federal employment may be brought before this Commission.

5. Consequences of Discrimination

177. In the case of discriminatory measures, there is no obligation to enter into a contract, but claims may be made for compensation for damage to or loss of property as well as for personal encroachment. In disputes, the alleged discrimination must be substantiated by prima facie evidence. After weighing all facts and merits of the case, the respondent must prove that another credible motive was the decisive factor in the unequal treatment, or confirm the existence of legal justification (§26 section 12 GlBG). Termination or dismissal of employment on the grounds of religion or belief may be appealed against in court.

178. So far, little case law has been developed in any of the courts (cf. above 2.). However, the Federal Equal Treatment Commission and the Ombudsman for Equal Treatment have had to deal with cases of discrimination on religious grounds. *In some cases, infringements of the Equal Treatment Act were observed and indemnifications were made.*[55] A few conflicts, especially ones concerning the wearing of Islamic headscarves (e.g., as an apprentice in a shop or a physician in a sanatorium with a conservative clientele) have been resolved through compensation payments recommended by the Commission for Equal Treatment. The rejection of a Muslim woman's application to work as a seamstress based on the argument that the headscarf might become entangled with the machine was considered to be in concordance with the prohibition of discrimination. The exclusion of a Sikh participant from a training course for the long-term unemployed for security reasons because he was wearing a Kirpan (a 20-cm long dagger) was considered justified by the Equal Treatment Commission, despite the impending loss of his benefits. Similarly, another Sikh had to relinquish his Kirpan when entering a courthouse.

179. A few years before the European anti-discrimination law was implemented, a Supreme Court decision[56] dealt with a Muslim employee who had been dismissed for worshipping daily in the presence of other employees, using a carpet and other religious objects for praying. He was also charged with leaving the business before closing time in order to go to the mosque on Friday afternoon, without taking working instructions into consideration. The Court stated that such behaviour disturbed the planned distribution of labour and irritated co-workers who also held the same fundamental right to religious freedom (in its negative dimension).

55. https://www.bmbf.gv.at/frauen/gleichbehandlungskommissionen/index.html.
56. OGH 27 Mar. 1996, 9 ObA 18/96.

Although the Court discussed the positive and the negative aspects of religious freedom, as it should, the question must be raised whether confrontation with forms of worship such as those described above is an unreasonable demand on the other employees.

E. Dress Requirements

180. In general, one has to assume the admissibility of wearing Islamic headscarves (hijabs) or Sikh turbans (dastars) as aspects of religious practice. The Anti-Face-Covering Act (AGesVG) 2017 introduced a ban on the covering of facial features in public places, whereby the legislator was referring to the Islamic niqab in particular. Section 1 states the aim of promoting integration by strengthening participation in society and ensuring peaceful coexistence in Austria. This law was criticized because although enabling interpersonal communication is an essential factor for peaceful, harmonious coexistence, constitutionally guaranteed liberties also include the right of the individual to refrain from participating in interpersonal communication if she or he should so choose.

181. A municipal decision in the system for operating city traffic in Vienna (Wiener Verkehrsbetriebe) was taken along similar lines: An adherent of the Sikh religion applied to the Viennese transport authority for a position as a tram driver, stating that he wanted to wear his turban as is required in his religious doctrine. The transport services agreed with his request, on the condition that the turban had the same colours as the usual drivers' caps and showed the transport system's logo. The passengers should be able to identify the Sikh driver as a member of staff.

182. During a trial by jury concerning the felony of a terrorist association according to §278b section 2 StGB and other acts liable to prosecution, the defendant refused to take off her face veil, a so-called niğab. This was classified as 'unseemly behaviour' which interfered with the order of judicial proceedings, and the woman was therefore excluded from attending the proceedings pursuant to §234 of the Code of Criminal Procedure (StPO).[57] The Supreme Court rejected the defendant's nullity appeal.[58] From the Court's point of view, the measure in question was justified, being neither based on bias or partiality of the Jury Court nor on any other procedural fault. Following the chief judge's reasoning in substance, the Supreme Court underlined that the defendant had been allowed to wear a headscarf and to attend the proceedings at any time provided she removed her veil. Because having one's face uncovered is considered an uncontested fundamental principle of common human communication in Austria it was the defendant's task to explain in a convincing way why her behaviour towards the Court could be considered not only as a politically but also ideologically motivated demonstration, for which, however,

57. Regional Criminal Court Vienna, 3 Mar. 2008, 442 Hv 1/08h.
58. OGH 27 Aug. 2008, 13 Os 83/08t. *See* B. Schinkele, 'Verschleierung einer Angeklagten im Gerichtssaal? Überlegungen aus grundrechtlicher Sicht', in *Islamophobie in Österreich*, eds. J. Bunzl & F. Hafez (Vienna & Innsbruck: Studienverlag, 2009), 156–167.

a courtroom was certainly not the right place. The Supreme Court took the position that the defendant had failed to allay these doubts and to show clearly her respect for the dignity of the Court irrespective of the disdain indicated by covering her face.

183. This decision was criticized because, according to the principle of proportionality, exclusion from Court proceedings must be the ultima ratio, taking into account the importance of the fundamental right of religious freedom and the guarantee of a fair trial (Article 6 ECHR).[59] The mere attendance of a veiled person in a courtroom, however, by no means endangers public order, national security, or any other object protected by legal order in the sense of Article 9 section 2 of the ECHR. Being present, even though without being heard on the substance of the charge would at least enable the defendant to follow the proceedings and, in case of need, to react with the help of her defence counsel and in particular, to bring forward a motion to give evidence according to Article 6 section 3 lit. d ECHR. This would be the way to guarantee to a certain degree the right to a fair trial and defence, although admittedly, in a considerably restricted sense.

F. Ritual Slaughter

1. Federal Act on the Protection of Animals

184. In 2004, after an extensive and quite emotionally charged public debate, a new Federal Act on Animal Protection (TSchG) was enacted, establishing a uniform legal situation throughout the whole federal territory.[60] According to this law, slaughter without previous stunning is principally forbidden. As regards 'compulsory religious precepts or bans of legally recognized churches and religious societies' which contravene this rule, ritual slaughter may be deemed lawful by administrative approval if it complies with certain detailed prerequisites concerning the slaughtering procedure. According to §11 Animal Welfare Slaughtering Regulation (Tierschutz-Schlachtverordnung)2015, Appendix A Z 3, the slaughter may only be carried out by a person who can prove their authorization by means of a certificate from a legally recognized religious society (for the Islamic concept of halal, cf., cf. 362). In any case, stunning must be carried out immediately after the act of incision and in such a manner that the animal does not suffer unnecessary pain, harm and fear. As a consequence, ritual slaughtering does not correspond to the offence of cruelty to animals according to §222 StGB which is an offence committed by a person who rawly mistreats or inflicts unnecessary torture on an animal.

59. *Ibid.*

60. Till then this subject matter fell within the sphere of competence of the *Bundesländer*, entailing diverging regulations, partly in contradiction with the constitutional guarantees. Cf. R. Potz & B. Schinkele, *Religionsrecht im Überblick*, 2nd ed. (Vienna: facultas.wuv, 2007), 86 et seq.; W. Wieshaider, 'Iterum: Schächten: Rund ums neue österreichische Tierschutzgesetz', *Österreichisches Archiv für Recht und Religion* 52 (2005), 227–262.

In this context, it must be underlined that experts have quite diverging views about the question of the animals' suffering pain during ritual slaughter by comparison with industrial slaughter.

185. In principle, this regulation is in concordance with the fundamental guarantees. The reference to 'compulsory religious precepts or bans', however, could give rise to misinterpretation. It should be clarified that the existence of different doctrines within a single religious community concerning this issue is of no importance from the point of view of the state. At any rate, the state must refrain from interpreting or assessing religious doctrines and precepts or their obligatory character. It must also be underlined that restriction of the exemption in question to legally recognized churches and religious societies constitutes unequal treatment. Ritual slaughtering falls within the scope of the fundamental right of religious freedom and as such it must be permitted to all religious groups irrespective of their legal status. At present, this seems to involve no practical problems owing to the fact that Sikhs do not perform ritual slaughter.

2. Case Law

186. If the aforementioned points of criticism are taken into consideration, this legal Act is essentially in conformity with the Constitutional Court and the Supreme Court's decision-making from the perspective of constitutional as well as penal law.[61] Accordingly, religious slaughter neither offends public morals nor infringes upon public order. In its recent decision on religious slaughter, the Constitutional Court ruled that public order only refers to actions that are incompatible with the peaceful coexistence of citizens and therefore only such provisions that are of essential significance from that point of view are permitted to restrict religious or denominational manifestations. Furthermore, this corresponds with the prevailing legislation from a legal comparative point of view, as well as with the opinion of the ECtHR and the law of the EU concerning the protection of animals at the moment of slaughtering or killing (cf. 421).

61. VfSlg. 15394/1998; OGH 28 Mar. 1996, 15 Os 27, 28/96; VwSlg. 10666/1897; 248 A/1907. Cf. R. Potz, B. Schinkele & W. Wieshaider (eds.), *Schächten. Religionsfreiheit und Tierschutz* (Freistadt-Egling: Plöchl, 2001).

Chapter 3. Collective Religious Freedom

187. The fundamental right of religious freedom comprises three dimensions, the individual, the collective and the corporative. Although there is a gradual increase in scale, the differentiation between the individual and the collective element is not of great significance. Every person involved in manifesting religion in a community with others is practising his or her individual right to religious freedom. Such activities are also covered by the fundamental right of freedom of assembly. Corporative religious freedom is of essential significance whereby a church, a religious community or another organization representing a philosophical belief (Weltanschauung) is the holder of the fundamental right. In this case, the scope of protection of the fundamental rights of freedom of religion and freedom of association overlap.

Chapter 4. Organizational Religious Freedom

§1. Corporative Religious Freedom

188. In Austrian legal language, the concept of 'corporative freedom of religions and belief' is used to describe the organizational component of this fundamental right. Religious and philosophical communities enjoy freedom of religion or belief in their own right (cf. 189). The individual and the corporative spheres are closely linked emanations of freedom of religion which has necessarily a fundamental status in a democratic secular state.

189. Though the historical legislator already stated in 1874 (Motivenbericht for the AnerkennungsG) that the purpose of this law was to realize the freedom of religion and conscience as well as the principle of parity of the confessions, thus accentuating the unity of both elements of religious freedom, the corporative sphere traditionally predominated in Austria. It was, however, combined with the state's right of supervision within the system of the so-called Staatskirchenhoheit.

190. Since 1945, the idea of human rights has been generally emphasized and for this reason, religious freedom as the right of every individual has become increasingly prominent. This development is reflected in the ECHR and the other instruments pertaining to human rights, particularly in the UN Covenants and the CSCE Documents (cf. 390 et seq.). Nowadays, it is stressed that it is the primary task of the state to promote religious communities in order to protect the religious interests of the individual adherents. This is one of the relevant aspects which illustrate why the use of the concept of Law on Religion is preferable to Ecclesiastical Law.[62]

§2. Different Categories of Religious Organizations

191. Another characteristic feature of the Austrian law on religion closely connected to the first-mentioned aspect is the strict differentiation between legally recognized churches and religious societies with public law status, on the one hand, and other religious communities on the other, as is constitutionally laid down in Article 15 StGG.[63] The Treaty of St. Germain extended the right to the free exercise of faiths, religions or denominations of every kind in public or in private to every inhabitant of Austria, thereby including adherents of legally not-recognized religious

62. H. M. Heinig & C. Walter, *Staatskirchenrecht oder Religionsverfassungsrecht. Ein begriffspolitischer Grundsatzstreit* (Tübingen: Mohr Siebeck, 2007); R. Potz & B. Schinkele, 'Europarecht – Wie hast du's mit der Religion?', in *Religion in Europa heute. Sozialwissenschaftliche, rechtswissenschaftliche und hermeneutisch-religionsphilosophische Perspektiven*, eds. K. Appel et al. (Göttingen: V&R unipress, 2012), 133 et seq.
63. VfSlg. 9185/1981; 11931/1988; cf. *248* et seq.

communities insofar as the exercise of their faith is not incompatible with public order or morality. However, corresponding provisions were not implemented at the corporative level.

192. Since the Federal Act concerning the Legal Personality of State-Registered Religious Communities (BekGG) was enacted in 1998 and the new Act on Associations 2002 (VereinsG), it has become possible for religious communities to obtain legal personality under private law. Despite this positive development, the differences in the treatment of both categories of religious communities in numerous legal fields have to be scrutinized with a view to reasonable justification, particularly insofar as legal positions are directly based on the fundamental right of religious freedom.

193. As far as non-religious philosophical communities (Weltanschauungsgemeinschaften) are concerned, these may attain the status of legal persons in the form of non-profit associations under private law on the basis of the Act on Associations 2002, however, without being identified by state bodies as philosophical communities. This represents a regulatory deficit in view of the equal treatment of religious communities and communities of non-religious belief which is required as a fundamental right.

194. In theory, the possibility also exists of founding a 'permissible society' (*erlaubte Gesellschaft*) according to §26 ABGB without state involvement. Nevertheless, apart from the fact that this possibility is merely of marginal practical importance, the acquisition of a legal entity is not undisputed.

195. The above-mentioned three categories of religious communities have the status of legal persons – be it under public or private law – and therefore the fundamental rights apply to them to the extent that the nature of such rights permits. To give an example, freedom of conscience as provided for by Article 14 StGG and Article 9 ECHR inherently presupposes an individual human person.

196. Public law status comprises the legal capacity of entities under private law. They may, therefore, own real property (church buildings and other assets) and take part in the ordinary course of legal transactions without restrictions, sharing equal status with other legal personalities. However, a specific Austrian problem exists, arising from §867 ABGB, which stipulates that 'presuppositions for validity of contracts with those communities upon which the special providence of the public administration is conferred are determined by their constitutions, respectively the political laws'. In practice, this provision only holds relevance for institutions of the Catholic Church, for which a specific provision in the Concordat exists (cf. 303 et seq.).[64]

64. H. Kalb, R. Potz & B. Schinkele, 'Rechtsgeschäfte mit kirchlichen juristischen Personen', *Österreichisches Archiv für Recht und Religion* 48 (2001), 353–418; R. Thunhart, 'Privatrechtlicher Vertrauensschutz und § 867 ABGB', *Österreichisches Archiv für Recht und Religion* 48 (2001), 419–454.

197. The Act on Responsibility of Associations (VbVG) refers to actions constituting a criminal offence according to state law. This Act indicates a fundamental reform, insofar as hitherto, criminal proceedings could not be pursued against juridical, but only physical persons. For the purpose of this Act, 'associations' include juridical persons, commercial partnerships, registered commercial companies and European economic communities of interest. Legally recognized churches and religious societies, as well as state-registered religious communities are explicitly exempt insofar as pastoral activities are concerned.

Chapter 5. Religious Freedom and Equality

§1. General Principle of Equality

198. Within the Constitution, the general principle of equality is enshrined in Article 2 StGG and Article 7 B-VG. The last-mentioned guarantee, *inter alia*, explicitly excludes privileges by reason of religion. In particular, in connection with the principle of equality, the Constitutional Court has transcended the understanding of fundamental rights as rights with a merely defensive effect.[65] As a result of this, it is now possible to derive state obligations – at least as a reflex – to render services in application of the principle of equality.[66]

199. By this approach to decision-making on the principle of equality, the Constitutional Court has compensated to a certain extent its principally positivistic attitude and its static understanding of fundamental rights. Thus, the efficiency of the protection of fundamental rights has been successively improved. Nowadays, the principle of equality is understood as a general precept of objectivity and reasonableness of legal regulations. For the judicial and administrative bodies, this means prohibition of arbitrary decision-making and the obligation to observe the principle of proportionality. This implies – safeguarding the legislator's margin of appreciation, primarily pertaining to legal policy – that it is the duty of the legislator to take care that any legal differentiation must be based on reasonable criteria and on the principle of proportionality in relation to the person affected as well as the concrete state of affairs.

200. In cases of interference with fundamental rights, the Constitutional Court has, moreover, the tendency to refer to the principle of equality instead of the fundamental right directly concerned. In compliance with this approach, §2 IsraelitenG was partially declared unconstitutional owing to a violation of the principle of equality and not of Articles 14 and 15 StGG respectively. The Court stated that it was incompatible with the principle of equality to prevent a group of Jewish people from founding another legally recognized religious community besides the only one already existing on a certain territory.[67]

§2. Prohibition of Discrimination According to §14 ECHR

201. Moreover, the ECHR in general and the prohibition of discrimination pursuant to Article 14 has an enormous impact on the legal system in Austria. Essentially, this derives from the fact that the ECHR is incorporated into the Constitution.

65. *See* K. Korinek, 'Betrachtungen zur österreichischen Verfassungsgerichtsbarkeit', in *Staatsrecht und Staatswissenschaften in Zeiten des Wandels*, eds. B.-C. Funk et al. (Vienna & New York: Springer, 1992).
66. R. Potz, 'Suum cuique – The Parity of the Recognized Churches and Religious Communities in Austria'. *European Journal for Church and State Research* 4 (1997), 196.
67. VfSlg. 9185/1987.

It must be underlined that these effects have become noticeable after a considerable period of hesitation. Later on, the Strasbourg case law generally had major implications in interpreting fundamental rights on the basis of dynamic comprehension. With regard to legislation, the equal treatment of men and women has been the initial turning point at the level of ordinary laws concretizing the constitutional prohibition of discrimination. Since then, this process has been successively intensified, mainly under the influence of European law (cf. 424 et seq.). As far as religious communities are concerned, Article 14 ECHR must be taken into consideration because according to Article 15 StGG, the principle of parity only applies to legally recognized churches and religious societies.

§3. Non-discrimination in Public Offices

202. Article 3 StGG stipulates that all public offices are accessible to all citizens. Exempt from this general rule are offices that are bound to confessions on the basis of objective and reasonable justification. This mainly applies to teachers of religious instruction in schools and the staff of theological faculties as well as clerics and other persons engaged in pastoral care in military or other institutions. A singular exemption also applies to the state official in the competent federal Ministry dealing with matters concerning the Protestant churches.

203. The Federal Act on Equal Treatment (B-GlBG) includes the entire sphere of employment with the Federal Republic as a whole (Bund), both under public and private law. Attention should be drawn to the special provision concerning discrimination on grounds of religion or belief in §13b section 2 B-GlBG,[68] which reads as follows:

> In case of occupational activities within public organizations the ethos of which is based on religion or belief, a difference of treatment based on a person's religion or belief shall not constitute discrimination where, by reason of the nature of these activities or of the context in which they are carried out, a person's religion or belief constitute a genuine, legitimate and justified occupational requirement, having regard to the organization's ethos.

204. According to the Explanatory Notes, the legislator presupposes that the organization of religious education classes in public schools as well as the institution for spiritual welfare within the armed forces could be deemed to be 'public organizations, the ethos of which is based on religion or belief' for the purpose of this Act. This construction implies a special meaning of the term 'public organization', taking into consideration the concrete factual and legal merits. As a consequence of this subsumption, the special exemption clause and its standard of evaluation (*lex specialis*) apply to the types of employment in question. Teachers of religious instruction as well as persons entrusted with pastoral welfare are essentially performing

68. § 13b section 1 B-GlBG comprises a general exemption clause, similar to § 20 section 1 GlBG (cf. *168*).

functions which are intrinsic core activities of church and religious communities. Any other interpretation would involve serious inconsistencies.[69] Pursuant to §41 section 1, the B-GlBG also applies to the members of a university as well as to applicants for employment, for any other legal relationship with the university, or for registration as a student (irrespective of certain exceptions). As far as studies are concerned, a direct and indirect anti-discrimination rule applies to students and university applicants.[70]

§4. Specific Guarantees of Equality Regarding Religion

205. According to Article 14 section 3 StGG, the enjoyment of civil and political rights is independent of religious belief. Nevertheless, duties incumbent on nationals may not be prejudiced by religious beliefs. This provision takes into consideration the general principle of equality from the perspective of individual religious freedom.

206. The principle of parity in its formal and substantial dimension as it is laid down in Article 15 StGG is seen as a special manifestation of the general principle of equality in the fields of state and church relationship, exclusively, however, with regard to legally recognized churches and religious societies (cf. 265 et seq.).

207. For historical reasons, a conception of special laws for several recognized churches and religious communities exists in Austria which is considered to be a sustainable instrument for realizing substantive parity, as reflected in §1 section 2 no. III ProtestantenG, which states:

> All acts of legislative and of executive power which concern the Protestant Church must observe the principle of equality before the law in relation to the legal and factual position of the other legally recognized churches and religious societies.

208. If this were to be affirmed, this provision would not merely be understood as a declaration of intent by the legislator, but rather in the sense of a most favoured (religion) clause with reciprocal effect. Accordingly, provisions that are expressly granted within the framework of the special law of religion of a legally recognized church or religious society would also apply to others as an adequate standard of law of religion. On the one hand, this raises very difficult questions and, on the other hand, such an interpretation – particularly with regard to the principle of equality and parity – has actually very little practical significance. As an example, only one Protestant agricultural public school is cited, which had been granted a subsidy on

69. Cf. B. Schinkele, 'Staat – Kirche – Schule und das neue Gleichbehandlungsrecht', *Österreichisches Archiv für Recht und Religion* 55 (2008), 290–303. For a different view cf. S. Schima, 'Die wichtigsten religionsrechtlichen Regelungen des Bundesrechts und des Landesrechts, Jahrgang 2005', *Österreichisches Archiv für Recht und Religion* 53 (2006), 292 fn. 32.
70. Special consequences with regard to the theological faculties must be left to a special contribution. Cf. R. Potz & J. Wallner, 'Antidiskriminierung und theologische Bildungseinrichtungen', *Österreichisches Archiv für Recht und Religion* 55 (2008), 304–326.

the basis of the aforementioned provision in the ProtestantenG in conjunction with Article II §2 of the 1962 School Agreement, as is provided for Catholic public schools of the same type.

Chapter 6. Limitations to Freedom of Religion or Belief

§1. General Characteristics of Limitations

209. The guarantees of fundamental rights in general contain different legal reservation clauses. The function of these reservation clauses has changed significantly in the course of establishing a state governed by the rule of law. Irrespective of their different wording, they should ensure initially that the administrative power adheres to the law. Since the principle of legality was incorporated into the Constitution in 1920 (Article 18 B-VG), the qualifications have lost their genuine meaning and have become more and more an instrument used by the legislator of ordinary laws in order to provide a basis for intervention. According to the StGG, a specific enactment is regularly required – except for the guarantees concerning religious freedom – if basic rights are to be restricted by statutes, without, however, any specifications for the ordinary legislator (*formeller Gesetzesvorbehalt*).[71]

210. In contrast, the differentiated and substantial legal reservations enshrined in the ECHR (Articles 8–12) – the so-called new type of restriction clauses – are to be understood in a substantive sense, implying a process of weighing the legal merits. In Austria, Article 9 section 2 ECHR includes the most important constitutional regulation in this respect:

> Freedom to manifest one's religion or beliefs shall be subject only to such limitations as are prescribed by law and are necessary in a democratic society in the interests of public safety, for the protection of public order, health or morals, or for the protection of the rights and freedoms of others.

211. The differentiated reservation clause of the ECHR is to be understood as a further step in a continuously progressive development of legalization. Therefore, the expressive enumeration of more objects protected by law found in the ECHR, in comparison to the former constitutional laws by no means implies an extension of the legislator's power to restrict fundamental rights. Such an approach would represent a fundamental misunderstanding, for two different reasons. First, it would imply an inadmissible abstraction from historical developments, and second, an unjustified inference from a numerical increase of expressively named legal objects to a quantitative enhancement of state power for intervention.

212. The most important instrument available for such an approach is the principle of proportionality. This restriction clause, therefore, requires reasonable, detailed examination, according to the criteria of aptitude, necessity and adequacy, i.e., proportionality in a narrower sense. In pursuance of the ultima-ratio principle, the least oppressive consequence must be taken in order to pursue the aim intended ('pressing social need'). The principle of proportionality can be considered to be the

71. *See* M. Holoubek, *Die* Struktur *der grundrechtlichen Gesetzesvorbehalte. System oder Schrankenwirrwarr?* (Vienna: Orac, 1997).

most important instrument in constructing fundamental rights as well as an unchallenged principle of the law of the European Union. It constitutes an elementary principle of justice permeating the legal order as a comprehensive unity.[72] In any case, this concept should be taken into consideration in a very strict sense, especially with regard to the objects of legal protection enumerated in the ECHR, which would otherwise almost amount to blanket clauses. The idea of a subsidiary is also encompassed in this principle, whereby the protection of the individual's fundamental rights is assessed to be of special value in comparison to public interests.

213. This is the correct procedure which must be followed, allowing for reasonable and appropriate coordination between the freedom to be protected and the legal provision restricting it to be established in individual cases. In accordance with the principle of proportionality, a fair balance between the conflicting legal positions concerned must be reached. This is the way by which the scope of protection of a fundamental right should be determined, or in other words, by which an ordinary statutory law can be qualified as a 'general law of the state'. It must be stressed that this discretion is neither uncontrolled nor unqualified. Specified argumentation is demanded here and the decisions are subject to a sequence of courts as well as to the final control of the Constitutional Court and the High Administrative Court. Of course, certain assessments are made within such procedures, whereby the scope of discretion for action rests with the legislator or – on a third level – to a lower degree, with the judicial and administrative bodies, respectively. The less concrete and tangible the formulation of the provision is, the greater the legislator's discretion for realizing his ideas within the constitutionally given standards. Within this margin of appreciation, the legislator is entitled to carry out his conceptions pertaining to legal politics.

§2. The Single Objects of Legal Protection According to the Reservation Clauses

214. As already mentioned, the different reservation clauses in Article 9 ECHR, Article 63 section 2 StVStGermain, and Articles 14 and 15 StGG present no hindrance to a harmonizing synopsis according to the construction of the guarantees concerned as an 'aggregated law on religious freedom' (cf. 112 et seq.). Though the wording of the individual reservation clauses is rather different, the subject matter seems quite similar. Essentially, the different legal reservations might amount to the same barriers. This is the way to attain genuine concordance, not only a conclusion

72. Cf. W. Berka, *Medienfreiheit und Persönlichkeitsschutz. Die Freiheit der Medien und ihre Verantwortung im System der Grundrechte* (Vienna & New York: Springer, 1982), 81; M. Holoubek, 'Zur Begründung des Verhältnismäßigkeitgrundsatzes – verwaltungs-, verfassungs- und gemeinschaftsrechtliche Aspekte', in *Grundfragen und aktuelle Probleme des öffentlichen Rechts*, eds. S. Griller et al. (Vienna: Orac, 1995), 97.

free of contradictions as a consequence of the most favoured principle, according to Article 54 ECHR.[73] Thus, there is no need to refer to it.

I. Citizens' Duties and Custody Rights (Article 14 StGG)

215. The relationship between the different sections of Article 14 StGG must be deemed a hierarchical correlation of norms. Consequently, in case of doubt, religious freedom takes precedence over the obligations inferred from the second and third sections. According to Article 14 section 2 StGG, the enjoyment of civil and political rights is independent of religious denomination. However, the duties may not be infringed upon by religious beliefs. This provision represents a specific clarification of the general principle of equality, which principally means that no individual may decline to fulfil a legal duty by referring to religious convictions. However, there are several legal exemptions, for instance, the exemption from giving evidence under the seal of confession as provided for under civil, penal, administrative or other specific procedural law. Concerning conscientious objectors (cf. 136 et seq.), Article 14 section 3 StGG states that no person may be compelled to perform acts of worship or to participate in church ceremonies or events, insofar as he or she is not subject to the legally justified power of a third person in that respect. According to the prevailing view, this provision only refers to custody rights of parents and other persons in charge of the upbringing of minors, before the latter have reached a responsible age in religious matters. No extension should be given to typical special-status relationships when the general status of civil liberty is limited by commitments under public law – for instance, during time spent in various institutions, during detention, or with regard to taking an oath.

II. Public Order and Public Safety (Article 63 Section 2 StVStGermain, Article 9 ECHR)

216. Reference to the protection of public order essentially indicates the functionality of the legal order, whereas public safety essentially implies the maintenance of internal and external peace. Preserving the functionality of the legal order, however, does not mean that public order should be considered equivalent to the legal order in its entirety. Such an interpretation has been explicitly rejected by the Constitutional Court.[74] Otherwise, the Court argued, the legislator of ordinary laws would be authorized to restrict or even abolish the freedom guaranteed for any reason. According to the Court's opinion, the term 'public order' comprises the 'embodiment of the prevailing fundamental conceptions of the legal order'. In a

73. According to this article, nothing in this Convention shall be constructed as limiting or derogating any human rights and fundamental freedoms which may be ensured under the law of any contracting party or under any other agreement to which it is a Party.
74. VfSlg. 2844/1955; VfSlg. 3505/1959.

decision from 1998 concerning religious slaughtering, the Court specified that insofar as public order only refers to actions which are incompatible with peaceful coexistence, only such provisions of essential importance from that point of view can therefore confine religious or denominational manifestations.[75] Therefore, mandatory religious precepts concerning ritual slaughtering do not constitute an offence to public morals nor do they infringe on public order (cf. 188).[76]

III. Good Morals (Article 63 Section 2 StVStGermain, Article 9 ECHR)

217. Courts very seldom refer to the restriction of 'good morals', an indefinite legal term, the legal interpretation of which, as a restriction of a fundamental right, is quite problematic. It encompasses an evolutional element, to a certain degree the implication of different moral standards under a local and temporal aspect. Consequently, the Strasbourg Conventional Instances stated that a uniform moral standard could not be deduced from the national legal orders of the Conventional parties. The Constitutional Court paraphrased this legal term as general fundamental ideas anchored in the population concerning a proper way of living, explicitly protected in a legal provision.[77] On the contrary, the doctrine often refers to 'pre-juridical categories'. With regard to the high and increasing closeness of legal codifications, by making reference to this limitation, the question at issue will usually not be whether 'good morals' could obtain legal relevance as non-codified law, but rather whether or not norms on the level of ordinary law could be qualified as concretizing 'good morals', and thus be able to legitimate an infringement of fundamental rights. In the case of *Otto Preminger Institute v. Austria*,[78] the ECtHR pointed out that as far as the term 'morals' is concerned it is not possible to discern one uniform conception of the significance of religion in society throughout Europe; even within a single country such conceptions may vary, as is the case in Austria with respect to the Province of the Tyrol (cf. 397).

IV. Health (Article 9 ECHR)

218. According to the case law of the Strasbourg Instances, health is to be understood in a broad sense insofar as it comprises the physical as well as the mental well-being of the individual. With regard to the law on religion, this potential restriction gains relevance primarily with regard to certain practices usually associated with certain new religious movements (sects). The legislator explicitly responds to such endangerments with the establishment of a public law institute for information on sects and similar institutions (cf. 464 et seq.).[79]

---

75. VfSlg. 15394/1998.
76. VfSlg. 15394/1998.
77. VfSlg. 15394/1998.
78. ECtHR 20 Sep. 1994, appl. no. 13470/87.
79. H. Kalb, R. Potz & B. Schinkele, 'Das Bundesgesetz über die Einrichtung einer Dokumentations- und Informationsstelle für Sektenfragen (EDISG)', *Österreichisches Archiv für Recht und Religion* 46 (1999), 353–400.

V. Rights and Freedoms of Others (Article 9 ECHR)

219. With regard to the rights and freedoms of others, reference is primarily made to the classic 'inherent limitations' comprising the human rights and freedoms embedded in the guarantees of fundamental rights. Furthermore, legal positions on the basis of ordinary laws might be protected in the same way, insofar as they reflect a common European standard. Altogether, a general commitment to tolerance as well as a prohibition of the misuse of fundamental rights must be deduced. To give an example: in principle, mission and even proselytising lie within the scope of fundamental rights. However, such activities must not infringe on other people's freedom of decision (cf. 558 et seq.).

VI. The General Laws of the State (Article 15 StGG)

220. Exactly this qualification is found in connection with the right of the churches and religious societies to determine and administrate their 'internal affairs' independently. Though their self-understanding is the main point of reference for the state legislator, it is, however, not the only decisive factor. The state itself has to formulate its own self-conception from its obligation to take care of the common weal. Therefore, a relationship to the legal reservation, reading as follows, should be established, '[...] but, like any association, is subject to the general laws of the state'. This formulation represents a restriction clause sui generis. Contrary to the other constitutional requirements of a specific enactment anchored in the StGG, this clause is to be understood as a material reservation implying, therefore, a process of weighing the legal merits. Due to the fact that the right to self-determination ensues directly from the human right of religious freedom, a comprehensive view of all religious guarantees is to be upheld according to the approach described above (cf. 119).

Part III. Legal Status of Religious Communities

Chapter 1. Formal Status of Religious Communities

221. There are three categories of religious communities:

- Legally recognized churches and religious societies with public law status.
- State-registered religious communities with legal entities under private law according to a special law on religious associations.
- Religious communities with legal entities under private law on the basis of the general Act on Associations.

222. It is to be assumed that all or almost all religious communities or movements operating within the federal territory which are neither legally recognized nor state-registered are organized on the basis of the Act on Associations.

§1. Legally Recognized Churches and Religious Societies

I. Overview

223. The constitutional basis of these religious communities is laid down in Article 15 StGG:

> Every Church and religious society recognized by the law has the right to joint public religious practice, arranges and administers its internal affairs autonomously, and retains possession and enjoyment of its institutions, endowments and funds devoted to worship, instruction and welfare, but is like every society subject to the general laws of the state (*allgemeine Staatsgesetze*).

224. The right of self-determination as it is encompassed there implies the status of an incorporated body under public law status (corporations sui generis). They are generally included, whenever state legislation relates to corporations under public law, unless explicitly excluded by law, as is the case, for instance, in the Act on Private Radio Broadcasting (PrR-G, cf. 726).

225. The following churches and religious societies enjoy public law status: the Catholic Church, the Protestant Church, the Greek-Oriental Churches, the Oriental-Orthodox Churches (the Armenian-Orthodox Church, the Syrian-Orthodox Church, the Coptic-Orthodox Church), the Hebrew Religious Community, the Islamic Religious Community, the Old-Catholic Church, the Evangelic-Methodist Church, the Church of Jesus Christ of Latter-day Saints (Mormons), the New-Apostolic Church, the Buddhist Religious Community, Jehovah's Witnesses, Free Churches in Austria and the Alevi Islamic Religious Community.

226. The provisions concerning churches and religious societies recognized by ministerial ordinance according to the Law on Legal Recognition of Religious Communities 1874 (AnerkennungsG) are laid down therein. The legal positions and the external legal relationships concerning 'historically recognized' churches and religious societies have been developed by means of special laws (Concordat 1933, ProtestantenG 1961, OrthodoxenG 1967, IsraelitenG 1890, as amended 2012). Furthermore, special acts exist for newly recognized religious communities, for Islam (1912, renewed 2015) and for the Oriental-Orthodox Churches 2003.

II. Preconditions for Recognition

227. As far as the preconditions for recognition are concerned, pursuant to §1 AnerkennungG, adherents of a hitherto not legally recognized faith are granted recognition as a religious community provided that their religious doctrine, forms of worship, statutes and chosen name do not contain anything illegal or morally offensive (section 1) and that the establishment and the continued existence of at least one religious community, fulfilling the requirements of this law, is guaranteed (section 2). Provisions concerning the inner structure of the religious community, the appointment of the board members, and their sphere of competence must be enclosed in the constitution or statutes, respectively. The names of the members of the board and the authorized representatives must be lodged formally with the administrative body.

228. In the Act on the Legal Status of Religious Denominational Communities 1998 (BekGG), comprising an amendment of the AnerkennungsG as a *lex fugitiva*, in §11 supplementary preconditions for recognition were decreed.[80] The number of

80. For the principal problems of the legal recognition, *see*: H. Kalb, R. Potz & B. Schinkele, 'Eintragung und Anerkennung von Religionsgemeinschaften nach dem Inkrafttreten des Bundesgesetzes über die Rechtspersönlichkeit von religiösen Bekenntnisgemeinschaften', *Österreichisches Archiv für Kirchenrecht* 45 (1998), 58–111; C. Grabenwarter, 'Kirchen, Religionsgesellschaften und andere', *Journal für Rechtspolitik* 5 (1997), 265–277; G. Lienbacher, 'Die rechtliche Anerkennung von Religionsgemeinschaften in Österreich', in *Standpunkte im Kirchen- und Staatskirchenrecht*, ed. C. Grabenwarter & N. Lüdecke (Würzburg: Echter, 2002), 154–176; K. W. Schwarz, 'Das Anerkennungsrecht aus der Sicht der Kultusbehörde', *Österreichisches Archiv für Recht und Religion* 57 (2010), 228–236; S. Hammer, 'Zur Ungleichbehandlung von Religionsgemeinschaften in der neueren Rechtsprechung', *Österreichisches Archiv für Recht und Religion* 52 (2005), 209–226; G. Lienbacher, 'Religiöse Rechte', in *Handbuch der Grundrechte VII/1: Grundrechte in Österreich*, ed. D.

followers must equal at least one two-thousandth of the Austrian population according to the most recent census. Income and assets must be used for religious purposes (for which the generally useful and charitable purposes, grounded in religious objectives, can be counted); the community must show a positive attitude to society and the state; there should be no illegal disturbance in relationships with existing legally recognized churches and religious societies or any other religious communities. Pursuant to the original version of the BekGG of 1998 (§11 section 1 no. 1) continued existence as a religious community for at least twenty years was a requirement, ten of which must have been spent as a religious denominational community with legal personality in the sense of this law.

229. Though the undifferentiated regulation of a 'waiting period' was heavily criticized by legal doctrine, the Constitutional Court had no problem in respecting the constitutionality of this provision, arguing that such a 'period of waiting time' seemed to be legitimate as a period of supervisory control carried out by the administrative body.[81] In two cases concerning the 'waiting period' in question, however, the ECtHR held that there had been a violation of Article 9, and also, owing to the difference in treatment, a violation of Article 14 as read in conjunction with Article 9 of the Convention.[82] A ten-year 'waiting period' for potential attainment of legal recognition could not be indiscriminately prescribed for all religious communities. This might be necessary in exceptional circumstances, such as in the case of newly established and unknown religious groups, but it hardly appeared justified with respect to religious groups with a long-standing existence internationally, which had also been long-established in the country and therefore familiar with the competent authorities. With respect to Jehovah's Witnesses, the state authorities should have been able to verify whether this religion fulfilled the requirements of the relevant legislation within a considerably shorter period. The Court reiterated its established case law, holding that a difference in treatment is discriminatory if there is not a reasonable relationship of proportionality between the means employed and the aim sought to be realized, taking into consideration a margin of appreciation which the contracting states enjoy.

230. The ECtHR's findings clearly show the necessity for making a distinction between religious communities with a long-lasting tradition and a worldwide spread on the one hand, and new religious movements on the other hand, which may possibly only recently have come into being, with only a little group of followers and completely dependent on a charismatic leader. Therefore, the legislator's schematic

---

Merten & H.-J. Papier (Heidelberg: Müller, 2009), 319–349; K. Pabel, 'Beobachtungen zum Religionsgemeinschaftenrecht im österreichischen Staatskirchenrecht', in *Die Zukunft der Verfassung – Die Verfassung der Zukunft? Festschrift für Karl Korinek*, ed. M. Holoubek, A. Martin & S. Schwarzer (Vienna & New York: Springer, 2010), 223–238.

81. VfSlg. 16102/2001, VfSlg. 16131/2001; cf. B. Schinkele, 'Kommentar zu VfGH 3 Mar. 2001, B 1713/98; VfGH 14 Mar. 2001, B 98/99; VfGH 14 Mar. 2001, G 68/99', *Österreichisches Archiv für Recht und Religion* 48 (2001), 239–261.

82. ECtHR, *Religionsgemeinschaft der Zeugen Jehovas – Jehovah's Witnesses – v. Austria*, 28 Jul. 2008, appl. no. 40825/98; ECtHR, *Verein der Freunde der Christengemeinschaft – Friends of the Christian Community – v. Austria*, 26 Feb. 2009, appl. no. 76581/01.

approach could not be objective or reasonable at all. Thus, the Constitutional Court had to change its above-mentioned approach, and from then on considered the provision in question to be unconstitutional due to a lack of differentiation in the sense of the ECtHR's findings.[83] Consequently, the legislator issued a re-enactment providing for graduations regarding the continuity of existence by taking into consideration various periods of existence combined with organizational and doctrinal connections to religious communities with international activities:[84] (a) continued existence as a religious community for at least twenty years, ten of which must have been spent in an organized form, at least five years as a religious denominational community with legal personality in the sense of this Law; or (b) organizationally and doctrinally integrated into an international religious community having existed for at least one hundred years and with at least ten years of activities in an organizational form in Austria; or (c) organizationally and doctrinally integrated into an international religious community having existed for at least two hundred years.

231. In both cases in question, the competent Federal Minister had dismissed the request for recognition as a religious community on the grounds that it had not existed as a registered religious community for a minimum of ten years, relying only on §11 section 1 no. 1 BekGG (original version). For this reason, the ECtHR did not find it necessary to examine the other preconditions of Article 11 BekGG, which had also been challenged by the applicants. Notwithstanding, the following reasoning of the ECtHR is of great significance, particularly with regard to the required number of members, the most problematic precondition of recognition. The Court stressed exactly the crucial issue in the Austrian law on religion deriving from the fact that the religious communities with public law status enjoy privileged treatment in many areas:

> These areas include exemption from military service and civilian service, reduced tax liability or exemption from specific taxes, facilitation of the founding of schools, membership of various boards. Given the number of these privileges and their nature, in particular in the field of taxation, the advantage obtained by religious societies is substantial and this special treatment undoubtedly facilitates a religious society's pursuance of its religious aims. In view of these substantive privileges, accorded to religious societies, the obligation under Article 9 of the Convention incumbent on the state's authorities to remain neutral in the exercise of their powers in this domain requires therefore that if a state sets up a framework for conferring legal personality on religious groups to which a specific status is linked, all religious groups which so wish must have a fair opportunity to apply for this status and the criteria established must be applied in a non-discriminatory manner.[85]

83. VfSlg. 19166/2010.
84. BGBl. I 2011/78.
85. ECtHR, *Religionsgemeinschaft der Zeugen Jehovas – Jehovah's Witnesses – v. Austria*, 28 Jul. 2008, appl. no. 40825/98, § 92.

232. For the future, therefore, for the required number of followers to equal at least one two-thousandth of the Austrian population would almost amount to a de facto prevention of legal recognition. Particularly, with respect to the privileged treatment legally recognized religious societies enjoy in many legal areas, partly directly emanating from freedom of religion, this precondition is inconsistent with the fundamental guarantees. Whereas the waiting period could 'merely' cause a delay in acquiring legal personality with public law status, the required number of followers, as the case may be, permanently prohibits this status. Unfortunately, the Constitutional Court has no doubts about respecting the constitutionality of this provision, without providing any reasonable substantiation.[86] The Court neither deals with the relevant highly significant considerations of the ECtHC mentioned above nor with the fact that half of the legally recognized religious communities have a lower or even a much lower number of members. Several complaints concerning this Constitutional Court case law which state-registered religious communities had lodged with the ECtHR, however, were dismissed according to Article 35 section 3 of the Convention, as amended by the 14th Additional Protocol 2010, i.e., on the basis of the decision of one single judge, without reasoning, and without any recourse of appeal. Regardless of serious doubts with respect to the principle of due course of law, these proceedings are entirely inconsistent with the ECtHR's own former reasoning in its judgments from 2008 and 2009 (cf. 231).[87]

III. Public Law Status

233. Legal recognition as presupposed in Article 15 StGG implies the status of an incorporated body under public law status (corporations sui generis) which is explicitly laid down in the special laws for individual churches and religious societies (Article II Concordat 1933, §1 section 2 I ProtestantenG 1961, §1 IsraelitenG 1890/2012, §1 IslamG 2015). Nevertheless, legally recognized churches and religious societies do not have the essential characteristics of public law corporations in the sense of administrative law. They are neither state-established institutions nor have they been conferred sovereign power. By their very nature, they lie outside state structures, and their legislative, administrative and judicial acts are not subject to state surveillance.

234. The legislator of the StGG 1867 considered public law status as an instrument for exercising state influence on churches and religious societies. Since then, the relationship between state and church as well as the constitutional reality and the methods of constructing fundamental rights have changed significantly. Consequently, the subject matter of public law status should be redefined. Based on the separation of state and church at the institutional level, conferring this status implies

86. VfSlg. 18965/2009, B 516/09; cf. S. Hammer, 'Kommentar zu VfGH 16. 12. 2009, B 516/09', *Österreichisches Archiv für Recht und Religion* 57 (2010), 286–302.
87. B. Schinkele, 'Aktuelle Fragen des österreichischen Anerkennungsrechts am Beispiel evangelischer Freikirchen und alevitischer Gruppierungen', *Religionen unterwegs* 19 (2013), 17–23.

the offer to cooperate with the state in certain aspects. The so-called legitimate constitutional expectations from the religious communities primarily concern their contributions in the sphere of education, social and welfare activities, as well as their role as dialogue partners regarding the complex ethical issues the modern state has to comply with. This status makes clear that the state accepts the activity of churches and religious societies in the public arena and does not wish to displace them into the private sphere.[88]

235. In many legal fields, significant consequences are derived from public law status. The difference in the treatment of legally recognized and non-recognized religious communities is constitutionally laid down in Article 15 StGG (cf. 225).

236. Communities (such as parishes) within a certain legally recognized church or religious society can also attain legal personality under public law. With regard to the Catholic Church, the Protestant Church and Islamic Religious Societies this possibility can be extended to institutions with legal personality according to internal law, such as foundations, social and charitable facilities (Article II and Article X Concordat, cf. 296; §4 section 1 ProtestantenG, cf. 310; §23 section 4 IslamG, cf. 357). Regardless of these special legal provisions, institutions of religious communities can make use of all other legal forms under private law.

IV. Revocation of Recognition

237. A further additional regulation is found in §11a BekGG concerning the revocation of recognition. Accordingly, the competent Federal Minister is obliged to revoke such recognition if one of the prerequisites – apart from the number of followers – is no longer met, if the religious society concerned has had no authorized representatives for at least a year, or if its activities contravene the statutes or constitute grounds for prohibition according to §5 BekGG (cf. 244). This provision only applies to religious communities legally recognized on the basis of the AnerkennungsG. A special provision is contained in §5 section 2 IslamG 2015, according to which the revocation of the recognition of an Islamic religious society requires a decision by the Council of Ministers. In the case of other legally recognized churches and religious societies, if need be, a revocation of recognition must be made possible by means of a special Act.[89]

---

88. B. Schinkele, 'Die öffentlich-rechtliche Stellung von Relgionsgemeinschaften', *Österreichisches Archiv für Recht und Religion* 56 (2009), 358–374; B. Schinkele, 'Zur öffentlich-rechtlichen Stellung von Religionsgemeinschaften', *juridikum* 13 (2001), 123–130; R. Potz, 'Zur öffentlich-rechtlichen Stellung der Kirchen und Religionsgesellschaften', in *Die 'Anerkennung' von Religionsgemeinschaften*, ed. R. Potz & R. Kohlhofer (Vienna: Verlag Österreich, 2002), 25–37.
89. S. Schima, 'Die Aufhebung der Anerkennung von Religionsgemeinschaften. Anmerkungen zum neu erlassenen § 11a des Bekenntnisgemeinschaftengesetzes', in *Recht – Religion – Kultur. Festschrift für Richard Potz*, ed. B. Schinkele et al. (Vienna: facultas.wuv, 2014), 756–773.

§2. STATE-REGISTERED RELIGIOUS DENOMINATIONAL COMMUNITIES

238. The BekGG created the legal basis for religious communities to obtain legal personality without at the same time giving them the status of a public law corporation. Registered religious denominational communities acquire juridical personality under private law and therefore do not enjoy the 'privileges' granted by law to legally recognized churches and religious societies. The following religious communities are state-registered as denominational religious communities: the Bahá'i Religion, the Christian Community – Movement for Religious Revival in Austria, the Church of Seventh Day Adventists, the Pentecostal Church – Community of God in Austria, the Hindu Mandir Society, the Schia Islamic Religious Community, the Old-Alevi Religious Community, the Unification Church, the Sikh Religious Community and the Free-Alevite Religious Community.

239. This law does not apply to philosophical communities (Weltanschauungsgemeinschaften). For this reason, should the situation arise, the administrative body could be faced with the necessity to distinguish religious and non-religious beliefs, quite a delicate task with respect to some of the new religious movements.

240. In 1999 this question was raised in the context of the 'Scientology Church Austria'. Scientology withdrew the application after expert opinions had raised doubts about the organization's religious nature and concerns regarding its developmental psychology:[90]

- In 2018 the application of the 'Church of the Flying Spaghetti Monster' was rejected as being neither a religion nor a religious community (cf. 125).
- In 2020, the Atheist Religious Community of Austria applied for registration as a religious denominational community. Their argument was that they do not believe that the gods created humans, but that humans created (and create) the gods, which means that they have a concept of God and are therefore to be qualified as a religion and religious community.[91]

241. Proof must be submitted with the application that the religious community has at least 300 followers residing in Austria belonging to the religious community, who do not belong to another religious denominational community with legal personality, legally recognized church or religious community. This number was criticized as being too high, especially with regard to new religious movements. The application must include the statutes, including the organization of the agencies and external representation, as well as supplementary materials showing the content and practice of the religious denominational community. The statutes must contain the name of the religious community, which must be such that it can be related to its

90. R. Potz & B. Schinkele, 'Die 'Scientology-Kirche Österreich' – die Voraussetzungen für den Erwerb der Rechtspersönlichkeit als eingetragene religiöse Bekenntnisgemeinschaft', *Österreichisches Archiv für Recht und Religion* 46 (1999), 206–251.
91. www.atheistisch.at/konzept/ (30.9.2023).

doctrine and there can be no confusion with existing religious communities. The doctrine must be differentiated from the doctrine of existing religious communities independent of their legal status.

242. The administrative body is obliged to deny acquisition of legal personality if this is necessary with regard to the doctrine or its practice for the protection of the interests of public safety, public order, health and morals or the protection of the rights and freedoms of others in a democratic society (Article 9 section 2 ECHR); this is especially the case regarding incitement to commit an illegal punishable action, hindering the psychological development of young adults, causing damage to psychological integrity by the use of psychotherapeutic methods especially aimed at winning converts.

243. The registration implies the qualification as a religious community and a 'seal of approval' as it were, which has legal relevance, where the legal order draws consequences from the fact of being a religious community and not from the status of recognition (for instance, the Act regulating public meetings or Penal Law). However, the legal position of registered religious denominational communities is quite different from that of legally recognized churches and religious communities (cf. 246 et seq.).

§3. Differentiation Between the Two Categories of Religious Communities

244. The differentiation between legally recognized and non-recognized religious communities is constitutionally laid down in Article 15 StGG (cf. 225 et seq.). As a result, legal consequences from public law status are provided for by ordinary law in numerous areas. The most important fields of law containing different regulations for both categories of religious communities are the right of self-determination, subsidising of private denominational schools, religious instruction classes, revenue law, labour law, military and non-military service and exemptions concerning the employment of foreigners. These differences in treatment within various legal spheres have remarkable consequences for the religious community concerned as well as its individual adherents.

245. This legal situation, therefore, is criticized because it could only be justified if there were no differentiations between the legal status of religious communities as far as legal positions are concerned, which are directly derived from the fundamental right of religious freedom. Consequently, the whole legal system must be scrutinized as to whether the consequences emanating from legal recognition can be deemed legitimate from that point of view. The differentiations provided for by the legal order must be justified on objective and reasonable grounds; otherwise, they represent non-objective infringements of the guarantees of fundamental rights and should be abolished. Unfortunately, for the time being, there is no indication whatsoever of any such intention, either with regard to the legislator, the Constitutional Court, the High Administrative or even the ECtHR. Therefore, this question remains the most crucial issue concerning the Austrian law on religion.[92]

246. In several cases, the High Administrative Court and the Constitutional Court had to deal with differences in the legal treatment of both categories of religious communities, especially concerning revenue law, military and non-military service and personal status law.[93] The question has regularly arisen as to whether the exclusion of the last-mentioned category of religious communities from numerous benefits (alternatives, reductions or exemptions) could be justified on reasonable grounds. Regardless of the specific context, both High Courts referred exclusively to the clear wording of the legal text. Neither an interpretation in accordance with the constitution nor a repeal of the provisions in question on the grounds of unconstitutionality was taken into account.

247. In three cases concerning military and non-military service, (*Lang v. Austria*,[94] *Gütl v. Austria*[95] and *Löffelman v. Austria*[96]) the ECtHR considered the relevant provisions of the Austrian Military Act and the Non-Military Service Act to be discriminatory. The applicants were Jehovah's Witnesses acting as 'elders' for the community which involved providing pastoral care, conducting church services and preaching. They argued that the exemption from military or non-military service did not apply to them as opposed to members of recognized churches and religious societies though they were charged with comparable religious functions. The Court established a connection to its judgment from July 2008 (cf. 231), and accordingly, to the fact that Jehovah's Witnesses had been denied legal recognition on the basis of a precondition (ten-year waiting period) contravening the Convention's guarantees. Regardless of the fact that this also held true for the 'Federation of Evangelical Communities in Austria' (*Bund evangelikaler Gemeinden* in Österreich), in the case of *Koppi v. Austria*, the Court dismissed the application of an evangelical preacher who had been entrusted with similar tasks.[97] In this case, the Court's findings were based on a wrong fact – the presumption that the Evangelical Community had not also applied for legal recognition as Jehovah's Witnesses had done – and, moreover, the Court denied in principle to consider the different treatment of both categories of religious communities in the context in question.

92. H. Kalb, R. Potz & B. Schinkele, 'Österreichisches Religionsrecht in der jüngsten Straßburger Rechtsprechung', *Österreichisches Archiv für Recht und Religion* 56 (2009), 400–432; B. Gartner, 'Aktuelle Herausforderungen für den Rechtsstaat einer plurireligiösen Gesellschaft', *Österreichisches Archiv für Recht und Religion* 57 (2010), 37–65.
93. For example cf. VwGH 10 Nov. 1998, 98/11/0175; VwGH 18 Mar. 2003, 2002/11/0256; VwGH 26 Feb. 2004, 2001/16/0366; VwSlg. 16508 A/2004; VwGH 27 Apr. 2006, 2005/16/0277; VfSlg. 16998/2003, VfSlg. 17021/2003.
94. ECtHR, 12 Mar. 2009, appl. no. 28648/03.
95. ECtHR, 12 Mar. 2009, appl. no. 49686/99.
96. ECtHR, 12 Mar. 2009, appl. no. 42967/98.
97. ECtHR, 10 Dec. 2009, appl. no. 33001/03.

248. Up to now, only in a few cases, the legislator has finally drawn consequences from criticism expressed in the legal doctrine. Since the amendment of the Personal Status Act (PStG) 2013,[98] legally recognized and state-registered religious communities are treated equally, i.e., members of both categories have the right to declare their religious affiliation in personal status certificates (concerning birth, marriage and death). Other examples to which equal treatment applies are the Executive Order Concerning School Report Forms (cf. 638) and the Act on Responsibility of Associations (cf. 199).

§4. Non-profit Associations

249. According to §1 section 1 Act on Associations 2002 (VereinsG) non-profit (ideological) associations are voluntary organizations consisting of at least two persons set up for a long period of time on the basis of statutes pursuing certain non-profit purposes. This law does not apply to those associations which must be constituted with another legal status according to other legal provisions or which have freely chosen another legal form under the appropriate legislation (§1 section 2). Henceforth, it is clear that religious communities can also obtain legal personality under private law on the basis of the VereinsG 2002.[99] With respect to the previous Act on Associations, such an option has been denied for a long period of time, and later on, the respective regulation was understood to be controversial, which resulted in an uncertain legal situation. Religious communities will refer to this possibility if they do not fulfil the conditions for legal recognition or state registration, or if a legal entity under public law is not in concordance with their self-understanding. These organizations enjoy equal status with other private associations. Contrary to the special categories of religious communities – legally recognized and state-registered religious communities – non-profit associations are not identified by state bodies as 'religious'. Therefore, if they require legal consequences to be derived from this qualification, the circumstances must be examined by the responsible administrative or judicial body in each case.

§5. Associations with Partly Religious Functions

250. Apart from this, every religious community – independent of its legal status – has the possibility to found associations with partly religious functions (religiöse Hilfsvereine), primarily related to the social and charitable activities of religious communities, regardless of their legal form. According to the revenue law, benefits (reductions or exemptions) are also attributed over and above 'religious' objectives to public utility and charitable purposes. As far as legally recognized churches and religious societies are concerned, the right to self-determination

98. BGBl. I 2013/16.
99. H. Tichy, 'Religiöse Gemeinschaften nach dem Vereinsgesetz 2002', *Österreichisches Archiv für Recht und Religion* 51 (2004), 379–397.

should not only be conferred on a church or religious society alone but also on those facilities which are in any way connected with it, independently of the legal structure of this link.

251. In a Constitutional Court decision of 2001[100] which was repeatedly referred to, the classification of an 'initiative circle' of Catholic laymen and priests in the Archdiocese of Vienna within the state legal sphere was at issue. Their purposes were focused on organizing and promoting lectures, prayer circles, spiritual exercises and pilgrimages, and the celebration of divine service according to the rite laid down in the Motu prorio 'Ecclesia Dei' [101] being at the centre of their activities. The proponents wished to found an association only according to state law which is, in principle, compatible with canon law (cf. mainly cc. 215 und 216 CIC). The Court took the position that the prohibition of such an association would not interfere with the fundamental rights of the proponents; rather, non-prohibition would violate the right of the Catholic Church to self-determination. The Court, however, made no differentiation regarding the various purposes, and did not deal adequately with the essential criterion as to whether an activity was carried out 'on behalf of the Church'.[102]

252. As part of measures for taking consistent action against terrorist organizations, section 2 was added to §11 VereinsG in 2021.[103] Accordingly, if the purpose of the association as described in the statutes is the practice of a cult, its statutes must be formally forwarded without delay to the department for religious affairs. The latter must examine whether the described practice of this cult is consistent with the practice of a legally recognized church or religious society. The result of the examination must be forwarded to the association authority without delay.

100. VfSlg. 16395/2001.
101. Apostolic Letter of 2 Jul. 1988, AAS 80 (1988) 1495 et seq.
102. R. Potz, 'Kommentar zu VfGH 11. 12. 2001, B 1510/00', *Österreichisches Archiv für Recht und Religion* 51 (2004), 321–334; cf. B. Schinkele, Vereinigungen von Gläubigen im Spannungsfeld von kirchlichem und staatlichem Recht. Überlegungen anlässlich des VfGH-Erkenntnisses Slg. 16395/2001, in *Recht – Bürge der Freiheit. Festschrift für Johann Mühlsteiger*, ed. K. Breitsching & W. Rees (Berlin: Duncker & Humblot, 2006),1031–1057.
103. BGBl I 2021/211.

Chapter 2. Autonomy of Religious Communities

§1. The Principle of Exclusivity

253. This historically developed principle should be seen in context with state neutrality in religious matters, the principle of parity and public law status. In its traditional meaning, it encompasses an exclusive right regarding name, notion, religious doctrine, worship and constitution. As a consequence, an individual cannot belong simultaneously to more than one church or religious society. The exclusive right to pastoral care also implies the obligation to refrain from extending such activities towards non-members, unless explicitly requested. The principle of exclusivity has traditionally been developed in the context of legally recognized churches and religious societies, and the legislator has expanded this principle to state-registered religious communities. Nowadays especially, the exclusivity of name and religious doctrine is in some way being questioned.[104]

254. Regarding the name in particular, reference must be made to the 'Alevi Case' of the Constitutional Court from 1 December 2010. According to this decision, the religiously neutral state is wrong in prohibiting the addition of the term 'Islamic' by an Alevite group, if the reference to Islam is essential to the group's self-understanding, and this can also be made plausible. Such an approach by state authorities would not only be an interference with the freedom of religion but would also constitute discrimination. In other words, the principle of exclusivity does not cover the use of a particular term as part of the name of a religious community, such as Catholic, Orthodox, Protestant, Israelite/Jewish, Islamic, etc.

255. Although §4 section 1 no. 2 BekGG also contains the principle of exclusivity, it is noteworthy that the administrative practice in connection with the BekGG refrained from adhering to it insofar as two Pentecostal churches – namely the 'Free Christian Church-Pentecostal Church' and the 'Pentecostal Church of God in Austria' – were registered as different denominational communities. The former was later legally recognized as being part of the 'Free Churches in Austria'. Since another group in the Pentecostal movement is constituted as being an association under the Associations Act 2002, three Pentecostal churches organized in different legal forms now exist.

256. The most problematic aspect of the traditional principle of exclusivity in the light of a contemporary law on religion is the requirement of distinctiveness in doctrine and creed -especially because such scrutiny of the requirement of doctrinal differences would regularly exceed the possibilities of a religiously neutral state. As

104. J. Schima, 'Ende des Ausschließlichkeitsrecht?', *Österreichische Juristenzeitung* 37 (1982), 141–147, 169–173; R. Potz, 'Das Ausschließlichkeitsrecht', in *Vom praktischen Wert der Methode. Festschrift für Heinz Mayer*, ed. C. Jabloner et al. (Vienna: Manz, 2011), 555–573; B. Gartner, 'Aktuelle Herausforderungen für den Rechtsstaat einer plurireligiösen Gesellschaft', *Österreichisches Archiv für Recht und Religion* 57 (2010), 37–65.

a consequence of the Constitutional Court's decision of 2010, the Islamic Alevi religious community was registered as a confessional community, whereas the request of the Alevi Federation[105] was rejected because of the substantial identity of doctrine and creed. After determining the differences in doctrine and creed, the Alevi Federation was registered under the name 'Free-Alevite Religious Community in Austria'.[106] The protracted proceedings in the Alevite cases make obvious that it would be more appropriate to take the organizational autonomy and distinctiveness primarily into account thus avoiding the risk of confusion with other religious communities In this way, criteria would be addressed which can be assessed solely by secular standards and would therefore have to be decisive for a state which is neutral in religious matters. According to the case law of the ECtHR, such a unique organization must not be enforced by the state.[107] In this respect, an end to the principle of exclusivity is called for in the doctrine.

§2. The Autonomy of Legally Recognized Churches and Religious Societies

257. Article 15 StGG is the central constitutional guarantee for legally recognized religious societies (cf. 225 et seq.).

258. An attempt to determine the actual meaning of Article 15 StGG must take into account that the StGG dates from an epoch with a completely different state-church relationship. The constitutional reality has significantly changed. Methods of assessing fundamental rights have been essentially modified[108] from the former dogmatic approach.[109]

259. In recent times, ordinary law – implementing the basic law directives – has also been amended, especially owing to the BekGG (cf. 230).

260. These developments can be seen in all aspects of the constitutional provisions of Article 15 StGG, with regard to the parity of legally recognized religious communities (cf. 264 et seq.), the right to self-determination of their internal affairs (cf. 268 et seq.), the guarantee of property (cf. 584) and the legal reservation of 'general laws of the state' (cf. 276 et seq.).

261. Today, the legal system of the relationship between state and church in Austria is based on the principles of religious neutrality and non-identification, of parity

105. R. Potz & B. Schinkele. 'Eintragung bzw gesetzliche Anerkennung alevitischer Gruppen in Österreich', *Österreichisches Archiv für Recht und Religion* 58 (2011), 137–155.
106. Cf. R. Potz & B. Schinkele. 'Zur Eintragung der Frei-Alevitischen Glaubensgemeinschaft in Österreich', *Österreichisches Archiv für Recht und Religion* 69 (2022), 301–345.
107. ECtHR, *Hasan and Chaush v. Bulgaria*, 26 Oct. 2000, appl. no. 30985/96.
108. B. Schinkele, 'Church Autonomy in Austria', in *Church Autonomy*, ed. G. Robbers (Frankfurt am Main et al.: Peter Lang, 2001), 561–575.
109. B. Schinkele, 'Church Autonomy in Austria', in *Church Autonomy*, ed. G. Robbers (Frankfurt am Main et al.: Peter Lang, 2001), 561–575.

and self-determination. In this system, parity is therefore a consequence of the general principle of equality and the guarantee of religious freedom in connection with the religious neutrality of the state. Because of this constitutional foundation of parity, public law status of churches and religious communities is only justified if two conditions are complied with: first, there is an enforceable claim by those who fulfil the legal qualifications and second, there is no difference in the legal status of the other religious communities as far as legal positions are concerned which derive directly from the fundamental law of religious freedom. This means that although there is separation between state and church at the institutional level, the principle of parity allows for cooperation with individual religious communities as long as this special regulation is in accordance with other 'spheres of justice'. According to a modern interpretation of the principle of separation of state and church, it is a grave misunderstanding to identify religious neutrality with the prohibition of referring to the religious dimension in all those social and cultural spheres of life which the state nowadays regulates.

I. The Principle of Parity

262. Article 15 StGG represents a specific guarantee of the general principle of equality in both of its forms, as formal parity and as substantial parity, as expressed in the wording, every recognized church or religious community arranges and manages its internal affairs independently. This means that parity can be a question of formal equality as well as a question of suum cuique.[110]

263. Historically, equality has always been postulated in connection with a concrete emancipatory interest. In the modern constitutional state ruled by law, the principle of parity requires an even more precise rendering. It is the task of the Constitutional Court's jurisdiction to ensure that the principle of equality ranks foremost in our complex modern society, and in fact, the subject matter of the principle of equality is determined to a great extent by the jurisdiction of the Constitutional Court.[111] In this sense, the specific principle of parity in law on religion constitutes an example of a step taken towards a more precise rendering of rules achieved at the constitutional level. Taking into account the unity of the legal system and in particular the interdependence of fundamental rights, a synopsis of all the relevant guarantees of fundamental rights must be made. Consequently, in handling questions of parity not only Article 15 StGG but also the general principle of equality must be included. This means that the legislator as well as the judicial and executive bodies dealing with problems of parity must observe all those special principles and rules which must be referred to in connection with the general principle of equality. While the wording 'equality before the law' (*vor dem Gesetz*) suggests

110. R. Potz, 'Suum cuique – The Parity of the Recognized Churches and Religious Communities in Austria', *European Journal for Church and State Research* 4 (1997), 187–204.
111. K. Korinek, 'Gedanken zur Bindung des Gesetzgebers an den Gleichheitssatz nach der Judikatur des Verfassungsgerichtshofes', in *Im Dienst an Staat und Recht. Festschrift für Erwin Melichar* (Vienna: Manz, 1983), 43–55.

only 'equality in application' (*Anwendungsgleichheit*), it has been made clear – especially in Austria since 1945 – that the legislator is also bound to the principle of parity and for this reason we can speak of 'equality in law' (*Gleichheit im Gesetz – Rechtsetzungsgleichheit*) as well.

264. The principle of substantive parity finds expression in the Austrian system of special laws for individually recognized churches and religious societies. In some legal provisions, explicit reference is made to parity. The Motivenbericht for the AnerkennungsG 1874 already stated that the purpose of this Act was to realize the freedom of religion and conscience as well as the principle of parity of the confessions.[112] A general provision is contained in §1 section 2 III ProtestantenG 1961: 'All acts of legislative and of executive power which concern the Protestant Church have to observe the principle of equality before law in relation to the legal and factual position of the other legally recognized churches and religious communities.' However, this provision is of limited practical significance (cf. 210 and 308). Another example is §7 OrthodoxenG, which refers to a number of paragraphs of the ProtestantenG and orders their analogous application, stating expressly in the Explanatory Notes that this provision takes the principle of parity into account.

265. The system of special laws for some recognized churches and religious communities as a consequence of substantive parity of course also causes the danger of distortions. Every single case, therefore, should be examined as to whether a different regulation is in accordance with the principle of substantive parity. One of the most discussed examples is the formal difference in special ecclesiastical law between the Catholic Church and the other communities: the special ecclesiastical law of the Catholic Church is traditionally governed by treaties with the Holy See. According to Austrian constitutional law, there is no other legal basis for treaties on ecclesiastical law. This problem, however, is diminished because the special laws for individual churches and religious communities are nowadays enacted in accordance with the corresponding religious community so that the formulation of the legal text in all cases is the result of negotiations.

II. The Right of Self-Determination Regarding 'Internal Affairs'

266. The understanding of the expression 'internal affairs' has undergone considerable development since 1867.[113] It is historically rooted, based on the iura in

112. Motivenbericht 43 Abgeordnetenhaus Session VIII 135 Beil StenProt, quoted in I. Gampl, R. Potz & B. Schinkele, *Österreichisches Staatskirchenrecht*, vol. I (Vienna: Orac, 1990), 145.

113. *See* especially R. Potz, 'Die inneren Angelegenheiten der anerkannten Kirchen und Religionsgesellschaften als Problem der Grundrechtsinterpretation', in *Ex Aequo et Bono. Festschrift für Willibald M. Plöchl*, ed. P. Leisching, F. Pototschnig & R. Potz (Innsbruck: Wagner, 1977), 409–422; H. Pree, *Österreichisches Staatskirchenrecht* (Vienna & New York: Springer, 1984), 63–68; B. Schinkele, 'Das Arbeitsrecht in der Kirche: Der verfassungsrechtliche und staatskirchenrechtliche Rahmen unterbesonderer Berücksichtigung der katholischen Kirche', in *Arbeitsrecht und Kirche. Zur arbeitsrechtlichen und sozialrechtlichen Stellung von Klerikern, Ordensangehörigen und kirchlichen Mitarbeitern in Österreich*, ed. U. Runggaldier & B. Schinkele (Vienna & New York:

sacra of the absolutistic Staatskirchentum. Like other constitutional terms, however, it is not determined once and for all but remains to a certain extent undecided in order to be capable of solving contemporary problems. Fundamental rights represent responses to actual experiences of injustice and thus have to be adapted to the needs of the time. Therefore, constitutional terms in general but especially fundamental rights are characterized by indefinite, vague wordings, and consequently, interpretation plays a most important role.

267. The term 'to arrange' refers to acts of legislation, while the term 'to manage' indicates measures of organization and administration. According to the doctrine and the court's decisions, the right of self-determination usually covers such aspects as dogma, teaching, religious service, own legislation and jurisdiction, disciplinary measures, appointment to and dismissal from a church office, conditions to be complied with by employees and administration of church property. Drawing a fairly clear line between 'internal affairs' and 'external affairs' seems to be impossible. For this reason, a definitive enumeration of internal affairs cannot be given, either in general or with regard to a particular community.

268. In accordance with the doctrine, the VfGH stated that to determine the 'internal affairs' of a religious community one must refer to the tasks of the community concerned, which should be determined in accordance with the principle of substantial parity by the religious communities as subjects of fundamental rights. For this reason, the self-understanding of the religious communities is relevant for the sphere of the state as far as it significantly co-determines the scope of this fundamental right. By analogy with the freedom of religion for individuals, which protects manifestations of religion or belief that are in some way recognizable as such, this self-understanding can include every activity which expresses the tasks of the religious community concerned.

269. The main point of reference for the legal and social status of religious communities is its self-understanding which must be derived from the characteristic features and special functions of each church or religious society. These criteria must be defined by the holders of the fundamental right themselves according to their genuine mandate in pursuance of the principle of substantial parity. Thus, the self-understanding of the religious community co-determines the scope of the fundamental right for the secular sphere. This concept has been worked out by the doctrine and has been accepted by the Constitutional Court as well as by the Supreme Court.[114]

Springer, 1996), 3–17; H. Kalb, R. Potz & B. Schinkele, *Religionsrecht* (Vienna: WUV, 2003), 65–71; R. Thienel, 'Religionsfreiheit in Österreich', in *Religionsfreiheit in Mittel- und Osteuropa zwischen Tradition und Europäisierung*, ed. G. Manssen & B. Banaszak (Frankfurt am Main et al.: Peter Lang, 2006), 35–78.

114. Cf. VfSlg. 7801/1976, VfSlg. 11859/1987; OGH 26 Nov. 1974, 4 Ob 41/74; OGH 13 Jul. 1976, 4 Ob 57/76; OGH 6 May 1987, 14 Ob A 29/87; OGH 16 Sep. 1987, 9 Ob A 71/87. OGH 6 May 1987, 14 Ob A 29/87; OGH 12 Apr. 1995, 9 Ob A 31/95.

270. Beyond a certain unalterable core, this self-understanding is to be understood in a dynamic way and insofar as it is variable. It is the task of the competent church authority to define this self-understanding. If the scope of the fundamental right depends on this, the courts or administrative bodies must lodge an inquiry with the competent authority. The term self-understanding refers to all activities carried out in accordance with the true mandate, the central objectives and genuine tasks of a certain community.

271. As far as individual religious freedom is concerned, the ECtHR has argued that the right mentioned in Article 9 ECHR protects acts which are intimately linked to these attitudes, such as acts of worship or devotion which are aspects of a religion or belief in a general recognized form.[115] In other decisions, the Court stated that the attitude must actually express the belief. Though one might criticize this line of jurisdiction as being too narrow, we can use it as an indication for transferring it to the corporative element.

272. A Supreme Court decision from 1974[116] can be deemed a leading decision, having been quoted in many cases. The Court then defined internal affairs as those affairs:

> concerning the inner core of church activity and those in which a lack of independence of the churches or religious societies would limit the proclamation of the religious truth and the practical exercise of the faith commandments; however, the churches are restricted by certain provisions on interdenominational matters as well as by certain constitutional provisions. The matter resulting from this definition can of course not be enumerated.

273. This formula represents quite a useable description. However, one must criticize the fact that the Supreme Court has failed to establish a relationship to the 'laws of the state'.

274. In summary, the term 'internal affairs' embodies a formula of variable contents, primarily depending on the self-understanding of the community concerned and ultimately resulting from a process of weighing the legal merits between the legal positions involved according to the principle of proportionality. Thereby, the 'democracy-clause' and the other limitations mentioned in Article 9 section 2 ECHR serve as important indicating measures.

III. 'General Laws of the State'

275. This self-understanding must be the argumentative starting point for establishing a relationship to the 'general laws of the state', but is not the only decisive

115. C. Grabenwarter & K. Pabel, *Europäische Menschenrechtskonvention*, 5th ed. (Munich: C.H. Beck, 2012), 292–296.
116. OGH SZ 47/135/1974.

factor. The state itself must formulate its own self-understanding deduced from its obligation to look after the common good. The next step, therefore, is to establish a relationship to the reservation clause which is a restriction clause sui generis. Contrary to the other constitutional requirements of a specific enactment in the StGG (*formelle Gesetzesvorbehalte*), it should be understood as a material requirement implying, therefore, a process of weighing the legal merits.

276. In the innermost core of church affairs, restrictions can only occur on account of inherent limitations or as a result of weighing up concurring legal positions based on fundamental rights. The more these central fields are left and church activities come into touch with the secular sphere, in addition to constitutional provisions of ordinary law representing potential limitations – the general laws of the state – come into effect. In some ways, we can speak of an 'open system'. Limitations ensuing from the 'general laws of the state' must be actualized in concrete cases if an object of legal protection in conflict with the right to self-determination is of equal or higher value than church autonomy. In such cases, an ordinary law creates impermissible barriers to a church's right of self-determination. Church autonomy and the other legal positions involved reciprocally determine and confine each other, taking into account the interdependence of fundamental rights and the unity of the legal order.

277. The procedure of weighing the legal merits is characteristic of the differentiated and substantial legal reservations embodied in the ECHR (Articles 8–12). The most important instrument available in such an approach is the principle of proportionality which implies weighing the legal and factual merits in every individual case. Thereby, the means applied must be placed in relation to the aims pursued. This new type of restriction clause requires a reasonable test of contemplation according to the criteria of aptitude, necessity and proportionality, in a narrower sense. In pursuance of the ultima-ratio principle, the least oppressive consequence should be chosen in order to achieve the intended aim ('pressing social need'). The principle of proportionality can be considered the most important instrument in constructing fundamental rights. It constitutes an elementary principle of justice, permeating the legal order as a comprehensive unity. The idea of subsidiarity is also encompassed in this principle, whereby the protection of the individual's fundamental rights is regarded as being of special value as compared to public interests.

278. This is the way to establish reasonable and appropriate coordination between the freedom to be protected – in our context, church autonomy – and the legal provision restricting it in concrete cases. In accordance with the principle of proportionality, a fair balance between conflicting legal positions must be found. This is the method by which the extent of the fundamental right should be determined and an ordinary law can be qualified as a 'general law of the state'. Primarily, it is not only incumbent upon the legislator but also to a lesser degree upon the judicial and administrative bodies to fulfil this task. To this extent, Article 15 StGG can be considered to be a constitutional provision immediately applicable by executive organs. Of course, certain assessments are made within such procedures. However, it must be stressed that this discretion is neither uncontrolled nor unqualified.

The less concrete and tangible the formulation of the provision is, the greater the legislator's discretion in realizing the underlying ideas within the constitutionally given standards. Detailed argumentation is demanded and the decisions are subject to the sequence of courts as well as to the control of the Constitutional Court and the High Administrative Court. In several cases, the legislator has expressively used his margin of appreciation by implementing a 'consideration-clause', for instance, in §132 section 4 Act on Labour Constitution (cf. 477), wherein the legislator has made clear that certain regulations may not be qualified as 'general laws of the state'.

IV. The Right to Have Justice Administered

279. The right to self-determination also encompasses autonomy with regard to offices and the right to have justice administered independently of the state. The internal legal system of churches and religious societies as well as their courts of law and their own system of judicature operate parallel to state law. Though churches principally act independently within these spheres, and their decisions are not subject to the state sequence of courts, this does not imply total exemption from state jurisdiction. The state has to comply with its duty to protect the requirement of church employees to seek judicial relief to a certain extent as well. Access to the courts concerning remuneration or other proprietary interests is even guaranteed to clergymen, other ministers and members of religious orders. The state courts are, however, bound to the preliminary questions which must be resolved by the church and are excluded from re-examination. A certain right to supervision can only be deduced from the prohibition of arbitrary decision-making, public morality and the ordre public. This results from the state's obligation to ensure the common welfare, including the right to have justice administered (Article 83 section 2 B-VG, Article 6 ECHR, §19 ABGB). The principle of due course of law indispensably requires that the matter can be brought before a court in case an encroachment on a subjective legal position approved by the legal system (order) is asserted. If such does not exist, recourse to the law is excluded and the motion for judgment (plaintiff's claim) must be dismissed on procedural grounds.[117]

§3. The Right of Other Religious Communities to Self-Determination

280. Against this background, the question of the right of not legally recognized religious communities to self-determination arises. This issue is closely related to the crucial problem of the Austrian law on religion, resulting from the fact that the

117. Established case law OGH 28 Feb. 1996, 9 ObA 12/96; VwGH 22 Jan. 2003, 98/08/0144; cf. H. Kalb, 'Kommentar zu OGH 9 Ob A 184/01a', *Das Recht der Arbeit* 52 (2002), 470–475; B. Schinkele, 'Zum Tendenzschutz von gesetzlich anerkannten Kirchen und Religionsgesellschaften – Überlegungen aus Anlass des OGH-Beschlusses 8. 1. 2009, 9 ObA 156/08v', *Recht der Wirtschaft* 27 (2009), 678–685.

provisions concerning the legal status of the different categories of religious communities are not in full concordance with fundamental law guarantees. This basic problem is also reflected in the following Constitutional Court statement regarding the right of state-registered religious communities to self-determination:

> Even though the religious denominational communities are given a non-insignificant autonomy by this Law (i.e., the BekGG), it has to be conceded, however, that their activities will be kept under observation of the authorities, so that during this period the comprehensive right of organizing and administering their internal affairs without state supervision and control – as it is guaranteed in Article 15 StGG for legally recognized churches and religious societies – is not guaranteed to state-registered religious communities.[118]

281. The Court statement clearly shows that the adaptation of the Austrian law on religion to the constitutionally given standards is not completely finished, although some improvements have been carried out by the BekGG. Therefore, it will be necessary to develop a concept in which all rights deriving directly from the fundamental right of religious freedom are guaranteed to both categories of religious community. Legal consequences provided by ordinary law which only apply to legally recognized religious communities must be scrutinized with regard to this aspect. Initially, this process seemed to have been accelerated by promising ECtHR's decisions. Unfortunately, however, reasonable expectations have not been met by any means, partly by virtue of the 14th Additional Protocol 2010 restricting the criteria for admissibility of applications (Article 35 section 3 ECHR).[119]

282. Nevertheless, it must be stressed that – independent of the construction of Article 15 StGG – the right to self-determination, at any rate, is constitutionally guaranteed to religious communities under private law status according to Article 9 ECHR. As a consequence of the approach described as a synopsis of all fundamental guarantees (cf. 111 et seq.), the substantial restriction clause in Article 15 StGG 'general laws of the state' just amounts to the same result as the limitations according to Article 9 section 2 ECHR. Consequently, traditional apprehension will subside and be replaced by the perception that the individual and corporative elements of religious freedom are closely linked. In this way, the institutional guarantee appears as a necessary emanation of the human right of religious freedom, essentially a fundamental status in a democratic secular state ruled by law. The corporative field, however, has a complementary function, i.e., the fundamental rights of churches and religious societies are guaranteed primarily for the benefit of individuals, in order to protect their religious interests effectively.

---

118. VfSlg. 16102/2001, VfSlg. 16131/2001.

119. B. Schinkele, 'Aktuelle Fragen des österreichischen Anerkennungsrechts am Beispiel evangelischer Freikirchen und alevitischer Gruppierungen', *Religionen unterwegs* 19 (2013), 20–22.

Chapter 3. Fundamental Rights and Religious Communities

283. Religious communities of the aforementioned three categories have the status of legal persons – be it under public or private law – and therefore they fully enjoy fundamental rights, except those which by their genuine nature only apply to individual persons, such as freedom of conscience. Of course, they are primarily holders of the fundamental right of religious freedom which is, however, functionally and systematically linked with other fundamental rights. Thus in addition, the following fundamental rights are of particular significance for religious communities: freedom of expression and information without prior censorship, freedom of association and peaceful assembly, and the right to the establishment and management of private schools and other educational institutions. As other legal persons, the religious communities have the right to bring a matter to the state courts according to the right to have justice administered.

284. The legally recognized churches and religious societies are incorporated bodies under public law status as corporations sui generis as laid down in Article 15 StGG. Regardless of this legal position, they are not incorporated into the state structure and have not been conferred sovereign power. In a very few cases, they exert state-like power, such as administering the former matriculation registers and providing for religious education within the public school system.

285. In principle, religious communities are not directly obliged by guarantees of fundamental rights, except for the right to data protection by which the religious communities are also directly bound. In general, fundamental rights are more and more understood nowadays as objective principles representing value judgments. Consequently, as such they might impose certain positive obligations the state must comply with, even in order to protect the rights of individuals against infringements by private parties (so-called third-party effect Drittwirkung). If the actual implications of the horizontal effect are at stake, the state has to take into consideration the particular legal position of legally recognized churches and religious societies.

286. The relationship between religious communities and the individual must be considered primarily from the perspective of the horizontal (indirect) application of fundamental rights, allowing for differences, however, between members belonging to the religious community concerned and other individuals. In the case of conflict between fundamental rights and legally protected interests, respectively, the different legal positions must be balanced carefully according to the principle of proportionality in order to render them as effective as possible. This also holds true when different aspects of religious freedom are in conflict – be it the individual and corporative dimension or the positive and negative dimension, as they are, in principle, of equal status and as such, subject to the same restrictions. A comparable procedure applies to other fundamental rights, with practical relevance especially relating to freedom of expression and freedom of association. Altogether, there exists a multi-dimensional relationship structure, for which a solution must be found that pays reasonable regard to the relevant fundamental rights at stake according to a substantive comprehension of human rights.

Chapter 4. Corporative Religious Freedom and Special Laws for Individual Churches and Religious Societies

§1. Overview

287. For historical reasons, special laws were created for legally recognized churches and religious societies which are of particular historical and social significance. This is a characteristic of the Austrian law on religion and is considered to be an adequate instrument for achieving substantive parity (cf. 266). While the provisions concerning churches and religious societies recognized by ministerial ordinance according to the AnerkennungsG are laid down therein, the legal positions and the external legal relationships concerning 'historically recognized' churches and religious societies have been developed by means of such special laws. The specific features of each of these laws are dealt with in this chapter.

288. According to Austrian constitutional law, no legal basis exists for public law treaties between the state and religious communities regarding their external legal relationships. With regard to the Concordat between the Austrian Republic and the Catholic Church, prima vista, there is a formal difference in terms of the legal position of the Catholic Church by comparison with the other churches and religious societies. This is so far not problematic since the special laws for churches and religious communities are drawn up nowadays in consultation with the corresponding religious community so that the formulation of the legal text is the result of negotiation in all cases. As a further consequence of the state's obligation to neutrality in religious matters, other recognized churches and religious societies participate in substance indirectly in Concordatarian regulations.

289. However, in recent times, there have been some agreements concerning joint matters between the state and legally recognized churches and religious societies – in particular in the organization of pastoral care in institutions and in the field of education and schools. The legal nature of such agreements is usually described as 'Verwaltungsverträge' (administrative agreements).

290. Special laws have been enacted with respect to the following churches and religious societies:

- The Concordat between the Holy See and the Austrian Republic with its Supplementary Protocol, dated 5 June 1933, complemented by Supplementary Treaties in the 1960s.
- The Federal Act of 6 July 1961 on the external legal relationships of the Protestant Church in Austria (ProtestantenG), representing the conclusion of a process which led to the equal treatment of the Protestant Church and the Catholic Church. In comparison with the Concordat, this more recent law guarantees a greater degree of religious freedom.
- The Federal Act of 23 June 1967 on the external legal relationships of the Greek-Oriental Church in Austria (OrthodoxenG), as amended 2011.

- The Federal Act on the external legal relationships of the Oriental-Orthodox Churches in Austria of 2003 (OrientKG).
- The Act of 21 March 1890 on the external legal relationships of the Israelite Religious Society (IsraelitenG), as amended 2012.
- The Federal Act on the external legal relationships of Islamic Religious Societies (IslamG 2015), replacing the IslamG 1912.

§2. The Catholic Church

291. The external legal relationships of the Catholic Church are traditionally governed by treaties with the Holy See which are recognized as bilateral international treaties sui generis and as such are subject to the process of transformation according to Article 50 of the Austrian Federal Constitution (B-VG).

292. The Concordat between the Holy See and the Austrian Republic with its Supplementary Protocol, dated June 5, 1933, complemented by Supplementary Treaties in the sixties.[120]

- The Treaty concerning the Regulation of Proprietary Relations (Vermögensvertrag) of 23 June 1960 (cf. 587).
- The Treaty concerning the Regulation of Questions relating to the School System and Concluding Protocol of 9 July 1962 (Schulvertrag – cf. 641 and 653).

293. Further treaties deal with the territorial organization of the Catholic Church in Austria by means of the establishment of dioceses, namely:

- The Treaty concerning the Elevation of the Apostolic Administration of Burgenland to a Diocese of 23 June 1960.
- The Treaty concerning the Elevation of the Apostolic Administration of Innsbruck-Feldkirch to a Diocese of 7 July 1964.
- The Treaty concerning the Establishment of the Diocese of Feldkirch of 7 October 1968.

294. The Republic of Austria guarantees the Holy Roman Catholic Church in her various rites the free exercise of her spiritual power and the right to make laws, decrees and orders without hindrance within her own field of competence (Article I §1 and 2).

295. The institutions of the Catholic Church which possess legal personality according to canon law also enjoy public law status in the sphere of state

120. E. Weinzierl-Fischer, *Die österreichischen Konkordate von 1855 und 1933* (Vienna: Verlag für Geschichte und Politik, 1960); I. Gampl, R. Potz & B. Schinkele, *Österreichisches Staatskirchenrecht*, vol. I (Vienna: Orac, 1990), 160–207; R. Potz, 'Ist das Konkordat noch zeitgemäß?', *Österreichisches Archiv für Recht und Religion* 53 (2006), 64–86.

legislation.[121] They are granted this status as soon as notice of their founding is lodged with the responsible ministry (Article II and Article X Concordat).

296. The founding of church provinces and dioceses as well as important boundary changes must be the subject of a treaty with the Federal government (Article III). In the Republic of Austria, there are at present two ecclesiastical provinces. The Ecclesiastical Province of Vienna consists of the Archdiocese of Vienna and the Dioceses of Linz, St Pölten and Eisenstadt. The Ecclesiastical Province of Salzburg consists of the Archdiocese of Salzburg and the Dioceses of Gurk, Graz-Seckau, Innsbruck and Feldkirch.

297. There is no state participation in appointments to church offices, with the exception of the operation of the 'political clause' in the case of bishoprics (Article IV). According to this clause, the Austrian Federal government must be informed of the name of the person chosen and has then the right to make 'objections of a general political nature'. If no agreement is reached, the Holy See is free to appoint the candidate of its choice. The 'political clause' is of little practical relevance nowadays; however, it might encourage the Holy See to consult the government at an early stage if the candidate appears likely to cause controversy. The same procedure applies, in principle, to the appointment of the Archbishop of Salzburg; however, the Archbishop is not appointed by the Holy See, but chosen by the Salzburg cathedral chapter from a list of three candidates nominated by the Holy See.

298. The existence of the state-maintained Catholic theological faculties in Vienna, Graz, Salzburg and Innsbruck is guaranteed by the Concordat (cf. 685 et seq.). Pursuant to Article V §1 section 3 of the Concordat, in principle, the internal organization and teaching activities must be regulated on the basis of the respective canon law. Regarding the provisions for implementation which are necessary with respect to the particularly state character of the theological faculties and where deviation from ecclesiastical regulations might be necessary, an agreement with the competent ecclesiastical authority is foreseen. According to §38 Act on Universities 2002, universities which offer studies in Catholic theology must take the Concordat into consideration 'when structuring their internal organization and the curricula and providing for teaching and research'. Obtaining permission for and dismissal from teaching activities, should the situation arise, must be ensured.

299. Article V §3 Concordat provides that the appointment or accreditation of professors or teachers at state-maintained Catholic theological faculties requires approval by the competent ecclesiastical authority, i.e., the competent diocesan bishop. Article V section 4 regulates subsequent ecclesiastical complaints by university teachers. The competent ecclesiastical authority may at any time withdraw consent. If the local bishop notifies the 'competent state educational administration' of the withdrawal, the administration is then responsible for the dismissal from teaching activities.

121. This possibility is also foreseen in the ProtestantenG (cf. *295*) and the IslamG (cf. *340*).

300. According to Article X §1 'orders and religious congregations' can be freely founded pursuant to the canonical provisions; there are no restrictions on the part of the state regarding their residences and housing, the number of and the characteristics of their members or their way of life, in concordance with the regulations approved by the Church.

301. Article XIII §1 contains a guarantee which covers church property and the acquisition of property by the Church within the framework of the general laws of the state, which must be seen in connection with Article 15 StGG (cf. 276 et seq.). Pursuant to Article XIII §2 – in practical terms, this is one of the most important provisions of the Concordat – the property of ecclesiastical legal entities is managed and represented by their organs appointed according to canon law. As far as religious orders are concerned, when concluding legal transactions, the local leader (abbot) or the superior of a higher-level unit is considered to be the competent representative within the legal sphere of the state. The financial management of church assets is carried out under the supervision and control of the competent church authorities or those of the religious order in question. Without their consent, such assets may not be alienated or encumbered.

302. In practice, the problem frequently arises as to which legal consequences should be drawn if rights of advice and consent provided for in canon law, particularly in the statutes of religious orders, have been disregarded, though they are necessary preconditions for the validity of contracts with ecclesiastical legal entities. According to the established case law of the Supreme Court[122] – strongly criticized in part by the scientific doctrine[123] – despite the *lex specialis* in Article XIII Concordat concerning legal transactions with religious orders, a legal transaction could be rendered void if it has been concluded without obtaining the assent or advice of certain ecclesiastical bodies in the religious order provided for in the respective statutes (e.g., a chapter or property administration council of a religious order). As the Supreme Court regularly observes, 'confidence in external matters of fact' (*Vertrauen auf den äußeren Tatbestand*) is not taken into consideration. This decision-making can result in unreasonable consequences for parties contracting with ecclesiastical legal entities, especially with regard to statutes of orders which are often not promulgated and not even available despite great efforts. Many intrinsic legal problems which ensue from this factual and legal situation have not yet been adequately dealt with.[124]

---

122. Of special significance are the following judgments: OGH 13 Apr. 1999, 4 Ob 46/99i; OGH 9 Sep. 1999, 8 Ob A 230/99b.
123. *See* H. Kalb, R. Potz & B. Schinkele, 'Rechtsgeschäfte mit kirchlichen juristischen Personen', *Österreichisches Archiv für Recht und Religion* 48 (2001), 353–418; R. Thunhart, 'Privatrechtlicher Vertrauensschutz und § 867 ABGB', *Österreichisches Archiv für Recht und Religion* 48 (2001), 419–454. Another approach is taken by H. Pree & B. Primetshofer, *Das kirchliche Vermögen, seine Verwaltung und Vertretung*, 2nd ed. (Vienna & New York: Springer, 2010), esp. 147 et seq.
124. It should be stressed that the Supreme Court's approach seems to be inadequate, irrespective of whether or not ecclesiastical legal entities are to be subsumed under the term 'communities' in the sense of § 867 ABGB and thus equal to municipalities.

303. In Article VIII of the Concordat, provisions are made for military chaplaincy. With the appointment of the Military Bishop by the Holy See, the state is involved in advance. Prior to the designation, the federal government can give the Holy See 'in a confidential manner through diplomatic channels' the names of appropriate personalities. In the case of the appointment of the Military Bishop, the procedure of the political clause has to be applied (cf. 298). The military chaplains are nominated by the Military Bishop, who has to reach an agreement with the Federal Ministry of Defence. This is followed by the appointment according to the state regulations. Personnel expenses for officers and support staff are borne completely by the Bund and the material costs are covered indirectly by means of transfers of material goods. Article XVI guarantees pastoral care in public hospitals, healthcare institutions and similar facilities as well as in prisons. This can be accomplished by establishing a chaplaincy for certain institutions with the agreement of the competent diocesan ordinarius, or by granting the competent local clergy (pastoral minister) or another minister charged with the task in his place free access to the inmates (cf. 744 et seq.).

304. Because the Concordat is an international treaty, in the case of difficulties in the interpretation of the Concordat or the occurrence of problems not yet treated which affect the state and church, an amicable solution or another ruling by mutual consent should be sought (Article XXII – Clause of Amicability).

305. In accordance with the obligation of Article 26 StVWien of 1955 (cf. 587) the Vermögensvertrag 1960 provides for an annual payment consisting of a fixed amount (currently Euro 20.754.000) and a payment in compensation for the remuneration of 1250 staff members, based on calculation of average income (article II section 1 lit b). Payments are made quarterly, the collecting point is the Archdiocese of Vienna.

§3. The Protestant Church

306. The Federal Act of 6 July 1961 on the external legal relationships of the Protestant Church in Austria (ProtestantenG) constitutes the conclusion of a process which has led to equal treatment of the Protestant Church with the historically dominant Catholic Church. In comparison with the Concordat the guarantees in this more recent law certainly reflect a higher standard of religious freedom.[125] According to an explicit request by the Protestant Church, in §1 section 1, the Church of the Augsburg Confession and the Church of the Helvetic Confession have been legally

125. *See* O. Fischer, *Das Protestantengesetz 1961* (Vienna: Herder, 1962); K. Schwarz, 'Die evangelischen Kirchen in Österreich von 1945 bis heute', in *Evangelische Kirchen und Europa*, ed. M. Bünker (Vienna: Evangelischer Presseverband, 2006), 131–155; C. Link, 'Der Protestantismus in Österreich', Evangelisch-Theologische Fakukltät, Gutachten und Studien Nr. 5: Wien 2007, https://etf.univie.ac.at/fileadmin/user_upload/fak_etf/Fakultaetspublikationen/Gutachten_und_Studien/gutachten_und_studien_05_2007.pdf; '150 Jahre Protestantenpatent – 50 Jahre Protestantengesetz' (contributions by different authors), *Österreichisches Archiv für Recht und Religion* 58 (2011), 225–327.

recognized as separate entities, in addition to the historically existing name: 'The Protestant Church of the Augsburg and the Helvetic Confession'.

307. §1 section 2 III ProtestantenG provides that 'all acts of legislative and executive power which concern the Protestant Church must observe the principle of equality before law in relation to the legal and factual position of the other legally recognized churches and religious communities.' This regulation implies an authentic interpretation by the legislator towards understanding the principle of parity in a substantive sense, indicating the meaning of a most favoured clause with reciprocal effect. All provisions specifically granted in special laws of recognized churches or religious societies should therefore be examined to determine to what extent they are linked to the specific conditions of the respective religious community. If this is not the case, these provisions would then also be applicable to other legally recognized churches and religious societies as an appropriate religious legal standard. However, this provision has only a limited practical significance (cf. 210 and 266).

308. The communities at all levels of the Protestant Church enjoy the status of public corporations. Newly founded communities and institutions[126] of the Church which possess legal personality according to internal ecclesiastical law become entities under public law from the date that the Church lodges the notification with the responsible ministry (§4 section 1).

309. The Protestant Church is completely independent of the state in all appointments of functionaries but is obliged to notify the members of the governing bodies in their capacity as legal representatives of Church institutions which possess legal personality under state law (§7 and §8).

310. Public support for the Protestant Church ceased during the Nazi regime. In accordance with the obligation of Article 26 StVWien of 1955 (cf. 587) the Protestant Church receives a fixed amount in annual grants (currently EUR 1.335.600) and compensation for the remuneration of 81 staff members, based on the calculation of average income (§20).

311. For the academic education of spiritual ministers and for the purpose of theological research and teaching, the existence of the Protestant Theological Faculty of the University of Vienna is guaranteed with at least six 'professorships' (§15 section 1). Faculty members and all persons involved in teaching are required to be members of the Protestant Church (§15 section 2). On the occasion of the appointment of a professorship provided for in this Law, the Rector of the University of Vienna must contact (Fühlungnahme) the Evangelical Supreme Ecclesiastical Council (Evangelischer Oberkirchenrat) concerning the persons proposed. According to §38 section 2 UnivG, the University of Vienna must observe §15 ProtestantenG 'when structuring the internal organization and the curricula and in ensuring teaching and research' in the Protestant Theological Faculty.

---

126. This possibility is also foreseen in the Concordat (cf. *283*) and the IslamG (cf. *340*).

312. According to §14 section 1 ProtestantenG, the Protestant Church is authorized to submit opinions, proposals and reports on matters concerning the recognized churches and religious societies in general or which affect the Protestant Church in particular to the legislative and other authorities of the Federal State (Bund) and the Bundesländer. According to §14 section 2 ProtestantenG, the federal authorities are also obliged to transmit draft laws to the Protestant Church for comment prior to their enactment, when external legal relationships of the Church are at issue. This right to submit opinions is a characteristic instrument of the civil activities of religious communities explicitly formulated for the first time in the ProtestantenG 1961 (cf. Part V).

313. The ProtestantenG guarantees pastoral care in the armed forces, in public hospitals, healthcare institutions and similar facilities as well as in prisons. §18 leg cit contains detailed regulations concerning pastoral care in hospitals. As far as permanently established pastoral care is concerned, a written authorization of the church leadership is required. With regard to the other institutions, the free access of the pastoral ministers charged with this task is granted. Moreover, §18 section 3 provides for transmitting the names of Protestant patients to the inquiring institution's pastor which has caused a discussion on its compatibility with the data protection (cf. 509 and 742).

314. In accordance with §22 section 2 ProtestantenG, the state official in the department responsible for the Protestant Church in the Ministry responsible for religious affairs must be a member of this Church. This exemption from the principle that all public offices should be accessible to all citizens does not interfere with the constitutional principle of equality or the prohibition of privilege on the grounds of religion, since this provision is considered a justified and reasonable denominational differentiation.[127]

§4. The Eastern-Orthodox Church

315. The Federal Act of 23 June 1967 on the external legal relationships of the Greek-Oriental Church in Austria (OrthodoxenG)[128] recognized the Greek-Oriental Church (Orthodox Church) in Austria for the first time as such, in addition to those Church Communities which already existed.[129]

127. VwSlg. 1379 A/1925.
128. *See* W. M. Plöchl, 'Das neue österreichische Orthodoxengesetz', *Österreichisches Archiv für Kirchenrecht* 20 (1969), 108–131; W. M. Plöchl, *Die Wiener Griechen* (Vienna: Herder, 1983); R. Potz, '30 Jahre österreichisches Orthodoxengesetz', in *Kirchenrecht und Ökumene. Festschrift Panteleimon Rodopoulos* (Kanon XV), ed. C. G. Fürst et al. (Eichenau: Kovar, 1999), 222–240.
129. In the Austro-Hungarian Monarchy four Metropolitan Churches were recognized. After World War I the system of autocephalous/autonomous churches within the Habsburg Monarchy ended and was changed according to the new political order, so that only three church communities (*Kirchengemeinden*) – two Greek and one Serbian – remained within the borders of the Austrian Republic (For the historical development *see 44* and *56*).

316. For the purposes of state law, membership results – according to § 1 section 2 OrthodoxenG – directly from the law pertaining to all persons of Orthodox faith who have permanent residence or habitual residence on federal territory, even if they are not members of any recognized 'Church Community' (*Kirchengemeinde*). Since that time, a two-fold membership in the Orthodox Church has existed, and thus it is possible to be an adherent of the Orthodox Church without at the same time being a member of a particular established church community. This construction is likely to cause legal problems since church membership as such is regulated by a state law which only refers to the statement of the person concerned.

317. In 2011, by the amendment of the OrthodoxenG,[130] an 'Orthodox Bishops' Conference' was established by the state (§ 1a) as a reaction to the establishment of the 'Orthodox Bishops' Conference of Austria' according to internal ecclesiastical law on 8 October 2010. However, membership of the state-established Orthodox Bishops' Conference is regulated differently, because the state recognizes only those bishops of autocephalous churches who are representatives holding the rank of a diocesan bishop 'recognized under this Act', as eligible for membership.

318. According to § 1a section 2, the range of responsibilities of the state-established Orthodox Bishops' Conference includes 'in particular': 1. the coordination of religious education in schools; 2. the right to give opinions and make proposals and reports in the sense of § 14 ProtestantenG (cf. 313); 3. the right to give opinions on the occasion of the recognition of Orthodox institutions according to the OrthodoxenG. This regulation is problematic because the state-established Bishops' Conference does not represent the Orthodox Church in its entirety, whereas the regulation regarding the internal 'Orthodox Bishops' Conference' established according to orthodox canon law requires the representation of the entire local Orthodoxy as well as unanimity of decision.

319. Only church communities and dioceses can be recognized as state-recognized institutions (§2); other intra-church organizations only have the possibility of founding associations or creating foundations.

320. According to the original version of the OrthodoxenG (§6), the Greek-Orthodox Metropolis of Austria was the only legally recognized diocese (§5) which, according to Greek-Orthodox canon law, belongs directly to the jurisdiction of the Ecumenical Patriarch of Constantinople. With the amendment of 2011, the possibility of establishing any other orthodox dioceses recognized by the state was granted (§3a). So far, the Russian Orthodox Diocese of Vienna and Austria is the only diocese which has been recognized by the state. The statutes were promulgated by the Ministry on 7 March 2012.

---

130. BGBl. I 2011/68. Cf. R. Potz & E. Synek, 'Zur Novellierung des Bundesgesetzes über die äußeren Rechtsverhältnisse der griechisch-orthodoxen Kirche in Österreich', *Österreichisches Archiv für Recht und Religion* 59 (2012), 391–404.

321. At the time that the OrthodoxenG came into force, four Church Communities which enjoyed the status of legal entities under public law already existed. These are dealt with in §§4 and 5 OrthodoxenG, i.e., two Greek-Orthodox Church Communities, subordinated to the Greek-Orthodox Metropolis of Austria, and the Serbian Orthodox and the Romanian Orthodox Church Community under the jurisdiction of the Patriarch of Belgrade and the Patriarch of Bucharest, respectively.

322. Since the OrthodoxenG came into force several new church communities have been created. In 1969, the establishment of the Russian Orthodox Church Community in Vienna and the Bulgarian Orthodox Church Community in Vienna was confirmed.[131] Since 2009, two further Russian Orthodox Church Communities in Graz and Linz have been confirmed as state-recognized institutions of the Orthodox Church in Austria. Both church communities belong under the jurisdiction of the Patriarchate of Moscow and are subordinated to the Russian Orthodox Diocese of Vienna and Austria. In 2013, a Church Community of Russian tradition was founded in Salzburg and its public law status was confirmed; however, it does not fall under the jurisdiction of the Vienna Diocese of the Moscow Patriarchate, but that of the German Diocese of the Russian Church Abroad, situated in Munich. In 2019 the Antiochian Orthodox parish of St. Peter and St. Paul in Vienna was officially recognized. Other proceedings for recognition of Serbian Orthodox Church Communities are currently (at the beginning of 2015) still pending.

323. Because of the internal structures of the Orthodox Church, which it is feared may lead to conflicts, the state has felt obliged to include in the Act provisions concerning the rights of supervision. If the applicable statutes of a church community do not meet legal requirements and deficiencies cannot be eliminated in due time despite a request for improvement by the state, the responsible Federal Minister must declare the competence of the respective church community to act in external affairs temporarily suspended. Simultaneously, a motion for the appointment of a curator must be brought before the civil court. If need be, the specific rights of the church community in its status as a corporation under public law must be suspended (§12 section 2).

324. By appointing a curator, the church community will no longer be able to draw up legally binding acts by self-selected organs presupposing full legal capacity. In scientific literature, reservations concerning compatibility with the constitution in this respect have been expressed, because intervention by a curator in Church administration in some areas – for instance, in staff matters – is in direct contradiction to the Church's right to self-determination.[132] The procedure described in §12

131. W. M. Plöchl, 'Errichtung und Satzungen der bulgarisch-orthodoxen Kirchengemeinde zum heiligen Ivan Rilski und der russisch-orthodoxen Kirchengemeinde zum heiligen Nikolaus in Wien', *Österreichisches Archiv für Kirchenrecht* 23 (1972), 195–211.

132. Cf. R. Potz & B. Schinkele, 'Das Orthodoxengesetz 1967 und die serbisch-orthodoxe Kirchengemeinde zum Hl. Sava in Wien', *Österreichisches Archiv für Kirchenrecht* 44 (1995–97), 197–224. The Supreme Court, however, is of a different opinion: OGH 4 Jun. 1987, 6 Ob 600/87.

must also be observed if the appointment of authorized representative bodies is carried out unlawfully or in violation of internal ecclesiastical regulations if deficiencies were not resolved in good time.

325. Pursuant to §7 section 1 OrthodoxenG, a series of provisions in the ProtestantenG in accordance with the principle of parity are to be applied to the legally recognized institutions and the religious ministers of the Greek-Oriental Church mutatis mutandis, taking into account the particular circumstances of the Orthodox Churches. These provisions relate to the special protection of church ministers, protection of professional secrecy, religious education in schools and youth education as well as spiritual care in the armed forces, in hospitals, other healthcare institutions and in prisons.

326. Orthodox religious instruction in public schools and private schools with public status is explicitly guaranteed. In Austria, religious education classes were introduced between 1992 and 1996 for Serbian Orthodox pupils in the form of group lessons, and since the school year 1993/94, a similar form of religious instruction was also organized for Romanian Orthodox pupils in Vienna. In 2007, at the Ecclesiastical College of Education in Vienna/Krems, a six-semester study course in Orthodox religious instruction for all school types in which religion is a compulsory subject was introduced (cf. 681).[133]

327. According to §7 section 3 OrthodoxenG, the regulation of state support in the enforcement of membership contributions has been allocated to a special legal provision, mainly because the different Orthodox church communities were unable to reach an agreement, most of them having refused state assistance in this matter. However, up to now, the proposed law has not yet been issued.

§5. The Israelite Religious Society

328. The IsraelitenG 1890[134] was based on the concept of the 'uniform Jewish community'. According to this concept, every Jew belonged to the cultus-community in the catchment area of permanent residence. However, this rule was modified by an amendment of 1984 allowing the recognition of another Israelite/Jewish religious society within the same territory according to the general rules of the AnerkennungsG.[135]

---

133. Cf. http://www.studienwahl.at/studien/lehramtsstudien/lehramtsstudium-theologie/2284-lehramt-fuer-religion-an-pflichtschulen-fuer-orthodoxe-oder-orientalisch-orthodoxe-religion-21-4-wien-und-krems.de.html.

134. *See* J. Budischowsky, *Die staatskirchenrechtliche Stellung der österreichischen Israeliten* (Vienna: Manz, 1995); R. Potz & B. Schinkele, 'Das neue Israelitengesetz 2012', *Österreichisches Archiv für Recht und Religion* 60 (2013), 303–335.

135. This amendment was a necessary consequence of the Constitutional Court's decision of Constitutional Court (VfSlg. 9185/1981); cf. J. Schima, 'Ende des Ausschließlichkeitsrecht?', *Österreichische Juristenzeitung* 37 (1982), 141–147, 169–173.

329. In 2012 an amendment to the IsraelitenG 1890, in effect a total revision of the law, was enacted.[136] This is principally based on the concept of 1890 but does not exclude the recognition of a further Israelite/Jewish religious society. The recognition of a further Israelite/Jewish religious society, however, is merely a theoretical possibility and far from realization because of the requirement of a minimum number of members (one two-thousandth of the Austrian population for recognition, as was introduced in §11 BekGG (cf. 225)). This number is considerably higher than the total number of Jews in Austria.

330. The first part of the IsraelitenG (§1 and §2) contains the usual description of the legal position of a legally recognized religious society which enjoys the status of a corporation under public law and its respective fundamental rights.

331. The second part deals with the organization and tasks of the Israelite Religious Society and the Israelite cultus-communities. The listing of certain issues which must be included in the constitution of the Israelite Religious Society to enable it to acquire legal force within the state legal field is consistent with those of other legally recognized churches and religious societies. Furthermore, as a Jewish specificum, this enumeration includes the obligation to ensure adequate representation of all existing traditions within the Israelite Religious Society. This must be seen in connection with the aforementioned de facto existing monopolistic position of the Israelite Religious Society.

332. In particular, the tasks of the Israelite Religious Society include the representation of the interests of its members, in as far as they exceed the scope of a religious community, the obligation to submit to the competent Federal Minister the constitution of the Israelite Religious Society as well as the statutes of the cultus-communities and their amendments, and notification of any changes in the composition of its organs. Decisions regarding distribution of the annual state payments according to §14 is another task which falls to the Israelite Religious Society.

333. Cultus-communities are autonomous bodies with legal personality under public law (§5). They must satisfy the religious needs of their members and provide the necessary facilities to carry out their tasks. Every cultus-community requires statutes, which must include all issues generally necessary to acquire legal force within the state legal field. Cultus-communities may establish and administer institutions and facilities in order to fulfil their duties as well as declare existing facilities under the administration of the cultus-community. New establishment of a cultus-community requires at least 300 members or 100 adult members plus a positive prognosis from the Israelite Religious Society regarding its future development.

---

136. *See* B. Gartner, 'Das neue österreichische Israelitengesetz: Eine historische Annäherung', in *Neuere Entwicklungen im Religionsrecht europäischer Staaten*, ed. W. Rees et al. (Berlin: Duncker & Humblot, 2013), 183–211; R. Potz & B. Schinkele. 'Das neue Israelitengesetz 2012', *Österreichisches Archiv für Recht und Religion* 60 (2013), 303–335.

334. The third part is dedicated to the rights and obligations of the Israelite Religious Society. These provisions predominantly correspond to those which usually apply to legally recognized churches and religious societies. The right to the use of a name and the protection of using religious designations in combination with the word 'Israelite' are guaranteed. Names that could give outside third parties the impression of a legal connection to the Israelite Religious Society or its institutions may only be used with the consent of the Israelite Religious Society.

335. The right to give opinions and make proposals and reports in the sense of §14 ProtestantenG (cf. 313) is explicitly guaranteed, as well as the protection of spiritual ministers, the protection of the professional secrecy of spiritual ministers and spiritual care in the armed forces, in prisons and in hospitals and other healthcare institutions.

336. Religious instruction in public schools and the establishment and operation of denominational private schools is guaranteed (§9 section 1). The Israelite Religious Society and its members have the right to instruct their children and youth – also outside of school – in all traditional customs and to educate them in accordance with their religious doctrines (§9 section 4). It may be assumed that ritual circumcision is implicitly included here, though the Explanatory Remarks to the amendment 2012 of the IsraelitenG 1890 contain no indication to this effect. Such an interpretation is consistent with a clarification made in the Explanatory Remarks to the IslamG 2015 (cf. 361).

337. According to §10 section 1, Jewish holidays and the Shabbat are granted state protection. The following Jewish holidays are specified: Rosh Hashanah (two days); Yom Kippur (one day); Sukkot (two days); Schemini Atzeret (one day); Simchat Tora (one day); Passover (four days); Schavuot (two days). Their dates are to be determined in accordance with the Jewish calendar. The provision has no consequences in the field of labour law but all avoidable activities on those days which cause noise or could disturb festivities, as well as public assemblies and processions, are forbidden in the vicinity of synagogues and other places or facilities used for worship by Israelite cultus-communities.

338. The Israelite Religious Society has the right to establish and operate ritual baths (mikvaot) according to internal religious regulations, which are not subject to regulatory approval for bathhouses.

339. The Israelite Religious Society has the right to organize the production of meat products and other food in accordance with internal regulations. With respect to meals for members of the Israelite Religious Society in the armed forces, in prison, in public hospitals and similarly, in public schools, the internal dietary regulations must be considered (§12).

340. According to Article 26 State Treaty of Vienna (StVWien 1955), Austria is obliged to indemnify persons who suffered financial losses resulting from Nazi legislation or destructions during the Nazi occupation (cf. 587). The Israelite Religious

Society, therefore, receives annual grants consisting of a fixed amount (currently EUR 600,000) and compensation for the remuneration of twenty-three staff members of Israelite cultus-communities, based on average income. Beyond this, there are further obligations for compensating Jewish institutions based on other laws; however, the necessary proof is often difficult to furnish, and thus the implementation of such laws was repeatedly delayed for a long time due to bureaucratic reasons (cf. 74).

341. The fourth part of the Law deals with the 'interaction of the Israelite Religious Society and the state'. The constitution of the Israelite Religious Society, the statutes of cultus-communities – in particular, the contribution scheme and electoral rules and amendments thereto – require the approval of the responsible Federal Minister to become valid. The names of the organs authorized as external representatives of the Israelite Religious Society and the cultus-communities and the spiritual ministers must be communicated to the Federal Minister immediately after the election or their appointment (§15).

342. Rabbis may not be examined as witnesses regarding information entrusted to them under the seal of secrecy, without prejudice to other relevant regulations. This also applies to the interrogation of rabbis as persons providing information or as parties in civil proceedings (§16).

343. According to Jewish law, cemeteries and cemetery departments are conceived as permanent (§19). Their dissolution, closure and exhumation of individual graves are prohibited. Exceptions require the approval of the competent religious authority. Burials in Jewish cemeteries and cemetery departments may only be carried out with the approval of the competent cultus-community.

344. If organs authorized as external representation or spiritual ministers are determined by election, the electoral process must be sufficiently outlined either in the constitution, the statutes or electoral rules so that a review of the electoral process is possible. If organs authorized as external representation or spiritual ministers are determined by election, according to the election rules, each qualified elector – after the exhaustion of all internal legal means – has the right to lodge a supervisory complaint with the Federal Minister. If, within fourteen days after receipt of the election results, neither an appeal according to internal law nor a complaint to the state authorities has been lodged, the Federal Minister must acknowledge the election results and issue a declaration confirming the election announcement. These provisions imply considerable governmental involvement in internal election procedures of the Israelite Religious Society. This right to state supervision might raise problems with respect to the fundamental right of self-determination, and should, if at all, only be exercised in the case of massive deficiencies in electoral proceedings. In general, the state is obliged to maintain neutrality in religious matters and should act very cautiously in view of conflicts within religious societies.

345. Following the example of the OrthodoxenG (cf. 324), the legislator of the IsraelitenG has provided for a further state supervisory tool, i.e., the possibility of appointing a state curator. If the term of function of organs authorized for external representation of the Israelite Religious Society or of a cultus-community has exceeded at least six months or these functionaries are unable to function for other reasons, the state authority must invite the Israelite Religious Society or the cultus-community within a period of at least one and at most six months to make provisions for elections or restore the capacity to function in another way than is foreseen in the Constitution or statutes. Should the Israelite Religious Society or the cultus-community fail to comply with this obligation and neither the Israelite Religious Society nor the cultus-community have brought in a motion for appointing a curator to the competent court, then it is the task of the Federal Minister to submit such an application to the competent court (§21). In comparison with the OrthodoxenG, the conditions for the appointment of a curator are much more tightly formulated, so that the risk of an intervention in internal affairs is significantly less here than in the case of Orthodox Churches. Thus, the handling of this provision in concordance with the Constitution seems, on the whole, to be guaranteed.

§6. The Islamic Religious Societies

346. In 2015, the IslamG 1912 was renewed by the Federal Act on the external legal relationships of Islamic Religious Societies which were long overdue.[137] The draft law has been the subject of intense political debate, which has not yet subsided, even after this law has come into force. In principle, this law differs from the other special laws concerning religious communities for two reasons. First of all, it is not a law concerning one single religious society but includes two different religious societies, namely, the Islamic Religious Society in Austria (Islamische Glaubensgemeinschaft in Österreich, IGGiÖ) and the Islamic Alevite Religious Society in Austria (Islamische Alevitische Glaubensgemeinschaft in Österreich, IAGÖ). This inclusion of the IAGÖ in the IslamG which was mainly based on the self-designation as 'Islamic' has been widely criticized because it disregards the fundamental differences between Islam and Alevism.[138] Moreover, this involvement means that the not yet legally recognized Alevi Federation of Austria – the IAGÖ originally was a part of it – should be recognized according to the AnerkennungsG, so that for these Alevi groups in future two different laws are to be applied (cf. 256).

347. Secondly, it is a law which not only regulates the external legal relationships of an existing religious society but also the preconditions for the legal recognition of further Islamic religious societies. Correspondingly, this concept is

137. *See* B. Gartner-Müller, 'Die Islamische Glaubensgemeinschaft und das Ausschließlichkeitsrecht der gesetzlich anerkannten Kirchen und Religionsgesellschaften', *Österreichisches Archiv für Recht und Religion* 59 (2012), 251–283; S. Schima, 'Das IslamG im Kontext des österreichischen Religionsrechts', *Österreichisches Archiv für Recht und Religion* 59 (2012), 225–250.

138. *See* M. Sökefeld, 'Sind Aleviten Muslime? Die alevitische Debatte über das Verhältnis von Alevitentum und Islam in Deutschland', in *Aleviten in Deutschland. Identitätsprozesse einer Religionsgemeinschaft in der Diaspora*, ed. M. Sökefeld (Bielefeld: transcript-Verlag, 2008), 195–218.

reflected in the structure of the law. The first part deals with the general legal position of Islamic religious societies and the prerequisites for the legal recognition of further Islamic religious societies. The second part includes provisions concerning Islamic religious societies. The third and fourth parts regulate the rights and obligations of the existing IGGiÖ and correspondingly, the IAGÖ. The fifth part deals with the 'interaction of the religious societies and the state' in the usual way, and the sixth part – 'final provisions' – includes, *inter alia*, the transitional rules for the two existing religious societies.

348. In 2021 an amendment was issued with the aim of ensuring the 'effective enforcement' of the Islam Act of 2015. To this end, a provision regarding the cooperation of all ministries with authority on religious affairs was added to the BekGG (§11b) as a general provision for dealing with religious communities. This continues a development towards state supervision in Austrian law on religion, which is increasingly being used as an instrument of integration and security policy. At the same time as the amendment to the Islam Act, the Counter-Terrorism Act was enacted as part of the package of measures targeting 'political Islam'. At the same time, the 'Austrian Fund for the Documentation of Religiously Motivated Political Extremism (Documentation Office for Political Islam)' was established as an independent fund. 'The task of the fund is scientific research into political Islam, its associated networks and structures. The center observes causes and trends with a view to strengthening and promoting pluralism, democratic awareness and religious freedom in Austria on the basis of its research. Accordingly, the documentation center undertakes research, and offers advice and information about the phenomenon of political Islam.'[139]

I. Legal Position and Acquisition of Legal Personality

349. §1 and §2 section 1 IslamG contain the usual description of the legal position and the fundamental guarantees concerning legally recognized churches and religious societies. The wording of §2 section 2 – which is not found in any other special law – is still a 'bone of contention' and has triggered quite a fundamental discussion. The first and second sentences which correspond with the IslamG 1912 state that 'Islamic religious societies enjoy the same legal protection as other recognized religious societies. Their teachings, institutions and customs enjoy the same legal protection, provided that they do not contradict legal regulations.' The third sentence, however, is new and reads as follows:

> Religious societies, cultus-communities or other subdivisions as well as their members may not rely on internal religious rules or teachings with respect to their duty to observe general norms of the state, provided that the applicable state law does not provide for such a possibility in the respective case.

139. https://www.dokumentationsstelle.at/ (15.7.2023). For a critical discussion of the term 'political Islam', *see* Islamische Glaubensgemeinschaft in Österreich (ed.), Politischer Islam - Versuch einer Definition, Vienna 2019.

350. This provision demonstrates a general distrust towards Islam and Muslims, respectively. The formulation is misleading from two perspectives. On the one hand, compliance with the standards of general laws of the state is a matter of course, and thus too superfluous to be expressly mentioned. On the other hand, it seems to imply that explicit legal permission is always required to give relevance to internal religious rules in the area of state law. Such an approach ignores the fact that the fundamental right to freedom of religion encompassing freedom of conscience might, because of certain facts and under certain circumstances involve difficult and complex balance of procedures. In order to strike a fair balance between conflicting objects of legal protection, simple reference to ordinary laws is by no means sufficient. Integration of the paraphrasing in question as applying to Muslims only has been partly legitimated in the public debate by pointing out that the predominance of the religious law of Sharia over human law-making is often asserted by Muslims.

351. Islamic religious societies acquire legal personality on application by ministerial ordinance of the responsible Minister. The preconditions for the acquisition of public law status are consistent with the general provisions of §11 BekGG (cf. 230 et seq.). Refusal of recognition also corresponds with the general law on recognition (§5 section 1). For the first time, the revocation of legal personality is regulated in a special law; nevertheless, it is in accordance with the respective provision of §11a BekGG which applies to churches and religious societies legally recognized according to the AnerkennungsG (cf. 239).

II. Constitution of Islamic Religious Societies

352. §6 section 1 IslamG outlines the issues which the constitution of an Islamic Religious Society must deal with within the framework of the society's internal affairs, in order to attain legal force within the sphere of the state. This enumeration corresponds with the respective provision in other special laws; however, it contains a significant supplement as regards the form of the required submission of its doctrine; as an additional requirement, a text outlining the essential sources of faith (Qur'an) must be presented, which must differ from the doctrine of existing legally recognized religious societies or state-registered religious denominational communities (no. 5). The required submission of the 'doctrine, including a text of the essential sources of faith (Qur'an) in the German language' gives rise to numerous problems. The requirement of a virtually authentic text of the Qur'an in German cannot be justified, either in terms of religious science or in terms of the law on religion. Such a suggestion does not take into account the complex processes involved in interpretation of religious sources which applies in general to the Holy Scriptures of revelational religions. The complexity of a translation of the Qur'an particularly calls for a detailed commentary. From the perspective of law on religion, it is questionable that the Explanatory Remarks try to legitimate the required submission of the Qur'an in the German language primarily on the grounds that the doctrine of an applicant religious society must be distinguishable from the teachings of already existing and legally recognized religious societies and state-registered religious denominational communities. There are assessments at issue which evidently demand too much of a state which is neutral in religious matters.

353. §6 section 2 IslamG determines that the financial means for ordinary activities aimed at satisfying the religious needs of the members must be obtained by the Religious Society, its cultus-communities, or their members from within the country. In particular, the employment of foreign public servants in the service of religious societies and cultus-communities as employees, clergy, pastors or officials is in any case prohibited by law, regardless of who pays them. This should serve the legitimate aim of preserving the independence of cultus-communities from governmental influence on the part of national and foreign governments (cf. 608). The Constitutional Court found that this regulatory objective is constitutional with respect to grants from other states and institutions, but not so with respect to grants from foreign private individuals insofar as they do not restrict the independence of the Religious Society or cultus-communities.[140]

354. The tasks of the Religious Society include, in particular, the representation of the interests of its members, in as far as they exceed the scope of a religious community, the obligation to submit the constitution of the Religious Society as well as the statutes of the cultus-communities and their amendments, and reports of changes in the composition of its organs to the competent Federal Minister (§7). The 2021 amendment additionally prescribes in §7 lit 4 the submission of accounting records, in particular financial statements and other related financial documents in order to control prohibited foreign financing (§6 section 2).

355. Cultus-communities are autonomous bodies with legal personality under public law (§8). They must satisfy the religious needs of their members and provide the necessary facilities to accomplish this task. Every religious community requires a statute, which must include a number of certain issues in order to acquire legal force within the sphere of the state, which corresponds essentially to the respective requirements of other special laws. Cultus-communities may establish and administer institutions and facilities in order to fulfil their tasks or declare existing facilities under the administration of the cultus-community. If such institutions are given legal personality by the internal law of the Religious Society, according to §23 section 4 IslamG they may also obtain legal status under public law by notification by the Religious Society to the competent Minister.[141] Institutions jointly administered by several cultus-communities – which are of great significance with regard to Islam – may only be founded with their mutual consent and the approval of the Religious Society (§8 section 2). New establishment of a cultus-community' requires a positive prognosis for the continuous existence and a sustainable economic basis and the approval of the Religious Society.

140. VfSlg 20.321/2019.

141. Also foreseen in the Concordat (cf. *283*) and in the ProtestantenG (cf. *295*).

III. Rights and Obligations of the Existing Islamic Religious Society in Austria

356. The third part is dedicated to the rights and obligations of the existing 'Islamic Religious Society in Austria'. The rules correspond predominantly with the usual regulations which apply to legally recognized churches and religious societies. The right to the use of a name and the protection of religious designations is guaranteed, although the fact that in the future there will probably be several Islamic Religious Societies could provoke difficulties and misunderstandings, involving complex questions regarding delineation. The right to give opinions and make proposals and reports in the sense of §14 ProtestantenG (cf. 313) is explicitly guaranteed.

357. The protection of spiritual ministers and the professional secrecy of spiritual ministers as well as the spiritual care of members who are in the armed forces, are detained in prison or housed in a public hospital or other healthcare institution is guaranteed. The material and personnel expenditure for the military chaplaincy is financed by the federal government.

358. With respect to persons entrusted with spiritual care in the aforementioned institutions, §11 section 3 IslamG requires these persons to be professionally and personally suitable to perform such activities. This professional qualification is only considered valid once the respective person has successfully completed studies in Islamic theology or comparable educational training. Personal qualification presupposes at least three years of relevant professional experience and knowledge of the German language at a level which qualifies the applicant for university studies. Furthermore, authorization from the respective Islamic Religious Society is required.

359. Islamic Religious Societies and their members are authorized to guide their children and youth through all traditional customs and to educate them in accordance with their religious doctrine (§11 section 4 IslamG). The Explanatory Remarks explicitly point out that circumcision according to Islamic tradition is covered by this provision.

360. The Islamic Religious Society has the right to organize the production of meat products and other food in accordance with its internal regulations. The IGGÖ, therefore, carries out certifications within the framework of the constitutionally guaranteed practice of religion. (Cf. 186 et seq.). The Islamic Information and Documentation Center Austria (IIDZ), which does not belong to the IGGÖ, certifies slaughtering as halal on the basis of a 'trade license', in which stunning is carried out that does not lead to heart arrest before death by bleeding has occurred. The IIDZ is thus in opposition to the IGGÖ but refers to an international acceptance of its certification and a standardization drawn up by 'Austrian Standards International' for products that are considered permissible (halal) under Islamic law. However, this rule raised the question of the permissibility of state standardization of halal slaughtering and was withdrawn on 1 March 2018.

361. Regarding holidays and weekly Friday prayers from 12.00 to 14.00, the protection of the state is guaranteed (§13). The dates of religious holidays are determined in accordance with the Islamic calendar. The following holidays are listed: the feast of Ramadan (Eid al-Fitr, three days), the feast of the Sacrifice (Eid al-Adha, four days) and the Schi'ite Day of Aschura (one day). This provision has no consequences in the field of labour law but all avoidable activities on those days which cause noise or could disturb festivities, as well as public assemblies and processions, are forbidden in the vicinity of houses of worship as well as other places and facilities used for worship by any Islamic religious community.

362. According to Islamic law, cemeteries and cemetery departments are conceived as permanent (§15). Their dissolution, closure, or exhumation of individual graves is prohibited. Exceptions require the approval of the competent religious authority. Burials in Islamic cemeteries and cemetery departments may only be carried out with the approval of the competent religious authority.

IV. Rights and Obligations of the Existing Islamic Alevite Religious Society (ALEVI) in Austria

363. The rights and obligations of the existing Islamic Alevite Religious Society in Austria[142][143] are predominantly formulated equivalent to the provisions which apply to the Islamic Religious Society in Part 3. This applies to the right to use the name and the protection of religious designations, to the right to give opinions, make proposals and reports in the sense of §14 ProtestantenG (cf. 313), the protection of spiritual ministers and the professional secrecy of spiritual ministers, as well as extending spiritual care to those members who are engaged in the armed forces, are inmates in prison or patients of public healthcare and similar institutions, the right to guide their children and youth through all traditional customs and to educate them in accordance with religious doctrines, taking into account dietary laws, regulations regarding public holidays and cemeteries. The Explanatory Remarks emphasize that ritual circumcision is encompassed by the right to educate children according to religious commandments. The provision referring to Alevite holidays refers to the following feasts: the weekly Cem-worship on Thursdays, the Lokma-days, the Memory of the Holy Hizir (three days), the Birth of Imam Ali (one day), the Proclamation of the Appointment of Imam Ali as Successor of Mohammed (one day), the Feast of Sacrifice (four days) and Asure (one day).

142. For the disputed inclusion of the IAGÖ in the IslamG. cf. R. Potz & B. Schinkele, *Opinion to the draft of the IslamG 2015*: http://www.parlament.gv.at/PAKT/VHG/XXV/SNME/SNME_02076/fname_371638.pdf. *See also* R. Potz & B. Schinkele, 'Eintragung bzw gesetzliche Anerkennung alevitischer Gruppen in Österreich', *Österreichisches Archiv für Recht und Religion* 58 (2011), 137–155.

143. Meanwhile three Alevite organisations with a specific status for religious communities exist in Austria *(cf. 240, 258)*.

V. Interaction Between Religious Societies and the State

364. The constitutions of the religious societies, the statutes of cultus-communities, in particular the contribution scheme, electoral rules and amendments thereto, require the approval of the responsible Federal Minister for their validity. The names of the organs authorized for external representation of the Religious Society and information about the cultus-communities and spiritual ministers must be communicated to the Federal Minister immediately after the election or appointment (§23 IslamG).

365. Unlike the other special laws, the IslamG does not contain an explicit provision concerning religious instruction, therefore, the general regulations for religious education classes (cf. 630 et seq.) are to be applied in Islamic religious instruction. Islamic religious education in schools was introduced in 1983.[144] The first teachers were mostly recruited from the countries of origin of the immigrants. For this reason, Muslim teachers who were often unfamiliar with the way of life in Western societies were faced with a young Muslim generation that had grown up in Austria. Against this background, Islamic religious education classes have caused conflicts, and thus occasionally rather exacerbated the identity problems of second- and third-generation Muslims. The conservative educational methods employed by these foreign teachers also gave rise to protests by parents.[145] The IGGiÖ, therefore, envisaged a domestic training course for Islamic teachers of religious education and proposed the establishment of an Islamic religious-pedagogical academy modelled on the lines of the existing Catholic and Protestant academies.[146]

366. Due to this initiative, the Islamic Religious-pedagogical Academy (IRPA) was founded in 1998 as a denominational private school pursuant to the Act on Private Schools and was conferred public status on this legal basis. In 1999, the Act concerning Studies at Academies and Establishing Colleges for Pedagogical Professions (AStG)[147] set in motion a process of development and organizational adaptation, transforming the 'Teachers' Training Academies' (Pedagogical Academies) into 'Colleges for Educational Professions' over an eight-year transitional period. The assignment of the academies of religious instruction according to the AStG had numerous consequences especially relevant for the Islamic Academies. The orientation on ideas and values required as a leading principle in §5 section 2 AStG, which must be seen in relation to the tasks of the Austrian schools, posed challenges to Islam, as do the three other leading principles: the range and freedom of

144. R. Potz, 'Der Islamische Religionsunterricht in Österreich', in *Bürgerliche Freiheit und Christliche Verantwortung, Festschrift für Christoph Link*, ed. H. de Wall & M. Germann (Tübingen: Mohr Siebeck, 2003), 345–369.

145. M. Schmied, 'Die Islamische Religionspädagogische Akademie', *Österreichisches Archiv für Recht und Religion* 46 (1999), 434–443.

146. *Ibid.*; R. Potz, 'Der Islamische Religionsunterricht in Österreich', in *Bürgerliche Freiheit und Christliche Verantwortung, Festschrift für Christoph Link*, ed. H. de Wall & M. Germann (Tübingen: Mohr Siebeck, 2003), 345–369.

147. M. Schmied, 'Die Islamische Religionspädagogische Akademie', *Österreichisches Archiv für Recht und Religion* 46 (1999), 434– 443.

scientific theories and opinions; the interconnection between research and teaching; and the equal treatment of men and women. For the first time, Islam experienced integration into a state university legislation. In 2007, the Islamic Teachers Training College for primary and secondary elementary schools was established, according to the Federal Act on the Organization of the Pedagogical Colleges and their Studies of 2005 (cf. 640 et seq.). Students complete their studies here with the degree of Bachelor of Education which enables them to continue their studies in various fields of higher education in Austria. Finally, in the winter term 2006/2007 the research department of 'Islamic Religious Pedagogy' was set up at the University of Vienna, with the main task of instructing Islamic teachers of religious education in secondary high schools.[148]

367. The introduction of regular studies in Islamic theology in addition to the study of Islamic religious pedagogy is a particular innovation of the IslamG. According to §24 section 1, six positions for professors will be established by 2019 for the purpose of theological research and teaching and to ensure the academic education of spiritual ministers of Islamic religious societies. Under this Act, a separate curriculum has to be drawn up for every Religious Society. On the occasion of the appointment of a professorship provided for in this law, the Rector of the University concerned must contact (*Fühlungnahme*) the Islamic Religious Societies regarding the proposed candidates. In this respect, it must be considered that the teachers of theological core subjects are adherents of a religious doctrine (law school) represented in the Islamic religious societies recognized under this Act (§24 section 4). These provisions cause some problems. First, the study of Alevite theology was incorporated into the Islamic theology degree program merely as a specialised branch. This means that the main subjects of Islamic theology, which are only of minor importance for Alevite theology, became basic subjects for Alevi students. This concept is inadequate. Second, if two or more religious societies exist in the future adhering to the same traditions, or if an Islamic religious society with a further tradition is recognized, the law will be difficult to apply.

368. With the integration of Islamic theology into the Austrian university landscape a gap has been closed.[149] It cannot be in the interests of Austrian society as a whole – and certainly not in the interest of its Muslim citizens – that Islamic theology remains out with state theological research and teaching. In particular, the current discussions within Islamic theology regarding a historical-critical method involve challenges and demand adequate guarantees of freedom of teaching and research and the possibility of interdisciplinary exchange.

369. The Religious Society and the Republic shall be obliged to inform each other of events affecting a matter covered by this Federal Act (§25 section 1). The Religious Society has to submit to the authority for religious affairs all institutions

148. E. Aslan, 'Religiöse Erziehung der Muslime in Österreich', *Österreichisches Archiv für Recht und Religion* 55 (2008), 1–13.

149. R. Potz, 'Islamische Theologie an der Universität', in *In mandatis meditari. Festschrift für Hans Paarhammer*, ed. S. Haering et al. (Berlin: Duncker & Humblot, 2012), 929–949.

of the religious society of cultus-communities and congregations as well as their functionaries, including religious functionaries, upon request (§25 section 2). In order to prove that the funds have been raised in accordance with §6 section 2, they are additionally obliged to submit the accounting records and related documents for all their facilities on request within a period to be set by the authority for religious affairs (§25 section 5).

370. Spiritual ministers may not be examined as witnesses with regard to information entrusted to them under the seal of secrecy, without prejudice to other relevant regulations. This also applies to the interrogation of spiritual ministers as persons providing information or parties in civil proceedings (§26).

371. In the case that organs authorized for external representation or spiritual ministers are determined by election, the electoral process must be sufficiently determined either in the constitution, the statutes or electoral rules so that a review of the electoral process is possible. If organs authorized for external representation or spiritual ministers are determined by an election, each qualified elector according to the election rules – after the exhaustion of all internal legal remedies – has the right to make a supervisory complaint to the Federal Minister. If, within fourteen days of receipt of the election results, neither an appeal according to internal law nor a complaint to the state authorities has been made, the Federal Minister must acknowledge the election results and issue a declaration confirming the election announcement (§28). These provisions, copied from the IsraelitenG (cf. 342) indicate a considerable involvement on the part of the government in the election of functionaries of religious societies. This right to state supervision might raise problems with respect to the fundamental right of self-determination, and should, if at all, only be exercised in the case of massive deficiencies in electoral proceedings. In general, the state is obliged to maintain neutrality in religious matters and should act very cautiously in view of conflicts within religious societies.

372. Following the example of the IsraelitenG (cf. 346) the possibility of appointing a curator is foreseen as a measure of state supervision (§29 IslamG). If the term of function of organs authorized for external representation of the religious society or of a cultus-community exceeds at least six months or if those organs are unable to act for other reasons, the state authority must invite the Religious Society or the cultus-community within a period of at least one and at most six months to provide for elections or restore the ability to act in another way, laid down in the constitution or the statutes. If the Religious Society or the cultus-community do not comply with this obligation and neither the Religious Society nor the cultus-community' has brought in a motion for appointing a curator to the competent court, the Federal Minister must submit such a request to the competent court.

373. §30 was completely revised by the 2021 amendment. In order to enforce decisions under the Islam Act, the state authority can issue a decision to revoke resolutions of any religious society, cultus-community or a recognized establishment that violates the law, constitution or statutes, can impose fines and use other lawful means. Although this provision stipulates fines of an appropriate amount, the fines are sometimes exorbitantly high – up to Euro 36,000 in special cases – and can therefore pose a real threat to the existence of Islamic communities and institutions.

374. Under the Act 2015, associations whose objective is the dissemination of religious doctrine of a Religious Society, and which already exist on the date the Act comes into force, are to be dissolved by decision of the Federal Minister of the Interior by the date of 1 March 2016, if the purpose of the association has not been adapted to fit the requirements of this Act (§31 section 3 IslamG). Therefore, associations must modify their aims in good time so that they no longer include the dissemination of religious doctrine. If the purpose of the association is converted into activities such as social and/or cultural activities, or the maintenance or establishment of a place of worship, the association may continue to exist. Drawing a line between associations which disseminate religious doctrine and those which fulfil partly religious purposes will make for great difficulties in practice. The provision in §31 section 3 could cause further legal problems, as the doctrine of the existing Islamic Religious Society in Austria covers the entirety of the Islamic law schools, according to the concept of the eight madhāhib recognized by the global Islamic community.[150] Therefore, all Islamic associations apart from the Islamic Religious Society in Austria relying on the mainstream Islam of the eight madhāhib must actually be dissolved.[151] Altogether, the provision in §31 section 3 raises a number of questions regarding the fundamental rights of freedom of association and freedom of religion.

§7. The Oriental-Orthodox Churches

375. In 2003, the Federal Act on External Relationships of the Oriental-Orthodox Churches in Austria (OrientKG)[152] put an end to the inequitable treatment between the Coptic-Orthodox Church and the two other Oriental-Orthodox churches which had already been recognized, the Armenian Apostolic Church since Joseph II, confirmed by a Ministerial Ordinance of 1973, and the Syrian-Orthodox Church, since 1988. The Coptic-Orthodox Church only has been a state-registered religious denominational community since 1998. The genesis of this law was closely linked with the generally given legal problems within the sphere of the law on recognition. Since 1985, several applications for recognition by the Coptic-Orthodox Church lodged with the competent Federal Minister have been rejected,

150. In July 2005, a conference of Islamic scholars from 50 countries adopted the so-called Amman Declaration, which contains the recognition of eight law schools, adopted on the summit of the Organization of the Islamic Conference in December 2005 and by the International Islamic Fiqh Academy in Jeddah. This recognition of the eight schools of law has a certain official character in the Muslim world.

151. This does not apply, of course, to the Islamic Alevi Religious Society in Austria, as the Alevis are not recognized by the Islamic world as Muslims.

152. B. Schinkele, 'Die Rechtsstellung der Orientalisch-orthodoxen Kirchen in Österreich unter besonderer Berücksichtigung der Koptisch-orthodoxen Kirche', in *Ius Canonicum in Oriente et Occidente. Festschrift für Carl Gerold Fürst*, ed. H. Zapp et al. (Frankfurt am Main: Peter Lang, 2003), 1041–1062, with further biographical data.

though without a formal administrative decision. In its reasoning, the Federal Minister made reference to the number of members as being too small to guarantee the continued existence of the church. However, this cannot be deemed a reasonable or objective ground for rejection – primarily, by comparison with the number of adherents of the Oriental-Orthodox Sister-Churches in Austria, which approximately equal those of the Coptic-Orthodox Church.

376. The coming into force of the BekGG 1998 involved another serious deterioration of the Coptic-Orthodox Church's legal situation. Besides creating a second category of religious communities, this Law includes an amendment of the AnerkennungsG 1874 encompassing additional prohibitive pre-requisites (cf. 230), in particular, the required number of adherents from now on – one two-thousandth of the inhabitants according to the last census – would have made any recognition of the Coptic-Church and thus, equal treatment with the sister churches impossible in future.

377. However, against this background, a way could still be found to eliminate discrimination against the Coptic-Orthodox Church in general and in particular, in relation to the Oriental-Orthodox Sister-Churches. Though these churches differ from each other in liturgy and canon law, from an ecclesiological point of view the unity of the Oriental-Orthodox Churches has never been questioned. Recently, more and more emphasis has even been placed on their uniform doctrine.

378. Faced with this situation, the Oriental-Orthodox Churches had to carry out a certain internal restructuring. As a common institutional organ, the OrientKG provides for a 'Church-Commission', composed of two representatives of each Oriental-Orthodox Church. Some common interests have been conferred on the competence of this Commission, such as coordinating religious instruction in schools or giving joint opinions on matters of relevance to the Oriental-Orthodox Churches as a whole.

379. §3 refers to the protection of church ministers and the professional secrecy of ministers, regulations on religious education and youth education, as well as the spiritual care of those members who are in the army, in prison or have been committed to public health or care institutions according to the relevant provisions of the ProtestantenG (cf. 314).

380. The OrientKG can be seen as a striking example of dynamic proceedings in the sphere of state law on religion. It is incumbent upon the denominationally neutral state to take into account the self-understanding of the various religious communities, reflecting the manifold religious doctrines and phenomena. In the actual case, the legislator has completely exhausted the legal instruments available with a view to highlighting the ecclesiological profile of the Oriental-Orthodox Churches as much as possible. This is the way to best achieve 'individual-case justice' as well as a high standard of religious freedom without interfering with the denominational neutrality of the state. However, it must not be forgotten that several other religious communities are also excluded from legal recognition – ultimately, as a consequence of arbitrary proceedings on the part of the responsible administrative body – with no comparable methods for solution whatsoever.

Part IV. International, Supranational, Transnational and Regional Effects on Religious Communities

Chapter 1. International Law Effects on Religious Communities

§1. Public International Law in the Austrian Legal System

381. According to Article 9 section 1 B-VG, the general rules of international law (i.e., customary law) are integral parts of the Austrian federal law. They rank lower than constitutional law but have priority over ordinary laws. Their significance lies in inter-governmental and diplomatic relations, whereas in matters of freedom of religion and law on religion, they play virtually no role.

382. International treaties may be a source of domestic law under Article 50 B-VG. Political state treaties and state treaties, the contents of which modify or complement existing laws or change the contractual basics of the European Union, require the approval of the First Chamber of Parliament (National Council). This is regularly the case with all international treaties relevant to religious freedom. The National Council may decide in each individual case that the treaty is non-self-executing, i.e., that it needs to be implemented by additional legislation (special transformation).

383. Public international law – other than general rules transformed by national laws into the Austrian legal system – has the same rank as ordinary law. If state treaties include matters of constitutional regulation they are subject to the requirements for constitutional amendments.

384. Some international conventions must be fulfilled by the issue of laws. If the guarantees of these international provisions are already ensured in the Austrian legal system, there is no further legal implementation. This applies, for example, to the two Covenants of 1966 aimed at concretizing the Universal Declaration on Human Rights 1948 (UDHR). Though they are neither directly applicable domestically nor oblige the legislator to respect them as a matter of constitutional law, they do have a certain political and interpretative significance.

§2. Freedom of Religion in the United Nations Treaty System

385. Based on the UDHR, the United Nations has developed a system of conventions to put into effect their commitment to human rights, practically all of which have been ratified by Austria.

386. Freedom of religion and the self-determination of religious communities are, *inter alia*, contained in a number of conventions and declarations. Of particular significance for the protection of religious freedom are the following:

- The International Covenant on Civil and Political Rights (ICCPR) 1966, whose Article 18 guarantees freedom of thought, conscience and religion. The Human Rights Committee is charged with the examination of the state reports and the formulation of General Comments. Freedom of religion is the subject of General Comment 22, containing detailed explanations with regard to Article 18 ICCPR which are also helpful for the interpretation of Article 9 ECHR. Notwithstanding this theoretical importance, General Comment 22 has no practical significance in Austrian jurisprudence.
- The International Covenant on Economic, Social and Cultural Rights (ICESCR) 1966, whose Article 13 section 3 guarantees the parents' right to ensure the religious and moral education of their children in conformity with their convictions and to choose other schools for their children than those established by public authorities.
- The Declaration on the Elimination of All Forms of Intolerance and of Discrimination Based on Religion or Belief of November 25, 1981, adopted by the General Assembly of the UN. It has practically no influence on Austrian jurisprudence.

§3. The Organization for Security and Cooperation in Europe

387. Of specific significance for Europe are the documents of the Organization for Security and Cooperation in Europe (OSCE), which has emerged from the Conference on Security and Cooperation in Europe (CSCE). Even though these Documents do not provide for enforceable rights, they represent political declarations of high rank, so that a certain normative commitment can be attributed to them.

388. Regarding law on religion, mainly the conferences of Helsinki 1975 and of Vienna 1989 have gained significance. In particular, in the Concluding Document of Vienna a restricted view of individual rights has been abandoned and the corporate and institutional component of religious freedom – and thus self-determination of religious communities – has been emphasized. Principle 16.4 of the Vienna Concluding Document provides that participating states will respect the right of religious communities not only 'to organize themselves according to their own hierarchical and institutional structure', but also 'to choose, appoint and replace their personnel in accordance with their respective requirements'.

389. In recent decades, the activities of the OSCE also reflect the tendency to focus increasingly on security issues and anti-discrimination laws related to freedom of religion or belief and law on religion. The 1994 Budapest Final Act and the 1999 Istanbul Final Act already established links to the misuse of religion for 'aggressive nationalist aims' and to 'xenophobia and anti-semitism'. In 2004, the OSCE established a department for tolerance and non-discrimination, which also focuses on freedom of religion or belief.

Chapter 2. Effects of European Law on Religious Communities

§1. European Legal Systems

390. With regard to Europe and consequently, to the European law on religion, two legal levels must be distinguished, the legal system of the European Union and the Council of Europe with its most important document, the European Convention on Human Rights (ECHR) as a 'law-making treaty'.[153] The number of the Member States of the Council of Europe is greater and more religiously and culturally diverse than that of the EU. All EU Member States are signatories to the ECHR. On the one hand, the EU law on religion shows a higher level of coherence; on the other hand, there has always been a corresponding mutual influence concerning fundamental rights between the two legal systems, gradually intensifying towards a certain degree of harmonization. This process reached its preliminary culmination in the Lisbon Treaty with the proposed accession of the ECHR to the EU.

§2. The European Convention on Human Rights

I. General Relevance

391. The ECHR has constitutional status in Austria and thus constitutes a significant stratum in the context of the fundamental rights' development. This becomes particularly clear in the field of religious freedom, where the constitutional norm of Article 9 ECHR overlaps the older specific guarantees, thereby forming a comprehensive fundamental right of freedom of religion and belief (cf. 84 and 112). Accordingly, by virtue of the Convention and the case law of the European Court of Human Rights (ECtHR) and the former Strasbourg organs, important stimuli have been introduced into the national case law, especially in respect of the decision-making processes of the Constitutional Court.

392. In a decision concerning religious slaughtering, the Constitutional Court[154] refers to a formula Austrian courts often invoke, following the case law of the European instances, especially used in connection with freedom of expression (Article 10 ECHR). The Court regards 'pluralism, tolerance and broadmindedness' as being of particular importance for a 'democratic society'.[155]

393. In order to reduce the risk of too extensive a European determination of the protection of fundamental rights, the Strasbourg case law repeatedly emphasizes the margin of appreciation of the individual states, whose duty it is to take reasonable and appropriate measures to protect the fundamental rights of the individual. It

153. C. Grabenwarter & K.Pabel, *Europäische Menschenrechtskonvention*, 5th ed. (Munich: C.H. Beck, 2012), 5.
154. VfSlg. 15394/1998.
155. Established case law since *Handyside v. the United Kingdom*, 7 Dec. 1976, appl. no. 5483/1972.

underlines, in particular, that the states are better able to assess the facts and circumstances of individual cases by taking into consideration the different cultures and needs, giving special consideration to the conditions under which interventions and limitations by the state are permitted (cf. 215). However, it is the ECtHR's task to examine whether appropriate use has been made of this discretionary measure, extending its control to both factors of reasonableness and necessity in accordance with the principle of proportionality.

394. In case law according to which the ECtHR has convicted Austria on the grounds of violation, the ECHR (II.) refers to a few issues of individual freedom of religion (mostly in conjunction with Articles 8 or 10 and Article 14 of the Convention, respectively), to preconditions for the legal recognition of religious communities and to different treatment of legally recognized religious communities and state-registered religious confessional communities. In general, the Austrian courts and doctrine refer to the European case law in the fields of law on religion primarily when questions of legal recognition and the status of religious communities are dealt with (III.).

II. Paradigmatic Austrian Cases

395. In the case of *Otto Preminger Institute v. Austria*,[156] the ECtHR held that there had been no violation of Article 10 of the Convention as regards either the seizure or the forfeiture of the film 'The Council of Love'. The movie is based on a play by Oskar Panizza, dating from 1894, in which the trial for blasphemy against the author serves as the frame story. Following a conviction for disparagement of religious doctrines, there had been a seizure and forfeiture of the film. The Court emphasized the right of citizens not to be insulted in their religious feelings by the public expression of views of other persons. The respect for the religious feelings of believers as guaranteed in Article 9 can legitimately be thought to have been violated by provocative portrayals of objects of religious veneration, and such portrayals can be regarded as a malicious violation of the spirit of tolerance, which must also be a feature of democratic society. Freedom of expression is applicable not only to 'information' or 'ideas' that are favourably received or regarded as inoffensive or as a matter of indifference, but also to those that shock, offend or disturb the state or any sector of the population. Referring to the duties and responsibilities as enshrined in Article 10 section 2, the Court holds that among them 'may legitimately be included an obligation to avoid as far as possible expressions that are gratuitously offensive to others and thus an infringement of their rights, and which therefore do not contribute to any form of public debate capable of furthering progress in human affairs'. Furthermore, the Court pointed out that in the case of 'morals' it is not possible to discern throughout Europe a uniform conception of the significance of religion in society, even within one single country. Therefore, a certain margin of appreciation must be left to the national authorities in assessing what

156. ECtHR 20 Sep. 1994, appl. no. 13470/87.

constitutes a permissible interference with the exercise of the right to freedom of expression where such expression is directed against the religious feelings of others.

396. The case *Hoffmann v. Austria*[157] dealt with the legality of taking into account the religious conviction of one of the parents being an adherent of Jehovah's Witnesses when deciding on the right of custody over the children after divorce. The ECtHR held (by five votes to four) that there had been a violation of Article 8 taken in conjunction with Article 14 of the Convention. 'Notwithstanding any possible arguments to the contrary, a distinction based essentially on a difference in religion alone is not acceptable.' The principal assumption that a child being educated by a member of a religious minority according to its rules would be pushed to the margins of society was considered to be incompatible with the concept of a democratic society. Therefore, the Court could not find that a reasonable relationship of proportionality existed between the means employed and the aim pursued. In fact, this judgment had great prejudicial effect on the judicial practice which strictly adheres to the Court's statement that interference in fundamental rights can only be legitimated and non-discriminatory if this would be the only way to ensure the child's well-being. Since then, in matters of custody rights relating to religion, the guardianship bodies and courts usually abstain from withdrawing the right to custody completely, but if need be, order a restriction concerning certain affairs, often concerning religious activities or health treatment.[158]

397. The case *Öllinger v. Austria*[159] dealt with the prohibition of a meeting at a municipal cemetery which was intended as a counter-event to a ceremonial wreath-lying of the SS Comradeship IV (Kameradschaft IV) expressing protest against such an action. The prohibition of the assembly was considered justified by the Austrian police authorities as well as the Constitutional Court with respect to the need for the undisturbed practice of religion and the protection of the 'religious feelings' of visitors to the cemetery, particularly regarding the special character of All Saints' Day. The ECtHR stated that the competing interests at stake had not been adequately assessed and, furthermore, that the local authorities had prioritized the interests of one group over the others without having been prepared to deploy the police forces which would have been able to ensure that the diverse claims at issue could have been settled, and simultaneously, satisfying the interests of cemetery-goers in protecting them against some rather limited disturbances. Therefore, the Court held (by six votes to one) that Article 11 of the Convention had been violated.

398. Taken as a whole, in quite a number of decisions the ECtHR had to deal with two crucial issues in the Austrian law on religion – the preconditions of legal recognition of religious communities on the one hand, and unequal treatment of legally recognized religious communities and state-registered religious denominational communities, on the other. It must be underscored that both aspects are closely linked and

157. ECtHR 22 Jun. 1993, appl. no. 12875/87.
158. OGH 4 Jun. 1996, 1 Ob 601/95; OGH 13 Aug. 1996, 2 Ob 2192/96h.
159. ECtHR 29 Sep. 2006, appl. no. 76900/01.

must not be considered in isolation. The Religionsgemeinschaft der Zeugen Jehovas (Jehovah's Witnesses)[160] and the Verein der Freunde der Christengemeinschaft (Friends of the Christian Community)[161] were affected. In its reasoning, the Court precisely described the main problem concerning legal recognition of religious communities in Austria:

> Given the number of these privileges and their nature, in particular in the field of taxation, the advantage obtained by religious societies is substantial and this special treatment undoubtedly facilitates a religious society's pursuance of its religious aims. In view of these substantive privileges, accorded to religious societies, the obligation under Article 9 of the Convention incumbent on the state's authorities to remain neutral in the exercise of their powers in this domain requires therefore that if a state sets up a framework for conferring legal personality on religious groups to which a specific status is linked, all religious groups which so wish must have a fair opportunity to apply for this status and the criteria established must be applied in a non-discriminatory manner (cf. §92).

399. Though the findings of these judgments are fundamental and of general significance, owing to the concrete facts and circumstances they only attained practical relevance with regard to the 'waiting period' but not to the far greater problem of the number of members necessary. These decisions resulted in an amendment of the BekGG, which henceforth provides for a differentiation with respect to the duration of existence as a precondition of recognition (cf. 230 et seq.).

400. In a few cases, the ECHR had to examine whether the difference in the treatment of registered religious denominational communities and legally recognized religious societies could be legitimated on objective and reasonable grounds. In the case of *Religionsgemeinschaft der Zeugen Jehovas (Jehovah's Witnesses) v. Austria*,[162] two 'privileges' granted to legally recognized churches and religious societies were at issue: (1) the exemption according to the Employment of Aliens Act as regards the employment of aliens with respect to pastoral activities (§1 section 2); (2) the exemptions from taxation of donations and inheritance[163] as provided for in the Inheritance Law Act 1955 (§15 section 1).

401. As regards the proceedings under the Employment of Aliens Act, the Court held that there had been a violation of Article 14 of the Convention taken in conjunction with Article 9 of the Convention. The regulation concerned showed the significance that the legislature attached to the specific function which representatives of religious groups charged with pastoral care activities fulfil within such groups:

160. ECtHR 28 Jul. 2008, appl. no. 40825/98.
161. ECtHR 26 Feb. 2009, appl. no. 76581/01.
162. ECtHR 25 Sep. 2012, appl. no. 27540/05.
163. Meanwhile the taxation of donations and inheritance has been totally abolished in Austria.

> As the privilege in issue is intended to ensure the proper functioning of religious groups as communities of individuals, and thus promotes a goal protected by Article 9 of the Convention, the exemption from the provisions governing the employment of aliens granted to specific representatives of religious societies comes within the scope of that provision.

402. With respect to inheritance and gift tax, the Court held that there had been a violation of Article 14 of the Convention taken in conjunction with Article 1 Protocol No. 1. In its reasoning, it exemplified that the privilege in issue was intended to ensure the proper functioning of religious groups as communities of individuals, thus promoting a goal protected by Article 9 of the Convention; exemption from the provisions governing the employment of aliens granted to specific representatives of religious communities comes within the scope of that provision. However, the court held that it was not necessary to examine the complaint about the proceedings under the Inheritance and Gift Tax Act under Article 9 taken alone and in conjunction with Article 14 of the Convention.

403. In the cases of *Lang v. Austria,*[164] *Gütl v. Austria,*[165] *Löffelman v. Austria*[166] and *Koppi v. Austria,*[167] the Court had to examine whether the authorities' refusal to exempt the applicants from alternative community service in lieu of compulsory military service was in concordance with the Convention (cf. 249).

404. In recent years, there have been two decisions relating to Islam. Accusing Muhammad of paedophilia, i.e., a frowned-upon sexual preference, and defaming him in this way without a factual examination of Islam or the phenomenon of child marriage constitutes defamation. The incriminating statements could not be regarded as a substantive contribution to public discourse.[168] Performing an autopsy despite the opposition of parents who wish to comply with their religious beliefs is a violation of Articles 8 and 9 ECHR if the private interests of the parents in burying their child's body intact are not considered alongside the public interest in performing the autopsy and the parents are not informed of the implications of the autopsy.[169]

III. Other Case Law with Special Importance for Austria

405. Apart from the ECtHR's decision mentioned above, the settled case law of the ECtHR in some areas of law on religion has influenced judicial practice and legal doctrine in Austria, particularly with regard to the following ECtHR reasoning.

164. ECtHR 12 Mar. 2009, appl. no. 28648/03.
165. ECtHR 12 Mar. 2009, appl. no. 49686/99.
166. ECtHR 12 Mar. 2009, appl. no. 42967/98.
167. ECtHR, 10 Dec. 2009, appl. no. 33001/03.
168. ECtHR 25 Oct. 2018, appl. no. 38450/12, *E.S. v. Austria.*
169. ECtHR 25 Jul. 2021, appl. no. 12886/16, *Polat v. Austria.*

406. According to the established case law of the ECtHR, freedom of thought, conscience and religion as enshrined in Article 9 ECHR is 'one of the most vital elements that go to make up the identity of believers and their conception of life, but it is also a precious asset for atheists, agnostics, skeptics and the unconcerned. The pluralism indissociable from a democratic society, which has been clearly won over the centuries, depends on it.'[170] The right to freedom of religion as guaranteed under the Convention 'excludes any discretion on the part of the state to determine whether religious beliefs or the means used to express such beliefs are legitimate'. Accordingly, the Court considered the authorization requirement provided by law was consistent with Article 9 of the Convention 'only in so far as it is intended to allow the Federal Minister to verify whether the formal conditions laid down in those enactments are satisfied'.[171] In delimiting the extent of the margin of appreciation the Court must have regard to what is at stake, namely the need to secure true religious pluralism, an inherent feature of the notion of a democratic society.[172]

407. Regarding religious communities, Article 9 of the Convention must be interpreted in the light of Article 11, which safeguards associative life against unjustified state interference:

> Indeed, the autonomous existence of religious communities is indispensable for pluralism in a democratic society and is thus an issue at the very heart of the protection which Article 9 affords. It directly concerns not only the organization of the community as such but also the effective enjoyment of the right to freedom of religion by all its active members. Were the organizational life of the community not protected by Article 9 of the Convention, all other aspects of the individual's freedom of religion would become vulnerable.[173]

408. The same holds if the leadership of religious communities is at issue:

> State action favouring one leader of a divided religious community or undertaken with the purpose of forcing the community to come together under a single leadership against its own wishes would likewise constitute an interference with freedom of religion. In democratic societies the state does not need to take measures to ensure that religious communities are brought under a unified leadership.[174]

409. In exercising its regulatory power concerning various religions, denominations and beliefs the state has a duty to remain neutral and impartial:

---

170. Established case law since *Kokkinakis v. Greece*, 25 May 1993, appl. no. 14307/88.
171. *Manoussakis v. Greece*, 26 Feb. 1996, appl. no. 18748/91.
172. *Manoussakis v. Greece*, 26 Feb. 1996, appl. no. 18748/91.
173. *Hasan and Chaush v. Bulgaria*, 26 Oct. 2000, appl. no. 30985/96.
174. *See Serif v. Greece*, 14 Dec. 1999, appl. no. 38178/97; *Metropolitan Church of Bessarabia and Others v. Moldova*, 13 Dec. 2001, appl. no. 45701/99.

> What is at stake here is the preservation of pluralism and the proper functioning of democracy, one of the principal characteristics of which is the possibility it offers of resolving a country's problems through dialogue, without recourse to violence, even when they are irksome […] For this reason 'the self-determination of religious communities is not only an essential part of freedom of religion, but the autonomous existence of religious communities also is indispensable for pluralism in a democratic society and is thus an issue at the very heart of the protection which Article 9 of the European Convention affords.' The role of the authorities in such circumstances is not to remove the cause of tension by eliminating pluralism, but to ensure that the competing groups tolerate each other.[175]

410. The choice of a name that corresponds to the self-understanding of the religious community falls under the protection of Article 9 ECHR.[176]

§3. European Union Law

I. Basic Principles

411. Austria acceded to the EU in 1995 after a referendum had been held on the Federal Constitutional Law on the accession of Austria.[177] The primary and secondary EU law (of whatever rank) takes precedence over any Member State's law comprising the constitutional law if contradicting national and European provisions apply to individual cases. In the sense of a 'primacy of application' the Member States' law that contradicts EU law would not become inoperative, but inapplicable in the case concerned.

412. According to the current state of integration, the EU has no far-reaching genuine competence in the fields of law on religion, but there is no 'field of exemption' regarding religion. Altogether, there is already a considerable amount of EU law relevant to religious matters, and thus European law increasingly extends to the religious sphere. Consequently, in legal doctrine, the term 'European law on religion' can more frequently be found.[178] This does not mean that a systematic, more or less closed compilation of relevant norms for religious matters would exist. It rather consists of a variety of European norms with different legal sources and of different legal nature and validity having impact on the religious dimension. In this

175. Cf. *Serif v. Greece*, 14 Dec. 1999, appl. no. 38178/97; *Hasan and Chaush v. Bulgaria*, 26 Oct. 2000, appl. no. 30985/96; *Metropolitan Church of Bessarabia and Others v. Moldova*, 31 Dec. 2001, appl. no. 45701/99.
176. *Bektashi Community v. Former Yugoslavian Republic of Macedonia*, 12 Mar. 2018, appl. no. 25176/13,
177. BGBl. 1994/498.
178. H. de Wall, 'Das Religionsrecht der EU – Grundstrukturen und Spannungen', *Zeitschrift für evangelisches Kirchenrecht* 50 (2005), 383–402; M. Krajewski, *Der religionsrechtliche Acquis Communautaire der Europäischen Union. Ansätze eines systematischen Religionsrechts der EU unter EU-Vertrag, EG-Vertrag und EU-Verfassungsvertrag* (Berlin: Duncker & Humblot, 2008).

sense, the existence of a 'European law on religion' not as a field of competence but as a cross-sectional matter is meanwhile evident.[179]

413. It finds its basis first of all in the right of religious freedom as part of the comprehensive protection of fundamental rights as a basic element of EU law and the recognition of the status of religious communities and institutionalizing a dialogue with them. Numerous guarantees against discrimination, the principle of subsidiarity as well as the obligation to respect the national identity of the Member States and their religious and cultural diversity are considered to be further supporting elements of a 'European law on religion' as well as certain regulations and exemptions within secondary European law. Finally, the case law of both European Courts, especially that of the ECtHR, must be emphasized as well as its significance in developing a certain 'ordre public européen'[180] from a law-on-religion perspective. Over and above this, the 'European law on religion' is determined by the single-market concept and the consequences of the 'four freedoms' demanding instruments of consideration clauses and exceptions in order to take account of the specific Proprium of religious communities.

II. Religion in Primary European Union Law

414. Since the Maastricht Treaty, fundamental rights, including freedom of religion and belief, have been considered to be an integral part of the EU law itself, being based on the common constitutional traditions of the Member States encompassing the ECHR which has often been described as a 'Part-Constitution' in the field of human rights.

415. Freedom of religion and belief is guaranteed in Article 10 of the Charter of Fundamental Rights of the European Union (CFR) and Article 21 prohibits discrimination on grounds of religion or belief. Pursuant to Article 22, the EU respects the multitude of cultures, religions and languages. The Charter entered into force in 2009 with the Treaty of Lisbon (Article 6 of the Treaty on European Union [TEU]) and since then has the same legal value as the European Union treaties. According to the limitation clause of Article 52 section 3 of the Charter, the meaning and scope of those rights which correspond to rights guaranteed by the ECHR, shall be the same as those laid down by the said Convention. Thus, the ECHR has become the standard for fundamental rights in EU law which is of special importance in Austria because of the constitutional status of the Convention. In addition, the Austrian Constitutional Court stated in 2012 that the fundamental rights guaranteed by the EU Charter can be asserted by Constitutional Court appeal as a constitutionally

---

179. R. Potz & B. Schinkele, 'Europarecht – Wie hast du's mit der Religion?', in *Religion in Europa heute. Sozialwissenschaftliche, rechtswissenschaftliche und hermeneutisch-religionsphilosophische Perspektiven*, eds. K. Appel et al. (Göttingen: V&R unipress, 2012), 129–160.

180. P. Häberle, 'Gemeineuropäisches Verfassungsrecht', *Europäische Grundrechte Zeitschrift* 18 (1991), 265.

guaranteed right[181] and that within its scope of application, the Charter will be used as a measure of constitutionality in judicial proceedings on the constitutionality of national laws and will eliminate conflicting general norms.[182]

416. As regards the amendments to Primary Law regarding religion by the Treaty of Lisbon, Article 17 of the Treaty on the Functioning of the EU (TFEU) is of particular significance for the status of religious communities in the Member States. Article 17 reads as follows:

1. The Union respects and does not prejudice the status under national law of churches and religious associations or communities in the Member States.
2. The Union equally respects the status of philosophical and non-confessional organisations.
3. Recognizing their identity and their specific contribution, the Union shall maintain an open, transparent and regular dialogue with these churches and organisations.

417. Article 17 sections 1 and 2 TFEU originate from Declaration number 11 attached to the Final Act of the Treaty of Amsterdam, which had the rank of ‘soft law’, and are nowadays part of the primary European Law. These provisions, in any case, guarantee the structural principles resulting from the fundamental conception of the law on religions of the Member States. Thus the EU and all its institutions are obliged to respect and not prejudice the national law on religion in a religiously and denominationally neutral manner. Finding out how far single legal positions are covered by this guarantee in individual cases will be a delicate boundary issue. The prohibition of interference will have to be applied the more a certain regulation is an expression of the basic state-church relationship in the Member State concerned.[183]

418. On the whole, Article 17 TFEU acknowledges churches and religious communities as factors within European law as well as civil society. This is expressed particularly in Article 17 section 3 which contains a ‘dialogue clause’: ‘Recognising their identity and their specific contribution, the Union shall maintain an open, transparent and regular dialogue with these churches and organizations’. The formulation ‘recognising their identity’ means that the respective self-understanding of churches and religious communities must be the decisive reference point for dealing with religion at the European level. By ‘their specific contribution’, the work of churches and religious communities to the common good, their social and charitable activities as well as their ethical competence and participation in the educational field are understood. The fact that a special dialogue clause regarding

181. VfSlg. 19632/2012.
182. Cf. Art. 139 and Art. 140 B-VG.
183. S. Muckel, ‘Die Rechtsstellung der Kirchen und Religionsgemeinschaften nach dem Vertrag über eine Verfassung für Europa’, *Die Öffentliche Verwaltung* 59 (2005), 191–198.

churches and religious societies has been implemented corresponds to the self-understanding of the churches and religious communities.[184] Due to their comprehensive mandate and their genuine Proprium, they do not or not only consider themselves as part of civil society. In this, they differ from other representative associations and organizations acting within civil society which merely pursue particularistic goals.

419. The Council Regulation (EC) No. 1099/2009 on the protection of animals at slaughter sets out specific rules governing the slaughter of animals bred or kept for the production of food, wool, skin, fur or other products as well as for the purpose of depopulation and related operations. As a general principle, animals shall be spared any avoidable pain, distress or suffering during slaughter and related operations. In recital no. 15 the regulation takes into account particular religious rites, cultural traditions and regional heritage according to Protocol No. 33 on the protection and welfare of animals (1997).[185] Austria has made use of the possibility to provide special rules for ritual slaughter (cf. 186).

420. The Regulation 2016/679 (General Data Protection Regulation – GDPR) contains the protection of natural persons with regard to the processing of personal data and the free movement of such data, and repealed Directive 95/46/EC. On the one hand, religious or ideological convictions are particularly protected ('sensitive') data, the processing of which is generally prohibited (Article 9). On the other hand, Article 91 takes into account existing data protection regulations of 'churches and religious associations or communities' in member states. In Austria, the GDPR came into force with the Datenschutzgesetz (DSG) 2018 (cf. 504 et seq.).

III. Religion in Secondary European Union Law

421. Secondary European Union Law – especially directives – contains provisions regarding religion as a cross-sectional matter. The majority of these provisions are special rules and exemptions resulting from the guarantee of freedom of religion. Other provisions have an indirect impact on religious communities as participants in economic and legal relations. In this context, the European anti-discrimination law in particular is of increasing importance for the Member States' law on religion.

422. The first Directive to be mentioned served as 'the implementation of the principle of equal treatment for men and women as regards access to employment, vocational training and promotion and working conditions' (76/207/EEC). After some amendments, it has been recast by the Directive 2006/54/EC 'on the implementation of the principle of equal opportunities and equal treatment of men and

184. Cf. Art. 11 section 2 TFEU.
185. Official Journal C 321 E, 29/12/2006, 0314.

women in matters of employment and occupation.' The Directive contains no special provision for religious organizations; there is merely an exemption clause formulated in general terms, which is applicable in principle (Article 14 section 2):

> Member States may provide, as regards access to employment including the training leading thereto, that a difference of treatment which is based on a characteristic related to sex shall not constitute discrimination where, by reason of the nature of the particular occupational activities concerned or of the context in which they are carried out, such a characteristic constitutes a genuine and determining occupational requirement provided that its objective is legitimate and the requirement is proportionate.

423. The next step was Directive 2000/43/EC implementing the principle of equal treatment between persons, irrespective of racial or ethnic origin. In this context, one has to take into consideration that a religious ground might happen to coincide with an ethnic ground, as could be the case with Jews, Muslims or Sikhs. A clear delimitation between ethnic and religious discrimination can sometimes hardly be drawn.

424. Finally, Directive 2000/78/EC has had the greatest impact on law on religion, establishing a general framework for equal treatment in employment and occupation, and prohibiting discrimination on the grounds of religion or belief, disability, age, or sexual orientation. Its basic objectives are partially not in accord with the internal law of several churches and religious communities. The Directive, therefore, contains a comprehensive exemption clause in Article 4 section 2:

> Member States may maintain national legislation in force at the date of adoption of this Directive or provide for future legislation incorporating national practices existing at the date of adoption of this Directive pursuant to which, in the case of occupational activities within churches and other public or private organizations the ethos of which is based on religion or belief, a difference of treatment based on a person's religion or belief shall not constitute discrimination where, by reason of the nature of these activities or of the context in which they are carried out, a person's religion or belief constitutes a genuine, legitimate and justified occupational requirement, having regard to the organization's ethos. This difference of treatment shall be implemented taking account of Member States' constitutional provisions and principles, as well as the general principles of Community law, and should not justify discrimination on another ground.
>
> Provided that it does not prejudice the right of churches and other public or private organisations, the ethos of which is based on religion or belief, acting in conformity with national constitutions and laws, to require individuals working for them to act in good faith and with loyalty to the organisation's ethos.

425. Whereas the equal treatment of men and women in matters of employment has already been established in Austria in the Act on Equal Treatment of 1979 and the Federal Act on Equal Treatment of 1993, on the basis of the above-mentioned

Directives two Acts on Equal Treatment have been rendered extending the anti-discrimination law to the criteria of a person's ethnic origin, religion or belief, age and sexual orientation.[186] The Equal Treatment Act 2004 (GlBG) and the amendment 2004 of the Equal Treatment Act in die Field of the Bund (B-GlBG) have implemented this Directive.[187] The Bundesländer have either issued separate anti-discrimination laws for their jurisdiction or implemented provisions prohibiting discrimination in their Equal Treatment Acts.

426. The European Directives themselves as well as the provisions of the Equal Treatment Acts – which in large parts adhere strictly to the European Directives – give rise to numerous awkward legal questions. As a whole, they represent a complex legal framework, corroborated due to some legislative deficiencies. This situation has already been reflected in quite diverging legal points of view.

427. According to the Audiovisual Media Services Directive (2010/13/EU), no television advertising or teleshopping shall be inserted during religious services (Article 20 section 2) and audiovisual commercial communications shall not include or promote discrimination based, *inter alia*, on religion or belief [Article 9 section 1 lit. c (ii)]. These provisions have been implemented in Austria in the relevant media laws (cf. 731 et seq.).

428. The Working Time Directive (2003/88/EC) enables Member States to derogate 'with due regard for the general principles of the protection of the safety and health of workers' from prescribed requirements, *inter alia*, in the case of 'workers officiating at religious ceremonies in churches and religious communities' (Article 17 section 1 lit. c).

429. The Directive on the Protection of Animals at the Time of Slaughter or Killing (93/119/EEC) was repealed by the Council Regulation (EC) No. 1099/2009 on the protection of animals at the time of killing (cf. 421).

430. The Directive establishing a general framework for informing and consulting employees in the European Community (2002/14/EC), formulating minimum standards, shall apply, according to the choice made by Member States, to undertakings employing at least fifty employees in any one Member State, or establishments employing at least twenty employees in any one Member State. The Directive contains an exemption clause:

> In conformity with the principles and objectives of this Directive, Member States may lay down particular provisions applicable to undertakings or establishments which pursue directly and essentially political, professional organizational, religious, charitable, educational, scientific or artistic aims, as well as

186. Special laws have been enacted with regard to disability: *Behinderteneinstellungsgesetz*, BGBl. 1973/329 as amended BGBl. I 2005/82, and *Bundes-Behindertengleichstellungsgesetz*, BGBl. I 2005/82.
187. BGBl. I 2004/65.

aims involving information and the expression of opinions, on condition that, at the date of entry into force of this Directive, provisions of that nature already exist in national legislation.

The corresponding Austrian labour law is in conformity with the Directive's standards and even goes beyond its provisions.

431. The Directive on the establishment of a European Works Council or a procedure in Community-scale undertakings and Community-scale groups of undertakings for the purposes of informing and consulting employees (94/45/EC, as amended 2009/38/EC) contains an exemption clause in Article 8 section 3:

> Each Member State may lay down particular provisions for the central management of undertakings in its territory which pursue directly and essentially the aim of ideological guidance with respect to information and the expression of opinions, on condition that, at the date of adoption of this Directive such particular provisions already exist in the national legislation.

432. Exemptions from customs duties and taxes in secondary law are of certain relevance for law on religion. According to Article 132 section 1 lit. k of the Directive on the Common System of Value Added Tax (2006/112/EC) exemptions are foreseen for the supply of staff by religious or philosophical institutions for the purpose of enumerated activities (regarding hospital and medical care, welfare and social security work, old people's homes, protection of children and young persons, social well-being, school or university education), and with a view to spiritual welfare. Also exempted is:

> […] the supply of services and closely related goods to their members in their common interest in return for a subscription fixed in accordance with their rules as non-profit-making organizations with aims of a political, trade-union, religious, patriotic, philosophical, philanthropic or civic nature, provided that this exemption is not likely to cause distortion of competition (Article 132 section 1 lit. l).

433. All of these exemptions are included in §6 Federal Act on the Taxation of Sales 1994.[188]

IV. The European Court of Justice

434. As far as matters of religion and belief are concerned, the ECJ deals mainly with labour or social law issues in a broader sense.

435. In the judgment *Prais v. Council* (ECR 1976, 1589), the ECJ acknowledged for the first time the fundamental right of religious freedom or at least the religious interests of individuals which must be respected by European institutions

188. Umsatzsteuergesetz BGBl. 1994/663 as amended BGBl. I 2014/40.

which the Court outlined in its reasoning though the complaint had been rejected.[189] On the one hand, the ECJ stated that neither Article 27 section 2 of the Staff Regulations nor the fundamental right at issue would require the appointing authority to avoid a conflict with a religious commitment the existence of which the Council had not been informed. On the other hand, the Court made an appeal to all European institutions to take known religious holidays into account and thus avoid such conflicts as in the case in question. In Austria, in individual cases when time off from work for religious reasons is at stake, as well as generally in discussions on respective provisions in collective labour agreements, reference is often made to the case of Prais.

436. The case *van Rosmaalen v. Bestuur van de Bedrijfsverenigingen*[190] concerned a priest and member of the Premonstratensian order whose activities the ECJ qualified as being characteristic of a self-employed person, though his income had been supplied by members of the missionary community benefiting from his services in his capacity as a missionary, but not by his religious order. Thus, on the basis of the fundamental freedom to provide services he was entitled to receive an invalidity pension (benefit) according to national social security rules. Though this result is deemed to be appropriate the Court's approach obviously shows difficulties in dealing adequately with the religious dimension within the given European legal framework at that time. This is, in principle, also true for the so-called Baghwan Case of 1988.[191]

437. A central topic has been and is the wearing of Islamic headscarves at the workplace in the private sector. The first two decisions in 2017 were contradictory. In the first case,[192] the Court ruled that the ban on the visible wearing of any political, philosophical or religious sign in the workplace, based on a neutral company policy, may be in line with the Directive. In the second case, it held that this is not the case if such a prohibition is based on a customer request.[193] On 15 July 2021, two further rulings on the wearing of Islamic headscarves at the workplace were issued.[194] The ECJ has made some changes, emphasizing the greater importance of the fundamental right of freedom of religion and granting the Member States a wider margin of appreciation by determining the minimum requirements within the meaning of Article 8(1) of Directive 2000/78/EC (cf. 426).

---

189. Cf. I. Pernice, 'Religionsrechtliche Aspekte im europäischen Gemeinschaftsrecht', *Juristen Zeitung* 32 (1977), 777–781.
190. ECJ 23 Oct. 1986, Case 300/84 (*A. J. M. van Roosmalen v. Bestuur van de Bedrijfsverenigingen voor de Gezondheid, Geestelijke en Maatschappelijke Belangen*), ECR 1986, 3097 et seq.
191. ECJ 5 Oct. 1988, Case 196/87 (*Steymann v. Staatssecretaris van Justitie*), ECR 1988, 6159 et seq.
192. ECJ 14 Mar. 2017, Case C-157/15 (*Samira Achbita & Centrum voor gelijkheid van kansen en voor racismebestrijding v. G4S Secure Solutions NV*).
193. ECJ 14 Mar. 2017, Case C-188/15 (*Asma Bougnaoui & Association de défense des droits de l'homme (ADDH) v. Micropole SA*).
194. ECJ 15 Jul. 2021 (GCh), Case C-804/18 (*IX v. WABE e.V.*) and Case C-341/19 (*MJ v. Müller HandelsGmbH*).

438. Concerning two German judgments, the Court of Justice had to deal with church employment law. The case *Vera Egenberger v. Evangelisches Werk für Diakonie und Entwicklung e. V.*[195] concerned the admissibility of religious affiliation as a recruitment requirement, i.e., discrimination in the application process, the case *IR v. JQ*[196] dealt with the dismissal of a divorced head physician at a denominational hospital on the grounds of remarriage. In both decisions, the ECJ emphasized the need for effective judicial review in compliance with the principle of proportionality. The aim is to guarantee the legal protection which individuals can derive from the general principles of Union law, such as the prohibition of discrimination on the grounds of religion or belief, now enshrined in Article 21 of the Charter, and to guarantee the full effectiveness of rights deriving from those principles and therefore, if necessary, to disapply any conflicting provision of national law. (cf. 779 et seq.).

439. In the much-discussed Austrian 'Good Friday decision',[197] the ECJ declared the provision of §7 section 3 ArbeitsruheG, according to which Good Friday is a public holiday for members of the Protestant Church, the Old Catholic Church, and the Protestant-Methodist Church to be discriminatory within the meaning of the Equal Treatment Framework Directive. (cf. 779 et seq).

195. ECJ 17 Apr. 2018, Case C-414/16.
196. ECJ 11 Sep. 2018, Case C-68/17.
197. ECJ 22 Jan. 2019, Case C-193/17, *Cresco Investigation GmbH v. Markus Achatzi.*

Chapter 3. Effects of Transnational Law on Religious Communities

440. Transnational law is neither international nor supranational nor national law; it refers, rather, to the activities of International Non-Governmental Organizations (INGO) appearing more and more as international actors with political and economic significance, independent of state control. These transnational corporations and international organizations also include religious actors. Until recently, scepticism towards religious global players referred almost exclusively to the Catholic Church and her cosmopolitan model. Over the last decades, American Evangelical Protestants, Islamic Organizations and Orthodox Churches have increasingly been acting as transnational players as well. These activities of new 'global religious identities' lead to greater religious engagement with regard to issues such as conflict resolution and transitional jurisdiction, and therefore people are turning to religious normative frameworks and authorities to a greater degree when dealing with those matters.

441. The global acting religions not only represent cross-border socio-political communities but also often support the interests of a – foreign – state. An example frequently cited is the external organizations of the state-run Turkish Presidency of Religious Affairs (Diyanet İşleri Başkanlığı), to which the Austrian Turkish-Islamic Union also belongs (Österreichische Türkisch-Islamische Union/Avusturya Türkiye İslam Birliği – ATIB) with its sixty Mosque-associations.

442. A special regulation is contained in §6 section 2 IslamG, providing that the means for normal activities aimed at satisfying the religious needs of its members shall be obtained by the relevant religious society, its cultus-communities or its members from within the country (cf. 355). Considering the importance for religious entities of receiving foreign funding, e.g., for charitable work and constructing religious edifices, subsidies from abroad are not generally prohibited as long as they are not used for the ongoing funding of religious societies or communities of worship, whether in cash or by provision of personnel. In the Explanatory Remarks of the law, the establishment of Austrian foundations is explicitly recommended. It is of decisive importance for the question of whether it can be regarded as legitimate domestic financing, if the seat of the foundation and the residence of the foundation's bodies are within Austria. The Explanatory Remarks further point out that the use of public employees in the service of religious societies and their individual communities as employees, clergy, pastors and officials, is in any case prohibited by law, regardless of who pays for them. This should serve the legitimate aim of preserving the independence of religions, especially from foreign governmental influence.

443. The application of transnational law is often encompassed by the right to self-determination in those spheres guaranteed by fundamental rights. In this way, the right of religious freedom gives appropriate scope for the application of religious law, including transnational religious law. Accordingly, the Concordat 1933 recognizes the right of the Catholic Church to make laws, decrees and orders within its own field of competence without hindrance (Article 1 section 2).

444. With regard to Islam and Muslims, the legislator obviously considers it necessary to emphasize explicitly the primacy of state law (§2 section 2 IslamG), a formulation which undoubtedly indicates a certain mistrust (cf. 352). It is held that religious societies, cultus-communities or other subdivisions as well as their members may not take recourse to internal provisions or teachings of their religious societies insofar as their duty to observe general norms of the state is concerned unless such a possibility has not been foreseen by the law applicable to the case in question.

Chapter 4. Regional Law Effects on Religious Communities

445. Due to Article 15 B-VG, matters that do not explicitly lie within the competence of the Federal Government in legislation and administration belong to the autonomous sphere of the Bundesländer. Although 'matters of cultus' are exclusively a federal area of responsibility, owing to the legal framework of competence, several laws of the Bundesländer exist which have implications for law on religion. This primarily applies to the laws on schools and kindergartens (cf. 623 et seq.), regional planning and building regulations (cf. 710 et seq.), law on public events (cf. 719), cemetery and funeral law (for reasons of sanitary police and preservation of piety) and some aspects of social welfare, especially youth welfare (cf. 757).

Part V. Religion and Politics

446. For a long time in Austria, the interaction between religion and politics was influenced by the Catholic traditions formed by the Habsburg counter-reformation and the concepts of the Josephinian established church and remained an influential factor until the twentieth century. In 1934, the Christian-authoritarian government thought it might be possible to found a 'Christian State', on the ideological basis of the social concept as laid down in the Encyclical Quadragesimo anno. The Preamble of the Christian-authoritarian Constitution of May 1, 1934 (cf. 55) has stated: 'In the Name of God, the Almighty, from whom all law emanates, the Austrian People for its Christian, German Federal State on a corporate fundament receives this Constitution.' This initiated the last phase of interpenetration between religion and politics, which was abruptly ended by the Nazi regime in 1938 when a strict system of separation was established for seven years (cf. 58 et seq.).

447. Though there is wide political acceptance in present-day Austria of the important social function exercised by churches and religious communities, they have not been granted the position of 'guardians of the democratic system and human rights', a function attributed to churches and religious communities by the German doctrine since the Second World War. It is generally accepted that religious communities rank among those social associations that create contexts for social and political communication. They are seen as important participants in the public dialogue by means of which citizens can be guided towards responsible action. This means that the religious communities are not only involved in the process of forming opinions regarding state legislation relevant to them in the broader sense but they are also represented on several advisory councils and committees, acting as cooperating partners of the state in various matters. Such a conception is in accordance with an understanding of the legal system as a participatory factor within a spreading civil society.

448. Since the beginning of the twenty-first century, law on religion in Austria – as elsewhere in Europe – has been influenced by new political categories – such as integration and security policies – which means that religious law is currently more than almost any other legal topic not only historically but also 'politically loaded' so that it appears to be the real 'political' law of our time.[198]

---

198. So C. Möllers, *Religiöses Recht als Gefahr?*, VVDStRL 68 (2009), 47–93, 49 et seq.

449. Integration law especially is an area of law of increasing importance for law on religion. This has to do with the fact that the perception of migrants by the receiving society is often shifted to the religious level, so that integration policy concepts are 'religionized', in particular, 'islamized'.[199] This becomes clear in a bundle of laws from 2017,[200] which creates a systematized legal basis for cross-institutional integration measures. Although the provisions strive for religiously neutral wording, the focus is clearly on Muslims. The legislative package contains two new laws, the Federal Act on the Integration of Legal Residents in Austria without Austrian Citizenship (IntG) and the Federal Act on the Prohibition of Face Covering in Public (AGesVG). In addition, other laws were amended, such as the Road Traffic Act (StVO), which now makes it possible to prevent distribution campaigns aimed at spreading radical ideas. In the Explanatory Notes, Salafist Koran distribution campaigns – the so-called street da'awa – were cited as examples. The IntG provides for an integration agreement (§7 IntG), which refers to values and orientation knowledge, in which freedom of religion and the relationship between religion and the state are particularly emphasized (3.2.1. Pkt 6 Integrationsvereinbarung-VO[201]). The AGesVG introduced a ban on covering the face in public places, whereby the legislator had the wearing of the Islamic niqab in particular in mind. With reference to the much-criticized ECtHR decision of 1.7.2014, 43.835/11 (*S.A.S. v. France*), the Explanatory Notes state that recognizing other persons and their faces is a necessary prerequisite for communication in European society. Due to the small number of women wearing a niqab, the law was often criticized as a symbolic political reaction.

---

199. S. Karakayali, *Zur 'Islamisierung' der Einwanderungsdebatte*, ed. *Ucar*, *Die Rolle der Religion im Integrationsprozess*, (Frankfurt/Main etc: Peter Lang, 2010, 173–183, 174).
200. BGBl I 2017/68 idF BGBl 2019/41.
201. BGBl II 2017/242.

Chapter 1. Religious Influence in Politics

§1. Austria on the Way to Becoming a Secular State in the Second Half of the Twentieth Century

450. After 1945, the Catholic Church – the most important religious community in Austria – had to come to terms with its past and specifically, its support for the authoritarian regime in power between 1934 and 1938 (cf. 55).

451. Against this background, the Mariazell Manifesto of 1952 represented a fundamental turning point in the relationship between the Catholic Church and the state, society and politics in general. The central issue was the commitment to a free church, which meant: 'No return to the state church of the past centuries, which degraded religion to a kind of ideological superstructure for the ethos of citizens and trained generations of priests to become mere state officials.' The Mariazell Manifesto also clearly rejected any alliance between 'throne and altar', 'which soothed the conscience of the faithful and blinded them to the dangers of an innerward hollowing-out'. Finally, the Mariazell Manifesto refused any connection with political parties: 'No return to the Protectorate of one party over the church, which was perhaps necessary at some times, but which alienated tens of thousands of the faithful from the Church.'[202]

452. Nonetheless, the Catholic Church continued to meet the state only in the form of a dialogue between institutions and its arguments in such encounters were mainly based on Austrian Catholic traditions, especially as far as marriage and the family were concerned. By the end of the 1950s which had linked cultural conservatism with revolutionary changes in technical and economic areas, the time was definitely over for the church to be successful with such a strategy. The relationship of the Catholic Church to political parties which were committed to religious concepts – especially the Christian Conservative People's Party (*Österreichische Volkspartei*) – had to be re-evaluated in principle according to the Mariazell Manifesto. For a long time, these parties were not seen as partners in the social dialogue, but rather as recipients of ecclesiastical directives. On the other hand, these parties sometimes tended to ask the churches to support their position in temporary political conflicts.

453. From the 1970s onwards, the churches, although their influence was waning, could still maintain their position as an important dialogue partner in civil society. This was evident for the first time in the conflict concerning the decriminalization of abortion and later, in debates on reforms to family law, ethical issues associated with

---

202. *See* R. Potz, 'Österreichs Weg zum säkularen Staat im dritten Viertel des 20. Jahrhunderts', in *Verdrängter Humanismus – verzögerte Aufklärung VI. Philosophie in Österreich 1951–2000. Auf der Suche nach authentischem Philosophieren*, ed. M. Benedikt et al. (Vienna: wuv.facultas, 2010), 911–926.

new technologies, and – most recently – with respect to the European anti-discrimination law. As everywhere else, the churches are strongly engaged in matters of asylum, immigration and social justice in general.

454. Since the 1990s, there have been some changes in the public perception of the churches. They were increasingly regarded as reminders of social problems, in particular concerning asylum and immigration law, development cooperation and ethical issues related to new technologies, in particular in the field of bio-sciences (cf. 533 et seq.).[203] Their social significance is nowadays concentrated on a largely positive perception of church activities in social welfare areas, especially those of the Catholic Caritas and the Evangelical Diakonia. More traditional church circles often complain that the public view of the churches is now mainly or even exclusively related to the positive aspect of their commitment to charitable work.

455. There is a tendency to recognize the significance of the religious dimension on the part of the state without valuing religion as such. As a whole, the state acknowledges religious communities as important groups in civil society, similar to other non-governmental organizations; however, it respects the fact that their specific mandate extends far beyond such aspects. To come straight to the point, religious communities constitute an essential part of the comprehensive 'ethics reservoir' – an essential basis for any state.

§2. Religion in Public Media

456. In accordance with its public mandate, Austrian Broadcasting (Österreichischer Rundfunk – ORF) in its capacity as a public law foundation is empowered to operate three radio programmes which can be received on a nationwide basis, nine programmes which can be received on each Bundesland and two television programmes which can be received on a nationwide basis (§1 section 1, §3 section 1 Federal Law on the Austrian Broadcasting Corporation [ORF-G]). §4 section 1 ORF-G specifies the task and functions of these programmes and mentions, among other things, the duty 'to consider adequately the importance of legally recognized churches and religious societies' (no. 12). An Audience Council (Publikumsrat) consisting of thirty-five members has been established to safeguard the interests of listeners. The Catholic Church and the Protestant Church are each entitled to nominate one member (§28 section 3 nos. 3 and 4 ORF-G). Among other tasks, the Audience Council must nominate six members of the Foundation's Council (Stiftungsrat). One member must be from the domain of the legally recognized churches and religious societies (§30 section 1 no. 2). According to the Programme Directives (1.6.4), compliance with the obligation to respect the significance of the legally recognized churches and religious societies not only means that events organized by

203. *See* U. Körtner (ed.), *Kirche – Demokratie – Öffentlichkeit. Ort und Auftrag der Kirchen in der demokratischen Gesellschaft* (Innsbruck & Vienna: Tyrolia, 2002); P. M. Zulehner & R. Polak, *Religion – Kirche – Spiritualität in Österreich nach 1945. Befund, Kritik, Perspektive* (Innsbruck & Vienna: Studienverlag, 2006).

them must be presented in their social relevance, but also that the contents of their faith must be considered and conveyed. According to §10 section 1 and 2 ORF-G, all programmes must respect human dignity and the fundamental rights of others with regard to their formulation and contents. They must not incite hatred on the grounds of religion (or others).

Chapter 2. Political Influence in Religions

457. As stated above, the institutional separation of church and state combined with the religious communities' right to self-determination also has the aim of preventing political influence on religion. However, it must not be overlooked that the public law status of legally recognized churches and religious societies implies an offer to cooperate in partnership, which the religious communities accept according to their self-understanding. This conception is based on the assumption that they are prepared to fulfil the 'institutionalized constitutional expectations of the state' connected with the act of recognition.[204] In this sense §11 section 4 BekGG and §4 section 3 IslamG 2015 demand 'a positive attitude towards society and the state' as a pre-condition of recognition (cf. 230).

458. State participation plays no part in appointments to church offices, apart from the procedure of the 'political clause' in the case of Catholic bishoprics (Concordat Article IV). According to this clause, the Federal Government must be informed of the name of the proposed person; should the situation arise, the Government might impose objections of a general political nature. If no agreement can be reached, the Holy See is free to appoint the candidate of its choice. The 'political clause' is of little practical relevance nowadays; however, it might encourage the Holy See to consult the Government at an early stage if the choice of candidate is likely to cause controversy.

459. The IslamG 2015 contains some specific regulations with a political background, namely that of restriction of foreign influence. §6 section 2 IslamG provides that the means for normal activities aimed at satisfying the religious needs of its members should be obtained by the religious society concerned, its affiliated communities, or its members from within the country in question. Especially the use of employees from a foreign public service as clergy, pastors or officials to a religious society and its communities is prohibited. The legitimate aim behind this is to preserve the independence of religions from foreign governmental influence (cf. 608). This policy was further strengthened by the 2021 amendment to the Islam Act (cf. 349).

204. *See* K. G. Meyer-Teschendorf, 'Der Körperschaftsstatus der Kirchen. Zur Systemadäquanz des Art. 137 V WRV im pluaralistischen Gemeinwesen des Grundgesetzes', *Archiv für öffentliches Recht* 103 (1978), 318.

Chapter 3. Interaction Between Religions and State on a Political and Legal Level

§1. The Right to Submit Opinions to State Authorities

460. Since the ProtestantenG 1961 (§14 section 1) the special laws for churches and religious societies have included the right to submit to the legislative bodies and the authorities of the Federal State (Bund) and the Bundesländer opinions, proposals and reports on matters concerning the recognized churches and religious societies in general or which affect the relevant church or religious society in particular (cf. 313). These rights are characteristic instruments of social activities of religious communities. The federal authorities are obliged to transmit bills to the churches and religious societies for comments prior to their enactment, whenever their external legal matters are affected.

§2. Public Law Institute for Sect-Related Questions

I. Background

461. As far back as 1992, the 'Committee on Legal Affairs and Human Rights' of the Parliamentary Assembly of the European Council presented a report on 'Sects and New religious movements'. Subsequently, the European Parliament passed a resolution requesting the membership states to increase the mutual exchange of information on the phenomenon of sects. As a result, the Austrian Parliament adopted a resolution in 1994[205] requesting the federal government to inform the public about the activities of 'sects, pseudo-religious groups, corporations and organizations as well as destructive cults' and to take appropriate measures for instruction and information in this respect. A direct result of this resolution was the Austrian Ministry for Environment, Youth and Family's informative booklet issued in 1996 (second edition 1999) entitled 'Sects – Knowledge Protects' (*Sekten – Wissen schützt*). These activities are to be regarded in connection with European initiatives.

II. The Establishment of a Federal Institute for Information on Sect-Related Issues

462. In 1998 the Federal Institute for Information on Sects was set up by the Federal Act on the Establishment of an Institute for Documentation and Information on Sect-Issues (EDISG).[206] The EDISG was established as an independent institution under public law acting in the field of non-sovereign administrative

205. Entschließung des Nationalrates (Resolution of Parliament) 14 Jul. 1994 (E 155-NR/XVIII.GP).
206. *See* H. Kalb, R. Potz & B. Schinkele, 'Das Bundesgesetz über die Einrichtung einer Dokumentations- und Informationsstelle für Sektenfragen (EDISG)', *Österreichisches Archiv für Recht und Religion* 46 (1999), 353–400.

power subject to the supervision of the Federal Minister for Family and Youth. According to §1 section 1, it is the duty of the Federal Institute to document and inform the public about possible dangers arising from sects and the activities of sect-like organizations. The legislator described the movements in question as communities based on religious or philosophical beliefs which may give rise to risks adversely affecting life or physical health, and the free development of personality; they include the freedom to join or leave religious or philosophical communities, the integrity of family life, property or the financial autonomy of the individual and the free mental and physical development of children and juveniles, provided that a well-founded suspicion to this effect exists.

463. Regarding the treatment of data and data protection according to §5 the Federal Institute for Information on Sects in the performance of its duties is especially entitled to collect, evaluate and pass on information, listen to advice from persons affected, cooperate and exchange information with domestic and foreign institutions and also develop, coordinate and manage research projects. It is committed to careful consideration of the relevant guarantees of fundamental rights, state neutrality in religious matters and the principle of tolerance towards all religious and philosophical convictions. Consequently, the Institute is strictly and legally bound to impart objective, reasonable and truthful information. Moreover, precise observance of the detailed regulations regarding the investigation, processing and conveying of data is one of the relevant aspects of its work.

464. Since the enforcement of this Law, the use of the term 'sect' in connection with a specific group implies a certain degree of damage to reputation, thus restraint should be exercised in this respect. At the very least, there can be no doubt that the term 'sect' has a somewhat negative connotation. Though the legislator's Explanatory Remarks stress that the Federal Institute for Information on Sects acts within the non-sovereign sphere of state administration, the Law on the Liability of the State for a Public Officer is to be applied, and not the civil law provisions concerning compensation for damage. This amounts to diminished liability in so far as, according to the Act on State Liability (AHG), the right to request an individual to revoke a defamatory allegation or to refrain from doing so is excluded. The annual report on sects of the Federal Institute for Information on Sects provides information on current developments in these fields. Since 2020, the Institute's information and advisory work has primarily focused on conspiracy theories directed against measures to contain the COVID-19 pandemic, an area in which the esoteric scene and Christian conservative and fundamentalist movements are also active.

III. Case Law

465. This legal position regarding judicial relief had already been exemplified by the Supreme Court[207] shortly before the EDISG came into force; the occasion

207. OGH 19 Jan. 1999, 1 Ob 306/98a, *Österreichisches Archiv für Recht und Religion* 46 (1999), 272 et seq.

was a lawsuit by the Sri Chinmoy Movement against the responsible Minister, requesting him to refrain from distribution of the information booklet entitled 'Sects – Knowledge protects', *in eventu* negating the allegation that the Sri Chinmoy Movement was operating commercial enterprises and abusing freedom of expression and freedom of religion under the pretence of activities which restricted personal freedom. Though the Court dismissed the complaint and the gap in legal protection has not yet been abolished, it must be emphasized that no other state booklet on 'sects' or any other comparable information from the state has been issued since then and that the Federal Institute for Information on Sects now operates quite cautiously with regard to the fundamental rights of the groups concerned.

466. Another judgment by the High Administrative Court[208] dealt with the same problem concerning the new religious movement Universelles Leben. The movement alleged that unlawful infringements of its fundamental right of religious freedom had been created by the text in the above-mentioned information booklet which clearly showed the state's intention to prevent young people in particular from joining this group because of its dangerous potential and susceptibility to conflicts. The Administrative Court confirmed the position that the groups concerned are deprived of the right of appeal against actual or supposedly harmful informational activities on the part of the state. This deficiency in legal protection is considered incompatible with a state ruled by law.

208. VwGH 6 Jul. 2003, 2003/11/0175 (Unabhängiger Verwaltungssenat Wien 5 Sep. 2002, GZ 02/A/12/10/1999/20).

Part VI. Labour Law Within Religious Communities

Chapter 1. Scope of Application of Labour Law

467. Religiously motivated activities can in principle be the subject of an employment contract (cf. §1151 ABGB). Persons whose activities are characterized mainly by religious, welfare or social purposes do not count as employees if they are not employed on the basis of a labour contract (§36 section 1 and section 6 Labour Constitution Act [ArbVG]). This is the case when the special motivation outweighs the normal economic objectives of the employment. Thus voluntary and honorary workers are not employees as prescribed by law.

468. Autonomy in terms of offices is encompassed by the right to self-determination according to Article 15 StGG and Article 9 ECHR.[209] Accordingly, the question of whether the clergy fall under the state definition of employment depends on the respective understanding of the sacraments and ministries of each religious community. In this context, it should be noted that priests and members of religious orders within the Catholic Church carry out their function on the basis of their being incardinated into a diocese or taking vows in connection with simultaneous integration into religious orders or similar institutions. Irrespective of the fact that they are not employees in legal terms, it should be taken into account that there are mutual rights and liabilities between these persons and the respective church institution which are of certain relevance under civil law. As a result, the legal position of priests and members of religious orders renders them not completely excluded from the right to have justice administered, mainly as far as claims safeguarding their personal and social existence are concerned. Insofar, internal ecclesiastical regulations for priests could attain relevance within the state legal order.[210]

469. As a peculiar legal feature, there is a certain interweaving of individual and collective labour law as laid down in §132 section 4 ArbVG. This aspect should be

209. *See* B. *Schinkele*, 'Das Arbeitsrecht in der Kirche: Der verfassungsrechtliche und staatskirchenrechtliche Rahmen unter besonderer Berücksichtigung der katholischen Kirche', in *Arbeitsrecht und Kirche. Zur arbeitsrechtlichen und sozialrechtlichen Stellung von Klerikern, Ordensangehörigen und kirchlichen Mitarbeitern in Österreich*, ed. U. Runggaldier & B. Schinkele (Vienna & New York: Springer, 1996), 3–40.

210. Ecclesiastical rules concerning ministry and remuneration of priests have been issued in all dioceses.

taken into consideration mainly with respect to its significant consequences for the individual employee in the case of termination of the labour contract, primarily as far as complying with obligations to loyalty is concerned.

470. In §132 section 1 and section 4 ArbVG the different treatment of legally recognized and other religious communities is reflected. According to §132 section 1 ArbVG, some provisions are wholly or partially not applicable to businesses and enterprises which directly serve political, coalitional-political, denominational, scientific, educational or welfare purposes. Thus, in order to prevent the participation of a works council in economic decision-making which could weaken the specific purpose of the institution, a certain exemption from co-determination of employees is also provided for religious denominational communities, though this is not so far-reaching as for legally recognized churches and religious societies. For the latter, the legislator has implemented an extended exemption from co-determination by employees according to §132 section 4 (so-called extended Tendenzschutz). This provision should be understood as a realization of the constitutionally guaranteed church autonomy on the level of sub-constitutional law in the fields of labour law (cf. 268 et seq.).

471. The amendment of the Equal Treatment Act (GlBG) implementing the European Directives 2000/43/EC and 2000/78/EC is of special significance (cf. 425 et seq.). Thus, §132 ArbVG has been complemented by the new anti-discrimination law providing for a specific measure (standard) for the justification of unequal treatment according to the exemption clause for occupational activities within churches and other organizations, the ethos of which is based on religion or belief (Article 4 section 2 2000/78/EC implemented in §20 section 2 GlBG). Therefore, a conjunction with the relevant legal framework as laid down in Article 132 section 4 ArbVG is required with respect to legally recognized churches and religious societies. As far as religious denominational communities are concerned, it must be emphasized that in contrast to the ArbVG, the anti-discrimination law makes no distinction between the different legal positions of both categories of religious community.

472. Another specific provision with relevance for religious communities is found in the Act concerning the Employment of Foreigners within the federal Territory (AuslBG). According to §2 section 1 of this Act, it is not applicable to foreigners as far as their pastoral work within a legally recognized church or religious society is concerned. As set forth in the legislator's explanations no reason exists for granting working permission to this group of persons, in the view of the labour market. While the explanations also mention teachers of religious education and advisers in religious affairs – among others – administrative practice prefers a narrower interpretation.

Chapter 2. Individual Labour Law

§1. General Basis in the Labour Constitution Act

473. Church employment is a part of civil law which is, in principle, variable within the legal limits of contractual liberty. Within the free elaboration of employment contracts the religious communities have the possibility to implement their genuine Proprium as regards the services rendered inside their institutions. Thus, state law can be modified regarding optional law, and even compulsory labour law must be interpreted in the light of the right to self-determination (Article 15 StGG). In this context, general clauses in need of substantiation and indeterminate legal terms are of paramount significance, such as socially not justified dismissal or specific peculiarities of church businesses and enterprises. Internal church statutes on employment and remuneration are a matter of contract law adopted by the churches and religious communities as holders of private law rights (*lex contractus*). These autonomous statutes are part of the 'internal affairs' of legally recognized churches and societies but are not statutory instruments in the meaning of constitutional state law and therefore not subject to the control of constitutionality.[211]

474. Apart from the partial exemption from co-determination by employees pursuant to §132 section 4 ArbVG, this Act principally applies to legally recognized churches and religious societies. As a consequence, their institutions and facilities such as dioceses, parishes or similar subdivisions within a certain religious community, parish kindergartens, denominational hospitals etc. are to be qualified as businesses or enterprises in the sense of this Act. Such a view is prevalent, even though this classification has partly been criticized in scientific literature.[212]

475. As mentioned above, it must be taken into consideration that individual and collective labour law are somehow interwoven, in particular with regard to the 'relative clause' in §132 section 4 ArbVG. Accordingly, the provisions regarding the organization of industrial relations as laid down in the Second Part of this Act (§§33–134b) are not applicable to businesses and enterprises which serve the denominational purposes of a recognized church or religious society, insofar as these regulations are in conflict with the very nature of the business or enterprise emanating from the specific assignment of the community concerned. Consequently, each case must be examined individually in order to determine whether the provision is compatible with the specific nature resulting from the right to self-determination. In pursuance of the established Supreme Court's case law the application of the Second Part of the ArbVG conflicts with the specific nature of a business or enterprise if the co-determination of the employees' representation is incompatible with the denominational purpose in question or if the co-determination

211. VfSlg. 3657/1976, VfSlg. 7801/1976, VfSlg. 11859/1987.
212. U. Runggaldier, 'Das Arbeitsrecht in der Kirche: kollektivrechtliche Aspekte', in *Arbeitsrecht und Kirche. Zur arbeitsrechtlichen und sozialrechtlichen Stellung von Klerikern, Ordensangehörigen und kirchlichen Mitarbeitern in Österreich*, ed. U. Runggaldier & B. Schinkele (Vienna & New York: Springer, 1996), 145–176.

of the employees entails unbearable or grossly inappropriate consequences.[213] In particular, the corresponding limited application of the ArbVG is of practical relevance concerning personnel matters of those staff members in charge of activities directly involving denominational purposes. Conflicts between a church or religious society and its officials in matters of private law employment contracts may, in principle, be taken to court. However, all preliminary questions, e.g., the validity of the removal from office, retirement, disciplinary measures, transfer to another place of work or function etc. are excluded from the court's assessment. Thereby, the Court makes no distinction as to whether or not the impugned conduct is directly connected with the specific purposes of the enterprise not fully subject to the ArbVG. This lack of differentiation has given rise to controversial discussion.[214]

476. As far as internal ecclesiastical statutes on employment and remuneration are concerned, the Supreme Court[215] has repeatedly held that the specific spiritual character of employment of consecrated ministers must be taken into consideration when examining the compatibility of an internal salary regulation order with good morals by the state. Correspondingly, a provision ensuring equal remuneration of religious ministers independently of the hours of religious instruction within the entire service obligation could by no means be said to offend good morals.

477. The interconnection of individual and collective labour laws shows practical implications mainly in context with the dismissal of employees subject to §105 ArbVG (in the Second Part). According to this provision, works councils must be involved in formulating a notice to terminate, and without their opinion dismissals are legally ineffective. The termination can be contested in court if the employee has been engaged in the business concerned for at least six months and – among other things – the termination is socially unjustified. This is the case if the essential interests of the employee are infringed upon unless the employer produces evidence that the dismissal is based on the personal circumstances of the employee which adversely affect the operational interests, or if operational requirements preclude continuance of employment.

478. This guarantee covers all activities carried out in pursuance of the true mandate, the fundamental tasks of the community concerned, thus primarily the spiritual and pastoral tasks but also all forms of social, educational, welfare or charitable activities. The formulation in §132 section 4 ArbVG indicates that partial exemption from this Law pertains to all facilities carrying out any functions of the legally recognized religious communities. This means that the legal framing of the factual connection of the individual institution is not important.

213. *See* especially OGH 26 Nov. 1974, 4 Ob 41/74; OGH 13 Jul. 1976, 4 Ob 57/76; OGH 6 May 1987, 14 Ob A 29/87; OGH 16 Sep. 1987, 9 Ob A 71/87.
214. *See* W. Schrammel, 'Probleme des Tendenzschutzes in der österreichischen Betriebsverfassung', in *Möglichkeiten und Grenzen der Rechtsordnung. Festschrift für Rudolf Strasser*, ed. W. Schwarz et al. (Vienna: Manz, 1993), 559–581.
215. OGH 6 May 1987, 14 OA b 29/87; OGH 12 Apr. 1995, 9 Ob A 31/95.

§2. ANTI-DISCRIMINATION LAW

479. According to §§17 and 19 GlBG, no person may be directly or indirectly discriminated against in the fields of employment and occupation[216] on the grounds of racial or ethnic origin, religion or belief, age or sexual orientation. For the purposes of this Act, direct discrimination shall be taken to occur where one person is treated less favourably than another is, has been or would be treated in a comparable situation on any of the grounds referred to in §17 section 1 GlBG; indirect discrimination shall be taken to occur where an apparently neutral provision, criterion or practice could, in particular, have a disadvantageous effect on persons having a certain religion or belief, a certain age, or a certain sexual orientation, placing them at a particular disadvantage compared with other persons unless that provision, criterion or practice is objectively justified by a legitimate aim and the means of achieving that aim are appropriate and necessary.

480. According to §20 section 2 GlBG – taking the European Directives practically word for word – in the case of occupational activities within churches and other public or private organizations the ethos of which is based on a person's religion or belief – a difference in treatment based on a person's religion or belief shall not constitute discrimination where, by reason of the nature of these activities or of the context in which they are carried out, a person's religion or belief constitutes a genuine, legitimate and justified occupational requirement with regard to the organization's ethos. The Council Directive continues that a difference of treatment shall take into account the Member States' constitutional provisions as well as the general principles of Community law, and should not justify discrimination on any other grounds. Provided that its provisions are otherwise complied with, this Directive shall thus not prejudice the right of churches and other public or private organizations, the ethos of which is based on religion or belief, acting in conformity with national constitutions and laws, to require individuals working for them to act in good faith and with loyalty to the organization's ethos. Those text passages which have not been implemented into the GlBG are of significance for a directive-compliant interpretation. Likewise, the 'opening clause' in Article 2 section 5 of the Council Directive constitutes an important indication for interpretation. Accordingly, the Directive should be without prejudice to measures laid down by national law, necessary in the interest of objects of legal protection similar to the reservation clause embodied in Article 9 section 2 ECHR.

§3. INTERNAL STATUTES ON EMPLOYMENT – SPECIAL ALLEGIANCE

481. A special relationship between churches and religious communities as employers and their employees results from direct participation in the pursuit of denominational aims. This expresses itself in a particular sort of allegiance – i.e., a

216. Additionally, a prohibition of discrimination in other areas according to the respective European Directives 2000/43/EC has been implemented on the grounds of gender and racial or ethnic origin (Part III GlBG).

principal acceptance of the doctrine of faith and the moral teaching of the church or religious society concerned and an appropriate way of life relating to the specific task of the employee in question, on the one hand, and to the church's spiritual mandate, on the other. This obligation of loyalty corresponds to the duty of responsibility on the part of the church employers. The allegiance may vary with the importance of a person's work to the church's spiritual mission. An important criterion to be taken into consideration is the credibility of the religious community on which, at its very core, the effectiveness of its activities depends. These aspects are reflected in the concept of understanding all employees as being members of a uniform community rendering church services (*christliche Dienstgemeinschaft*). Considering that starting point, a concept of grading loyalties owed by employees of religious communities according to their self-understanding by referring to certain bases within universal and particular canon law has been established.[217] With regard to the relevant decisions of the VfGH and the Supreme Court, the right to self-determination has been constructed in quite a broad sense (cf. 270 et seq.).[218]

482. Internal ecclesiastical statutes on employment and remuneration as a matter of contract law adapted by legally recognized churches and religious societies belong to the 'internal affairs' in the sense of Article 15 StGG. These autonomous statutes are to be qualified as leges contractus which become part of the individual employment contracts. Reference is made therein to a special allegiance whose substance matter is usually prescribed in a more or less general manner. This legal framework is partly completed by collective labour agreements (cf. 497).

483. In principle, each diocese within the Catholic Church has individual statutes on employment and remuneration and frequently, specific regulations for certain occupational groups such as pastoral assistants, parish secretaries, church musicians, sextons, etc. To give an example regarding the special allegiance of employees: among the grounds for giving notice the Viennese Statutes on employment and remuneration make reference to 'gross or repeated infringements of the employees' obligation as laid down in the respective service regulation', as well as conducting 'a way of life detrimental to the credibility of the Church'.[219] Comparable formulations are found in the other diocesan Statutes on employment, altogether in compliance with framework regulations for church service issued by the Austrian Bishops' Conference.[220] As far as the Protestant Church is concerned, numerous Church Laws of the Augsburg and Helvetic Confessions of the Evangelical Church contain detailed provisions for church services depending on the different categories of personnel, such as the 'Order of the Sacred Ministry' (*Ordnung des*

217. *See* primarily cc. 208, 210, 1290 CIC.
218. *See* especially OGH 6 May 1987, 14 Ob A 29/87; OGH 12 Apr. 1995, 9 Ob A 31/95.
219. § 14 section 2 lit. a and b Statutes on Employment and Remuneration, http://www.zentralbetriebsrat.at/content/site/service/gesetze/index.html [9. 10. 2014].
220. Cf. current reports on Austrian particular canon law written by W. Rees in *Österreichisches Archiv für Recht und Religion*.

geistlichen Amtes),[221] provisions for vicars, for other employees, for special ecclesiastical services such as those provided by church musicians, and directives for pastoral care in hospitals and prisons. Furthermore, the Disciplinary Regulations apply to religious ministers as well as other categories of church employees. Altogether, the provisions relating to a special allegiance have the character of general clauses.

484. Against this background and through the integration of the European anti-discrimination law, one can assume that the established special concept of grading loyalties owed by employees to denominational employers according to the self-understanding of the latter will continue to endure with its essential features – primarily with regard to church activities within the inner core of 'internal affairs' such as spiritual tasks and pastoral care. As far as charity and social welfare activities are concerned – also regularly covered in a similar way by the specific ecclesiastical mandate – the new anti-discrimination law could involve certain modifications. Nevertheless, depending on the particular facts and circumstances of the case, the legal merits will need to be weighed more thoroughly and more precise arguments will have to be formulated to reach reasonable decisions.[222]

485. The main points of conflict which are estimated to arise will concern homosexual partnerships and questions regarding membership and withdrawal from church membership, as already reflected in the scientific discourse. As far as the first issue is concerned, both discrimination criteria – 'religion' and 'sexual orientation' – might happen to coincide in the case of employees of churches and religious societies as regards the practice of homosexuality. Starting from the fact that a distinction must be made between a homosexual orientation as such and its practice or living in a homosexual partnership, such circumstances cannot be qualified as intersectorial (multiple) discrimination in its genuine sense, though the situation is somehow similar. The peculiarly dogmatic difficulty lies in the fact that the refusal of an application or a dismissal refers directly to the sexual orientation of a person while this criterion becomes relevant only with regard to an employer whose ethos is based on religion or belief. In other words, the church employer demands a certain attitude corresponding to the relevant doctrinal and moral teachings and simultaneously, another explicit anti-discrimination criterion applies here. The Council Directive's wording in Article 4 section 2 suggests that the application of this exemption clause should be restricted to religion or belief only and should not justify discrimination on other grounds. Taking this aspect into account as well as the precondition that the other provisions are complied with, two legal dogmatic approaches seem to be practicable. Reference might be made to Article 4 section 1

221. Ordnung des geistlichen Amtes der Evangelischen Kirche in Österreich, http://www.evang.at/kirche/intern-evang-at/rechtsdatenbank/mitarbeiterinnen/ [9. 10. 2014].

222. ECtHR, *Obst v. Deutschland,* 23 Sep. 2010, appl. no. 425/03; ECtHR, *Schüth v. Deutschland,* 23. Sep. 2010, appl. no. 1620/03; ECtHR, *Siebenhaar v. Deutschland,* 3. Feb. 2011, appl. no. 18136/02. Cf. B. Schinkele, 'Kirchliches Arbeitsrecht in der aktuellen Rechtsprechung des Europäischen Gerichtshofs für Menschenrechte', *Österreichisches Archiv für Recht und Religion* 55 (2008), 155–173.

of the Directive (§20 section 1 GlBG) generally providing for a difference in treatment, however, in compliance with a stricter evaluation standard regarding justification of unequal treatment in comparison with Article 4 section 2 (20 section 2 GlBG). Such a construction seems to meet the Council Directive's aforementioned requirement. Another approach could be found by means of a teleological interpretation or reduction by reading the relevant wording in the Directive that it 'should not justify discrimination on an entirely other ground'.[223] It can be assumed that both procedures would essentially lead to the same result. Such approaches seem to be necessary, not at least in order to avoid inconsistencies regarding other loyalty infringements which are sanctioned by corresponding labour law measures, in particular, in the case of pastoral assistants and teachers of religious education classes or other persons charged with functions of the inner core of a religious community.

486. Another matter of dispute could arise in the case of a church employee leaving the church, who is, however, engaged in tasks not exclusively reserved for members of the church concerned. The question arises as to whether a dismissal on the grounds of withdrawal from church membership can be justified as a reason for dismissal in any case, while membership as a precondition of employment is only required for persons with pastoral, catechistical and usually educational tasks, in certain cases for persons in leading positions. Questions of this nature will apply particularly to the fields of social welfare activities, for instance, within the staff in a hospital with a denominational holder.[224]

487. As far as divorced and remarried persons are concerned, such factual circumstances as regards access to employment or termination, as far as one can see, have never been the subject of Courts' adjudications. It may be assumed that such cases are usually resolved unanimously. It must be underlined that church institutions and subunits, in principle, are prepared to take into account a change in the legal situation as well as in societal realities, to a certain – though quite different – extent. Thus the specific facts and circumstances of an individual case can be brought to effect considering also the genuine instruments of case-by-case justice as part of the ecclesiastical legal order such as aequitas canonica and salus animarum.

488. The Supreme Court had to discuss the labour law consequences of public criticism of the Catholic Church,[225] making reference to the decision of the German Constitutional Court from 1985.[226] In a public letter, a development cooperation

223. *See* E. Holzleithner, 'Das Diskriminierungsverbot aufgrund der sexuellen Orientierung: Reichweite und Grenzen', *Österreichisches Archiv für Recht und Religion* 55 (2008), 251–265; B. Schinkele, 'Religionsfreiheit und europäisches Antidiskriminierungsrecht – Einige grundsätzliche Überlegungen', *Österreichisches Archiv für Recht und Religion* 55 (2008), 198–203.
224. B. Schinkele, 'Kirchenmitgliedschaft, Kirchenaustritt und europäisches Antidiskriminierungsrecht', in *In mandatis meditari. Festschrift für Hans Paarhammer,* ed. S. Haering et al. (Berlin: Duncker & Humblot, 2012), 1099–1117.
225. OGH 12 Apr. 1995, 9 ObA 31/95.
226. BVerfGE 70, 138.

worker engaged as a teacher at a private Catholic school in Papua New Guinea criticized the attitude of the Catholic Church regarding questions of birth control as moralistic and harsh. The court qualified his dismissal as socially legitimate and not arbitrary. Pursuant to the established case law, the state courts are bound to decisions on preliminary questions which are to be resolved by the church. A certain right to supervision can be deduced from the prohibition of arbitrary decision-making, offence against good morals and the ordre public. This judgment has been criticized for refraining from dealing with the reservation clause 'subject to the general laws of the state' according to Article 15 StGG.[227]

489. Religious education instructors, irrespective of whether they are employed by the state or a religious society, need a professional qualification as well as the delegation of power from the community concerned (missio canonica). Conferring the power to teach belongs to the 'internal affairs' in the sense of Article 15 StGG which is regulated in detail in the Act on Religious Education at School (for details see 606 et seq.).

§4. Employment Safety and Labour Inspection

490. The Employment Safety Act (ASchG) provides for several exemptions with respect to the self-understanding of legally recognized churches and religious societies. On the one hand, consecrated ministers are not deemed employees in the meaning of this Act and therefore it does not apply to them. On the other hand, numerous regulations concerning construction, composition, and equipment of workplaces and construction sites are not applicable to buildings and other facilities dedicated to the purposes of worship of legally recognized communities. Similarly, the scope of the Labour Inspection Act (ArbIG) extends neither to religious ministers nor to institutions carrying out denominational functions of these religious communities.

227. H. Kalb, 'Kommentar zu OGH 12. 4. 1995, 9 Ob A 31/95', *Das Recht der Arbeit* 46 (1996), 36–43.

Chapter 3. Collective Labour Law

§1. Partial Exemption from Co-determination by Employees

491. According to the second sentence of §132 section 4 ArbVG, several provisions of this Act are by no means applicable to enterprises and administrative organizations charged with the administration of the internal affairs of legally recognized churches and religious societies, actually concerning company agreements in certain matters, rights to economic information, intervention and consultation, as well as to some extent the right to be involved in operative changes. This provision is to be understood as a realization of the fundamental right of self-determination on the level of ordinary laws in the fields of labour law. Thus it has been made clear that certain provisions of the Act on Labour Constitution are not qualified as 'general laws of the state' (cf. 276 et seq.).

§2. Establishment of Works Councils

492. In principle, according to §132 section 4 ArbVG, the establishment of works councils is in concordance with the right to self-determination of legally recognized churches and religious societies, while the exercising of certain rights must be examined case by case. This legal view has been confirmed by a Supreme Court's decision concerning a Protestant parish community comprising several institutions pursuing social or educational purposes such as running kindergartens, student hostels and hospitals.[228] Though these legal issues might raise many theoretical legal questions, in practice the cooperation of both sides, representatives of employers and works councils, seems to work quite well.

493. Works councils are established within the facilities of Catholic and Protestant Church businesses or enterprises with more than five employees who are entitled to vote. To give an example, the Archdiocese of Vienna shows a tripartite structure of fictive operative areas each electing their own staff committee body: the Financial Chamber, the Ordinariate and the Centre of Apostolate/Pastoral Office. Since the coming into force of the ArbVG a central staff committee was established in 1977. It operates starting from an equal labour and remuneration law basis, cautiously observing the principle of subsidiarity and the different requirement profiles. In principle, one can qualify the negotiations and agreements between the central staff committee and the employer's representatives to a certain extent as an internal social partnership.

228. U. Runggaldier, 'Kommentar zu OGH 5. 9. 2001, 9 Ob A 184/01a', *Österreichisches Archiv für Recht und Religion* 49 (2002), 488–505.

§3. Collective Labour Agreements

494. According to §7 ArbVG, legal entities under public law in their function as employers are subsidiarily capable of concluding collective labour agreements. Consequently, legally recognized churches and religious societies are empowered to conclude collective labour agreements as well as individual work agreements (company agreements). Subsidiarity in this context means, for instance, that a diocese has this capability with regard to its own employees but not to those of subordinate entities such as parishes. For a long time, this opportunity has rarely been used but nowadays this practice is becoming increasingly popular. In this context, it must be underlined that internal ecclesiastical statutes on employment and remuneration are becoming part of individual employment contracts as leges contractus and thus pursue a similar purpose as collective labour contracts do.

495. Within the Catholic Church, three Austrian dioceses (Linz, Graz-Seckau, Innsbruck)[229] have concluded a collective labour agreement with the Trade Union for private employees which has been adapted several times. A few religious orders as holders of denominational hospitals have been pioneers in this respect. Caritas Austria has had a collective labour agreement in force since 2001 which includes all staff members of the individual Caritas-organizations and the Caritas-Central. In this case, the ability to contract a collective agreement was based on conferring it by the competent administrative body as is legally provided for. As far as the Protestant Church is concerned, after inclusion of the religious ministers in comprehensive social insurance schemes in 1996 (cf. 499) the governing bodies of the Protestant Churches (Evangelischer Oberkirchenrat A. und H.B, Evangelischer Oberkirchenrat A.B., Evangelischer Oberkirchenrat H.B.) as employers and the Association of Protestant Pastors (Vereinigung Evangelischer Pfarrerinnen und Pfarrer) as a recognized voluntary professional organization concluded a collective labour agreement with the approval of the Synodal Committees which has been continuously adjusted.[230] This collective agreement is focused on salary and pension schemes.

229. *See* the collective labour agreement of the diocese Linz, http://www.kollektivvertrag.at/kv/dioezese-linz-ang, the diocese Graz-Seckau, http://www.kollektivvertrag.at/kv/dioezese-graz-seckau-ang and the diocese Innsbruck http://www.kollektivvertrag.at/kv/dioezese-innsbruck-ang.

230. Collective labour law of the Protestant Church, *see* http://www.evang.at/fileadmin/evang.at/doc_rechtsdatenbank/kollv.pdf.

Chapter 4. The National Insurance System

§1. Exemption from Obligatory Social Insurance

496. General obligatory social insurance, as laid down in §4 of the General Social Insurance Act (ASVG), covers health, accident and retirement pension insurance. According to §7 section 1 no. 7, priests as well as members of religious orders and similar institutions of the Catholic Church are exempted from full insurance liability regarding their pastoral work and other activities which they exercise in fulfilling their spiritual commitments such as religious education classes if they do not have contractual relations with other corporations apart from their church or its institutions. Some of these persons have partial insurance, which covers only illness, accidents or retirement. Priests and members of religious orders in general have the possibility of self-insurance or continued voluntary insurance. Holders of a spiritual office in the Protestant churches, who had previously also been exempted, were included in the full insurance by the ASVG amendments from 1980 and 1996.

497. If a person who is exempt from full insurance ceases to be a member of the clergy, religious order or similar institution a certain amount must be transferred by the respective institution or facility to the new pension insurance institution (§314 ASVG). With regard to their alternative maintenance on the basis of internal supply systems the existential protection of such persons becomes relevant only in the case of their leaving the diocese or the religious order.

§2. Care Allowance for Priests and Members of Religious Orders

498. The Federal Act on Care Allowance 1993 (BPfGG) has introduced a nationwide and, in principle, homogenous re-organization of payments to persons who are in need of care. In this context, the crucial issue was whether priests and members of religious orders could be deemed to have a valid claim 'for a retirement benefit or income or an equivalent performance based on a private contract' as is demanded in §3, and thus were entitled to benefits according to this Act. A Ministerial Decree of 2002[231] made clear that priests of the Catholic Church belong to this category of beneficiaries if they are incardinated or temporarily integrated into a diocese within the federal territory which has a valid claim for benefits. In several decisions,[232] the Supreme Court has stated that incardination represents a relationship with private law relevance and that the internal ecclesiastical retirement benefit for priests is to be qualified as a functionally comparable equivalent in the meaning of §3 cited above. In this respect, the Ministerial Decree has put the Supreme Court's opinion into practice. With regard to the fact that priests are exempted from

231. BGBl. II 2002/72.
232. OGH 22 Oct. 1996, 10 Ob S 267/95; OGH 5 Sep. 2000, 10 Ob S 121/00t; cf. H. Kalb, 'Kommentar zu OGH 22. 10. 1996, 10 Ob S 267/95', *Das Recht der Arbeit* 47 (1997), 369–374; H. Kalb, 'Kommentar zu OGH 5. 9. 2000, 10 Ob S 121/00t', *Österreichisches Archiv für Recht und Religion* 48 (2001), 272–281.

full social insurance; a certain amount of money should be transferred commensurate to the additional expenditure arising. An analogous rule should be provided for members of religious orders.

Part VII. Religious Communities and Protection of the Individual

Chapter 1. Protection of Privacy

499. The relationship between religious communities and the individual must be considered primarily from the perspective of the horizontal (indirect) application of fundamental rights, allowing for differences, however, between the members belonging to the religious community concerned and other individuals (cf. 134). In the case of conflict between fundamental rights and legally protected interests, respectively, the two legal positions must be balanced carefully according to the principle of proportionality in order to render both as effective as possible. This also holds true when both aspects of religious freedom, the positive and the negative, are conflicting, as they are, in principle, of equal status and as such, subject to the same restrictions.

500. Over and above these aspects, registration of residents, as well as religious affiliation, are dealt with in this chapter. In principle, the concealment of one's religious or philosophical belief falls within the scope of the fundamental right to religious freedom, implying the exclusion of an enforced divulgement. There are only a few exemptions in which the state is authorized to request information about religious affiliation. However, there is partly a lack of transparency regarding the right to refuse disclosure.

§1. Registration of Residents

501. The Registration Act (MeldeG) distinguishes between 'identity data' and 'registration data'. 'Identity data' refers to name, residence, date of birth and nationality and additionally, for foreigners, passports. Religion belongs to 'registration data', and as far as 'registration data' are concerned according to §22 section 1 no. 1 MeldeG a sanction is imposed for a missing declaration, but not, however, for a false declaration of 'registration data'. An applicant was sentenced to an administrative penalty owing to his refusal to declare his religious belief on the registration form. Undoubtedly, the different legal consequences – whereby a sanction provided for a declaration which was (merely) deficient but not for a wilful and knowingly false declaration – obviously amount to a 'contradiction in valuation'. With regard to the genesis of the MeldeG, the Constitutional Court proceeds from the assumption that this incoherence is the result of several draft alterations during the process of becoming law. Though the wording of this text is quite unambiguous, the Constitutional Court did not repeal the regulation because it was unconstitutional but resolved the problem on the basis of an interpretation in conformity with the Constitution by making clear that no liability exists to divulge one's religious belief in connection with registration of residence.[233]

§2. Data Protection

502. Data protection law covers both individual religious convictions and constitutionally protected activities of religious communities in their capacity as clients of data processing. The first Austrian Act on Data Protection (DSG 1978)[234] was replaced in 2000 by the EU Directive on Data Protection 95/46/EC, which was implemented by a new Data Protection Lw (DSG 2000). On 25 May 2018, the directly applicable (cf. 422) text of the General Data Protection Regulation (GDPR) replaced the statutory provisions of the DSG 2000 with the Data Protection Amendment Act 2018 (hereinafter referred to as DSG 2018), which entered into force on the same day. The DSG 2018 can be regarded as a kind of accompanying law and addresses constitutional protection of the fundamental right of data protection (§1), provisions for implementation of the GDPR (§§2 to 33) as well as further security provisions (§§34 to 77).

503. According to §1 DSG, every person has a fundamental right to the confidentiality of his or her personal data – especially concerning private and family life, in as far as a legitimate interest in secrecy can be claimed. In Austria, data protection also includes juridical persons, thus religious communities are affected by data protection in as far as this fundamental right is meaningful for them. The direct horizontal effect of the fundamental right to data protection (cf. 286) also applies to religious communities.

504. According to Article 9 section 1 GDPR, religious and philosophical beliefs are data whose processing is generally prohibited. Article 9 section 2 cites exceptions, some of which are particularly relevant for data processing by religious communities. The collection, processing or transfer of data by religious communities is generally permissible if the use of this data takes place within the framework of the religious community's legally guaranteed right to self-determination. This could concern, for example, the linking of membership data with data on church-contributions, religious education and data of employees in church service, which has been recorded through data applications; finally, health data, which is important for many church health service facilities, will have to be considered.

---

233. VfSlg. 15541/1999; cf. H. Kalb, 'Kommentar zu VfGH 24. 6. 1999, B 1253/98', *Österreichisches Archiv für Recht und Religion* 47 (2000), 404–410.

234. *See* R. Potz, 'Das Datenschutzgesetz 2000 im religionsrechtlichen Kontext', *Österreichisches Archiv für Recht und Religion* 47 (2000), 384–394.

505. Legal provisions permit state authorities to solicit information regarding membership in a religious community which might be of relevance to the state sector, insofar as rights and obligations in the public sector are concerned, such as in connection with religious education (cf. 632 et seq.), registration information (cf. 504 et seq.), the activities of the Federal Institute for Information on Sects (cf. 465), the law on church-contributions (cf. 590 et seq.) and security police measures in accordance with the SPG and SNG.

506. Hospitals' obligation to notify recognized churches and religious societies of patients' religious beliefs is also covered by a data transfer regulation. This obligation has led to a controversial debate concerning data protection within the context of pastoral assistance in healthcare institutions. Some hospitals with public law status had refused to transmit the names of Protestant patients to the inquiring institution's pastor as stipulated in §18 ProtestantenG (cf. 314 and 742). The hospital management argued that the DSG had derogated from this regulation which assumes that patients are asked to state their confession on admission to a hospital. On the contrary, the competent Federal Minister took the position that explicit consent by patients allowing the authorities to forward their names to the institution's pastor would also not be necessary in future. It would only be forbidden to pass on the names of those inmates who had explicitly rejected pastoral care. Based on this opinion, it should be added that the best procedure would be to inform patients that they are not obliged to disclose their religious beliefs. According to the principle of parity, this should apply to all legally recognized churches and religious societies (cf. 264 et seq.).

507. The GDPR created a scope exception from Union law within the definition of Article 17 TFEU,[235] which must also be seen in the context of the fundamental rights guarantee of corporate freedom of religion.[236] Pursuant to Article 91 section 1 GDPR, comprehensive data protection rules of 'churches or religious associations or communities' existing in a Member State at the time of this Regulation's coming into effect may continue to apply to the protection of natural persons with regard to processing, provided that they are brought into line with this Regulation.

508. The Catholic Church[237] and the Protestant Church[238] have issued internal protection regulations for church data which Article 91 GDPR applies to. Other recognized churches, religious societies and other religious communities have not yet adopted such a regulation. Unlike the Catholic Church, the Protestant Church has also made use of the authorization in Article 91 section 2 GDPR and established an independent supervisory authority in the form of the Data Protection Senate.

235. Cf. Recital 165.
236. Krömer & Brandner 2022, Rz 6ff.
237. *Decretum Generale* über den Datenschutz in der Katholischen Kirche in Österreich und ihren Einrichtungen (Church data protection regulation), ABl-ÖBK 74/2018.
238. ABl 54 (2018).

Chapter 2. Freedom to Marry

509. Following a decision by the VfGH on 4 Dec. 2017, same-sex partners have been able to marry since 1 January 2018 and opposite-sex partners can establish a registered partnership, which was previously reserved for same-sex couples.

510. In Austria, the religious orientation of marriage law ended in 1938 with the laicization by the Act on the Unification of the Law of Marriage and Divorce in the Country of Austria and the Rest of the Reich (EheG 1938, cf. 61). After 1945 this law was transferred to the legal system of the Republic with the exception of provisions containing ideological traits of National-Socialism, in particular the 'impediment of difference in race'. Since then, the system of compulsory civil marriage has been realized and religious marriages have had no consequences under civil law (cf. 696).

511. According to §16 section 1 of the Federal Act on International Private Law (IPRG), a marriage can only be deemed formally valid by the state registrar, even if the personal statute of the foreign fiancé permits another form of marriage. Foreign religious marriages can only be recognized if they have legal effect according to the relevant state law.

512. The Austrian marriage law includes the prohibition of bigamy. Polygamy is incompatible with the basic values of Austrian law.[239] According to §8 EheG, a person may not marry before his or her former marriage has been annulled or dissolved. A marriage is considered void if, at the time of the wedding, either person is already living with a third person in a valid marriage or registered partnership (§24 EheG). In such a case, the second marriage of the partner with Austrian citizenship must be dissolved judicially. Moreover, bigamy is a criminal offence pursuant to §192 of the StGB. A (merely) religious marriage does not fall under the prohibition of bigamy.

513. According to §17 section 1 IPRG, the preconditions of marriage for each of the engaged partners must be judged according to their personal status, whereby the personal statute of a fiancé at the time of marriage is relevant. According to the rules of private international law, there are some restrictions based on the Austrian ordre public.

514. The secular marriage law does not include impediments based on religion. Therefore, any foreign legal impediment to a marriage or annulment on the grounds

239. Regarding the experience of Austrian authorities with polygamy, it is remarkable that a systematic guide to the 'Matrimonial law, family law and inheritance of the Muslims of the Hanafite rite', published 1883 for monitoring the administration of justice in Islamic courts, explicitly recognized the institution of polygamy for Bosnia.

of religion – especially in the case of an interconfessional marriage – is not in accordance with the Austrian ordre public. The recognition of such a marriage annulment would contradict the principle of state secularity.[240]

515. A contradiction to the Austrian ordre public occurs if there is serious direct or indirect pressure to marry a certain person, such as a contractual penalty in the contract of engagement, a payment for the necessary consent of a minor to the marriage or a foreign provision which considers an appropriate payment as valid.[241] 2006 forced marriages have been qualified as severe coercion under §106 section 1 no. 3 Penal Code.[242] In implementation of Article 37 of the Council of Europe Convention on preventing and combating violence against women and domestic violence (Istanbul-Convention), the particular injustice of such acts was defined more clearly in the Amendment of the StGB in 2015 (StRÄG 2015) by reassessing them as a separate criminal offence.[243] Due to the socio-cultural significance of the family in connection with the precarious minority situation, the wording of the law expressly extends the means of coercion to include the particularly effective threat of breaking off or withdrawing family contact. Forcing someone to enter into a (merely) religious marriage is not covered by the offence but can be subsumed under the general offence of coercion. However, due to the practical importance of religious marriages in some immigrant communities, it would be worth considering including these marriages, designating them as forced marriages and as such as an offence.

516. A further measure against forced marriages of girls – implementing the Council Directive on Family Reunification 2003/86/EC – was the increase of the age limit of spouses to 21 years for the claim of family reunification with effect from 1 January 2010 (prohibition of 'importation of underage brides').[244]

517. So-called marriages by proxy are permissible, for instance, in Islamic law. As long as there is only a 'proxy in the declaration', it is a question of form and sufficient to satisfy the relevant provisions of local law. A representation in the will (with the authority of partner selection or discretionary freedom to conclude or not by the representative) contradicts the public order.

240. VwSlg. 11436 A/1984, VwSlg. 13374 A/1991.
241. OGH 13 Sep. 2000, 4 Ob 199/00v. A respective agreement falls under the nullity sanction for a violation of good morals (§ 879 section 1 ABGB).
242. Whosoever commits an assault by forcing a person – *inter alia* – into marriage is now to be punished with imprisonment of from six months to five years. Forced marriage became an 'official offence'.
243. ErlRV 869 BlgNR XXV. GP, 18.
244. § 2 section 1 no. 9 Act on Settlement and Residence (NAG).

Chapter 3. Freedom of Expression

518. The fundamental right to freedom of expression is comprehensively guaranteed according to §13 StGG and §10 ECHR. Moreover, the Resolution of the Provisional National Assembly (Beschluss der Provisorischen Nationalversammlung) from 1918[245] should be mentioned here, which prohibits any censorship as a violation of the fundamental right of citizens and establishes the full freedom of the press.

519. The fundamental right to free expression of thought in speech, writing and any other form of communication is principally guaranteed to all individuals and groups (comprising religious communities themselves) and thus includes their right to free criticism of the doctrinal and moral teachings of a religion and the speech and actions of authorities and members of a religious community. Such expressions are subject to the general reservations provided in the fundamental guarantees mentioned above. The offences within the Penal Code such as 'Disparaging Religious Doctrines' (§188 StGB) and 'Incitement' are dealt with in Chapter 8 (523 et seq.).

520. As far as the relationship between a certain religious community and its own members is concerned, these persons are also free to express their disagreement with the official doctrines or their criticism of statements and actions of the church authorities. However, the right to self-determination of religious communities (cf. 268 et seq.) implies their right to impose sanctions on members whose statements are considered unacceptable, which can even include their exclusion. The right to have justice administered before the state courts against such measures does not exist. With regard to employees, religious communities can to a certain degree demand that they act in conformity with the doctrinal and moral teachings of the respective religious community (cf. 426 and 483). Moreover, special rules are provided with regard to teachers of religious education classes (cf. 647 et seq.).

245. StGBl. 1918/3.

Chapter 4. Due Process Norms and Religious Groups

521. The right to self-determination encompasses the right to have justice administered independently of the state. The internal legal system of churches, religious societies and their own judicial organization operates parallel to the legal sphere of the state. Churches and religious societies principally act independently regarding their 'internal affairs' and their decisions are not subject to a procedure of state courts. This, however, does not imply total exemption from state jurisdiction. The state has to comply with its duty towards church employees to protect their requirement to seek judicial relief to a certain extent. The possibility of access to courts, mainly concerning remuneration or other proprietary interests, also exists to a certain extent for clergymen, other ministers and members of religious orders. The state courts are, however, bound to preliminary questions which must then be resolved by the church and are excluded from re-examination (cf. 280).

Chapter 5. Professional Secrecy

§1. General Protection

522. In order to avoid unreasonable conflicting situations, the Austrian procedural norms distinguish two categories of exemptions from the principally existing duty to bear testimony, in fact, the prohibition from interrogating a person on the one hand, and the witness's right to refuse to answer certain questions on the other. Within the first group, one must distinguish between persons who are absolutely incapable of being witnesses and persons relatively unable to testify. Besides state officials, the last-mentioned group particularly includes spiritual ministers, whereby the incapacity to bear testimony is restricted to certain facts and perceptions within their immediate area of activity.

§2. General Denominational Protection

523. The seal of confession and other forms of spiritual secrecy are taken into account in two respects, irrespective of the legal status of the church or religious community in question. Within the Penal Code provision 'Omission of preventing an action liable to prosecution' an exemption is provided for spiritual ministers.[246] According to §286 section 1 StGB:

> a person shall be punished who wilfully and knowingly omits the intentional commitment of a punishable action imminent or which has already begun, or omits to notify the appropriate state authority or the threatened person, when such notification would prevent the commitment of the offence.

524. §286 section 2 provides for the impunity of the delinquents 'in so far as they got to know about the imminent action on the basis of information confided to them in their capacity as spiritual ministers'. This means that it is up to the spiritual minister to decide whether or not he makes use of this exemption.

525. Moreover, the different procedural rules provide for protection of the confessional secret. Clergymen and other pastors may not be interrogated as witnesses in criminal, civil, administrative or taxation proceedings, or, additionally, in Constitutional Court or High Administrative Court proceedings with regard to information confided to them during sacramental confession or otherwise under the seal of strict confidence as spiritual ministers in their specific capacity (§320 Code of Civil Procedure [ZPO], §151 no. 1 Code of Criminal Procedure [StPO]).[247] However, with respect to knowledge or information which goes beyond this, clergymen and

246. Cf. B. Schinkele, 'Beichtgeheimnis und geistliche Amtsverschwiegenheit aus kirchen-, straf- und religionsrechtlicher Sicht', in *Recht – Religion – Kultur. Festschrift für Richard Potz*, ed. B. Schinkele et al. (Vienna: facultas.wuv, 2014), 797 et seq.

247. *Ibid.* 790 et seq.

other pastors are bound to testimony. Pursuant to §144 no. 1 StGB, the seal of spiritual secrecy must not be circumvented, particularly as regards the regulation and execution of certain investigative measures. In any case, the optic or acoustic surveillance of clergymen by technical means is prohibited in confessionals or rooms destined for spiritual conversation.

526. A dispensation is not allowed, given by the person suspected of a criminal offence or by the church authority, even if the clergyman was willing to give evidence. Which persons are deemed to be 'spiritual ministers' and how far-reaching the seal of confession is, follows from the self-understanding of the respective church or religious community. Examinations interfering with these regulations present grounds for appeal within the ZPO (§321) and grounds for nullity according to §§281 and 345 StPO.

527. In practice, both regulations are likely to involve problems of delimitation with regard to the fact that non-clerics or non-consecrated ministers, respectively, are increasingly being charged with pastoral care tasks, not at least in the sphere of religious assistance in institutions such as prisons.

528. Taking into account the serious consequences that the absolute prohibition of witness interrogation could have, this legal situation has been criticized for leaving no scope for consideration of the facts and circumstances of individual cases. Consequently, it should be the spiritual minister's decision whether or not he or she is willing to give testimony. This means that the absolute prohibition of witness interrogation should be replaced by the right to refuse testimony, however, but by no means disregarding the internal ecclesiastical sanctions which could be imposed for breaching the seal of confession. Such a regulation would be in concordance with freedom of conscience, especially taking into consideration the understanding of fundamental rights as also implying a status positivus (cf. 129 et seq.).

§3. Specific Denominational Protection

529. Several laws regulating the external relationship of individual churches and religious societies contain provisions with the corresponding protection of denominational secrecy, which are, however, of little relevance with respect to general protection. According to Article XIII Concordat, clergymen may not be asked by juridical and administrative bodies for any information on persons or things which they have received under the seal of spiritual secrecy. Comparable regulations are embedded in the ProtestantenG (§11 section 1), OrthodoxenG (§7 section 1), OrientKG (§3 section 1), IsraelitenG (§16) and IslamG (§26). Due to the principle of parity and the most favoured clause in the law on religion, other legally recognized religious communities could indirectly benefit from the additional international legal guarantee based on the Concordat (cf. 267).

Chapter 6. Medical Deontology

530. In the field of bioethics and bio-laws existential questions of life and death are at issue, and therefore, regulating this is one of the most difficult tasks facing the legislation in a pluralistic system. Of course, religious and philosophical regards are also of great significance, so that churches and religious societies regularly participate in the respective public debates.

§1. ABORTION

531. The Penal Code (StGB) 1975 introduced the so-called Fristenlösung which introduced a limitation of the punishability of abortion, and simultaneously a 'conscience clause' for the medical staff. According to §97 section 1 StGB, termination of pregnancy is not punishable if it is undertaken by a physician during the first three months of pregnancy after a preceding medical consultation. No criminal prosecution shall take place after the expiration of the three-month period in the case of medical or eugenic indication or in the case of the minority of the pregnant female (section 2).

532. Freedom of conscience in context with abortion is granted according to §97 section 2 and 3 StGB:

(2) No physician is obliged to undertake a termination of pregnancy or to participate in such a termination, unless the termination is necessary without delay because of imminent danger to the life of the pregnant woman, which cannot otherwise be averted.
(3) No person shall be discriminated against in whatsoever way on the grounds of a termination of pregnancy under the law or for participation in such a termination, or for the refusal to undertake or to participate in such a termination. This also applies to the persons working in nursing service, in medical-technical service, or in medical emergency service.

533. The question of introducing the Fristenlösung resulted in the most serious conflict between the Catholic Church and the Austrian state after 1945. It shows a nearly perfect example of the possibilities and limits of political action regarding the different ethical perspectives of the churches and the pluralistic state (cf. 78).[248]

534. Following a complaint, the Constitutional Court had to examine the constitutionality of the Fristenlösung with regard to Article 2, Article 8, and Article 12 ECHR, as well as Article 63 section 2 StVStGermain, holding that there was no interference with any of the constitutional guarantees referred to:[249] The term 'inhabitant' in Article 63 section 1 and section 2 StVStGermain explicitly refers to

248. *See* R. Potz, 'New Liberties and Church-State Relationships in Austria', in *'New Liberties' and Church and State Relationships in Europe*, ed. European Consortium for Church-State Research (Milan: Giuffrè, 1998), 313 et seq.
249. VfSlg. 7400/1974.

human beings who have already been born, therefore this guarantee cannot be a criterion for the constitutionality of §97 StGB. The 'right to life' pursuant to Article 2 ECHR only relates to a person's own life. The concept of 'person' underlying Article 2 ECHR is independent of that conceived by the national legal orders. No consequences regarding protection under Article 2 ECHR may be drawn from the fact of conferring a legal or a partly legal personality (to a nasciturus) within a national legal order. Article 8 ECHR does not exclude the enactment of penal law provisions in order to protect the right to respect for family and private life; however, it does not contain any obligation on behalf of the legislator to penalize for disregarding it. Similarly, Article 12 ECHR does not imply the state's obligation to issue protective penal laws.

535. According to §6 section 3 Act on Healthcare Institutions (KaKuG), the statutes of the institution regulating the internal operation of the hospital should contain no provision which prohibits the unpunished termination of pregnancy or the participation in such a termination, nor any provision which combines the refusal to undertake or to participate in such a termination. The Constitutional Court held that this regulation does not interfere with the right to religious freedom according to Article 14 StGG, Article 63 section 2 StVStGermain, and Article 9 ECHR. It restricts the internal regulatory authority; however, it does not prevent the holder of the hospital from excluding the admission of pregnant women for undertaking an abortion, unless in cases of non-rejectable sick persons or necessary medical assistance.[250]

536. With regard to the practical handling of this subject, non-denominational healthcare institutions with public status in some Bundesländer or certain regions also refuse to carry out abortions. For this reason, politicians from time to time firmly and publicly stress the importance of respecting the legal claim of the persons concerned and of adjusting the practice appropriately.

§2. Reproductive Medicine

537. The Act on Medical Assistance for Reproduction 1992 (FMedG) as amended 2015 provides for medically assisted reproduction for women living in a conjugal, a registered partnership (heterosexual or homosexual) or long-term relationship, while single women are excluded whereas all methods of fertilization with the help of sperm donation are allowed. Moreover, although egg donation is permitted, negotiation and commercialization are forbidden. The donor may not be older than 30 and the recipient not be older than 45 years. For the first time, examination of the artificially fertilized embryo before implantation into the uterus (preimplantation diagnostic) is allowed, however, in compliance with strict prerequisites. The inclusion of homosexual partnerships has become necessary due

250. VfSlg. 7720/1975.

to a Constitutional Court decision of 2014.[251] Therein the Court stated that prohibition preventing female homosexual partners from fulfilling their desire for children by means of sperm donation is a form of discrimination.

§3. Euthanasia

538. After a lengthy public debate in Austria, in which the churches and religious societies in particular took part, the Constitutional Court declared the criminal offence of 'assisted suicide' in §78 StGB unconstitutional on the grounds that it violates the right to self-determination, prohibiting any form of assistance under any circumstances.[252]

539. As a result, the Dying Will Act (SterbeverfügungsG 2022) was passed. Pursuant to §2 section 1 SterbeverfügungsG, no natural or legal person is obliged to provide assistance, such as the dispensing of the pharmaceutical product by a pharmacist, to provide medical information or to participate in drawing up a dying will. Assistance in the definition of this legal provision is understood to mean the physical support of the person willing to die by carrying out life-ending measures, but not the provision of medical information or assistance in drawing up a dying will. No person may be disadvantaged in any way whatsoever because of such assistance, medical consultation or cooperation in the preparation of a dying will or the refusal to provide assistance, carry out a medical consultation or cooperate in the preparation of a dying will (§2 section 2). From the perspective of law on religion, these regulations raise the question of whether and to what extent churches and religious societies should permit assisted suicide (without participation) in their denominational institutions.

§4. Medical Treatment

540. Medical treatment requires the consent of the patient after appropriate information, thus an 'informed consent'. Unauthorized medical treatment, i.e., the treatment of a person without his or her at least implied consent is forbidden by criminal law. If it is not possible to apply for consent without serious risks to the patient's life or health, consent will be presumed unless the supposed danger did not exist of which one could have been aware with due diligence (§110 StGB). For quite a long time now, the autonomy of patients has become the most important aspect in balancing the values involved. Furthermore, the possibility of patients' advance directives in a binding or considerable form as well as a healthcare proxy has become established.

251. VfGH 11 Dec. 2014, G 119/2014 et al.
252. VfGH 11 Dec. Slg 20.433/2020.

541. Consequently, a legally responsible person who rejects medical treatment whether for religious or any other reasons must not be forced to receive it. In practice, difficulties could arise, mainly with regard to underage persons. In as far as minors are mentally competent and capable of discernment their consent must be obtained. Special therapeutic treatment including surgery can only be carried out with the additional agreement of the parents or other persons in charge of the minor's upbringing. A special problem concerning therapeutic treatment derives from the refusal of blood transfusions motivated by religious conviction, especially in the case of Jehovah's Witnesses. Persons having the care and custody of a child are obliged to care for the 'protection of the physical well-being and health of the child' (§146 ABGB), regardless of their religious commandments. The child's well-being must be taken into account as the supreme principle. Thus, if the well-being of a child conflicts with the parents' religious conviction, such decisions must not be a question of conscience and these persons cannot refer to their constitutionally guaranteed right of religious freedom. In the case of the refusal of consent presenting a serious danger to the life or health of the minor, the physician must contact the competent guardian court (Pflegschaftsgericht). After a partial withdrawal of the parents' custody of the child, a legal representative must be appointed to give the substitute approval. No consent is required if there is imminent danger (§8 section 3 KaKuG in conjunction with §176 ABGB).

542. A legally responsible person who rejects medical treatment for whatever reasons must not be forced to receive it. However, in specific cases, problems might arise with regard to legal consequences, mainly concerning claims for damages. In principle, the injured person is legally obliged to minimize damages. The crucial question is whether a person who has caused a traffic accident is liable for higher compensation payments arising from the refusal of a certain medical treatment (blood transfusion) for religious reasons by the injured person. This could result in higher treatment costs or even death, and thus in compensation claims for the pain and suffering of the bereaved as well as for funeral costs. The Supreme Court – contrary to another judgment of the OLG Innsbruck[253] – held that the freedom of decision-making by reason of conscience does not exclude the obligation to bear the subsequent disadvantages personally.[254] Its position was criticized for being in complete disregard of the fundamental right of freedom of conscience.[255] However, a compromise solution, i.e., sharing the additional costs as proposed in the literal doctrine,[256] cannot be implemented because of the contradiction in the transacted case law, although it would seem to be an adequate settlement.

253. OLG Innsbruck 16 Aug. 1994, ZVR 1996/48; cf. *Juristische Blätter* 119 (1997), 756.
254. OGH 22 Jun. 2011, 2 Ob 219/10k.
255. H. Kalb, 'Verletzung der Schadensminderungsobliegenheit durch Verweigerung von Bluttransfusionen aus religiösen Gründen. Kommentar zu OGH 22. 6. 2011, 2 Ob 219/10k', *Juristische Blätter* 134 (2012), 251–256.
256. J. Schacherreiter, 'Kommentar zu OGH 22. 6. 2011, 2 Ob 219/10k', *Österreichisches Archiv für Recht und Religion* 60 (2013), 221 et seq.

543. The clear limitations to the principle *volenti non fit iniuria* with reference to good morals, especially in the case of physical injuries, mainly regarding Female Genital Mutilation are dealt with in Chapter 8 (cf. 577).

§5. Epidemic Legislation

544. The state's measures to combat the epidemic necessarily interfere with the constitutionally protected guarantee of freedom of religion, in particular the freedom to practice religion. The campaign against the ' 2019-nCoV' therefore often had implications for law on religion. On 26 January 2020, the applicability of the Epidemics Act was ensured by including the '2019-nCoV' in the classification of notifiable diseases.

545. Although epidemic laws, as 'general state laws' within the meaning of Article 15 StGG, may constitute limits to the right of self-determination of the recognized churches and religious societies, the Austrian government has decided to leave the corresponding regulations to the churches and religious societies as their 'internal affairs'.

546. The representatives of all recognized churches and religious societies were therefore invited to the Federal Chancellery on 12 March 2020 in preparation for the first measures to deal with the pandemic. They were informed about the upcoming measures and asked to 'voluntarily and of their own decision abstain from worship gatherings'.[257]

547. An agreement was reached in which the recognized churches and religious societies undertook to adopt the state measures in their own regulations. According to the government, this 'preservation of the autonomy of the religious communities' did not indicate any privileges, but was based on their given 'structure, organization and power of enforcement.'[258]

548. After this meeting, the legally recognized churches and religious societies decided to strictly adhere to the government measures and to largely suspend activities in the religious communities for the next few weeks. However, the places of worship were to remain open for prayer and pastoral advice was to be offered. After the expiry of the 'Corona agreements' concluded with the Ministry of Culture on 30 June 2021, the recognized churches and religious societies agreed to 'continue to take precautionary measures for the protection of the faithful at their own discretion'.

---

257. P. Schipka, Zwischen staatlicher Erwartungshaltung und Aufrechterhaltung kirchlicher Sendung: Institutionalisierte Kontakte zwischen Staat und Kirche in der Corona-Krise in der Republik Österreich, ed. S. Mückl, Religionsfreiheit in Seuchenzeiten, Berlin 2021, 253–263, 256.
258. Quote from the Federal Government's statement on the Constitutional Court complaint (V 312/2021-15).

549. These arrangements, the content of which was only made public through press conferences, had the character of gentlemen's agreements, as they were not legally binding and their implementation depended on the willingness of the churches and religious societies to ensure appropriate protection against infection through internal regulations.

550. For their part, the churches and religious societies adopted the requirements of the large number of governmental COVID-19 regulations that were amended and renamed several times in quick succession.[259] Only during the fourth lockdown in the autumn of 2021 did they partially deviate from the uniformity of the measures.

551. The VfGH, which has been called upon many times, has only in a few cases found violation of fundamental rights by state measures to contain the COVID-19 pandemic, mostly due to insufficient documentation of the decision-making basis or unobjective differentiations in the respective system of measures. One decision of the Constitutional Court was of particular significance for law on religion,[260] wherein it considered an undifferentiated exception regarding 'gatherings for religious practice' in comparison to 'a general prohibition on entering facilities that serve cultural edification and participation in cultural life' as a 'categorically unequal treatment' in view of the protective purposes of religious freedom pursuant to Article 9 ECHR and artistic freedom pursuant to Article 17a StGG.

552. The court was unable to recognize the special factual justification necessary for such a 'priority status' of religious practice. It could not be inferred that the freedom of either category was more or less deserving of protection. Even if differences between the fundamental right to both religious and artistic freedom are undoubtedly extremely difficult to identify from a state perspective, it is possible to find points of reference that allow for a certain differentiation, albeit not 'categorical unequal treatment', within the scope of the state's margin of discretion.[261] What is particularly remarkable about this decision is that the Constitutional Court does not mention the right to self-determination of the churches and religious societies under Article 15 StGG, which has no comparable equivalent in the area of artistic freedom.[262]

259. An overview of all corona measures of the Catholic Church can be found at https://www.katholisch.at/corona (30.6.2023).

260. VfGH 30. Jun. 2022, V 312/2021-15.

261. A. Kowatsch, Die freie Religionsausübung in Zeiten der Pandemie – ein religionsrechtlicher und kanonistischer Zwischenbericht, *Österreichisches Archiv für Recht und Religion* 69 (2022), 225–297; R. Potz & B. Schinkele, Religions- und Kunstfreiheit während der Corona-Pandemie. Überlegungen aus Anlass des VfGH-Erkenntnisses V 312/2021 vom 30. Juni 2022, in ed. W. Rees, H. Kalb & C. Niemand, Kanonist, Ordensmann und Gestalter. FS Lederhilger, Berlin 2023, 553–571, 565–569.

262. R. Potz & B. Schinkele, ibid., 567 et seq.

Chapter 7. Non-discrimination

553. Non-discrimination is dealt with in Part II (165 et seq. and 204 et seq.) and Part VI (482 et seq.).

Chapter 8. Penal Law and Religion

554. The Penal Code does not specifically provide for offences attenuated by religious motivation or as a matter for one's conscience to decide. Neither Austrian doctrine nor the Courts deal thoroughly with the problems arising from offences committed because of the religious convictions of offenders; this issue is addressed mainly from the perspective of guilty knowledge. According to the prevailing opinion, the fundamental assumption is that offenders are conscious of the wrongful nature of their acts. Thus, error as to the prohibited nature of an action is regularly precluded. However, in relation to crimes of omission – referring to the criterion of reasonableness – moral conflicts arising from religious or philosophical convictions are taken into account appropriately. Finally, religious motivation may be considered with regard to the assessment of punishment or even as a legal reason for exemption from punishment. Such matters are relevant, most especially with regard to religious precepts concerning medical treatment (e.g., prohibitions concerning blood transfusions), in connection with the offence of failure to discharge the duty to render help to others (§75 StGB) or even murder by way of omission (§2 in conjunction with §75 StGB).

555. The Penal Code currently in force does not include any offence concerning proselytising and apostasy. Apostasy was neither an offence in the Penal Code of 1803 nor in the Penal Code of 1852 (however, there was an exclusion from intestate succession up to 1868). According to the Penal Code of 1803 (§107 lit. c) as well as that of 1852 (§122 lit. d in conjunction with §123) a person who induced a Christian to apostasy or intended to disseminate unbelief or to disseminate heresy regarding the Christian religion, was to be punished with imprisonment of between six months and one year. Although these offences were in the re-enactment of the Penal Code in 1945, the prevailing opinion suggests that they expired *per consuetudinem*.

556. Penal law is one of the few areas where the different legal categories of churches and religious communities have no significance.

§1. Religious Peace

I. Defamation or Outrage Against a Church or Religious Community

557. There is no offence corresponding to blasphemy as such. Blasphemy was abolished in the great revision of the Penal Code in 1975 (StGB), though this had already been a field of 'dead law' for a long time. Since then the Penal Code simply provides for 'Disparaging Religious Doctrines' (§188 StGB):

> A person who disparages or derides in public a person or a thing which is an object of worship in a church or religious community within Austria, a religious doctrine, a legally admissible observance, or a lawful establishment of such a church or religious community, and does so in circumstances which are

calculated to give rise to public nuisance, is to be punished with imprisonment of up to six months or a fine of up to 360 daily rates.

558. This statutory provision aims to protect the practices of religious cults against disturbance as well as manifestations of personal convictions without interference and compulsion; in other words, it aims, primarily, at the peaceful coexistence of citizens with different religious and philosophical convictions. However, this also implies the protection of the religious feelings of believers.[263] As far as the typology is concerned, this offence represents an 'abstract strict-liability tort' and actual realization is not required.[264]

559. Philosophical convictions or corresponding associations are not treated in the same way. However, it may be noted that regarding such associations, the occurrence of analogous facts is rather unusual. Depending on the factual circumstances, the offence according to §111 StGB 'Defamatory remark' or §115 'Personal insult' might be relevant here.

560. A more serious punishment is available for 'Incitement to violence' for which the level of criminal law relevance is higher. According to §283 StGB:

- a person who publicly in a manner calculated to endanger public order, or perceptible by a broad public provokes or incites explicitly to violence towards a church or religious community or towards another group defined by the criteria of race (ethnicity), colour, language, religion or belief, birth, national or ethnic origin, gender, disability, age, sexual orientation, or towards a member of such a group, is to be punished with imprisonment of up to two years;
- The same applies to any person who perceptible by a broad public stirs up hatred towards one of these groups, or humiliates it in such a way as to interfere with human dignity and thus intending to disparage it.[265]

561. Apart from the specific offence of §283 StGB, menace, violence or application of force against another person's freedom of religion are punished according to the general offences of assault, coercion, etc.

---

263. Cf. ECtHR, *Otto Preminger Institute v. Austria*, 20 Sep. 1994, appl. no. 13470/87. *See* C. Grabenwarter, 'Filmkunst im Spannungsfeld zwischen Freiheit der Meinungsäußerung und Religionsfreiheit', *Zeitschrift für ausländisches öffentliches Recht und Völkerrecht* 55 (1995), 128–165; D. Kolonovits, 'Meinungsfreiheit und Blasphemie in der jüngeren Rechtsprechung des EGMR', in *Kontinuität und Wandel der EMRK. Studien zur Europäischen Menschenrechtskonvention*, ed. C. Grabenwarter & R. Thienel (Kehl, Straßburg & Arlington: Engel, 1998), 188 et seq.
264. *See* J. Wallner, 'Strafrecht und Kunstfreiheit im Kontext der religiös-weltanschaulichen Sphäre. Überlegungen anhand eines Anlassfalls', *Österreichisches Archiv für Recht und Religion* 49 (2002), 239–259.
265. *See* H. Kalb, 'Religionsstrafrecht – aktuelle Änderungen', in *Recht – Religion – Kultur. Festschrift für Richard Potz*, ed. B. Schinkele et al. (Vienna: facultas.wuv, 2014), 255 et seq.

II. Desecration of a Place of Worship or a Sacred Object of any Religion and Hindrance or Disruption of a Religious Meeting

562. §189 StGB 'Disturbing the Practice of Religion':

(1) A person who hinders or disrupts a legally admissible sacred service or an act of worship of a church or religious community with violence or threats of violence is to be punished with imprisonment of up to two years.

(2) A person who gets up to mischief in circumstances calculated to give rise to public nuisance:

1. at a place dedicated to the lawful practice of a church or religious community,
2. during a lawful sacred service, or
3. concerning an act of worship of a church or religious community, is to be punished with imprisonment of up to six months or a fine of up to 360 daily rates.

563. There is no equivalent protection for ceremonies of philosophical associations (Weltanschauungsgemeinschaften). Usually, however, such associations neither have similar places of worship nor practice their belief in a comparable manner. In the case of hindrance or disruption to a meeting, every assembly enjoys the general protection afforded by the Security Police Act (SPG). A person who disrupts public order by unjustified and inconsiderate behaviour is charged with an administrative offence.

§2. Religious Property

564. Two of the offences aggravated by religious motivation relate to religious property:

> 'Aggravated damage to property' (§126 StGB)
>
> A person who commits damage to property being an object dedicated to sacred service or religious worship of a church or religious community, or to a grave or other burial place, a tomb or a memorial located in a cemetery or in a place used for religious practice, is to be punished with imprisonment of up to two years or a fine of up to 360 daily rates; in the event that the action causes damage exceeding EUR 50,000, it is to be punished with imprisonment of between six months and five years. This provision – among others – also applies to public monuments or objects preserved for their historical or artistic value.
>
> 'Aggravated theft' (§128 StGB)
>
> A person who commits theft at a place used for religious worship or steals an object dedicated to sacred services or religious worship of a church or religious community is to be punished with imprisonment of up to three years. If the value of the stolen object exceeds EUR 50,000, the penalty may be more severe.

§3. Religious Titles, Garment and Emblems

565. As far as the protection of religious garment is concerned, the Austrian Concordat 1933 as well as the ProtestantenG 1961, the OrthodoxenG 1967 and the OrientKG 2003 refer to the legal provisions on the improper use and public vilification of military uniforms. The criminal offence of abusing a uniform was abolished by the Criminal Law Amendment Act 1934. This Act was abrogated on the basis of the Federal Act Repealing Obsolete Statutes 1999 without providing an alternative. Therefore, since then, reference can only be made to §35 Military Service Act, regulating the admissible wearing of uniforms of soldiers and militia, violation of which meets with an administrative fine of up to EUR 700 (§53). There are no rules on false impersonation of office with regard to clergy.

§4. Confessional Secret

566. Disclosure of a secret obtained in the exercise of the ministry does not constitute an offence under the Penal Code. Criminal Law, however, takes account of the confessional secret with regard to the 'Omission of preventing an action liable to prosecution'. Moreover, there are procedural rules providing for the protection of the confessional secret (cf. 528 et seq.).

§5. Position of Religious Communities in Penal Law

567. If a criminal offence against honour (§111 'Defamatory remark', §113 'Reproach for a criminal offence already served or remitted', §115 'Personal insult') is committed against a spiritual minister[266] of a church or religious community during the exercise of office or a sacred service, the public prosecutor must prosecute the perpetrator with the authorization of the injured person and the appropriate higher authority of the body in question. The same applies when an offence is committed against such spiritual ministers with regard to their professional actions in a printed form, on the radio or in any other way which renders them accessible to a broad public (§117 section 2 StGB). The definition of spiritual ministers is determined on the basis of the self-understanding of the church or religious community in question (cf. Article I §3 Concordat, §9 ProtestantenG, §3 OrthodoxenG).

§6. Disruption of a Funeral and Abuse of a Corpse or Desecration of a Sepulchre

568. A person who knowingly disrupts a funeral ceremony by noise impact or other behaviour calculated to commit nuisance is to be punished with imprisonment of up to three months or a fine of up to 180 daily rates (§191 StGB).

266. The same applies to state officials.

569. A person who takes a corpse or parts of it or the ashes of a deceased person from the custody of the person or authority entitled to dispose of them, removes a corpse or parts of it or the ashes of a deceased person from a burial or other resting place, or abuses or dishonours a corpse, the ashes of a deceased person or a burial, resting or memorial place is to be punished with imprisonment of up to six months or with a fine of up to 360 daily rates. A person who takes away jewellery from a burial, resting or memorial place is to be punished with imprisonment of up to three months or with a fine of up to 180 daily rates (§190). The object protected by these offences is the general feeling of piety towards the dead.

§7. Strengthening the Fight Against Religious Terrorism

570. In response to an Islamist terrorist attack in Vienna on 2 November 2020, the Counter-Terrorism Act 2021 (TeBG) was enacted, which therefore contains some of the problems characteristic of such measure legislation. Thus, regardless of the different manifestations of extremism, by restricting the law to a purely religious motivation, gives the impression that extremist ideas punishable under criminal law are an exclusively religiously motivated phenomenon. While the text of the law strives for neutral wording, it is clear from the Explanatory Notes that the provisions have only Islam in mind. The central political objective of the TeBG is explicitly stated as combating 'political Islam'.

571. The TeBG amended the Criminal Code as well as the Code of Criminal Procedure and the Prison Act. In §33 section 1 StGB, no. 5a was added as a further aggravating circumstance if the offender 'acted out of religiously motivated extremist motives'. §52b StGB introduced judicial supervision for 'anti-state and terrorist offences as well as genocide, crimes against humanity and war crimes' in the same way as for sex offenders. §247b StGB created the offence of 'religiously motivated extremist association'.

§8. Crimes Against International Law

572. The Austrian Penal Code contains crimes against international law implementing rules of the Convention on the Prevention and Punishment of the Crime of Genocide 1948:

'Genocide' (§321 StGB)

(1) Who with the intent to destroy a group as such in whole or in part, being characterized by affiliation to a church or religious community, race, nation, ethnic group or state, kills members of the group or causes serious bodily or mental harm to members of the group, inflicting on the group conditions of life calculated to bring about their physical destruction in whole or in part, imposes measures intended to prevent births within the

group, or forcibly or by threat of force transfer children of the group to another group, shall be punished with imprisonment for life.

(2) Who arranges the joint commitment of one of the offences specified in section 1 shall be punished with imprisonment of one to ten years.

573. Moreover, §321a ('Crimes against humanity') and §§321b to 321f StGB deal with war crimes.

§9. Female Genital Mutilation

574. According to §90 StGB, a physical injury or danger is not contrary to law if the injured or endangered person agrees to it in advance and the injury or danger as such does not contravene good morals (section 1). However, it is inadmissible to agree to genital mutilation or any other genital injury which causes a lasting impairment of sexual sensation (section 3). Female Genital Mutilation qualifies as a serious physical injury with serious continuing effects and is to be punished with imprisonment of between one and ten years (depending on the concrete circumstances of the case).[267]

§10. Cruelty to Animals

575. Who cruelly mistreats an animal, or inflicts unnecessary torture on it, is to be punished with imprisonment of up to one year or with a fine of up to 360 daily rates (§222 StGB). This offence must be considered with regard to ritual slaughtering, which is dealt with in Part II, 180 et seq.

267. B. Schinkele, 'Religionsfreiheit, Reichweite und Grenzen im Kontext religiös-kultureller Praktiken – unter besonderer Berücksichtigung von Female Genital Mutilation und Zirkumzision', in *Interkulturell kompetent. Ein Handbuch für Ärztinnen und Ärzte*, ed. M. Peintinger (Vienna: facultas.wuv 2011), 103–118.

Part VIII. Church Financing

576. As elsewhere in Europe, we can find in Austria an amalgam of sources of revenue.[268] These include membership contributions, voluntary grants, such as donations, inheritances, charity benefit contributions, income from estates and capital assets, profits from businesses and enterprises etc. As far as recognized churches and religious societies are concerned, there is a mixed system nowadays in Austria consisting of direct and automatic financing (grants by the state for social services and in the field of schooling), indirect financing (tax exemptions) and church membership contributions which churches can sue members for through state courts.

577. At the time of Emperor Joseph II, church financing was initially based on incomes from the Church itself as well as governmental grants. Essentially, this system existed until new legal provisions were introduced in 1939 by the national-socialist legislator. Thus the state gave subsidiary support to remuneration of the Catholic clergy known as Kongrua (based on minimum earnings, corresponding to position) by means of a religious fund. This fund has been created out of property originating from his closure of monasteries and from previous religious funds. Expenditure for the construction and maintenance of buildings was borne by the state in the form of 'public patronage'. The Protestant Church was granted 'Public Assistance Payments' according to §20 of the Protestants Patent 1861. The Israelite Religious Society benefited from the enforcement of obligations to be carried out as stipulated in §§19 and 22 of the IsraelitenG 1890. The Old-Catholic Church was given nominal annual support by the state for the first time in 1917 in the form of an assistance grant for remuneration of the clergy.

578. With the AnerkennungsG 1874, a system of membership contributions was introduced. §14 provides for the administrative enforcement of church levies.

579. The Act on Church-Contributions of 1 May 1939 and three implementing ordinances stipulated that the Catholic Church, the Protestant Church and the Old-Catholic Church had to raise funds from that time on by mandatory subscription. State grants were suspended and the property of the religious funds was transferred to the German state. After 1945, legislation on church-contributions fell under those

268. H. Kalb, 'The Financing of Religious Communities in Austria', in *The Financing of Religious Communities in the European Union*, ed. European Consortium of Church & State Resarch (Leuven et al.: Peeters, 2009), 87–96.

laws and statutory instruments which, in principle, remained in force on the basis of the Transitional Act of 1945 (cf. 66). This decision brought about a fundamental change in church funding in Austria.

580. An example illustrates the dimension of the incoming revenue: The global budget of the Austrian Catholic dioceses showed revenues of EUR 670.5 million in the year 2022. The majority of the proceeds came from church-contributions amounting to EUR 500 million (75%); in 2013, state compensation for Nazi damages (cf. 586) generated EUR 55.7 million (8.3%) and other sources yielded approximately EUR 114.8 million (17.1%). This income was used almost entirely to cover personnel expenses and material expenditure, in particular for building maintenance.

Chapter 1. Direct Financing of Religious Communities

§1. Protection of Property

581. Pursuant to Article 15 StGG, legally recognized churches and religious societies 'remain in possession of and continue to enjoy the fruits of their institutions, foundations and funds intended for the purpose of worship, education and welfare', and 'are, however, subject to the general laws of the state'. This guarantee is a specific application of the general fundamental guarantee for property in Article 5 StGG. Nevertheless, Article 6 section 2 StGG provides for the possibility that the state may legally impose limitations on acquisitions of real estate by ecclesiastical legal entities in favour of the public good ('amortization laws'). In the case of the Catholic Church, such 'amortization laws' were explicitly excluded by Article XIII Concordat 1933 (cf. 302), a fact which – due to the principle of parity – has consequences for other Churches and Religious Societies, too. Nowadays, however, amortization law no longer exists in Austria.

582. According to the unanimous opinion of the high courts and specialist literature, the independent administration of property constitutes an 'internal matter' with regard to churches and religious societies (cf. 268 et seq.). In connection with the relevant recognition procedure for gaining status as recognized churches or religious societies, one of the preconditions for recognition pursuant to §11 no. 2 BekGG is 'the use of income and assets for religious purposes' (cf. 230). This provision has also been included in §4 section 2 IslamG; however, the paraphrasing here is quite ambiguous. It needs to be interpreted according to the constitutional guarantees, and therefore can only refer, if at all, to the period prior to recognition. Otherwise, this would amount to interference with the 'internal affairs' of legally recognized churches and religious societies – in other words, a relapse back into the structures of the nineteenth century. This development was reinforced by the amendment to the IslamG 2021 (cf. 349).

§2. State Subsidies (Indemnifications)

583. In Austria, no general state funding exists for churches and religious communities. State payments to religious communities exist only on the basis of indemnity for financial losses caused during the Nazi occupation. According to Article 26 StVWien of 1955, Austria is obliged to indemnify those who have suffered financial losses resulting from Nazi legislation or destruction during the Nazi occupation. This obligatory compensation concerns the nationalization of Church funds and the cancellation of state grants to the Catholic Church, the Protestant Church, and the Old-Catholic Church as well as the pillage and destruction of cultural objects (synagogues, cemeteries, cultural objects, etc.) of the Israelite Religious Society (cf. 341). As far as the Austrian state budget is concerned, these financial obligations have lost their formal character as indemnification. Since 1967, payments based on Article 26

StVWien 1955 have no longer been listed as a separate budget item, but have been integrated into subsidies for cultural purposes, despite the fact that the legal title as indemnification still persists.

584. This obligation of the StVWien 1955 was implemented in the Agreement on the Regulation of Property Relationships of June 23, 1960 (Vermögensvertrag) with the Catholic Church (cf. 306), in §20 ProtestantenG (cf. 311), in §14 IsraelitenG 1890 as amended in 2012 (cf. 341) as well as in a separate law for the Old-Catholic Church. Since the Federal Law BGBl I 2020/166, the amounts are adjusted in the case of a permanent deflation of 20%, if necessary also retroactively. A permanent reduction in value is deemed to occur in the first of four consecutive months in which a reduction in value of 20% has been exceeded. The adjustment is to be announced by decree by the Federal Chancellor in agreement with the Federal Ministry of Finance.

585. A special problem was – and still is – posed by the rights of the Israelite Religious Society and its institutions to restitution and indemnity, since the necessary proof required by law is often difficult to furnish and implementation of these laws has repeatedly been delayed by state authorities. The second Reserve Rights Act 1951[269] gave the Israelite Religious Society the right to raise claims by legal persons who had served in religious, cultural, welfare or social fields, including those of Jewish foundations and funds. Finally, the Federal State (Bund) established a general compensation fund for Jewish property which had been confiscated or destroyed during the Nazi period, which can also serve as a basis for claims by cultus-communities and other Jewish institutions according to the Compensation Funds Act 2001.[270]

§3. Church-Contributions

586. According to the Act on Church-Contributions (KBG) of 1 May 1939, church-contributions are qualified as membership fees under private law, a fact which, in principle, contradicts the public law status of legally recognized churches. Furthermore, it is constitutionally not unobjectionable in view of the concessions regarding administrative enforcement laid down in the AnerkennungsG 1874, the IsraelitenG 1890 and the IslamG 2015.

587. According to §1 KBG, the Catholic Church, the Protestant Church and the Old-Catholic Church are entitled to levy church-contributions pursuant to an internal ordinance on church-contributions (Kirchenbeitragsordnung, KBO) which has

269. Bundesgesetz vom 11. Juli 1951 über die Übertragung der Ansprüche auf Rückstellung von Vermögen einiger juristischer Personen, die ihre Rechtspersönlichkeit während der deutschen Besetzung Österreichs verloren und später nicht wiedererlangt haben (2. Rückstellungsanspruchsgesetz), BGBl. 1951/176.

270. Bundesgesetz über die Einrichtung eines Allgemeinen Entschädigungsfonds für Opfer des Nationalsozialismus und über Restitutionsmaßnahmen (Entschädigungsfondsgesetz), BGBl. I 2001/12 as amended BGBl. I 2002/114.

been adopted by the church to cover their personnel expenses and material expenditure. §1 KBG does not constitute a commitment on the part of the state to collect church-contributions since the right to levy contributions is part of the right to self-determination enshrined in Article 15 StGG.[271] Compliance with the standards of the KBG is only the *conditio sine qua non* for making use of state assistance in asserting the right to obtain contributions through court action as laid down in §3 section 1 KBG.

588. Adult members are obliged to pay church-contributions (§2 section 1). Obligation to contribute consists, regardless of whether members avail themselves of the services offered by the churches or not. Liability for contribution ends with departure from the respective church or by death. In the case of withdrawal (cf. 156) from church membership the obligation ends three months after the first of the following month. The churches, however, make no use of their option to claim church-contributions for this period.

589. Church access to state-registered data has become an increasingly less important factor. According to the amendment of the Registration Act (MeldeG) 1991, mayors are obliged to transfer the registration data of residents in their municipality who are declared members of a legally recognized church or religious society (cf. 504).

590. Assessment of financial requirements for material and staff is an internal matter for legally recognized churches or religious societies. Responsibility for assessment and collection of church-contributions, therefore, lies with the churches (§3 section 1 KBG). These activities are classified as non-state administrative and 'internal affairs' under Article 15 StGG. The internal 'ordinances on contributions' issued by the three churches are not ordinances in the sense of state law and therefore, not subject to review by the Constitutional Court. These 'ordinances on contributions' must include the principles on which church-contributions are determined, especially the preconditions for members' obligation to pay these contributions and the criteria for calculating the amount due. Furthermore, the administrative facilities employed in the assessment and collection of contributions and the ecclesiastical organs responsible for extrajudicial and judicial representation in matters of church-contributions must be indicated.

591. According to §3 section 2 KBG, church regulations and decisions about the level of church-contributions are subject to state supervisory approval by the competent Federal Ministry. This administrative act is the precondition for the enforceability of outstanding church-contributions with state courts. In this context, it must be emphasized that setting and collecting church-contributions is primarily an 'internal affair'. A legal provision which grants state support for enforcing the collection of outstanding church-contributions as such, however, does not interfere with the internal affairs of churches. It is up to the churches whether they make use

271. VfSlg. 3657/1959.

of state assistance or not. If a church takes advantage of state jurisdiction, church-contributions matters no longer constitute an 'internal affair', but thereby become an 'external affair' of the respective church.[272]

592. The contribution rate of the Catholic Church and the Old-Catholic Church amounts to 1.1% and that of the Protestant Church 1.5% of taxable income, after deduction of tax exemptions.

§4. CULTUS-CONTRIBUTIONS

593. Based on the AnerkennungsG 1874, other recognized churches and religious societies are entitled to levy a cultus-contribution for which they have access to administrative enforcement in keeping with their status as legal entities under public law.

594. §15 IsraelitenG provides for the issuing of a 'cultus-contribution regulation' (Kultusumlagenordnung). According to §103 of the Statute of the Israelite Cultus-Community in Vienna, the cultus-contribution amounts to 1% of income before deduction of tax exemptions; this equals a minimum of EUR 120 and a maximum of EUR 10,000. The possibility of administrative enforcement is provided for by law, but the Israelite Religious Society currently rarely makes use of this instrument.

595. §23 IslamG 2015 provides for a 'cultus-contribution regulation' (*Kultusumlagenordnung*). According to §4, every member of the Islamic Religious Society of Austria has to pay an annual fee of a maximum of EUR 60. The possibility of administrative enforcement is provided for by law but the Islamic Religious Society makes no use of this instrument at the present time.

596. As far as the Eastern-Orthodox Church is concerned, according to §7 section 3 OrthodoxenG §7 section 3 OrthodoxenG, the regulation of state support in the enforcement of membership contributions has been reserved to a special legal act, which, however, has never been enacted. It must be assumed that the Oriental-Orthodox Churches (the Armenian-Orthodox Church, the Syrian-Orthodox Church and the Coptic-Orthodox Church) also have access to administrative enforcement for collecting contributions levied according to internal rules, regardless of the misleading or even incorrect paraphrasing in the Explanatory Remarks to the OrientKG 2003. At present, no church or religious society recognized under the AnerkennungsG 1874 takes advantage of the possibility of administrative enforcement by the state.

272. VfSlg. 3816/1960; VwSlg. 7188 A/1967; OGH 14 May 1958, 2 Ob 143/58; OGH 27 Aug. 1952, 3 Ob 509/52.

§5. ADDITIONAL STATE SUBSIDIES

597. Additional state subsidies are granted either directly – primarily for specific religious activities in the field of education and pastoral care in public institutions (cf. 739 et seq.) – or indirectly, mainly in tax laws.

I. Religious Instruction

598. In compulsory schools, secondary high schools, teaching colleges, agricultural colleges and colleges of forestry, religious instruction according to denomination is a compulsory subject for all pupils who are members of a legally recognized church or religious society. However, students have the possibility of opting out. These religious education classes are totally financed by the state (cf. 630).

II. Denominational Private Schools

599. Only schools operated by these religious communities are granted subsidies towards the costs of teaching personnel in denominational private schools with public status, so-called living subsidies, or, if this is not possible, by transfer of an equivalent sum of money. No legal entity other than a legally recognized church or religious society has a legal claim to be granted state subsidies; however, provision for staff expenditure is a matter for the discretion of the Federal Minister. This differential treatment seems to be unconstitutional on the grounds that it infringes on the principle of equality and the right to non-discrimination (cf. 668).

III. Theological Studies

600. The continuous existence of the four Faculties of Catholic Theology at the Universities of Vienna, Graz, Innsbruck and Salzburg as well as the Faculty of Protestant Theology in Vienna which are financed by the state, is guaranteed (cf. 687 and 691). Likewise, regular funding for the study of Islamic theology in accordance with the IslamG 2015 (cf. 692 et seq.).

IV. Chaplaincy

601. The financing of personnel expenses and material expenditure for chaplaincies in the armed forces is regularly stipulated in the special laws (cf. 751 et seq.). In fact, up to now the wages and expenditures are fully state-financed only for the Catholic Church and the Protestant Church. As regards other churches and religious societies, only agreements without institutional embedding and only a small reimbursement for expenditures have so far been provided (see, e.g., for the Orthodox Military Chaplaincy, cf. 754).

602. Apart from occasional minimal personal subsidies on the basis of regional provisions, pastoral care in healthcare institutions is not financed by the state. However, a certain degree of infrastructure is provided.

603. With respect to Roman Catholic pastoral care in prisons, provisions have been made for a small number of official positions for pastoral advisers, who are engaged on an employment contract basis and financed by the state. According to an agreement dating from 2002, the Evangelical Church receives a small subsidy; the number of persons sent by the church is not determined.[273] A more or less identical agreement regarding pastoral care in prisons was reached with the Islamic Religious Society in Austria in 2010.[274]

§6. State-Registered Religious Denominational Communities

604. State-registered religious denominational communities – legal entities under private law – are financed by donations and legacies, etc. The Austrian legal system, which focuses on legally recognized churches and religious societies, does not take other religious communities into account. This fact presents a challenge for future legislation (e.g., identification of ecclesiastical aims with those of recognized churches and religious societies in tax laws).

§7. Foreign Financing of Normal Activities

605. §6 section 2 IslamG stipulates that the financial means for normal activities aimed at satisfying the religious needs of its members must be obtained by the Religious Society, its worship communities or its members from within the country (cf. 355). This provision has led to heated discussions on the draft bill and has also drawn remarkable attention internationally. In the Explanatory Remarks, it was considered – for the first time and not undisputed – that prohibition of core funding from abroad was implicitly included in §5 AnerkennungsG 1874. This provision stipulates that recognition is based on evidence that sufficient funds are available or can be applied in a legally permitted manner to secure the necessary liturgical facilities and the upkeep of the regular religious minister.

273. Agreement between the Republic of Austria and the Protestant Church in Austria of 2002 as amended 23 Mar. 2009.

274. Agreement between the Republic of Austria and Islamic Religious Society in Austria, BMJ-VD53101/0005-VD 2/2010 of 18 Mar. 2010.

Chapter 2. Indirect Financing of Religious Communities

§1. Reimbursement of Activities in the Social Field

606. Church activities in the field of social assistance and healthcare, education and culture, though hardly ascertainable, represent a significant instrument for legitimating their status. Primary statistical data for this non-profit sector is not available. Although the expenditures or welfare services rendered by churches are reimbursed by public funds to a great extent, this form of 'contracting out' actually saves the state money in this sector, because it would be more expensive to run such institutions.

§2. Tax Law

607. The provisions of tax law which are relevant to religious communities are, on the one hand, based on the consequences in revenue law resulting from the public law status of legally recognized churches and religious societies, hence mainly in regard to corporate income tax liability and value added tax liability. On the other hand, Austrian tax law provides for benefits, i.e., reductions or exemptions for corporations which pursue 'ecclesiastical aims' in addition to those with public utility or charitable purposes. According to §38 section 1 Federal Revenue Act 1961 (BAO) 'ecclesiastical aims' are those aims which help to promote legally recognized churches and religious societies. As a consequence, state-registered religious denominational communities are granted tax benefits for welfare and charitable purposes but not, however, for religious purposes in a stricter sense. §34 section 2 contains a representative list of such 'ecclesiastical purposes' which must be met if a tax law, in connection with preferential treatment of private law corporations, associations and assets refers, *inter alia*, to religious purposes:

> Ecclesiastical purposes include in particular the establishment, maintenance and decoration of buildings of worship and parish houses, the holding of religious services, prayers and other religious or pastoral events, the training of religious ministers, religious education classes, funerals and religious commemoration of the dead, furthermore, the administration of church property, remuneration of the clergy and church employees, provision for their old age and invalidity, care of their widows and orphans including the establishment and maintenance of special facilities for this group (§38 section 2 BAO).To obtain these benefits, the statutes of the corporations concerned must expressly and precisely describe the exclusive and immediate activities involved in such 'ecclesiastical purposes'.

608. The unequal treatment of both categories of religious communities in the area of tax law as outlined before, seems problematic because of its discriminatory character. The administrative and judicial practice does not allow to subsume 'religious purposes' of state-registered religious denominational communities under 'non-profitable and charitable purposes'. This constitutes discrimination as far as the innermost activities of religious communities are concerned. Adequate consideration of those religious communities remains an urgent legislative challenge within law on religion.

609. Contributions to legally recognized churches and religious societies are tax deductible up to an annual amount of EUR 400 as special payments.

Part IX. Education

610. The Austrian school system[275] must be seen as a structural unity, as described in §3 section 1 of the Act on School-Organization (SchOG). From the age of six, each child has to go to primary school (Volksschule) for four years. As far as secondary education is concerned, there is a choice between (junior) high school (Gymnasium/Unterstufe) and secondary elementary school (Mittelschule). Beginning with the school year 2008/09, a school experiment concerning a form of common secondary education for pupils from the age of 10 to 14 has been carried out (the so-called Neue Mittelschule). Since 2011-2012, this school type has successively been incorporated into the regular school system. After the age of 14, a further streaming of pupils takes place; they may choose between (secondary) high school (Gymnasium/Oberstufe), secondary vocational school or one year of 'polytechnic training' (polytechnischer Lehrgang). After this course, their compulsory education is completed. The Gymnasium takes another four years (eight altogether), while secondary vocational schools usually take five years. Both courses of education end with a final examination (Reifeprüfung) which entitles students to university entrance. Students on vocational apprenticeships have to attend the so-called Berufsschule for a certain number of weeks.

275. *See* F. Jonak & L. Kövesi, *Das österreichische Schulrecht*, 13th ed. (Vienna: Österreichischer Bundesverlag, 2012).

Chapter 1. General Principles of Public Education

611. Although compulsory schooling was introduced by the state in 1774, the Catholic Church remained responsible for public education until the end of the neo-absolutist era in the 1860s. Then the state educational system was secularized and a system of interconfessional schooling was established, which was constitutionally laid down in Article 17 StGG and set out in detail in the Act Concerning the Relationship between Church and Schools 1868 (cf. 41).

612. Pursuant to Article 17 section 2 StGG the establishment and management of private schools and other educational institutions is guaranteed provided the legal qualifications can be assured. The right of parents to educate their children privately at home without their attendance at school is guaranteed in section 3. Section 4 stipulates that the respective churches or religious societies are responsible for the teaching of religious education in schools. The entire educational and schooling system is subject to the supreme control and supervision of the state (section 5).

613. Similar to the whole ECHR, Article 2 of the 1st Additional Protocol has constitutional status in Austria. This guarantee must always be understood in conjunction with the right of children to education and must be perceived in the light of Article 9 ECHR.[276] The obligation of the state to respect the right of parents to a form of education and teaching in conformity with their own religious and philosophical convictions does not imply that the state has a duty to establish a form of education which is fully in accordance with the religious and philosophical convictions of the parents. An objective and pluralistic educational (system), free from indoctrination, is required. This is a central guarantee from the perspective of a pluralistic conception of the state-church relationship.[277]

614. With regard to the Austrian federal system and the fact that the substantive bases of the public educational system have always been an ideological issue between the main political groups in Austria, the structures of competence in the public education administration are quite complex. The main powers lie with the Bund, whereby since the B-VG 1920, federal legislation on schooling has been made subject to the requirement of a two-thirds majority with fifty per cent of the Members of Parliament present. In 2005 a relevant B-VG amendment was issued in order to make this field of law more flexible. Henceforth, these prerequisites have been restricted to some subject matters deemed to be of paramount significance, among which are 'affairs concerning state-church relations' including religious school instruction. This regulation is in need of interpretation: on the one hand, private schools are no longer explicitly mentioned, and on the other, matters concerning denominational private schools (*konfessionelle Privatschulen*) are to be reasonably subsumed under 'affairs concerning state-church relations'. This wording suggests that the qualified quorum

276. Established case law of the ECtHR, cf., e.g., *Lautsi v. Italy* (Grand Chamber), 18 Mar. 2011, appl. no. 30814/06.

277. *See* ECtHR, *Kjeldsen and other v. Denmark*, 7 Dec. 1976, appl. no. 5920/71.

requirement should still be applied to the special regulations concerning private denominational schools. The Explanatory Remarks may also be understood to favour such a construction.

615. According to §2 section 1 of the Act on School-Organization (SchOG), the aim of Austrian schooling is to further the development of young people's aptitudes as regards religious values – among other things – by way of appropriate instruction. The inclusion of religious values in a legal provision describing the aims of education is based on the objective of making education comprehensive, giving a choice to persons open to religious education and development.

616. In 2005, the main objectives of Austrian schooling were incorporated into the Constitution.[278] By this implementation, tolerance as a legal term found its way into the Constitution for the first time. According to Article 14 section 5a B-VG, democracy, humanity, solidarity, peace and justice, as well as broadmindedness and tolerance towards all people are fundamental values for schools, and should serve as a basis for guaranteeing the highest standards of education in continuous development for the entire population, irrespective of birth, social or financial background. With regard to these criteria as an adequate substratum, young people should learn to take responsibility for themselves, for others, the environment and the following generations, with a firm basis of social, religious and moral values. The article explicitly stresses that each pupil should be guided towards social comprehension and broadmindedness with regard to the political, religious and philosophical convictions of others. The inclusion of religious values is designed as an offer for persons who are open to religious education within a comprehensive school education.

617. In addition, a legal definition of the term 'school' was implemented in this constitutional amendment, following the case law of the Constitutional Court.[279] Accordingly, besides imparting general and/or vocational knowledge and skills, a comprehensive educational concept is an essential mandatory characteristic of any institution qualified as a school.

618. As far as the fundamental right of parents to educate their children privately at home without their attending school is concerned (Article 17 section 3 StGG), the requirements of compulsory schooling are only considered to be met pursuant to §11 Act on Compulsory Schooling (SchPflG), if home education has the same quality as that of public schools or private schools with public status, though any state influence on the structure of home instruction is excluded. The success of homeschooling has to be validated by taking an examination at an appropriate public school every year. Parents need not give any reasons for their decision to instruct their children at home; therefore, it is not possible to determine the share of religiously motivated homeschooling cases, all the more so as no official nationwide statistics exist.[280]

---

278. BGBl. I 2005/31.
279. VfSlg. 4290/1962.
280. S. Hammer & J. Franck, 'Religion in Public Education – Report on Austria', in *Religion in Public Education*, ed. European Consortium of Church & State Resarch (Trier 2011), 61 et seq.

Chapter 2. Kindergartens

619. A kindergarten is an institution which has the task of supporting the family education of children from the age of three until they reach the age of compulsory schooling. Since regulations on kindergartens fall under the competence of the Bundesländer (Article 14 section 4 lit. b B-VG), each Bundesland has its own law concerning kindergartens. Austrian children are obliged to attend a kindergarten one year before entering school, but they usually go to kindergarten from the age of 3 to 6 years.

620. Though the individual laws differ somewhat in detail, the objectives of education in kindergartens are very similar in each Bundesland. On the one hand, the respective laws, in general, refer to a form of education which takes the social, ethical and religious aspects into consideration. In Lower Austria, it is cited that one responsibility of the kindergarten is to provide a fundamental contribution to religious and ethical education.[281] On the other hand, religious instruction is explicitly foreseen,[282] following the example of the school system. Moreover, the exhibition of a cross is legally envisaged, with minor differences.[283] The Constitutional Court[284] had to deal with this issue of crosses in kindergartens (cf. 657) on the occasion of an application concerning a crucifix in a Lower Austrian kindergarten.

621. In 2009, on the basis of Article 15a B-VG, an agreement concerning the introduction of a half-day,cost-free and compulsory form of support in institutional child-care facilities was concluded between the Bund and the Bundesländer (so-called 15a-Vereinbarung).[285]

622. Mostly, the respective laws refer to a form of education which takes social, ethical and religious aspects into consideration (cf. 623).

623. Public kindergartens are established and maintained by the municipality of the Bundesland. Analogous to the regulations for public schools, public kindergartens are generally open to children without distinction of birth, sex, race, status, class, language or religion (Article 14 section 6 B-VG).

624. Private kindergartens are those which are not established and maintained by the municipalities and the Bundesländer. Private kindergartens can limit the admission to children of a certain language, a certain confession, etc. In practice, churches and religious societies are important providers of private kindergartens,

---

281. § 3 section 1 Lower Austrian Kindergarten Act (NÖKindergartenG 2006).
282. § 29 NÖKindergartenG.
283. *See, e.g.*, § 12 section 2 NÖKindergartenG.
284. VfSlg. 19349/2011; *see* R. Potz & B. Schinkele, 'Gutachten zu den religionsrechtlichen Aspekten des Niederösterreichischen Kindergartengesetzes', *Österreichisches Archiv für Recht und Religion* 57 (2010), 395–412.
285. BGBl. I 2009/99.

and in the meantime, in addition to kindergartens run by the Catholic Church and the Protestant Church, a large number of kindergartens also exist with Islamic providers.

625. In 2019, an agreement between the Federal government and the Bundesländer on the elementary sector stipulated that children in elementary educational institutions (kindergartens) may not wear ideological or religious clothing that includes a head covering. Following the abolition of the parallel prohibition in elementary schools by the VfGH (cf. 657), the follow-up agreement from 2022 no longer contains this provision, particularly at the insistence of the Federal States.

Chapter 3. Religious Education in Public and Private Schools

626. On the basis of a separation between state and church, public schooling belongs to those fields which are characterized in Austria by a productive interaction, each part taking care of its genuine tasks and responsibilities. In this area, core matters of the state's sovereignty are not at issue, and thus the denominational neutrality of the state must be carried out in a way that integrates religion and belief, however, without the state identifying with any confession, the so-called inclusive neutrality (cf. 100 et seq.).

§1. Constitutional Basics

627. Religious instruction is guaranteed by Article 17 section 4 StGG which provides that the respective churches or religious communities are responsible for classes in religious instruction in school.[286] Viewed systematically, religious instruction must be seen in relation to the fundamental right of religious freedom and the guarantees in Article 2 of the 1st Additional Protocol ECHR, with regard to the pupils as well as the parents, on the one hand, and the organizational religious freedom of the religious communities on the other.

628. However, owing to historical reasons, religious instruction in schools is restricted to legally recognized churches and religious societies. Nowadays, such a concept must be questioned, with respect to the perspective of the rights of the individual as well as corporate rights. Against this background, religious education in schools has been strongly criticized for granting privileges to legally recognized churches and religious societies, occasionally in connection with a call for abolition. However, this conception should not primarily be qualified as a privilege of the legally recognized religious communities but rather as a form of discrimination against the other religious communities and their adherents, respectively. It seems to be an infringement of the right to non-discrimination according to Article 14 ECHR since there are no reasonable grounds for justifying this differential treatment. In view of the systematic justification of religious education classes with regard to religious freedom and parental rights, it is on the one hand constitutionally problematic to connect the right to give religious instruction with the fact of legal recognition. On the other hand, one has to ask whether, in such an important area as the public school system, the willingness of the recognized churches and religious societies to cooperate with the state can be required. The 'institutionalised constitutional expectation of the state' which is expressed in the act of recognition should in fact imply an obligation to give religious instruction.

286. Cf. the contributions in A. Rinnerthaler (ed.), *Historische und rechtliche Aspekte des Religionsunterrichts* (Frankfurt am Main et al.: Peter Lang, 2004).

§2. The Concept of Religious Instruction

629. Currently, religious instruction is governed by the Act on Religious Education at School of 1949 (RelUG).[287] According to §1 RelUG, all pupils who are members of a legally recognized church or religious community must take religious instruction in their denomination as a compulsory subject in primary and secondary schools, colleges of education, academies for social work, teacher training colleges, agricultural colleges and colleges of forestry. At other schools, religious instruction is an optional subject which means that pupils have to state at the beginning of the school year if they wish to attend religious instruction classes.

630. These regulations apply to public schools and private schools with public status, thus also to schools run by operators with other religious or philosophical orientations, as well as to schools operated by state-registered religious denominational communities.

631. For pupils who belong to a recognized church or religious society, religious instruction is compulsory, but opting out is possible. In this case, instruction in ethics is compulsory (cf. 643). Pupils under the age of 14 may withdraw from religious education if their parents make a written request to that effect during the first five days of every school year. Pupils older than 14 may apply for withdrawal in their own writing. Opting out during the school year is only allowed if the pupil leaves the respective religious community.

632. The curricula for religious education as part of the 'internal affairs' are adopted by the churches and religious societies; the Ministry of Education must be informed and must publish them in the Federal Law Gazette (Bundesgesetzblatt), though this is merely of declaratory significance. State approval is not necessary. One restriction is the requirement that only such books and teaching materials may be used as are not in conflict with the aim of educating responsible citizens (§3 section 2 RelUG). The state is neither authorized to prohibit ecumenical cooperation between churches nor to promote such activities.

633. Textbooks for religious instruction classes are included in the school book programme according to the Act on Equalization of Family Burdens 1967 (FamLAG) and are financed by the state.

---

287. G. Luf, 'Religionsunterricht – Ein Privileg der Kirchen?', in *Ex Aeqo et Bono. Festschrift für Willibald M. Plöchl*, ed. P. Leisching et al. (Innsbruck: Wagner, 1977), 457–472; K. Schwarz, 'Der Religionsunterricht in der Schule – eine 'gemeinsame Angelegenheit' von Staat und Kirche zur Gewährleistung religiöser Interessen in der Gesellschaft', *Schulfach Religion* 21 (2002), 225–242; K. Pabel, 'Verfassungsrechtliche Rahmenbedingungen des Religionsunterrichts in Österreich', *Österreichisches Archiv für Recht und Religion* 59 (2012), 64–86; B. Schinkele, 'Religions- und Ethikunterricht in der pluralistischen Gesellschaft – Überlegungen aus religionsrechtlicher Sicht', *Österreichisches Archiv für Recht und Religion* 58 (2011), 13–24.

634. Principally, members of legally recognized churches or religious societies are not allowed to attend religious instruction classes of another confession.[288] Pupils who belong to no confession or who are members of state-registered religious communities or any other religious communities may take part in confessional religious instruction of a legally recognized church or religious society, provided the respective teacher of religious instruction has agreed. For these pupils, religious instruction is an optional subject which is mentioned as such in the school reports, but without being graded (assessed). Under exceptional circumstances, pupils who are not members of the respective confession can be admitted to the final exam in religious instruction.[289]

635. According to §3 section 2 of the Executive Ordinance Concerning School Report Forms[290] an entry is made in both the annual and the half-term school report concerning the pupil's membership in a legally recognized church or religious society and – as an innovation – in a state-registered religious denominational community as well.

636. Before the determination or change of the weekly number of lessons in religious instruction, the state must consult the religious community concerned. The mandatory standard of two lessons of religious instruction per week may be reduced in relation to the number of pupils attending. If less than three pupils participate in religious instruction, lessons are only offered if the church or religious society pays for the teachers. If less than half of the pupils in a class attend religious instruction of one confession, it is possible to form a class combining pupils from other classes or schools, as long as this appears practical with regard to the requirements of school organization and religious instruction (§7a section 1 RelUG).

637. The organization, implementation and direct control of religious education classes is the responsibility of the respective church or religious community. The state has the right to supervise religious instruction in organizational and disciplinary matters by means of its school supervisory bodies (§2 section 2 RelUG). Therefore, it is the religious community and not the state, which organizes religious instruction classes, despite the fact that religious instruction as a compulsory subject enjoys equal standing with other subjects.

638. With respect to the Catholic Church, specific regulations apply in the Schulvertrag 1962, replacing the respective part on schooling in the Concordat 1933 (cf. 649 and 653). Apart from several rather marginal deviations, the specific regulations correspond with the general legal rulings.

639. Since the introduction of Islamic religious instruction in Austrian public schools in 1983 the school administration has been faced with several problems,

288. *See* GZ BMBWK-10.014/2-III/3/2007, Rundschreiben no. 9/2006.
289. Implementing ordinance, BMUKK GZ 10.014/2-III/3/2007.
290. Zeugnisformularverordnung, BGBl. 1989/415, as amended BGBl. II 1999/320.

though the system works well on the whole. In 1998 the Islamic Religious Pedagogical Academy, established according to the regulations for pedagogical academies under the Austrian Private School Act (PrivSchG) was founded. This was effected in the interests of the Islamic community and the Austrian school administration. Meanwhile, the legal foundation of this Academy has been changed according to the Federal Act on the Organization of the Pedagogical Colleges and their Studies of 2005 (HochschulG). In the academic year 2006/2007 the research department of 'Islamic Religious Pedagogy' was established at the University of Vienna and in 2013 at the University of Innsbruck. Its main task is the instruction of teachers of religious education in secondary high schools (cf. 368).

§3. Ethics Instruction

640. After a twenty-year-long school experimental phase, ethics lessons were transferred into the regular system in the 2020/2021 school year by the SchOG amendment, BGBl I 2020/133. This provides for ethics to be a compulsory subject with two lessons per week from the 9th school level for those pupils who do not take part in religious education (§39 section 1 SchOG). According to the Explanatory Notes ethics lessons should enable pupils to reflect independently on ways to shape their lives successfully, provide them with guidance and lead them to a well-founded examination of the fundamental questions of life. By exploring different philosophical, ideological, cultural and religious traditions and concepts of humanity, ethics lessons should contribute to individual personal development.

641. According to §43 section 3 SchOG, the compulsory subject of ethics is to be taught at the same time as the religious education of the legally recognized church or religious society to which the highest number of pupils in the school belong.

642. Since the 2021/22 academic year, the universities of Vienna, Innsbruck, Graz, Salzburg, Klagenfurt and the Catholic Private University of Linz offer a teacher training course in ethics and the universities of Vienna and Graz offer master's degree courses in ethics (120 ECTS credits).

§4. Teachers of Religious Instruction

643. Teachers of religious instruction in state schools are employed either by the state (Bund, Bundesländer) or by churches and religious societies.[291] Although teachers employed by the religious community have no employment contract with the state, they are paid by the Bund or the Bundesländer (§6 RelUG).

291. B. Schinkele, 'Zur Rechtsstellung kirchlich bestellter Religionslehrer unter besonderer Berücksichtigung der katholischen Kirche', in *Arbeitsrecht und Kirche. Zur arbeitsrechtlichen und sozialrechtlichen Stellung von Klerikern, Ordensangehörigen und kirchlichen Mitarbeitern in Österreich*, ed. U. Runggaldier & B. Schinkele (Vienna & New York: Springer, 1996), 121–141.

644. Only qualified persons who have been approved by the competent authority or the respective church or religious society may be appointed as teachers of religious instruction (§3 RelUG), by the so-called missio canonica with regard to the Catholic Church and the 'vocatio' with regard to the Protestant Church. Should the authorization of the church or religious community be withdrawn, the teacher may no longer be employed as a teacher in religious education classes (§6 RelUG). For teachers employed by a church or religious community, withdrawal constitutes a reason for termination of employment. The same applies to state-employed teachers; however, it is up to the responsible body, in the case of agreement, to entrust him or her otherwise with a state function.

645. The decision to grant, deny or withdraw confessional authorization is covered by the fundamental right of self-determination of the respective religious community. Relevant questions constitute a quite sensitive field in state-church relationships. No justification for withdrawal of authorization is legally demanded of the confessional authority, which seems to be in conflict with the principle of due course of law. Thus, it is the task of the church or religious society to ensure at least a minimum of legal standards.[292] The state courts may exert control as far as the examination (verification) of concrete facts is concerned, or if an arbitrary decision or a decision contrary to good morals or the ordre public is at issue.

646. As regards this issue, there is a specific regulation in the Schulvertrag (cf. 293), in so far as the teacher concerned must be transferred (moved) to another state occupation, must retire or his employment must be terminated.

647. The teachers of both categories are obliged to adhere to the curriculum and to follow the instructions and precepts of the respective church or religious community. Control of religious education classes is exerted by school inspectors who are appointed by the church or religious society and a certain number are paid by the state (§7c RelUG). Apart from this, all teachers of religious instruction are subject to the general rules of state school law.

648. Teachers employed by a legally recognized church or religious society are subject to the respective disciplinary authority according to internal ecclesiastical law, and not to the school supervisory authority. The administration in public schools is not entitled to impose disciplinary measures on them. According to the Constitutional Court,[293] the public school administration can only inform the respective confessional school authority of any infringements of school rules. It would be at the discretion of the respective church or religious community to take

292. Cf., e.g., Framework Regulations for the Religious Instructors of the Austrian Dioceses (Rahmenordnung für Religionslehrer der österreichischen Diözesen [c. 804 CIC]), Amtsblatt der Österreichischen Bischofskonferenz 1996/17/II.2, 8–10.
293. VfSlg. 2507/1953.

disciplinary sanctions with respect to such teachers. However, state school authorities could ban a teacher from classes, if necessary, in order to maintain general school discipline and a controlled process of instruction.[294]

649. According to §2a RelUG, pupils and teachers are free to participate in services and ceremonies, usually organized by legally recognized churches or religious communities for special religious or state occasions, particularly at the beginning and the end of the school year. The same applies to other religious exercises and events. Pupils who would like to join in such activities are granted permission for absence from lessons 'to the previous extent'. This wording correlates with a respective provision in the school treaty with the Holy See, thus implying that any reduction of this level would presuppose the assent of the Catholic Church.

294. In 2009, in an agreement with the Federal Minister of Education regarding Islamic teachers of religious education the Islamic Religious Society in Austria committed itself to immediately revoke the teaching authorization of any teacher who evidently distances himself or herself from democratic values or human rights, cf. http://www.ots.at/presseaussendung/OTS_20090202_OTS0193/bm-schmied-vereinbart-mit-der-islamischen-glaubensgemeinschaft-massnahmenpaket-fuer-den-islamischen-religionsunterricht [17. 3. 2015].

Chapter 4. Special Issues

§1. Exhibition of Crosses in Classrooms

650. In all public schools and those schools with equal status, in which religious instruction is a compulsory subject, the school operators are obliged to exhibit a cross in each school classroom, presupposing the majority of the pupils of the school belong to a Christian denomination (§2b section 1 RelUG). According to the Concluding Protocol of the Schulvertrag 1962 (cf. 293), any changes to this regulation require the consent of the Holy See.

651. From the perspective of positive religious freedom, a cross (crucifix) or other religious symbols in schools might be interpreted as an 'offer' for those pupils who adhere to the respective religion, and additionally, as a concretization of their parents' right under Article 2 of the 1st Additional Protocol ECHR to have their religious convictions respected in state schooling.[295] Though the cross is primarily a religious symbol, the character of its cultural form must not be completely disregarded. In the specific historical context in Austria, the fact should not altogether be ignored that crosses in classrooms have been exhibited per consuetudine for a long time and were removed in the Nazi era under protest by some parents.[296] In general, the cross as a religious, namely Christian, symbol is open to the interpretation of the beholder and is therefore to a certain degree a symbol of varying content.

652. For pupils who are not adherents of the respective religion or who have no religious confession, a religious symbol in classrooms may usually be considered to have only extremely marginal interference with their negative freedom of religion. In potentially specifically embarrassing cases, an appropriate solution should be found by careful consideration of the conflicting interests.

653. With respect to state neutrality in religious matters, a certain tension may still remain, even within the concept of 'inclusive neutrality' (cf. 100 et seq.). Taking this perspective into account, Austrian legal regulations in this respect seem to be in need of improvement. The legal possibility should exist for both school and kindergarten governors to make decisions deviating from general regulations, considering all the facts and circumstances of individual cases. Moreover, bearing in mind the aspect of non-discrimination, the exhibition of symbols of other religions should also be considered.[297] Acceptance of different religious symbols in classrooms would have a favourable effect on the development of a tolerant attitude towards other confessions, one of the explicitly mentioned objectives of public education in the Austrian Constitution (cf. 619). Finally, the majority criterion seems,

---

295. H. Kalb, R. Potz & B. Schinkele, *Das Kreuz in Klassenzimmer und Gerichtssaal* (Freistadt: Verlag Plöchl, 1992), 67; *see also* vol. 3 of *Österreichisches Archiv für Recht und Religion* 57 (2010), which deals with the topic *Schulkreuze in österreichischer und europäischer Perspektive*, 353–524.
296. *See* H. Engelbrecht, *Die Geschichte des österreichischen Bildungswesens*, vol. 5 (Vienna: Österreichischer Bundesverlag, 1988), 414.
297. Cf. § 6 Act on Education and Care for Children of Styria 1999, LGBl. 22/2000, as amended LGBl. 88/2014.

in general, to be inadequate in matters of fundamental rights. Beyond this, the regulation in question is problematic insofar as the number of Christian pupils in a school is the relevant factor as opposed to the number in a particular class.

654. For the first time, the Constitutional Court[298] had to deal with this issue on the occasion of an application concerning a crucifix in a Lower Austrian kindergarten (cf. 623 et seq.).[299] The Court considered the provision concerned to be in compliance with the Constitution, as regards fundamental rights as well as the state's neutrality in religious matters, on the reasoning that a legally ordered crucifix in a kindergarten neither implied a preference for a certain religious conviction nor an infringement with the prohibition of indoctrination. Due to the relationship of state and church in Austria based on an institutional separation the interpretation of the cross as symbolizing a State Church could be excluded. Though one may agree with the result and the essential parts of the Court's reasoning, it should not go without mentioning that the negative component of religious freedom has not been adequately considered.

§2. Headscarf and Other Forms of Religious Dress

655. In 2019, an amendment to the SchUG, BGBl I 2019/54, introduced a 'headscarf ban' for primary school girls, according to which girls may not wear a headscarf that covers all or significant parts of their hair until the end of the school year in which they turn ten (§43a). In 2020, this headscarf ban was declared unconstitutional by the VfGH after careful consideration of the complex and difficult issues involved. The VfGH saw the ban, which, according to the Explanatory Remarks, was aimed at Muslim girls, as a violation of the principle of equality and the right to freedom of religion. Such a selective prohibition would not be suitable to promote social integration of the girls concerned in accordance with local customs and traditions. By prohibiting a certain type of clothing in contrast to other non-prohibited religious clothing habits, the repealed regulation contains a violation of the requirement of religious and ideological neutrality of the state (VfSlg 20.435/2020).

656. In principle, it can be assumed that the wearing of an Islamic headscarf by a teacher during lessons is permissible. It could only be prohibited in specific individual cases, primarily to maintain peace at school. If necessary, the provisions concerning employment duties of civil servants could be used as a legal basis.

§3. Opting Out for Religious Reasons

657. Apart from religious instruction, pupils may not opt out of other subjects or certain lessons – for instance, in biology or natural science – for religious or any

298. VfSlg. 19349/2011.
299. According to the Federal Structure Act on Kindergarten this falls within the competence of the *Bundesländer. See* § 3 section 1 and § 12 section 2 NÖKindergartenG.

other reasons.[300] This is in concordance with the case law of the ECtHR concerning Article 2 of the 1st Additional Protocol. Parents do not have the right to request a curriculum in conformity with their religious or philosophical convictions. However, the parents' right to have their conviction respected implies an objective, critical and pluralistic education, free from indoctrination (cf. 616).[301] The only legitimate grounds for non-participation in physical education are health reasons.

300. S. Hammer & J. Franck, 'Religion in Public Education – Report on Austria', in *Religion in Public Education*, ed. European Consortium of Church & State Resarch (Trier: 2011), 58 et seq.
301. Cf., e.g., ECtHR, *Kjeldsen v. Denmark*, 7 Dec. 1976, appl. no. 5095/71.

Chapter 5. Denominational Private Schools

§1. Denominational Private Schools (in the Strict Sense)

658. According to Article 17 section 2 StGG the establishment and running of private schools and other educational institutions is guaranteed provided the legal qualifications can be approved. Systematically seen, like the right to religious instruction, this article also concretizes the parents' right to have their religious or philosophical convictions respected and the children's right to education according to Article 2 of the 1st Additional Protocol ECHR.[302]

659. Apart from special provisions concerning the establishment, maintenance and closure of schools, in principle, the state school law also applies to private schools. However, there are a few exemptions. In our context, it should particularly be emphasized that school admission is based on a private contract between the school's operators and the pupils or their parents. Such contractual agreements allow for a certain freedom of arrangements within the compulsory state law, such as the membership of certain confessions, school fees, or further grounds for termination of the contractual relationship.

660. According to the Private School Act (PrivSchG), schools which are not founded and operated by the respective legal school provider are 'Private Schools' (§2 section 3). Schools which are operated by legally recognized churches or religious societies or by trusts or funds recognized by them are known as denominational private schools (*konfessionelle Privatschulen*); certain special regulations apply to them. Private schools are granted public status which empowers them to issue school reports legally equivalent to those of state-run schools of the same type, if their operators, heads and teachers can guarantee proper and regular instruction in accordance with the aims of Austrian schooling. If private schools are operated by legally recognized churches and religious societies, the fulfilment of those conditions is legally presumed (§14 section 3 PrivSchG).

661. This legal presumption does not apply to private schools run by other religious communities or any other private entities, so the conditions for the achievement of public status must be approved in every single case. However, this differentiation between the two categories of private schools is considered to be in concordance with the Constitution. This differentiation in treatment seems to be justified with regard to the centuries-long activities and experience of churches in the fields of education and training.[303]

662. In the case of legally prescribed school types the results achieved in class must be equivalent to those in a state school of the same type (sustainable operation

302. Cf. the contributions in A. Rinnerthaler (ed.), *Das kirchliche Privatschulwesen – historische, pastorale und ökonomische Aspekte* (Frankfurt am Main et al.: Peter Lang, 2007).
303. VfSlg. 5034/1965.

in conformity with the tasks of the public school system). The fulfilment of these conditions is legally presumed in the case of recognized churches and religious societies (§11 section 3 PrivSchG).

663. The state has the duty to operate public schools of different types but both private physical and legal persons may also run these schools. According to the constitutional allocation of competences, state-run schools are financed either by the Bund, the Bundesländer or local authorities and are open to all children. Private schools may define certain preconditions of attendance, such as membership in a certain confession.

664. Only schools operated by these religious communities are granted subsidies towards the costs of teaching personnel for denominational private schools with public status, the so-called living subsidies (§17 PrivSchG). This means that the teachers needed by denominational schools to meet the requirements of the school curriculum are employed and paid for by the competent state governing body, not by the respective religious community. Both the teacher concerned and the competent authority in the church or religious community have to agree to the teacher's appointment at the denominational school as a corollary of the right to religious freedom in its individual and organizational dimensions. This also means that the employment of a teacher must be terminated if his or her consent or the religious authority in question no longer exists. In exceptional cases, instead of a 'living subsidy' an equivalent financial subsidy may be granted.

665. Any legal entity other than a legally recognized church or religious community has no legal claim for the granting of state subsidies, though their schools disburden the state's budget for education to the same extent. The operators of such schools are allowed to apply for financial support; however, the state may refuse, taking into account the means of disposal related to the Federal Finance Act. This differential treatment seems to infringe on the right to non-discrimination under Article 14 ECHR, read in conjunction with Article 9 and Article 2 of the 1st Additional Protocol to the Convention. Though a right to public subsidies for denominational private schools as such cannot be derived from the ECHR,[304] there is no reasonable and objective reason for the differential treatment of legally recognized churches and religious communities compared with other religious communities. This is primarily true with regard to state-registered religious denominational communities, all the more de lege lata since no 'fair opportunity' exists for such communities to acquire public law status (cf. 233 et seq.).[305]

666. Following a request for a preliminary ruling from the Administrative Court, the ECJ had to deal with State subsidies of private schools with public law status in relation to a school operated by the Seventh-day Adventist Church. The applicant was the co-financing 'Free Church of the Seventh-day Adventists in Germany

304. *See* ECtHR, *Verein Gemeinsam Lernen v. Austria*, 6 Sep.1995, appl. no. 23419/94.
305. *See* ECtHR, *Religionsgemeinschaft der Zeugen Jehovas and others v. Austria*, 31 Jul. 2008, appl. no. 40825/98, § 92.

KdöR'. The question was whether Union law was applicable in the present case constellation and whether the freedom of establishment guaranteed by Article 49 TFEU was affected (ECJ 2. Feb. 2023, C-372/21). Now the BVwG has to clarify whether teaching at the private primary and secondary school in question constitutes an economic activity within the meaning of Union law.

§2. Private 'Statutes Schools'

667. §14 PrivSchG differs for private schools which, due to their organization and their curriculum, are entitled to use a legally regulated school designation, and private schools, which do not correspond to a public school type (Statutarschulen). While those schools which have an equivalent in the public school system are bound to the same regulatory requirements which apply to similar public schools, in the case of private 'schools on statutes' providers can realize their own pedagogical and organizational school concept.

668. A private Islamic association which was not integrated into the Islamic Religious Community in Austria applied to the education authority for the approval of an organizational statute concerning the establishment of a private 'School for Islamic Education/Al-Azhar of Austria'. According to its statutes, besides imparting general knowledge, theological Islamic studies and accordingly, lessons leading to professions in pastoral care should be included. The High Administrative Court dismissed the application – as the educational authority had before – on the grounds of interference with the 'internal affairs' of the Islamic Religious Society in Austria.[306]

669. First of all, the Court confirmed the established case law regarding the right to order and administrate the 'internal affairs' of legally recognized churches and religious societies according to Article 15 StGG (cf. 271). The ambit of the 'internal affairs' inherently follows from the essence and the special mandate of the religious community concerned in correspondence with its self-understanding. As the Court argued, the purposes of the Private Islamic School in question outlined in the statutes – the organization and substantial determination of education in pastoral care – were to be classified as 'internal affairs'. In such matters, no legal basis would then exist for any approving authority or supervisory competence on the part of the state educational body. The fact that the statutes, apart from theological studies, provided for the imparting of general knowledge had no significance to the relevant findings. Such a private school as the planned Islamic school cannot be established or run as a denominational private school pursuant to the PrivSchG. The administration of schools of this type is exclusively reserved for legally recognized churches and religious societies (and specially authorized private or juridical persons).

306. B. Schinkele, 'Kommentar zu VwGH 31 Jan. 2005, 2002/10/0015', *Österreichisches Archiv für Recht und Religion* 53 (2006), 120–135.

Chapter 6. Religious Holidays

670. The Act on Teaching-time at Schools 1962 (SchZG) provides for a number of religious holidays for different confessions in public schools and private schools with public status over and above the general regulations for holidays. Apart from weekends, most public holidays described in the Act on Holidays (FeiertagsruheG) are Catholic or at least Christian feast days. In addition, the feast of the patron saint of the individual Bundesland is declared a school holiday. Likewise, the days around Christmas and Easter are school-free days.

671. Apart from these general rules, some special provisions exist for pupils of other confessions according to the Act on the Teaching-time at Schools (§13 section 1 and 2 SchZG). Pupils who are members of the Lutheran and Reformed Protestant Churches do not have to attend school on Reformation Day (October, 31). Jewish children are exempted from attending school on the two first and the two last days of Pesach, on the two days of Shavuot, on the two days of the New Year's feast, on Yom Kippur as well as on the two first and the two last days of Sukkot.

672. Moreover, exemptions are provided for children whose religion does not allow them to attend school or to perform certain activities on Saturdays (§13 section 3 SchZG), mainly Jews and members of the Seven-Day-Adventists. On these days, the headmaster must release pupils who are members of such religious communities from classes at their parents' request. More details have been decreed by the Federal Ministry of Education.[307] Parents belonging to religious communities other than legally recognized communities must provide proof that this principle corresponds to a general precept of their confession.

673. The permission to be absent from lessons upon request (cf. §9 section 6 SchPflG, §45 section 4 SchUG) is granted to Muslim pupils with regard to Id-al-Fitr at the end of Ramadan, to Id–al-Adha and the Aschura-Day; pupils with Alevite confession with regard to Hizir-Feast, the Nevruz-Feast, to the Sacrificial-Feast and the Gadir'Hum Feast; pupils of the Islamic-Schiite Community with regard to the Fastbreaking-Feast, the Sacrificial-Feast und des Ghadir-Feast; orthodox pupils with regard to the Christian high feasts (Christmas, Good Friday, Easter Monday, Pentecost Monday) according to the Julian calendars as well as at the annual feast of the Patron saint of the church (In the Serbian-Orthodox Church the Day of St. Sava).

674. Pupils who have been absent for religious holidays have to catch up on lessons in the missed curriculum on their own. When giving grades, teachers may not take into account pupils' lack of knowledge due to absences from lessons due to religious reasons (§13 section 5 SchZG).

307. Implementing Decree on Religious Education Classes (*Durchführungserlass zum Religionsunterricht*), BMUKK-10.014/2-III/3/2007.

Chapter 7. Pedagogical and Religious-Pedagogical Colleges of Higher Education

675. The Federal Act on the Organization of the Pedagogical Colleges and their Studies of 2005 (HochschulG) provides for an independent incorporation of the 'Teachers' Training Academies' into the tertiary sector of education including the bachelor's degree for teaching appointments. The Act Concerning Studies at Academies and Establishing Colleges for Pedagogical Professions of 1999 (AkStG) set in motion a process of development and organizational adaptation, transforming the Pedagogical Academies into 'Colleges for Educational Professions' within an eight-year transitional period.

676. The legislator – as highlighted in the Explanatory Notes of the HochschulG – has taken into account that the subject matter of religious instruction as well as teachers' training fall within the ambit of the 'internal affairs' of the legally recognized churches and religious societies. Therefore, the right to religious freedom comes into effect, primarily as far as the curricula are concerned. With respect to the fact that denominational colleges are private institutions, the legal relationship with their students is based on a contract under private law. Regarding the structure and organization of the colleges, the same quality and academic level as provided at the public institutions must be guaranteed. As a consequence, denominational colleges are obliged to observe the general provisions concerning qualification of the teaching staff including performance review, academic autonomy, student co-determination and allowance for previous studies, personnel and material equipment. Among the general leading principles, the development of social competence in connection with the imparting of social, moral-ethical and religious values is explicitly mentioned. In order to ensure the comparability of these studies and degrees with those of the public Teachers' Training Colleges, the law provides for recognition proceedings (§§4-7 HochschulG).

677. With regard to the Schulvertrag 1962 (cf. 293), the Catholic Church was faced with the problem that pursuant to its Additional Protocol, colleges of higher education were excluded from its scope of application. Therefore, in an exchange of notes between the Republic of Austria and the Holy See it was clarified that the provisions of the Schulvertrag concerning the education and vocational training of teachers – above all with regard to financing – should also be applied to the Teachers' Training Colleges run by the Catholic Church.[308]

678. For the time being, four Catholic Religious-Pedagogical Colleges have been established. The Protestant, Orthodox, Old-Catholic and Eastern-Oriental studies are connected with the Viennese Catholic College in an Ecumenical Board.

---

308. It was discussed, whether there was a need for an alteration of the Concordat instead of a mere exchange of notes.

679. In addition to this ecumenical cooperation, agreements were concluded with the Israelite Religious Society, the Islamic Religious Society, the Alevi Religious Society (ALEVI), the Buddhist Religious Society and the Austrian Free Churches, whereby these were integrated into the courses offered by the Ecclesiastical Teachers' Training College in Vienna.

Chapter 8. Theological Faculties and Religious Universities

§1. Theological Faculties at State Universities

680. The Austrian constitutional system contains no explicit guarantee for theological research at state universities or academies.[309] Although the constitutional foundations of the school law presuppose the existence of religious instruction in public schools, in principle no obligation exists on behalf of the state to provide for the training of teachers of religious education, because the legally recognized churches and religious societies and not the state are the entrepreneurs of religious instruction. There is, therefore, no constitutional obligation for the state to integrate theology into the canon of objects of research and teaching at universities. Nonetheless, an overall view of the constitutional principles of law on religion shows that fulfilling this task is in absolute conformity with the constitutional system in Austria.

681. Basically, the training of spiritual personnel as well as the entire office and employment law belongs to the internal affairs of the legally recognized churches and religious societies in accordance with Article 15 StGG. Therefore, the state itself cannot take over the training of spiritual personnel. However, an appropriate state education such as is provided in theological faculties can be approved by the churches and religious societies. The theological faculties, therefore, belong to those areas where cooperation with churches and religious societies as socially effective forces acting in the public sphere is not only permissible but even necessary.[310]

682. There is no contradiction to the guarantee of freedom of teaching and science if the specific nature of theology is considered within the framework of state universities. To cultivate the scientific field of religion with the exclusion of theology, from the point of view of social politics as well as science politics would be a questionable reduction. The organization of theological research and teaching at state universities, however, must take three interacting aspects into account: the religious and ideological neutrality of the state, the self-determination of the religious communities, the guarantees for teaching and research as well as the fundamental rights of the theologians concerned.

683. There are not only secular standards to be considered but also the theological concept of the religious communities in particular. First, the fundamental question is raised whether, and if so, in what form the respective religious society has a scientific concept of theology. Second, it must be clarified if the respective religious society entrusts the research and teaching of theology to the state universities. The

309. R. Potz, 'Islamische Theologie an der Universität', in *In mandatis meditari, Festschrift für Hans Paarhammer,* ed. S. Haering et al. (Berlin: Duncker & Humblot, 2012), 929–950; S. Hammer 'Zur konfessionellen Bindung der Theologie aus Sicht der Wissenschaftsfreiheit', in *Recht – Religion – Kultur. Festschrift für Richard Potz*, ed. B. Schinkele et al. (Vienna: facultas.wuv, 2014), 117–132.

310. Deutscher Wissenschaftsrat, *Empfehlungen zur Weiterentwicklung von Theologien und religionsbezogenen Wissenschaften an deutschen Hochschulen*, Drs. 9678–10, 29 Jan. 2010: http://www.wissenschaftsrat.de/download/archiv/9678–10.pdf [23. 10. 2014].

Concordat (Article V §1), the ProtestantenG (§15 section 1) and the IslamG (§24 section 1) emphasize that the theological faculties and institutes are maintained by the state for the purpose of the scientific education of spiritual ministers. Thus, there is a consensus that the Catholic Church, the Protestant Church and the Islamic Religious Societies have in principle agreed to recognize and accept graduates of state universities in the fields of theology and religious pedagogy into their service.

§2. Faculties of Catholic Theology

684. There are Faculties of Catholic Theology at the Universities of Vienna, Graz, Innsbruck and Salzburg. Article V of the Concordat guarantees the continued existence of these faculties, financed by the state, for the purpose of the academic education of the clergy. Their internal organization and educational practice are regulated by the state according to the law on universities. The term 'internal organization' in this context refers to the organizational provisions of the Act on Universities (UnivG) 2002; the term 'educational practice' refers to the provisions of this law on academic studies, which includes an explicit proviso in favour of the terms of the Concordat (§38 section 1 UnivG).

685. Academic degrees in theology awarded by a papal academy in Rome or any other papal academy are recognized as having the equivalent legal status of state degrees in Austria.

686. The appointment or admission of professors and lecturers must be agreed upon by the competent church authority. If church authorization is withdrawn, the teacher must be excluded from exercising the respective teaching activity. According to the majority opinion, the disciplinary measure of the compulsory redundancy of a professor of theology whose authorization has been withdrawn according to Article V section 4 of the Concordat does not violate the fundamental rights of freedom of religion and conscience, freedom of opinion or of academic teaching and research, since its aim is to educate pastors and teachers of religious education.[311]

687. On the basis of Article V of the Concordat, theology may also be studied at theological colleges established by the competent church authorities.

§3. Faculty of Protestant Theology

688. The Federal State (Bund) is obliged to maintain a Faculty of Protestant Theology with at least six permanent chairs at the University of Vienna to guarantee the academic education of ordinands and theological research and teaching (§15 section 1 ProtestantenG). Faculty members and all persons involved in teaching must be members of the Protestant church (§15 section 2). Before appointing a professor to a chair, the university must consult (Fühlungnahme) the Protestant Church

311. VfSlg. 6998/1973, VwSlg. 8419 A/1973.

authorities. According to §38 section 2 UnivG, as regards the Protestant Theological Faculty, the University of Vienna must observe §15 ProtestantenG 'when structuring the internal organization and the curricula and in ensuring teaching and research activities'.

§4. Islamic Theology

689. The introduction of regular studies in Islamic theology in addition to the study of Islamic religious pedagogy was a particular innovation of the IslamG 2015.[312] According to §24 section 1 for the purpose of theological research and teaching and to ensure the academic education of spiritual ministers of Islamic religious societies up to six positions for teaching staff will be provided at the Austrian universities (cf. 369).

690. According to §24 section 3 IslamG, a separate curriculum must be prepared for every Islamic religious society. On the occasion of the appointment of a professorship provided for in this Act, the Rector of the University of Vienna must contact (Fühlungnahme) the Islamic religious societies regarding the persons proposed. Thereby, it must be taken into consideration that the persons teaching theological core subjects are adherents of a religious doctrine (Islamic law school) represented in the Islamic religious societies recognized under this Act (§24 section 4). In future, these provisions could lead to some problems if the number of Islamic religious societies increases due to the splitting of an existing Islamic Religious Society or the recognition of a further Islamic religious society.

691. The study of Alevi theology was merely incorporated as a branch of study – a term foreign to Austrian university law – into the Islamic theology degree program. This meant that the main subjects of Islamic theology, which are only of minor importance for Alevi theology, became main subjects for Alevi students. This concept has turned out to be inadequate, as the extremely low number of students shows.

§5. Private Universities

692. The Act Concerning Studies at Academies and Establishing Colleges for Pedagogical Professions (UniAkkG) of 1999, replaced in 2011 by the Act on Private Universities (PUG), put an end to the state monopoly in Austria and made the organization of private universities possible. In 2000, the 'Catholic Theological Private University of Linz' was established. The foundation was set up by means of an administrative decision of the accreditation council, an administrative body not bound by any instructions nor needing ministerial consent. The 'Catholic Theological Private University of Linz' is therefore entitled to grant academic graduate

312. R. Potz, 'Islamische Theologie an der Universität'. In *In mandatis meditari. Festschrift für Hans Paarhammer*, ed. S. Haering et al. (Berlin: Duncker & Humblot, 2012), 929–950.

degrees with equal legal status (magisterium, licentiate and doctorate) to state universities, to carry out habilitation procedures for obtaining a venia legendi and enjoys the same legal status in various other respects (e.g., public scholarships, the social-insurance-position of and tax regulations for students).[313]

313. H. Kalb, 'Die Katholisch-Theologische Universität Linz'. *Österreichisches Archiv für Recht und Religion* 47 (2000), 363–383; B. Schinkele, 'Church and State in Austria 2000', *European Journal for Church and State Research* 8 (2001), 236 et seq.

Part X. Matrimonial and Family Law

Chapter 1. Legal Position of Religious Marriage

693. Since the coming into force of the Act on the Unification of the Law of Marriage and Divorce in the Country of Austria and the Rest of the Territory of the Reich from 6 July 1938 (EheG 1938 cf. 61 and 513), the marriage ceremony before an organ of a religious community had no legal effect for the state. According to §67 of the former Act on Personal Status from 1955, an administrative punishment (fine or imprisonment) should be imposed on a person who participated in a religious marriage ceremony before the marriage had been contracted in front of a registrar. After 1945, both laws – the EheG and the PStG – were transferred to the legal system of the Republic with the exception of provisions containing ideological traits of National-Socialism, especially the 'impediment of difference in race'. Since then in Austria the system of compulsory civil marriage has been realized and religious marriages have no civil consequences.

694. The aforementioned provision of §67 has been repealed by the Constitutional Court as being unconstitutional because of its incompatibility with Article 15 StGG and Article 63 section 2 of the StVStGermain.[314] Pursuant to the Constitutional Court's reasoning, religious marriage ceremonies of legally recognized churches and religious societies represent an act of public manifestation of one's religion in the sense of Article 15 StGG. Since this procedure and the determination of the moment in time now fall within the scope of 'internal affairs', legally recognized church or religious societies are entitled to regulate and administer independently.

314. VfSlg. 2944/1955.

Chapter 2. Legal Position of Religious Family Law

695. Religious family law has no legal relevance in Austrian family law. Nevertheless, all persons are free to organize their family life according to religious rules and personal convictions.

696. According to §582 section 2 ZPO family law is exempt from arbitration. Therefore, decisions by religious courts cannot have civil law consequences in matters of family law, except foreign decisions according to the rules of international private law.

Part XI. Religion and Culture

Chapter 1. Religion and Art

§1. Protection of Monuments

697. There is a close link between the protection of cultural property and freedom of art on the one hand and the protection of freedom of religion, on the other. State activities must be aware of the fact that religious monuments usually serve directly religious purposes and their use is therefore of central importance for the practice of religion. As a consequence, the specific features of religious monuments must be considered in any provision regarding their preservation, destruction or alteration. Furthermore, this means that consideration of changed cultic-liturgical rules must not be regarded as a disturbing element in the protection of cultural property, but as proper observance of functional monument protection.

698. Protection of monuments in Austria is based on a wide interpretation of the term 'monument'. According to §1 section 1 of the Act on Protection of Monuments (DMSG), it includes moveable (in particular archaeological and artistic objects) and immovable (constructions and archaeological sites) monuments of historical, artistic and other cultural significance, created by humans.[315] Collections of moveable monuments or ensembles of immovable monuments are also protected, but not complexes of cultural landscapes which are subject to the individual townscape protection of the Bundesländer (cf. 714 et seq.).

699. Up to 31 December 2009, the criterion of legal presumption was to be applied for the protection of immovable monuments in the sole or majority ownership – *inter alia* – of churches or religious societies including their institutions, as long as the Federal Office for the Protection of Monuments had not rendered an administrative decision as to whether or not preservation was actually in the public interest, either ex officio or by application from a party (§2 section 1 and 4 DMSG). This concept was criticized because of the uncertainty of preservation on the basis of legal presumption.

---

315. *See* N. Helfgott, 'Denkmalschutzgesetz und kirchliches Eigentum', *Österreichisches Archiv für Kirchenrecht* 29 (1978), 426–445; W. Wieshaider, 'Auswirkungen der Novelle 1999 zum Denkmalschutzgesetz auf die Religionsgemeinschaften', *Österreichisches Archiv für Recht und Religion* 49 (2002), 395–403.

700. As far as immovable monuments are concerned, this criterion of legal presumption was replaced by protection on the basis of a decree of the Federal Office for Monuments. Therefore, since 1 January 2010, immovable monuments are only protected on the basis of an ordinance confirming the public interest in their preservation (§2 section 4 DMSG).[316] However, rightful claimants may still apply for an administrative decision on the basis of a separate procedure on the question of existing public interest (§2a section 5).

701. As before, however, movable monuments in the sole or majority public ownership of bodies with public law status are preserved by virtue of legal presumption.

702. Another form of protected status is based on an administrative decision by the Federal Office for Monuments and mainly affects objects in private ownership (§3 DMSG).

703. According to §4 DMSG, destruction of or any alteration to monuments is only allowed with the consent of the Federal Office for Monuments, except if delay would result in imminent danger (section 2).

704. The applicant is obliged to give evidence of the reasons justifying the intended destruction or alteration and to enclose appropriate plans – except measures necessary for repairing and maintenance. The office has to compare the facts and merits in favour of destruction or alteration with those in favour of unchanged preservation of the monument (§5 section 1 DMSG).

705. Notwithstanding this provision, consent must be given to an application for alteration if the monument is used for worship by a legally recognized church or religious society and the alteration is necessary for the practice of worship on the basis of mandatory or at least generally applied liturgical instructions. In any case, observance of those liturgical instructions must be considered necessary in the sense of this provision in order to allow for the regular practice of worship as well as those circumstances which enable the faithful to attend church services to a sufficient degree and in a reasonable and dignified manner. From that point of view, the legal claim primarily comprises necessary expansions of churches, especially parish churches, if there is not enough room for parishioners to fulfil their worship obligations. Direct participation must also be understood as a liturgical necessity. The manner and extent of this necessity must be proved by means of a certificate from the competent supreme authority of the church or religious society concerned on demand of the Federal Office for Protection of Monuments. This certificate must include details of the expected consequences if the application for alteration is not granted in the manner or to the extent requested therein. Thus, the aforementioned Office is given a basis for submission of an alternative proposal. If the Office has already made some suggestions the church authority is obliged to comment on them (§5 section 4 DMSG).

316. Since 30 Jun. 2010 the objects under monument preservation are listed at http://www.bda.at.

706. The Council for Historic Monuments is an advisory committee to the Federal Office for Protection of Monuments, whose responsibility is to give specialist expertise. One representative of the church or religious society concerned takes part in the meetings of the Council as an ad hoc member if a monument in majority church ownership is affected (§15 DMSG).

§2. Regional Planning and Building Regulations

707. Freedom of religion and belief guarantees full freedom to the undisturbed exercise of religious and non-religious convictions, thus encompassing the construction of churches and other buildings or places of worship. A substantive approach in the interpretation of fundamental rights as well as state neutrality in religious matters requires the state to consider the religious interests and needs of the faithful when preparing plans for land use.

708. Provisions regarding urban and regional planning as well as building regulations fall under the competence of the Bundesländer. Consequently, in the context of systematic and future-oriented structuring of the national territory, the Regional Planning Acts of the Bundesländer must be adequately sensitive to the cultural requirements and needs of the population. The cultural environment, as one of the foundations of the development of a comprehensive personality, also includes the religious dimension and, consequently, religious buildings, as a requirement for the practice of worship and related activities, according to the respective religious concept. After having assessed the appropriate space requirements of each religious community irrespective of their legal status, municipal development planners must reserve areas to include facilities for pastoral care, among other things. Churches are, of course, explicitly mentioned in the areas designated for community institutions, including any other place of worship.

709. Urban and regional planning programmes must be presented to the legally recognized churches and religious societies, or at least to the Catholic Church and the Protestant Church, for their opinions. In a few Bundesländer, representatives of the Catholic Church and the Protestant Church are members of the Regional Planning Boards.[317]

710. Similarly, in compliance with the aforementioned requirements, building regulation laws must guarantee the undisturbed practice of religion with regard to buildings intended for worship, such as churches, mosques, synagogues and other buildings of this kind. Consequently, the general rules concerning construction height do not regularly apply to such buildings as long as the urban image and landscape are not impaired. However, structural engineering requirements concerning general criteria such as safety, strength of buildings, fire protection, environmental protection or the like are also relevant as regards religious buildings. In particular,

317. Cf., e.g., § 11 section 4 no. 2 Act on Regional Planning of Upper Austria (OÖ-ROG); § 11 section 1 Act on Regional Planning of Styria (Stmk-ROG).

with reference to some intentions concerning the implementation of restrictions on building mosques at the level of the Landes-legislature, it must be stressed that even seemingly neutral building regulation laws which prohibit building mosques must, in fact, be considered unconstitutional.

711. In 2008, a special procedure for townscape care was introduced in Vorarlberg.[318] Since then, the Government of the Land Vorarlberg is entitled to determine by ordinance which construction projects due to type, size and shape affect the interests of townscape or landscape protection. Furthermore, in the Vorarlberg Act on Regional Planning the concept of 'locations for large audiences' has been established (§16a).[319] Under this provision, the municipal council can determine by ordinance that locations for large audiences need a special dedication in the zoning plan. An appropriate location must be designed for at least 150 people; examples mentioned are cinema centres, discotheques, sports facilities and buildings for worship.

712. In Bad Vöslau, a small town in Lower Austria near Vienna, an approach which in some ways can be considered exemplary was found in 2009. On the basis of a continuous dialogue between all persons and groups affected, a reasonable agreement was reached with regard to the site of the mosque, its construction and its specific design – a minaret consisting mostly of glass.[320]

713. With regard to buildings for worship, the question of noise-immissions also arises. In these cases, one has to consider the protection of religious practice and observances on the one hand, and the limitations of religious manifestations in order to protect legitimate conflicting interests, on the other. In practice, the problems are mainly related to the ringing of church bells and the Muezzin call. As regards church bells, one must distinguish between bell-ringing for liturgical and secular reasons. Ringing before and during holy service or other forms of worship is considered to be an admissible religious manifestation and, as such, a reasonable and socially adequate noise annoyance.[321] However, the ordinary laws on protection against immissions and the respective restrictions are relevant in the case of hourly ringing to indicate the time, especially at night and in residential areas. Accordingly, an appropriate level of noise molestation must not be exceeded. Case by case, a fair balance must be struck between religious interests and the needs of neighbours and the general surroundings. The same is true with regard to the Muezzin call which is, in principle, allowed and can, after all, also be transmitted via loudspeaker.

714. Under public law, the various Security Laws of the Bundesländer contain provisions concerning 'undue excitation of disturbing noise' as an administrative offence.[322] Usually, such conflicts can be settled by mutual agreement. To give an

---

318. Vlbg-BauG 2001, as amended LGBl. 34/2008.
319. Vlbg-RaumplG 1996, as amended LGBl. 35/2008.
320. E. Fürlinger, *Moscheebaukonflikte in Österreich. Nationale Politik des religiösen Raums im globalen Zeitalter* (Vienna: University Press, 2013), 289 et seq.
321. VwSlg. 7921 A/1911.
322. Cf. Steiermärkisches Sicherheitsgesetz, LGBl. 2004/24, as amended; Wiener Landessicherheitsgesetz, LGBl. 1993/51, as amended.

example, the Archbishop of Vienna has decreed that within urban areas bells must not ring before seven o'clock in the morning.[323] The regional planning regulations also provide for a certain degree of protection against disturbing nuisance by being oriented on the criterion of reasonableness depending on the zoning category concerned. A fair balance must be struck between the right of the religious communities to self-determination and the needs of neighbours and the general public.

715. §364 ABGB stipulates that private owners of real estate must pay attention to limitations ensuing from the laws which serve the preservation and promotion of the common good. Accordingly, impacts by immissions are forbidden if they exceed the customary usual standards or interfere with the common terms of use. As far as the Muezzin call is concerned, local standards are to be interpreted with respect to the fundamental guarantee of religious freedom as well as changed demographic conditions.

§3. Public Events

716. The law on organizing public events is part of the area of competence of the Bundesländer. In principle, these Acts on Public Events also apply to cultural events organized by churches or religious societies either in their religious buildings or facilities. However, most of these laws provide for exemptions with regard to 'events which are manifestations of a faith, a religion or a confession', 'events in the context of religious exercise' or comparable formulations. Such definitions might involve awkward delineations whereby criteria such as the religious self-understanding, the actual organizer, the subject of an exhibition or any performance, the visitors or the profit motive might be useful.[324]

§4. Religion in the Arts

717. From the very beginning of mankind, religion and art were deeply connected and their unbundling constitutes a significant process in the history of both fields. Until today, the artistic design of rooms serving cult purposes and the artistic arrangements of rituals and ceremonies are of great significance in religious practice. In this way, art has always served an important function in imparting religious content.

718. The history of the relationship between art and religion has not only been characterized by its complementary relationship but – especially since the twentieth century – by fundamental conflicts. The respective case law clearly illustrates that

323. *Wiener Diözesanblatt* 100 (1962), 70.
324. B. Moser-Zoundjiekpon, 'Organisation von kulturellen Veranstaltungen in Einrichtungen der römisch-katholischen Kirche bzw durch solche', *Österreichisches Archiv für Recht und Religion* 52 (2005), 393–423.

the democratic state, legitimized primarily by ensuring basic rights and freedoms, quickly finds itself at the limits of its possibilities when such sensitive human rights come into conflict.

719. According to the Copyright Act (UrhRG), religious communities have some rights to freedom of use. For non-commercial purposes, individual written works may be copied, distributed and made available to the public in a collection that includes works by several authors and designated for the use of churches or schools to an extent justified by these aims (§45 section 1 no. 1 UrhRG). Appropriate remuneration must be paid; this is a claim which can only be made by bodies which can enforce performing and artistic rights. Public performance of a piece of music is also permitted if it is performed, *inter alia*, within a church ceremony and admission is free of charge (§53 section 1 no. 2 UrhRG).

720. The case law concerning conflicts between freedom of art and freedom of religion usually refers to §188 of the Criminal Code concerning disparagement or public ridicule of persons or things which are objects of worship in churches or religious communities, religious doctrines or legally admissible observances (cf. 560 et seq.).

Chapter 2. Religion and the Media

721. Freedom of the media is guaranteed in Article 13 StGG and Article 10 ECHR in connection with the prohibition of censorship in the Provisional National Assembly's Resolution of 1918,[325] all of which have constitutional status. According to the formulation of the Constitutional Court's decisions, the scope of Article 10 ECHR is wider than that of Article 13 StGG because it explicitly also includes the right to receive and impart information without interference by public authorities and regardless of frontiers.[326] On the basis of a synoptic approach, both the legal as well as the doctrinal practice proceed from the assumption of a comprehensive freedom of communication encompassing its different forms of expression and thus also the freedom of the media.[327] Freedom of communication is one of the most important basic features of a democratic society and is, therefore, also of high relevance within the law on religion from different perspectives. On the one hand, religious communities use all forms of communication – in particular, the media – as an instrument of mission and proclamation of faith; on the other hand, religion is subject to reporting and critical analysis, also protected by freedom of communication.

§1. Audiovisual Media

I. Public Law Broadcasting

722. The ORF (Österreichischer Rundfunk) is a public law foundation (§1 section 1 ORF-G) which for the purpose of fulfilling its public mandate is obliged to run three nationwide radio programmes and nine which can be received in each Bundesland as well as two nationwide television programmes (§3 section 1 ORF-G). §4 section 1 ORF-G enumerates the duties and functions of these programmes and mentions, among other things, their obligation 'to consider adequately the importance of legally recognized churches and religious societies' (no. 12). To safeguard the interests of listeners, the Audience Council (Publikumsrat), was established, at present consisting of thirty members, (§28 section 1 ORF-G). The Catholic Church and the Protestant Church are entitled to nominate one member each (§28 section 3 nos. 3 and 4 ORF-G).[47] Among its other duties, the Audience Council nominates six members of the Foundation Council (Stiftungsrat). According to Programme Directives (1.6.4), compliance with the obligation to respect the significance of the legally recognized churches and religious societies not only means that events organized by them must be presented in their social relevance, but also that the content of their faith must be taken into consideration and appropriately conveyed.

325. Beschluss der Provisorischen Nationalversammlung, StGBl. 1918/3.
326. VfSlg. 11297/1987; VfSlg. 12104/1989.
327. W. Berka, 'Präambel', in *Mediengesetz*, ed. W. Berka (Vienna: LexisNexis/Orac, 2002), 16.

II. Private Broadcasting

723. After the decision of the ECtHR in the case *Lentia and Others v. Austria*,[328] holding that a (public) broadcasting monopoly violates Article 10 ECHR, the first legal framework for the operation of private radio on a regional level only was enacted in 1993. In 2001, a fundamental reform was carried out by bringing into force the Act on Private Radio Broadcasting (PrR-G), with the aim of further development of a dual broadcasting system by promoting commercial as well as non-commercial private radio (§1 section 2 PrR-G). Juridical persons with public law status are excluded from operating private radio programmes because of their closeness to the state. Because this exclusion explicitly does not apply to legally recognized churches and religious societies, they are allowed to run such radio stations, regardless of their public law status (§8 no. 1 PrR-G). The reason is that they do not fulfil state functions characteristic of public law corporations. According to §16 section 4 PrR-G, all programmes must respect human dignity and the fundamental rights of others with regard to their formulation and contents. They must not incite hatred on the grounds of race, gender, religion or nationality.

724. There are two radio stations which explicitly reflect their fundamental religiously based orientation. Radio Stephansdom, run by the Catholic foundation of the same name with public law status, conveys content related to religion, deals with social and ethical issues and provides listeners with information about the Catholic Church.[329] Moreover, the station is well known for its classical music programme.

725. Radio Maria Austria, run by a private association with the same name, aims to disseminate religious and ethical content with the intention of promoting a 'value-based culture of life in all areas of society'. It broadcasts liturgy, issues on catechism and spirituality, counselling programmes, news from the Catholic Church and music, with a focus on spiritual music.[330]

III. Private Television/Audiovisual Media Services

726. The Act on Audiovisual Media Services (AMD-G) 2010 regulates the organization of terrestrial and satellite television, the provision of other audiovisual media services and the operation of multiplex platforms. Legally recognized churches and religious societies are to be accepted as private providers of media services, regardless of their public law status (§10 section 2 no. 1), the reason being that they do not fulfil state functions characteristic of public law corporations. According to §30 section 1, presentations of audiovisual media services must

---

328. ECtHR 24 Nov. 1993, appl. no. 13914/88, 15041/89, 15717/89, 15779/89, 17207/90; *see also Europäische Grundrechte Zeitschrift* 21 (1994), 549 et seq.
329. http://www. radiostephansdom.at [17. 3. 2015].
330. http://www.radiomaria.at [17. 3. 2015].

respect human dignity and the fundamental rights of others with regard to their formulation and contents. They must not incite hatred on grounds of race, gender, religion, disability or nationality.

727. Pursuant to §54d no. 1 AMD-G, content whose public availability on a video platform constitutes, among other things, incitement to commit terrorist offences and approval of terrorist offences (§282a StGB) as well as incitement to hatred (§283 StGB) is prohibited. Insofar as it does not already fall under §283 StGB, any incitement to violence or hatred against a group or against a member of such a group on grounds of religion or belief, among other things, is prohibited (§54d no. 2 AMD-G).

IV. Advertising in Audiovisual Media

728. The provisions concerning advertising in audiovisual media are largely determined by EU law (cf. 429). On three days of the year – Good Friday, All Saints' Day (1 November), and Christmas Eve (24 December) – commercial advertising is forbidden (§13 section 5 ORF-G). The broadcasting of religious services must not be interrupted by advertisements or teleshopping. The same applies to any other programmes with religious content shorter than thirty minutes (§15 section 6 ORF-G). Audiovisual commercial communication must not offend human dignity, nor contain or promote any form of discrimination, *inter alia*, on the grounds of religion and belief (§31 section 3 AMD-G). This also applies to religious advertisements, which are generally not forbidden. Product Placement in broadcasts of religious content is forbidden (§31 section 1). Broadcasts of religious services must not be interrupted by any advertisements or teleshopping (§44 section 4).

§2. Print Media

729. Freedom of the press is one of the classic individual rights and, in connection with freedom of expression, represents the starting point for a comprehensive guarantee of freedom of the media.

730. The Catholic Church and the Protestant Church each operate a press agency: the Catholic press agency kathpress [331] and the Evangelische Pressedienst (epd).[332]

731. Media enterprises related to the Catholic Church are prominently represented in the Austrian media landscape. One of the two leading print media companies in Austria is the 'Styria Media Group', which belongs to the private foundation Katholischer Medienverein. It issues, among other things, three national daily newspapers, the weekly magazine Die Furche as well as several periodicals in

331. http://www.kathpress.co.at.
332. http://www.evang.at/presse/epd-newsletter/.

Slovenia and Croatia. Moreover, part of this media company is willhaben.at, the most frequently visited online ads platform.

732. The Austrian Press Council (Österreichischer Presserat) is an institution for the voluntary self-control of the press, founded in 1961 and re-established in 2010, after its self-dissolution in 2002 because of internal conflicts. The Presserat has published a Code of Ethics for the Austrian press.[333] The Code refers twice to religion: 'Any discrimination on racial, religious, ethnic, sexual or other grounds is inadmissible' (Article 7.2), and 'Disparagement or ridiculing of religious doctrines or of recognized churches and religious communities which causes unjustified offence, is inadmissible' (Article 7.3). Although the Code is not legally binding it is important for the interpretation of legal norms regulating the protection of journalistic professional practice (§2 and §3 MedienG), protection of privacy in the media (especially §6 and §7 MedienG) as well as defamation and offence according to §1330 ABGB and according to §111 StGB (cf. 570).

333. http://www presserat.at/show_content.phphid=2 [27. 2. 2015].

Part XII. Religious Assistance in Public Institutions

Chapter 1. General Principles

733. The field of religious services and pastoral care must be seen in terms of both the individual and the organizational dimensions of the right to religious freedom. While pastoral care in the armed forces has traditionally been a field of cooperation between state and church, emphasis has increasingly been placed on religious assistance in hospitals as well as in other healthcare facilities, prisons and other public institutions. This is not least a consequence of the interpretation of fundamental rights using a more substantial approach, encompassing a certain state obligation to take measures to ensure the practice of religious freedom even under difficult circumstances. Any form of religious assistance that the religious communities are permitted to provide may only be carried out in the form of an offer without any manner of compulsion.

734. Although state provisions regarding religious assistance in the aforementioned institutions substantiate the fundamental right of religious freedom, the concrete method of implementation differs somewhat, depending on the legal status of the relevant religious community and the number of its adherents. This has certain effects on the individuals concerned.

735. Apart from general legal provisions, additional provisions exist which guarantee pastoral care in the armed forces as well as in hospitals and prisons by special laws for the legally recognized churches and religious societies, for example, in the Concordat, the ProtestantenG, the OrthodoxenG, the OrientKG, the IsraelitenG, and the IslamG. Accordingly, there are two categories of religious assistance in these institutions, depending on whether it is permanently established in the respective institution or not.

Chapter 2. Different Forms of Categorical Pastoral Care

§1. Pastoral Care in Healthcare Institutions[334]

736. The Federal Act on Hospitals and Healthcare Institutions (KaKuG) describes the patient's right to pastoral care on demand (§5a no. 5). According to the distribution of competencies between the Bund and the Bundesländer, the latter must ensure that the holders of hospitals and healthcare institutions comply with this legal duty, taking into account the specific purpose of the respective institution. This precept has been regularly implemented in all individual laws of the Bundesländer together with the right to psychological support. This reflects the legislator's endeavour to provide for the comprehensive care of patients.

737. Apart from occasional minimal personal subsidies on the basis of regional provisions, pastoral care in healthcare institutions is not financed by the state, although infrastructure is financed to some degree.

738. In principle, hospitals may ask patients to state their religious affiliation before admission. However, this is a crucial issue insofar as no explicit obligation exists to inform the patient at the same time that he or she actually has the right to refuse to answer this question. In practice, one may assume that this will be handled differently. However, it must be underlined that informing the patient in advance is the only fully consistent way to deal with the negative dimension of the right to religious freedom.

739. The problem in question has resulted in a controversial debate, particularly with regard to data protection. Some hospitals with public status refused to transmit the names of Protestant patients to the inquiring institution's pastor as stipulated in §18 ProtestantenG (cf. 314). The hospital management argued that the DSG had derogated this regulation which takes for granted that patients are asked to state their confession on admission to the hospital. On the contrary, however, the competent Federal Minister took the position that the explicit consent of patients before the authorities forward their names to the institution's pastor would also not be necessary in future. It would only be forbidden to pass on the names of those patients who explicitly reject pastoral care. Based on this opinion, it should be added that the most satisfactory procedure would be to inform patients that they are not obliged to disclose their religious beliefs at all. According to the principle of parity, this should apply to all legally recognized churches and religious societies.

740. Disclosure of confession is, however, necessary if the patient wishes to adhere to religious dietary regulations. This is explicitly guaranteed in special laws

334. R. Potz, 'Recht auf seelsorgliche Betreuung aus der Sicht der Patienten und der Religionsgemeinschaften', in *Spiritualität, Religion und Kultur am Krankenbett*, ed. U. Körtner et al. (Vienna & New York: Springer, 2009), 108–118.

for several legally recognized churches and religious societies, although it is, in fact, already comprehensively ensured on the basis of the individual's right to religious freedom.

741. In practice, pastoral care in hospitals is an important field of cooperation between care staff and pastoral advisers on the one hand, and ecumenical and even interreligious activities on the other. To give an example, the Allgemeine Krankenhaus in Vienna provides a common place of worship, offering a platform for ecumenical and interreligious cooperation, with the participation of the Catholic Church, the Protestant Church, the Orthodox Churches, the Israelite Religious Society and the Islamic Religious Society.

742. Usually, a cross is exhibited in hospital rooms, even if the hospitals are not run by a particular denomination, somehow per consuetudinem, since there is no legal basis for or against this. One must assume that this issue must mainly be decided at the discretion of the holder of the healthcare institution, though taking into account that this is a highly sensitive matter which must be carefully dealt with case by case, with a view to achieving a balance between conflicting interests.

§2. Pastoral Care in Prisons

743. The individual's right to practice his or her religion in penal institutions is governed by §85 Act on Imprisonment (StVG). This guarantee includes the prisoner's right to attend services or other religious events of his or her 'own confession' usually held in the institution. Moreover, communication with a pastoral adviser who is appointed or admitted to the institution concerned must be guaranteed at reasonable intervals. On a case-by-case basis, after having heard the pastoral adviser, a prisoner can be excluded from participating in worship or other religious ceremonies for reasons of security or requirements of prison regime. If a pastoral adviser of the inmate's confession is neither appointed nor admitted and the prisoner asks for pastoral care, the prison governor is obliged to nominate a spiritual adviser from the respective religious community, as far as this is possible according to the particular circumstances.

744. In a decision of 1999,[335] the Constitutional Court interpreted the wording 'own confession' in §85 StVG in a broad sense, comprising not only the actual affiliation but also former membership in the case of withdrawal of membership – even including any other confession the inmate sympathizes with, without formally adhering to it. Of course, as the spiritual adviser may not be forced to carry out any activities, it is completely his or her decision whether or not to comply with such a request.

335. S. Schima, 'Kommentar zu VfSlg. 15.592/1999', *Österreichisches Archiv für Recht und Religion* 47 (2000), 260–268.

745. Besides the supervision of the denominational authority, the pastoral staff is subordinate to the Department of Justice, the president of the respective Court or the head of the institution in question. Inmates are allowed to receive pastoral advisers during the office hours of the institutions but outside visiting times. It is forbidden to supervise the content of the conversation.

746. Regarding Roman Catholic pastoral care in prisons, a small number of official positions are provided for pastoral advisers who are engaged on the basis of an employment contract and financed by the state. Protestant and Islamic pastoral care in prisons consists entirely of full-time and part-time persons who are employed by the respective religious society. According to an agreement dating from 2002, the Protestant Church receives the amount of EUR 30,000; the number of persons sent by the church is not specified.[336] A largely identical agreement for pastoral care in prisons was reached in 2010[337] with the Islamic Religious Society in Austria.

747. In the meantime, an Orthodox, an (Islamic) Alevi and a Jehovah's Witness prison chaplaincy have also been set up as well as a Buddhist prisoner support service.

§3. Pastoral Care in the Armed Forces

748. Military chaplaincy[338] is provided for the Catholic Church (Article VIII of the Concordat), the Protestant Church (§17 ProtestantenG), the Israelite Religious Society (§8 section 1 no. 1 IsraelitenG), the Islamic Religious Societies (§§11 and 18 IslamG), the Orthodox Churches and the Oriental-Orthodox Churches (§7 OrthodoxenG and §3 OrientKG refer to the ProtestantenG). In all these cases, the personnel expenses and material costs are covered by the state. For a long time, in fact, only Catholic and Protestant Military Chaplaincies were established; personnel expenses for officers and support staff were borne completely by the Bund and the material costs were covered indirectly by means of transfers of material goods. The establishment of additional military chaplaincies was not initially planned. Therefore, the Orthodox, Islamic, (Islamic)Alevi and Jewish military chaplains are not integrated into army administration and only receive a small remuneration. This constitutes unequal treatment contrary to parity.

749. As a result of the increasing diversity in the religious composition of Austrian conscripts in the 1990s, the Austrian Armed Forces issued numerous decrees dealing with members of religious minorities, which were finally summarized in a decree of 2003.[339]

---

336. Agreement between the Republic of Austria and the Protestant Church in Austria from 20 Apr. 2004 as amended 23 Mar. 2009.
337. Agreement between the Republic of Austria and Islamic Religious Society in Austria, BMJ-VD53101/0005-VD 2/2010 from 18 Mar. 2010.
338. K.-R. Trauner, 'Wandel von Staat und Kirche am Fallbeispiel Militärseelsorge', *Österreichisches Archiv für Recht und Religion* 59 (2012), 174–198.
339. The version currently in force dates from 2006, BMLV-VBl I 53/2006.

750. In the IslamG 2015 a legal basis for the installation of an Islamic Military Chaplaincy was created. In 2011, the Orthodox Military Chaplaincy was established on the basis of §7 section 1 OrthodoxenG and an agreement between the Austrian Republic and the Orthodox Bishops' Conference.[340] However, the law provides for an institutional incorporation comparable to the Catholic and the Protestant Chaplaincies, the person designated by the Orthodox Bishops' Conference is not a member of the armed forces. The remuneration is paid by the Greek-Orthodox Church in Austria, which receives an expenditure reimbursement from the Ministry of Defence amounting to only EUR 4,100 per annum.

751. Over and above, in general, the individual right of religious freedom within the armed forces is taken into consideration to a great extent and in a differentiated manner, as regards, for example, religious holidays and service time, food, the wearing of beards, and prayer rooms. There are manifold precautionary measures for guaranteeing the possibility of observing religious commandments consistent with different individual adherence to religious rules. With regard to Jewish and Sikh soldiers, strict orthodoxy is taken into account, and with regard to Muslim soldiers three categories are distinguished, namely strict believers, extremely strict believers and non-strict believers.

752. Within the institutionalized Military Chaplaincy provision is made for ethics education (Lebenskundlicher Unterricht) for which the respective pastoral advisers are responsible. This instruction is obligatory for soldiers in basic military service or service training who are members of the Catholic Church, the Protestant Church or the Methodist-Evangelical Church; however, it is possible for individuals to withdraw from this.

§4. Pastoral Care in the Police Forces

753. Spiritual care in the Federal Police Forces[341] is based on agreements in private law with the Austrian Bishops' Conference[342] and the Evangelical Supreme Ecclesiastical Council (Evangelischer Oberkirchenrat),[343] as well as on an Administrative Ministerial Ordinance of the Home Office on Pastoral Care in the Police Forces.[344] The establishment of pastoral care for police officials explicitly aims to provide ethical-moral assistance in order to help individuals achieve an even more

---

340. Agreement on the Establishment of an Orthodox Military Chaplaincy *ad experimentum* between the Republic of Austria and the Orthodox Churches of 17 Jun. 2011, BMLVS 590597/4-Präs/2011 of 4 Aug. 2011, A.2. The permanent establishment took place 2013 (BMLVS 590597/6-Präs/2012 from 4 Jan. 2013).
341. *See* K. Schwarz, 'Polizeiseelsorge – berufsfeldbezogene Supervision vor dem Hintergrund der Religionsfreiheit', *Österreichisches Archiv für Recht und Religion* 55 (2008), 30–46.
342. Agreement between Archbishop Christoph Schönborn and the Federal Minister of the Interior of 12 Dec. 2002.
343. Agreement between Bishop Mag. Herwig Sturm and the Federal Minister of the Interior of 26 Sep. 2006.
344. BMI-OA 1000/0308-II/1/b/2006, 2 Jan. 2007.

conscientious and satisfying degree of fulfilment in their work, taking into consideration the particular mental and physical stresses involved in their profession and the resulting challenges to their family life and social contacts. Pastoral care in the police forces is subordinate to the Diocesan Bishop or the Evangelical Supreme Council, respectively. The appointment of pastoral ministers is carried out in consultation with the Federal Ministry of the Interior.

Part XIII. Religions in the Social Field

Chapter 1. Basic Principles and Activities

754. In almost all religions, social activities play an important role in religious practice. Especially in Christian tradition, charity is a major focus of the gospel. Since the beginning of Christianity, questions concerning the administration of charity in welfare organizations have stood at the centre of ecclesiastical activities. Although the achievements of medieval towns and their welfare foundations were of great importance for the history of charity in Europe, social services were predominantly integrated into ecclesiastical bodies. As in other European countries, during the time of enlightened absolutism (Maria Theresia and Joseph II) the Austrian state started to establish a system of welfare administration. The most important step was the organizational separation of matters of social welfare and healthcare (re-organization of the Viennese Groß-Armenhaus and the foundation of the Allgemeines Krankenhaus in 1784). In the constitutional period, the first important legislative measure came into force in 1870, when the Act on the Organization of the Public Health Service (Reichssanitätsgesetz) was issued, which included fundamental provisions for healthcare and nursing institutions. The right of supervision was conferred on the state. The municipalities were responsible for providing the necessary assistance in cases of illness and childbirth delivery. After the end of the monarchy, the Health Care Institutions Act of 15 July 1920 clarified that it was the responsibility of the Bundesländer to determine the necessity of establishing such institutions.

755. In Austrian constitutional law, no special clause exists concerning the principle of social justice or a welfare state, as such. Notwithstanding, it can be taken from the competence Articles (Article 10 section 1 nos. 11, 15 and 17 and Article 12 section 1 no. 1 B-VG) that the constitution presupposes a state that is obliged to comply with a number of social and welfare activities. Principally, the prevailing competence in welfare matters lies with the federal legislation. In accordance with Article 12 section 1 no. 1 the federal framework legislation is provided for social assistance for people in need, youth welfare, nursing homes, hospitals and other homes offering public assistance, whereas the passing of implementation laws is incumbent on the Bundesländer. Against this background, it must be noted that the welfare state in Austria is, on the level of ordinary law, realized in a comprehensive way.[345]

756. In general, voluntary charitable work must fulfil several functions: an integrative function, which consists of integrating people in need into the state system of social security as far as possible; an alternative function, that of offering temporary or permanent aid to people who fall through the network of social security; an advocatory function which should represent the requirements of persons in need against the state, thus indicating the efficiency of such operations in a sociopolitical sense. Cooperation with other organizations and charitable associations is an important precondition for closing gaps in the social system by joint political action and making proposals to remedy grievances.[346]

757. Owing to more distinct flexibility and being better geared to innovation, private charities are presently counteracting deficiencies and shortcomings of state facilities, which are characterized to a growing extent by excessive diversification of central regulation and bureaucracy. Recently, legal standards – which must be taken into account by church facilities and church-related institutions – have been significantly enhanced, particularly with respect to the legal embodiment of patients' rights, providing for secure standards of quality, establishing ethic commissions and supervisory instruments for staff, and accompanied by increasing regulations for healthcare institutions. All this is a great challenge for church-related non-profit organizations.

758. To a great extent, the expenditures of welfare services rendered by churches are refunded by public funds. By this form of 'outsourcing', the state saves costs in this sector because running such institutions by itself would cause more expenses. As far as the relationship and interaction between public welfare institutions and non-profit-making private charities are concerned, the principle of subsidiarity is carried out to a certain degree. Making use of voluntary charities is provided for according to the Public Welfare Acts of the Bundesländer if two preconditions are fulfilled: the private charities must be qualified and disposed to render the services concerned and their contributions are seen to promote the pursued objectives.

759. Voluntary charitable work in Austria is dominated by the organizations of the Catholic Church and the Protestant Church. In some fields such as homes for refugees, foreign aid and development cooperation, Catholic and Protestant institutions are the leading organizations. Their representatives are also prominent players in civil society in political discussions on immigration and integration.

345. *See* R. Potz & B. Schinkele, 'State and Church in the Social Field in Austria', in *Social Welfare, Religious Organizations and the State*, ed. I. Dübeck & F. O. Overgaard (Milan: Giuffrè, 2003), 157–178.

346. M. Lehner, *Caritas – Die soziale Arbeit der Kirche. Eine Theoriegeschichte* (Freiburg & Breisgau: Herder, 1997), 353 et seq.

760. By far, the most important organization performing charitable work within the Catholic Church is the Caritas.[347] This organization does not have a unitary organization and inner structure. Each diocesan Caritas has its own administration that works together in a parent organization, the so-called Austrian Caritas Centre. This is an institute with a legal entity according to cc. 312 et seq. CIC. Its tasks are primarily the coordination and promotion of the Caritas agencies as well as cooperation with the Caritas Internationalis. The Bishops' Conference nominates one Caritas Bishop who works within the Directory Conference, the most important decision-making body. The canon law differentiation between public and private associations with or without legal personality is of great importance. The fact that both the latter do not act on behalf of the church has the consequence that they are much less bound to instructions from or subject to the vigilance of the ecclesiastical authorities. The diocesan Caritas agencies have different legal statuses, according to canon law as well as state law. With regard to their juridical position in both legal spheres, one can, therefore, distinguish three categories of Caritas agencies. Most of them are public juridical persons according to canon law, partly also with public law status according to the Concordat (cf. 296). The Caritas of the Archdiocese of Vienna is established according to the State Associations Act, thus gaining legal personality governed by private law. The Caritas of the Diocese of Innsbruck has neither legal personality according to canon law nor state law.

761. Caritas Austria employs about *17,694* salaried employees, while another 46,000 persons work as volunteers. Financing is composed of public revenues and public subsidies, private revenues, donations (inclusive inheritances), sales and membership contributions. The annual budget of Caritas Austria amounts to EUR 1,128.30 million, three-quarters of which comes from public funds paid for carrying out public services, or as state subsidies for performing other charitable activities.[348] The main specialized fields of Caritas' activities according to its statutes are: homes for aged people with and without nursing care, centres for disabled persons and socio-psychological facilities, mobile services for aged persons and families, institutions for the homeless, advisory bureaus, homes for refugees, foreign aid and development cooperation, schools and kindergartens, parish Caritas and special work projects.

762. The Diakonische Werk (Diakonia) is the umbrella organization of thirty-four Protestant charitable organizations, including institutions of the Old Catholic Church, the Baptist Church of Austria and the Salvation Army as well. It is organized as an ecclesiastical association according to §219 of the Protestant Church

347. *See* P. Gantner, *Die verbandliche Caritas in Österreich. Eine staatskirchenrechtliche Bestandsaufnahme* (Linz: Trauner, 1998); C. Grabenwarter, 'Staatsrechtliche Rahmenbedingungen katholischer Caritas', *Österreichisches Archiv für Recht und Religion* 55 (2008), 373–398; M. Landau, 'Die Tätigkeit der Caritas vor dem Hintergrund ihres kirchlichen Anspruchs', *Österreichisches Archiv für Recht und Religion* 55 (2008), 413–458; B. J. Berkmann, 'Österreichische Caritas im europäischen Wettbewerb', *Österreichisches Archiv für Recht und Religion* 55 (2008), 462–493.

348. https://www.caritas.at/ueber-uns/was-wir-tun/ [15.11. 2023].

Constitution,[349] being recognized by the Evangelical Supreme Ecclesiastical Council (Oberkirchenrat) after approval of the statutes. Diakonia Austria employs about 10.317 persons in full-time positions, with a further 3,000 persons working as volunteers. The annual budget of the Diakonia amounts to EUR 568 million, of which about three-quarters come from public funds, either paid for the undertaking of public services or as state subsidies for performing other charitable activities.[350] The special fields in which Diakonia is active according to its statutes correspond with the activities of the Catholic Caritas. In most areas, the two institutions work together.

763. The large number of Jewish social and charitable organizations and foundations in Austria which generally used to be of great importance, especially in Vienna, for the development of welfare institutions ended with the destruction and annihilation of Jewish life during the Nazi era.[351] The Sanatorium Maimonides Centre exists today as an institution of the Israelite Cultus-Community of Vienna.[352] It combines many functions under one roof; as Vienna's Jewish old people's home, it includes a retirement home, nursing wards, outpatient clinics and a day-care centre. Many residents who were traumatized by events during the Nazi period and have returned to their original home country after years of residence abroad need special care and assistance.

764. The idea of establishing an Islamic charitable institution goes back to 1999, after the great earthquake in Izmir in Turkey, when the general under-representation of immigrants in the field of disaster relief in Austria became evident.[353] In 2022, the social and charitable institution 'Karima' was established as an association. The main focus is on supporting people in Austria. In the future, however, international aid projects will also be considered. It also supports the work of the Islamic Religious Society's social department. This includes hospital prison and military chaplaincy as well as telephone chaplaincy.

349. http://www.evang.at/fileadmin/evang.at/doc_rechtsdatenbank/kv.pdf.
350. http://diakonie.at/sites/default/files/jb_gesamt_fertig.pdf [03.04.2015].
351. A. S. Duizend Jensen, 'Jüdische Gemeinden, Vereine, Stiftungen und Fonds', in '*Arisierung' und Restitution*, ed. Österreichische Historikerkommission (Vienna: 2002): www.hakoah.at/ressourcen/pressetexte/INTJUEDVEREINE.pdf [3. 4. 2015].
352. *www.maimonides.at/.*
353. *See* K. *Tomenendal et al., Ramadan in Österreich. Zur muslimischen Selbstdarstellung im Fastenmonat* (Klagenfurt: Wieser-Verlag, 2010), 151 et seq.

Part XIV. Protection of Sundays and Religious Holidays

Chapter 1. General Remarks

765. The Austrian Federal Constitution does not include recognition or protection of Sundays and religious holidays. The Constitutions of a few Bundesländer (Lower Austria, Upper Austria and Salzburg)[354] provide for the protection of Sundays as a state objective. In general, public holiday observance constitutes a cultural-anthropological constant with a primarily cultic dimension, thus reflecting the history of a particular country and its specific approach to religion. This applies to Sundays as the Christian day of rest from work on the one hand and holidays of confessional origin, on the other.

766. In Austria because of the historically rooted situation concerning legal holidays, the question arises as to how and to what extent the legislator should protect those specific religious holidays as days of rest which are not explicitly protected by general laws on holidays on the one hand and the religious interests of individual adherents based on their freedom of religion or belief, on the other. Focus on these aspects has increased since the European anti-discrimination law came into force.[355]

767. Article 13 Act on the Interconfessional Relations of Citizens (InterkonfG) stipulates that no person should be forced to abstain from work on holidays of a religious community to which he or she does not belong. During religious services on Sundays, public work is prohibited if avoidable and not urgently necessary. The significance of this provision is relative, however, since Sundays and the most important Christian holidays are days of general rest from work.

354. Article 4 no. 2 Constitional Law of Lower Austria, Art. 9 Constitutional Law of Salzburg, Art. 15 section 3 Constitutional Law of Upper Austria.

355. *See* H. Hopf, K. Mayr & J. Eichinger, *GlBG: Gleichbehandlung – Antidiskriminierung* (Vienna: Manz, 2009); K. Mayr, 'Feiertage und Diskriminierung aufgrund der Religion im österreichischen Arbeitsrecht', *ecolex* 15 (2004), 428–431; W. Wieshaider, 'Das staatliche Feiertagsrecht als vergessene Umsetzungsmaterie der Richtlinie 2000/78/EG', *Österreichisches Archiv für Recht und Religion* 55 (2008), 279–289; A. Potz 'Dienstverhinderung aus religiösen Gründen', in *Recht – Religion – Kultur. Festschrift für Richard Potz*, ed. B. Schinkele et al. (Vienna: facultas.wuv, 2014), 639–662.

768. Legislation in several Bundesländer provides for various special regulations concerning public events on Good Friday and Christmas Eve. On those days, celebrations in general, partly including sports events, other events that are considered detrimental to the genuine character and significance of the days concerned or events that offend 'religious feelings'[356] are prohibited.

769. Extensive protection of religious holidays is provided for pupils according to school regulations (cf. 670–674) and for persons serving with the armed forces.

356. *See*, *e.g.*, § 17 section 2 Viennese Act on Cinemas, LGBl. 1955/18, as amended.

Chapter 2. Protection of Religious Holidays

770. Pursuant to §2 section 1 ARG, weekend rest in the sense of this Act generally comprises a continuous rest period of thirty-six hours including Sundays. On legal holidays the employee has the right to a continuous rest period of at least twenty-four hours beginning at the earliest at 0.00 am and at the latest at 6.00 am (§7 section 1).[357]

771. In line with the historical background, most of the holidays recognized by the state and protected by law as days of rest from work are Christian, or more precisely, Catholic holidays; only two holidays are of secular nature (1 May, 26 October). The following days have been recognized as holidays according to §7 section 1 Act on Rest from Work (ARG): 1 January (New Year), 6 January (Epiphany), Easter Monday, 1 May (National Holiday), Ascension of Christ, Pentecost Monday, Corpus Christi, 15 August (Assumption Day), 26 October (National Holiday), 1 November (All Saints' Day), 8 December (Immaculate Conception), 25 December (Christmas Day) and 26 December (St. Stephen's Day).

772. After hearing the Regional Chamber of Industry and Trade and the competent Chamber for Workers and Employees, the head of a Bundesland (Landeshauptmann) is authorized to determine by ordinance those times during holidays in which activities necessary to meet the respective regional needs are allowed as far as they are not or not sufficiently referred to in the Operation Period Act (§3 BZG). From this perspective, problems repeatedly arise with regard to the Day of the Immaculate Conception.[358]

773. Article IX Concordat 1933 differs somewhat from this general enumeration, insofar as Easter Monday, Pentecost Monday and St. Stephen's Day are not mentioned; however, the Feast of the Apostles St. Peter and Paul (29th June) is added. The latter holiday was later repealed by papal dispensation.

774. The ARG applies to employees of legally recognized churches and religious societies who are not engaged in business (enterprise) unless no equivalent internal rules exist (§1 section 3 ARG). To give an example: The Decree of the Austrian Bishops' Conference concerning Exemptions from Weekend and Holiday Rest[359] contains supplementary rules regarding the various diocesan statutes on employment and remuneration. Altogether, these inner-ecclesiastical regulations constitute equivalent internal rules in the sense of the aforementioned norm. They regularly provide for a few more days free from work in addition to the legal provisions of the state, such as Christmas Eve, Maundy Thursday and the Day of the Regional Patron.

---

357. Act on Holiday Rest (FRG), BGBl. 1957/153, as amended. With regard to the ARG and the Operation Period Act (BZG), BGBl. 129/1984, as amended, the significance of the FRG has been marginalized.
358. Cf. VfSlg. 10510/1985.
359. Amtsblatt der Österreichischen Bischofskonferenz no. 2/1984, 29.

775. Good Friday has been a holiday for members of the Protestant Church only, namely the Augsburg Confession and the Helvetic Confession, the Old-Catholic Church and the Evangelical-Methodist Church (§7 section 3 ARG). This form of protection of special days for religious minorities has been called into question for quite some time with regard to the European anti-discrimination law (European Directive 2000/78/EC) because of possible implications of preferential treatment of those churches.

776. Accordingly, questions were referred to the ECJ for a preliminary ruling. Due to the underlying facts of the case – the plaintiff, who does not belong to a religious community, had claimed an additional payment of public holiday pay in accordance with §9 section 5 ARG for work performed on Good Friday – the focus was on the entitlement to public holiday pay in the case of work performed on Good Friday. The ECJ considered the establishment of Good Friday as a public holiday and the entitlement to public holiday pay in the case of work on this day only for members of certain Christian churches to be direct discrimination on the grounds of religion, contrary to Article 21 CFR. The ECJ left it up to national legislation to make Good Friday a public holiday for everyone or for no one.[360]

777. The Austrian legislator has complied with the ECJ's Good Friday ruling and introduced a 'personal leave day' in 2019 by amending the ARG (§7a section 1). Accordingly, the employee can unilaterally determine the date of this vacation day to which he or she is entitled once per vacation year ('unilateral vacation start'). The employee must give written notice of this day at least three months in advance. According to section 2, the employee is free not to take the announced 'personal vacation' at the request of the employer, whereby the entitlement to this day of leave is retained. Furthermore, in addition to vacation pay, the employee is entitled to due remuneration for the work performed for the announced day, i.e., a total of double the remuneration, which means that the right pursuant to section 1 has been consumed.

778. The ARG amendment adds a no. 28 to §33a, according to which provisions in collective labour agreements that provide for special regulations for Good Friday only for employees of the churches concerned are ineffective and will be inadmissible in the future. This provision requires revisions in existing collective labour agreements, for which there are already some models.

779. Since the middle of last century several Administrative Decrees, Circulars and similar announcements or collective labour agreements have already taken into account the specific holidays of religious minorities. For example, a Decree of the Federal Chancellery[361] allows Protestant public servants to attend church services on Reformation Day provided this does not interfere with the operational requirements of their posts, and Resolutions of the Viennese Town Senate allow time off from work on Reformation Day. A collective labour contract between the Austrian

360. ECJ 22.1.2019, C-193/17, Cresco Investigation GmbH / Markus Achatzi.
361. Decree of 23 Oct. 1956, Zl 60591-3/1956.

Trade Union Federation (Österreichischer Gewerkschaftsbund) and the Federal Chamber of Trade and Industry has granted a release from work on Yom Kippur.[362]

780. Meanwhile, it is clearly evident that efforts are generally being made to remedy the situation at the level of collective labour agreements and administrative decrees, respectively. Thus, for instance, the Collective Labour Agreement for University Employees[363] stipulates that employees who are members of a 'state-recognized church or religious society' are granted time off work for two days at most, with the continued payment of salary to enable them to comply with their essential religious duties on holidays (§16 section 7). The formulation 'state-recognized church or religious society' does not precisely correspond with legal terminology, however. Therefore, by interpretation in conformity with constitutional guarantees, it may be assumed that (at least) the state-registered religious denominational communities are to be subsumed under this regulation, as this would otherwise constitute discrimination.[364]

781. In the recently revised versions of the IsraelitenG 1890 and the IslamG 2015, 'state recognition' of certain religious Jewish, Muslim and Alevitic holidays (including prayer times on Fridays or Thursdays, respectively) has been included, although without direct consequences in the field of labour law as clarified in the Explanatory Remarks. However, disturbing and avoidable emissions surrounding places of worship have to be omitted.[365] The discussion of such questions in general is currently ongoing and concrete results are not yet predictable.

---

362. 18 Feb. 1953, Ke 23/53.
363. Cf. D. Schöberl, '§ 16 Kollektivvertrag', in *Personalrecht der Universitäten*, ed. W. Pfeil (Vienna: Manz, 2010), Rz 13.
364. A. Potz, 'Dienstverhinderung aus religiösen Gründen', in *Recht – Religion – Kultur. Festschrift für Richard Potz*, ed. B. Schinkele et al. (Vienna: facultas.wuv, 2014), 639–662.
365. Cf. the corresponding general regulation regarding holidays in Art. 13 section 3 InterkonfG (cf. *734*).

Chapter 3. Free Time off Work for Fulfilling Religious Duties

782. According to §8 section 1 ARG employees who work at weekends or during periods of holiday rest have a legal claim to have time off work on the grounds that it is necessary for them to fulfil their religious obligations unless it is possible for them to do so outside normal working hours and if the exemption is compatible with the operating requirements of the business or enterprise. The employee must inform the employer about his or her religious obligations at the same time as the agreement on the weekend or holiday rest, two days in advance at the latest, and in the case of a later agreement, immediately.

783. In this context, giving this information to the employer in good time, out of general loyalty of employees towards employers, is of great significance. The Supreme Court had to deal with the case of a disc jockey who was a member of the Protestant Church and had agreed more than one week in advance to work on Maundy Thursday and Good Friday. After having complied with his official duties on Maundy Thursday, he then confronted the employer with his refusal to work on the morning of Good Friday. The Supreme Court confirmed the legality of his dismissal on the grounds of his late notification (delay in communication) of his refusal to work.[366]

784. In another case, a Muslim employee had informed the employer during the week that he would not be able to work on the coming Saturday after 2 p.m. (following a week's working time of 46.5 hours) because of Bayrami, one of the highest religious feasts. The competent Labour and Social Court judged this a legitimate ground for his exemption from work.[367]

785. Over and above the legal framework of the ARG, there are a few more provisions on the basis of which a claim for a free time from work could be asserted, in particular §8 Act on Salaried Employees (AngestelltenG) and §1154 ABGB. These provisions make a claim for continued payment of salary in cases where an employee is prevented from working for important personal reasons which are no fault of his or hers. The desire to participate in a religious celebration is considered – in addition to disease and misfortune – an important reason in this sense. This can also be a relevant factor for employees who belong to religious communities which are not covered by the ARG.

786. In this context, the question of correct procedure arises in cases where adherents of certain religions are obliged not only to attend worship services, perform prayer rituals or other shorter religious activities but also when they have to rest from work throughout the day. There is no general legal basis which covers

366. OGH 23 Sep. 1975, 4 Ob 33/75.
367. Labour and Social Court (Arbeits- und Sozialgericht) Vienna, 27 Oct. 2003, 9 Cga 52/03m, ARD-Betriebsdienst (ARD) 5526/5/2004.

such conflicts. A substantial interpretation of fundamental rights, flexible and generous handling of leave claims and respective relevant labour law rules should, however, help resolve such problems. Accordingly, a fair balance must be struck between the religious interests of the employees or public servants and the requirements of the employers or state bodies. However, if this problem arises repeatedly (every Saturday, for example) it then becomes a matter for the employee's conscience to decide whether or not he or she is able to exercise the profession concerned. Thus, the High Administrative Court stated that a refusal to work by reference to the Bible neither constitutes a reason for legal justification nor a lawful excuse for the violation of official duty.[368]

368. VwSlg. 12509 A/1987.

Table of Statutes

ABGB General Civil Law Code (*Allgemeines Bürgerliches Gesetzbuch*) JGS 1811/946
AHG Act on State Liability (*Amtshaftungsgesetz*) BGBl. 1949/20
AMD-G Act on Audiovisual Media Services (*Audiovisuelle Mediendienste-Gesetz*) BGBl. I 2001/84
AnerkennungsG Law on Legal Recognition of Religious Communities (*Gesetz betreffend die gesetzliche Anerkennung von Religionsgesellschaften*) RGBl. 1874/68 as amended BGBl. I 1998/19
AngestelltenG Act on Salaried Employees (*Angestelltengesetz*) BGBl. 1921/292
ArbIG Labour Inspection Act (*Arbeitsinspektionsgesetz*) BGBl. 1993/27
ArbVG Act on Labour Constitution (*Arbeitsverfassungsgesetz*) BGBl.1974/22
ARG Act on Rest from Work (*Arbeitsruhegesetz*) BGBl. 1983/144
ASchG Employment Safety Act (*ArbeitnehmerInnenschutzgesetz)* BGBl. 1994/450
AStG Act concerning Studies at Academies and Establishing Colleges for Pedagogical Professions (*Akademien-Studiengesetz*) BGBl. I 1999/94
ASVG General Social Insurance Act (*Allgemeines Sozialversicherungsgesetz*) BGBl. 1955/189
AuslBG Act concerning the Employment of Foreigners within the Federal Territory (*Ausländerbeschäftigungsgesetz*) BGBl. 1975/218
BAO Federal Revenue Act (*Bundesabgabenordnung*) BGBl. 1961/194
BekGG Act on the Legal Status of Religious Denominational Communities (*Bundesgesetz über die Rechtspersönlichkeit von religiösen Bekenntnisgemeinschaften*) BGBl. I 1998/19
B-GLBG Federal Act on Equal Treatment (*Bundes-Gleichbehandlungsgetz*) BGBl. 1993/100
BPfGG Federal Act on Care Allowance (*Bundespflegegeldgesetz*) BGBl. 1993/110
B-VG Federal Constitution Act (*Bundes-Verfassungsgesetz*) BGBl. 1930/1 (Reenactment)
BZG Operation Period Act (*Sonn- und Feiertags-Betriebszeitengesetz*) BGBl. 1984/129
CIC Codex Iuris Canonici AAS 75 (1983) Pars II
CIC 1917 Codex Iuris Canonici AAS 9 (1917) Pars II
Concordat 1855 Imperial Patent, promulgating the Agreement of 18 August 1855 between His Holiness Pope Pius IX and His Imperial-Royal Apostolic Majesty Franz Joseph I, Emperor of Austria (Kaiserliches Patent, womit das zwischen Seiner Heiligkeit Papst Pius IX. und Seiner kaiserlich-königlichen Apostolischen

Majestät Franz Joseph I., Kaiser von Österreich, am 18. August 1855 [...] abgeschlossene Übereinkommen (Concordat) kundgemacht [...] wird, [...] RGBl 1855/195)

Concordat 1933 Concordat between the Holy See and the Austrian Republic with its Supplementary Protocol of 5 June 1933 (*Konkordat zwischen dem Heiligen Stuhl und der Republik Österreich samt Zusatzprotokoll vom 5. Juni 1933*), BGBl. II 1934/2

DMSG Act on Protection of Monuments (*Denkmalschutzgesetz*) BGBl. 1923/533

DSG Act on Data Protection (*Datenschutzgesetz*) BGBl. I 1999/165 in the version of BGBl. I 2018/23 ECHR European Convention on Human Rights (*Europäische Konvention zum Schutze der Menschenrechte und Grundfreiheiten*) BGBl. 1958/210

EDISG Federal Act on the Establishment of an Institute for Documentation and Information on Sect-Issues (*Bundesgesetz über die Einrichtung einer Dokumentations- und Informationsstelle für Sektenfragen*) BGBl. I 1998/150

EheG Act on the Unification of the Law of Marriage and Divorce in the Country of Austria and the Rest of the Reich (*Gesetz zur Vereinheitlichung des Rechts der Eheschließung und Ehescheidung im Lande Österreich und im übrigen Reichsgebiet*) dtRGBl. I S 1938/807

EidG Act on Oath (*Gesetz zur Regelung des Verfahrens bei den Eidesablegungen vor Gericht*) RGBl. 1868/33

FamLAG Act on Equalization of Family Burdens (*Familienlastenausgleichsgesetz*) BGBl. 1967/376

FeiertagsruheG Act on Holidays (*Feiertagsruhegesetz*) BGBl. 1957/153 (Reenactment)

FMedG Act on Reproductive Medicine (*Fortpflanzungsmedizingesetz*) BGBl. 1992/275

GDPR General Data Protection Regulation (*DSGVO-EU-Datenschutz-Grundverordnung* (EU) 2016/679)

GlBG Act on Equal Treatment (*Gleichbehandlungsgesetz*) BGBl. I 66/2004 HochschulG Federal Act on the Organization of the Pedagogical Colleges and their Studies of 2005 (*Hochschulgesetz*) BGBl. I 2006/30

ICCPR International Covenant on Civil and Political Rights, BGBl. 1978/591

ICESCR International Covenant on Economic, Social and Cultural Rights, BGBl. 1978/590

InterkonfG Act on Inter-Confessional Relations (*Gesetz über interkonfessionelle Verhältnisse der Staatsbürger*) RGBl 1868/49

IntG Act on Integration (Bundesgesetz zur Integration rechtmäßig in Österreich aufhältiger Personen ohne österreichische Staatsbürgerschaft) BGBl. I 2017/68 (Integrationsgesetz)

IPRG Federal Act on International Private Law (*Bundesgesetz über das internationale Privatrecht*) BGBl. 1978/304 IslamG 1912 Act on the Recognition of the Adherents of Islam as a Religious Community (*Gesetz betreffend die Anerkennung der Anhänger des Islams als Religionsgesellschaft*) RGBl. 1912/159

IslamG 2015 Act on External Legal Relationships of Islamic Religious Societies (*Bundesgesetz über die äußeren Rechtsverhältnisse islamischer Religionsgesellschaften – Islamgesetz 2015*) BGBl. I 2015/39

IsraelitenG Act on the External Legal Relationships of the Israelite Religious Society (*Gesetz betreffend die Regelung der äußeren Rechtsverhältnisse der israelitischen Religionsgesellschaft*) RGBl. 1890/57 in the version of BGBl. I 2012/48

JournalistenG Act on Legal Positions of Journalists (*Journalistengesetz*) BGBl. 1920/88

KaKuG Act on Hospitals (*Bundesgesetz über Krankenanstalten und Kuranstalten*) BGBl. 1957/1

KatholikenG Act on the External Relationships of the Catholic Church (*Gesetz, wodurch Bestimmungen zur Regelung der äußeren Rechtsverhältnisse der katholischen Kirche erlassen werden*) RGBl. 1874/50

KBG Act on Church-Contributions (*Gesetz über die Erhebung von Kirchenbeiträgen im Lande Österreich*) GBlLÖ 1939/543

Ktn-BauO Carinthian Building Regulation Act (*Kärntner Bauordnung*) LGBl. 1996/62 (Re-enactment)

Ktn-OrtsbildpflG Carinthian Act on Townscape Care (*Kärnter Ortsbildpflegegesetz*) LGBl. 1990/32

MedienG Act on Media (*Mediengesetz*) BGBl. 1981/314

MeldeG Registration Act (*Meldegesetz*) BGBl. 1992/9

NAG Act on Settlement and Residence (*Niederlassungs- und Aufenthaltsgesetz*) BGBl. I 2005/100

NÖKindergartenG Lower Austrian Kindergarten Act (*Niederösterreichisches Kindergartengesetz*) LGBl. 2006/49

OÖ-ROG Act on Regional Planning of Upper Austria (*Oberösterreichisches Raumordnungsgesetz*) LGBl. 1993/114

ORF-G Federal Act on Austrian Broadcasting (*Bundesgesetz über den Österreichischen Rundfunk*) BGBl. 1984/379 (Re-enactment)

OrientKG Federal Act on External Relationships of the Oriental-Orthodox Churches in Austria (*Bundesgesetz über äußere Rechtsverhältnisse der Orientalisch-orthodoxen Kirchen in Österreich*) BGBl. I 2003/20

OrthodoxenG Federal Act on External Legal Relationships of the Greek-Oriental Church in Austria (*Bundesgesetz über äußere Rechtsverhältnisse der griechisch-orientalischen Kirche in Österreich*) BGBl. 1967/229

PrivSchG Private School Act (*Bundesgesetz über das Privatschulwesen*) BGBl. 1962/244

PrivUniG Act on Private Universities (*Privatuniversitätengesetz*) BGBl. I 2011/74

ProtestantenG Federal Law on External Legal Relationships of the Protestant Church in Austria (*Bundesgesetz über äußere Rechtsverhältnisse der Evangelischen Kirche*) BGBl. 1961/182

PrR-G Act on Private Radio Broadcasting (*Bundesgesetz, mit dem Bestimmungen für privaten Hörfunk erlassen werden*) BGBl. I 2001/20

PStG Act on Personal Status (*Bundesgesetz über die Regeln des Personenstandswesens*) BGBl. I 2013/16

PUG Act on Private Universities (*Privatuniversitätengesetz*) BGBl. I 2011/74

RelKErzG Act on the Religious Upbringing of Children (*Bundesgesetz über die religiöse Kindererziehung*) BGBl. 1985/155 (Re-enactment)

RelUG Act on Religious Education at School (*Religionsunterrichtsgesetz*) BGBl. 1949/190

R-ÜG Act on the Transition of Laws (*Rechts-Überleitungsgesetz*) StGBl. 1945/6
SchOG Act on School-Organization (*Schulorganisationsgesetz*) BGBl. 1962/242
SchPflG Act on Compulsory Schooling (*Schulpflichtgesetz*) BGBl. 1985/76
Schule-Kirche-G Act Concerning the Relationship between Church and School (*Gesetz, wodurch grundsätzliche Bestimmungen über das Verhältnis der Schule zur Kirche erlassen werden*) RGBl 1868/48
Schulvertrag Treaty between the Holy See and the Austrian Republic concerning the Regulation of Questions relating to the School System and Concluding Protocol of 9 July 1962 (*Vertrag zwischen dem Heiligen Stuhl und der Republik Österreich vom 9. Juli 1962 zur Regelung von mit dem Schulwesen zusammenhängenden Fragen*) BGBl. 1962/273
SchZG Act on Teaching-time at Schools (*Schulzeitgesetz*) BGBl. 1985/77 (Re-enactment)
SPG Security Police Act (*Sicherheitspolizeigesetz*) BGBl. 1991/566
StG 1945 Penal Code 1945 (*Strafgesetz*) StGBl 1945/25
StGB 1975 Penal Code 1975 (*Strafgesetzbuch*) BGBl. 1974/60
StGG Constitutional Act on the Fundamental Rights of Citizens (*Staatsgrundgesetz über die allgemeinen Rechte der Staatsbürger für die im Reichsrathe vertretenen Königreiche und Länder*) RGBl 1867/142 incorporated in the B-VG StGBl. 1920/303
Stmk-ROG Act on Regional Planning of Styria (*Steiermärkisches Raumordnungsgesetz*) LGBl. 2010/49
StPO Code of Criminal Procedure (*Strafprozeßordnung*) BGBl. 1975/631 (Re-enactment) StVG Act on Imprisonment (*Strafvollzugsgesetz*) BGBl. 1969/144
StVStGermain Treaty of Saint-Germain-en-Laye (*Staatsvertrag von Saint-Germain-en-Laye vom 10. September 1919*) StGBl 1920/303
StVWien Treaty for the Re-establishment of an Independent and Democratic Austria. Signed at Vienna, on 15 May 1955 (*Staatsvertrag betreffend die Wiederherstellung eines unabhängigen und demokratischen Österreich vom 15. Mai 1955*) BGBl. 1955/152
TEU Treaty on European Union, consolidated version of 26 October 2012 (2012/C 326/01)
TFEU Treaty on the Functioning of the European Union, consolidated version of 26 October 2012 (2012/C 326/01)
TSchG Federal Act on Animal Protection (*Tierschutzgesetz*) BGBl. I 2004/118 UniAkkG Act Concerning Studies at Academies and Establishing Colleges for Pedagogical Professions (*Universitäts-Akkreditierungsgesetz*) BGBl. I 1999/168
UnivG University Act (*Bundesgesetz über die Organisation der Universitäten und ihre Studien*) BGBl. I 2002/120
UrhRG Copyright Act (*Urheberrechtsgesetz*) BGBl. 1936/111
VbVG Act on Responsibility of Associations (*Verbandsverantwortungsgesetz*) BGBl. I 2005/151
VereinsG Act on Associations (*Vereinsgesetz*) BGBl. I 2002/66 Vermögensvertrag Treaty concerning the Regulation of Proprietary Relations of 23 June 1960 (*Vertrag zwischen dem Heiligen Stuhl und der Republik Österreich vom 23. Juni 1960*

zur Regelung von vermögensrechtlichen Beziehungen) BGBl. 1960/195 Vlbg-BauG Vorarlberg Building Regulation Act (*Vorarlberger Baugesetz*) LGBl. 2011/52

Vlbg-RaumplG Vorarlberg Act on Regional Planning (*Vorarlberger Raumplaungsgesetz*) LBGl. 1985/31

WehrG Military Service Act (*Wehrgesetz*) BGBl. I 2001/146 (Re-enactment)

ZDG Act Concerning Non-Military Service (*Gesetz über den Zivildienst*) BGBl. 1986/679 (Re-enactment)

ZPO Code of Civil Procedure (Zivilprozessordnung) RGBl 1895/113

Selected Bibliography

I. Books

Barta, E. *Krankenanstalten in kirchlicher Trägerschaft*. Linz: Trauner, 1998.

Berka, W. *Medienfreiheit und Persönlichkeitsschutz. Die Freiheit der Medien und ihre Verantwortung im System der Grundrechte*. Vienna & New York: Springer, 1982.

Berka, W., Binder, C. & Kneihs, B. *Die Grundrechte. Grundfreiheiten und Menschenrechte in Österreich*. 2nd ed. Vienna: Verlag Österreich, 2019.Berkmann, J. B. *Katholische Kirche und Europäische Union im Dialog für die Menschen. Eine Annäherung aus Kirchenrecht und Europarecht*. Berlin: Duncker & Humblot 2008.

Bleckmann, A. *Von der individuellen Religionsfreiheit des Art. 9 EMRK zum Selbstbestimmungsrecht der Kirchen. Ansätze zu einem 'Europäischen Staatskirchenrecht'*. Cologne et al: Heymann, 1995.

Blum, N. *Die Gedanken-, Gewissens- und Religionsfreiheit nach Art. 9 der Europäischen Menschenrechtskonvention*. Berlin: Duncker & Humblot, 1990.

Böckenförde, E.-W. *Staat, Gesellschaft, Freiheit. Studien zur Staatstheorie und zum Verfassungsrecht*. Frankfurt: Suhrkamp, 1976.

Brünner C. (ed.). *Diskriminierung aus religiösen Gründen*. Vienna: Verlag Österreich, 2009.

Bucher, A. A. *Ethikunterricht in Österreich*. Innsbruck & Vienna: Tyrolia, 2001.

Budischowsky, J. *Die staatskirchenrechtliche Stellung der österreichischen Israeliten*. Vienna: Manz, 1995.

Burckhard, M. *Gesetze und Verordnungen in Cultussachen*. 2 vol. 3rd ed. Vienna: Manz, 1895.

Denk, M. *Die Berücksichtigung religiöser Interessen im Steuer- und Abgabenrecht*. 2 vol. Linz: Trauner, 1995.

Dreier, H. *Staat ohne Gott. Religion in der säkularen Moderne*. 2nd ed. Munich: C.H. Beck, 2018.

Duizend Jensen, A. S. *Jüdische Gemeinden, Vereine, Stiftungen und Fonds – 'Arisierung' und Restitution*. Vienna: Österreichische Historikerkommission, 2002.

Dullinger, T. *Arbeitsrechtliche Relevanz religiöser Bedürfnisse*. Vienna: Manz, 2020.Eibensteiner, C. *Die Kirche und ihre Einrichtungen als Tendenzbetriebe unter besonderer Berücksichtigung der Katholischen Kirche*. Linz: Trauner, 1994.

Selected Bibliography

Ermacora, F. *Handbuch der Grundfreiheiten und der Menschenrechte.* Vienna: Manz, 1963.

Ermacora, F. *Grundriß der Menschenrechte in Österreich.* Vienna: Manz, 1988.

Fischer, O. *Das Protestantengesetz 1961. Mit erläuternden Bemerkungen.* Vienna: Herder, 1962.

Frowein, J. & W. Peukert. *Europäische Menschenrechtskonvention. EMRK-Kommentar.* 3rd ed. Kehl am Rhein: Engel, 2009.

Fürlinger, E. *Moscheebaukonflikte in Österreich. Nationale Politik des religiösen Raums im globalen Zeitalter,* Vienna: University Press, 2013.

Gampl, I. *Österreichisches Staatskirchenrecht.* Vienna & New York: Springer, 1971.

Gampl, I., R. Potz & B. Schinkele. *Österreichisches Staatskirchenrecht. Gesetze, Materialien, Rechtsprechung.* Vol. 1. Vienna: Orac, 1990.

Gampl, I., R. Potz & B. Schinkele. *Österreichisches Staatskirchenrecht. Gesetze, Materialien, Rechtsprechung.* Vol. 2. Vienna: Orac, 1993.

Gantner, P. *Die verbandliche Caritas in Österreich. Eine staatskirchenrechtliche Bestandsaufnahme.* Linz: Trauner, 1998.

Gartner, B. *Der religionsrechtliche Status islamischer und islamistischer Gemeinschaften.* Vienna-New York: Springer, 2011.Grabenwarter, C. & Pabel, K. *Europäische Menschenrechtskonvention.* 7th ed. Munich & Vienna: C.H. Beck, 2021.

Graf-Stuhlhofer, F. *Eckdaten zur Geschichte österreichischer Freikirchen.* Pforzheim: Martin-Bucher-Seminar, 2021.

Haring, J. *Kommentar zum neuen österreichischen Konkordat.* Innsbruck, Vienna & Munich: Tyrolia, 1934.

Haunschmidt, F. *Das Arbeitsrechtsverhältnis der Laienmitarbeiter im Bereich der katholischen Kirche.* Vienna: Verlag des Verbandes der Wissenschaftlichen Gesellschaften Österreichs, 1989.

Heimerl, H. & H. Pree. *Handbuch des Vermögensrechts der katholischen Kirche unter besonderer Berücksichtigung der Rechtsverhältnisse in Bayern und Österreich.* Regensburg: Pustet, 1993.

Heine, S., R. Lohlker & R. Potz. *Islam in Österreich.* Innsbruck & Vienna: Tyrolia-Verlag, 2012.

Heinig H. M. & C. Walter. *Staatskirchenrecht oder Religionsverfassungsrecht. Ein begriffspolitischer Grundsatzstreit.*Tübingen: Mohr Siebeck, 2007.Hengstschläger, J. & Leeb, D. *Grundrechte.* 3rd ed. Vienna: Manz, 2019.

Herrnritt, R. H. *Grundlehren des Verwaltungsrechts.* Tübingen: Mohr Siebeck, 1921.Hiersche, A., Holzinger, K. & Eibl, B. *Handbuch des Epidemierechts.* Vienna: Manz, 2020.

Hilf, J.M., Urtz, C. & Handstanger, M. Strafrecht. *Verbandsverantwortlichkeit aus strafrechtlicher, abgabenrechtlicher und verwaltungsstrafrechtlicher Sicht. 20. ÖJT 2018.* Vol. 3/1. Vienna: Manz 2018.

Hinkelmann, F. *Bibliographie zu Freikirchen und Evangelikaler Bewegung in Österreich.* Petzenkirchen: Verlag für Glaube, Theologie und Gemeinde, 2021

Höhl, M. & Hartleib, G. *Integrationsgesetz. Kommentar unter Einbindung der Durchführungsbestimmungen sowie der relevanten Nebenbestimmungen.* Vienna & Graz: NWV, 2020.

Holoubek, M. *Die Struktur der grundrechtlichen Gesetzesvorbehalte. System oder Schrankenwirrwarr?* Vienna: Orac, 1997.Hopf, H., Mayr, K., Eichinger, J. & Erler, G., GlBG. Gleichbehandlung – Antidiskriminierung. 2nd ed. Vienna: Manz, 2021.

Höpfel, F. & Ratz, E. *Wiener Kommentar zum Strafgesetzbuch.* 2nd ed. Vienna: Manz, 2022.

Hussarek, M. *Grundriß des Staatskirchenrechts.* 2nd ed. Leipzig: Duncker & Humblot, 1908.

Huster, S. *Die ethische Neutralität des Staates.* 2nd ed. Tübingen: Mohr Siebeck, 2017.

Isak, A. *Das Selbstverständnis der Kirchen und Religionsgemeinschaften und seine Bedeutung für die Auslegung staatlichen Rechts.* Berlin: Duncker & Humblot, 1994.Jonak, F. & Kövesi, L. *Das österreichische Schulrecht.* 14th ed. Vienna: ÖBV, 2016.

Juranek, M. *Das österreichische Schulrecht. Einführung in die Praxis.* 6th ed. Vienna: Verlag Österreich, 2022.Kahl, W. *Lehrsystem des Kirchenrechts und der Kirchenpolitik.* Freiburg im Breisgau & Leipzig: Mohr Siebeck, 1894.

Kalb, H., R. Potz & B. Schinkele. *Das Kreuz in Klassenzimmer und Gerichtssaal.* Freistadt: Plöchl, 1996.

Kalb, H., R. Potz & B. Schinkele. *Religionsgemeinschaftenrecht. Anerkennung und Eintragung.* Vienna: Verlag Österreich, 1998.

Kalb, H., R. Potz & B. Schinkele. *Religionsrecht.* Vienna: WUV, 2003.

Kasiri, H. *Der Schia-Islam. 14 Volumes.* Vienna: iLogos Internationaler Verlag des schiitischen Wissensdiskurses, 2020.

Kirste, S. *Theorie der Körperschaft des öffentlichen Rechts: verwaltungshistorische, organisationstheoretische und verwaltungsorganisationsrechtliche Aspekte.* Heidelberg: heiBOOKS, 2017.

Klecatsky, H. R. & H. Weiler. *Österreichisches Staatskirchenrecht.* Vienna: Verlag der Österreichischen Staatsdruckerei, 1958.

Klein, B. *Privatschulen im kanonistischen Kontext. Eine staatskirchenrechtliche Bestandsaufnahme.* 2 vol. Linz: Trauner, 1995.

Kohlhofer, R. (ed.). *Gewissensfreiheit und Militärdienst.* Vienna: Verlag Österreich, 2000.

Koja, F. *Wissenschaftsfreiheit und Universität.* Salzburg: Pustet, 1976.

Koja, F. *Konkordat und Wissenschaftsfreiheit.* Salzburg: Pustet, 1980.

Korinek, K. *Entwicklungstendenzen in der Grundrechtsjudikatur des Verfassungsgerichtshofes.* Vienna: Orac, 1992.

Körtner, U. (ed.). *Kirche – Demokratie – Öffentlichkeit. Ort und Auftrag der Kirchen in der demokratischen Gesellschaft.* Innsbruck & Vienna: Tyrolia, 2002.

Krajewski, M. *Der religionsrechtliche Acquis Communautaire der Europäischen Union. Ansätze eines systematischen Religionsrechts der EU unter EU-Vertrag, EG-Vertrag und EU-Verfassungsvertrag.* Berlin: Duncker & Humblot, 2008.

Kremsmair, J. *Der Weg zum österreichischen Konkordat von 1933–34.* Vienna: Verlag des Verbandes der Wissenschaftlichen Gesellschaften Österreichs, 1980.

Leitner, A. *Anspruch der Kirchen und Religionsgesellschaften auf Präsenz im öffentlich-rechtlichen und privatrechtlichen Rundfunk.* Linz: Trauner, 2000.

Lichtblau, A., B. Staudinger, C. Lind, M. Keil, & E. Brugger. *Geschichte der Juden in Österreich.* Vienna: Ueberreuter, 2006.

Liebmann, P., G. Tropper, G. Scheibelreiter & R. Leeb, *Geschichte des Christentums in Österreich: Von der Spätantike bis zu Gegenwart.* Vienna: Ueberreuter, 2003.

Link, C. *Kirchliche Rechtsgeschichte. Kirche, Staat und Recht in der europäischen Geschichte von den Anfängen bis ins 21. Jahrhundert.* 3rd ed. Munich: C.H. Beck, [3]2017.

Mayer, H. (ed.). *Staat und 'Sekten'. Staatliche Information und Rechtssschutz*, Vienna: Verlag Österreich, 2001.

Mayerhofer, E. *Handbuch für den politischen Verwaltungsdien*st. Vol. 4. Vienna: Manz, 1898.

Mischler, E. & J. Ulbrich. *Österreichisches Staatswörterbuch. Handbuch des gesamten österreichischen öffentlichen Rechts.* 4 vol. 2nd ed. Vienna: Hölder, 1905–1909.

Mock, E. *Gewissen und Gewissensfreiheit. Zur Theorie der Normativität im demokratischen Verfassungsstaat.* Berlin: Duncker & Humblot, 1983.

Muckl, S. *Religions – und Weltanschauungsfreiheit im Europarecht.* Heidelberg: Winter, 2002.

Noll, J. *Jehovas Zeugen als Bekenntnisgemeinschaft. Rechtsfragen um eine religiöse Minderheit.* Vienna: Verlag Österreich, 2001.

Öhlinger, T. & H. Eberhard. *Verfassungsrecht.* 10th ed. Vienna: facultas.wuv, 2014.

Ortner, H. *Religion und Staat. Säkularität und religiöse Neutralität.* Vienna: Verlag Österreich, 2001.

Paarhammer, H. (ed.). *Vermögensverwaltung in der Kirche.* 2nd ed. Thaur in Tirol: Österreichischer Kulturverlag, 1988.

Paarhammer, H., F. Pototschnig & A. Rinnerthaler (eds.). *60 Jahre österreichisches Konkordat.* Munich & Eichenau: Kovar, 1994.

Plöchl, W. M. *Vom Grundrecht der Kirchenfreiheit.* St. Pölten: NÖ Pressehaus, 1977.

Plöchl, W. M. *Die Wiener Griechen.* Vienna: Herder, 1983.

Potz, R & R. Kohlhofer (eds.). *Die 'Anerkennung' von Religionsgemeinschaften.* Vienna: Verlag Österreich, 2002.

Potz, R. & B. Schinkele. *Religionsrecht im Überblick.* 2nd ed. Vienna: facultas.wuv, 2007.

R. Potz, B. Schinkele & W. Wieshaider (eds.). *Schächten. Religionsfreiheit und Tierschutz.* Freistadt-Egling: Plöchl, 2001.

Pree, H. *Österreichisches Staatskirchenrecht.* Vienna & New York: Springer, 1984.Pree, H. & Heckel, N. *Das kirchliche Vermögen, seine Verwaltung und Vertretung. Handreichung für die Praxis.* 3rd ed. Vienna: Verlag Österreich, 2021.

Primetshofer, B. *Ehe und Konkordat. Die Grundlinien des österreichischen Konkordats-Eherechtes 1934 und das geltende österreichische Eherecht.* Vienna: Herder, 1960.

Rinnerthaler, A. (ed.). *Historische und rechtliche Aspekte des Religionsunterrichts.* Frankfurt am Main et al.: Lang, 2004.

Rinnerthaler, A. & H. Paarhammer (ed.). *Das kirchliche Privatschulwesen – historische, pastorale, rechtliche und ökonomische Aspekte*. Frankfurt am Main et al.: Peter Lang 2007.

Robbers, G. (ed.). *State and Church in the European Union*. 2nd ed. Baden-Baden: Nomos, 2005.

Rumpler, H. *Österreichische Geschichte 1804-1914: Eine Chance für Mitteleuropa: Bürgerliche Emanzipation und Staatsverfall in der Habsburgermonarchie*. Vienna: Ueberreuter, 1997.

Runggaldier, U. & B. Schinkele (eds.). *Arbeitsrecht und Kirche. Zur arbeitsrechtlichen und sozialrechtlichen Stellung von Klerikern, Ordensangehörigen und kirchlichen Mitarbeitern in Österreich*. Vienna & New York: Springer, 1996.

Schinkele, B. et al. (eds.). *Recht – Religion – Kultur. Festschrift für Richard Potz*. Vienna: facultas.wuv, 2014.

Schlaich, K. *Neutralität als verfassungsrechtliches Prinzip*. Tübingen: Mohr, 1972.

Schnizer, H. *Schuldrechtliche Verträge der Katholischen Kirche in Österreich*. Graz & Cologne: Böhlaus, 1961.

Schwendenwein, H. *Religion in der Schule. Rechtsgrundlagen. Das Österreichische Religionsunterrichtsrecht*. Graz, Vienna & Cologne: Styria, 1980.

Schwendenwein, H. *Österreichisches Staatskirchenrecht*. Essen: Ludgerus, 1992.

Schwerhoff, G. *Verfluchte Götter. Die Geschichte der Blasphemie*. Frankfurt/Main: S. Fischer, 2021.

Silbernagl, I. *Verfassung und gegenwärtiger Bestand sämtlicher Kirchen des Orients*. 2nd ed. Regensburg: C. G. Manz, 1904.

Stelzer, M. *Das Wesensgehaltsargument und der Grundsatz der Verhältnismäßigkeit*. Vienna & New York: Springer, 1991.

Strupp, K. (ed.). *Ausgewählte diplomatische Aktenstücke zur Orientalischen Frage*. Perthes: Gotha, 1916.

Tomenendal, K. et al. Ramadan in Österreich. Zur muslimischen Selbstdarstellung im Fastenmonat. Klagenfurt: Wieser-Verlag, 2010.

Vachek, M. *Das Religionsrecht der Europäischen Union im Spannungsfeld zwischen mitgliedstaatlichen Kompetenzreservaten und Art. 9 EMRK*. Frankfurt am Main et al: Lang, 2000.

Wakolbinger, D. *Was heißt denn hier normal? Ausgewählte Fragen zum Antidiskriminierungsrecht: Religion, Weltanschauung, sexuelle Orientierung, ethnische Zugehörigkeit*. Vienna: Neuer Wissenschaftlicher Verlag, 2011.

Wallner, J. *Health Care zwischen Ethik und Recht*. Vienna: facultas.wuv, 2007.

Wandruszka, A. & P. Urbanitsch (eds.). *Die Habsburgermonarchie 1848-1918*. Vol. 4. 2nd ed. Vienna: Verlag der Österreichischen Akademie der Wissenschaften, 1985.

Werni, F. *Religionsgemeinschaften und Gleichheit*. Vienna: Verlag Österreich, 2022.

Wieshaider, W. *Denkmal und öffentliches Interesse*. Vienna: Verlag Österreich, 2016.

Wieshaider, W. (ed.). *Die Veränderung von Denkmalen. Das Verfahren gemäß §5 DMSG*. Vienna: facultas, 2019.Winter, J. *Die Wissenschaft vom Staatskirchenrecht im Dritten Reich*. Frankfurt am Main et al: Peter Lang, 1979.

Wunderli, A. & Mann, C. (eds.). *Die gesetzliche Anerkennung der 'Freikirchen in Österreich'. Ein ökumenisches Gesamtkunstwerk*. Vienna: LIT, 2023.

II. Articles

1. Articles in Books

Berka, W. 'Rechtliche Probleme im Hinblick auf die Tätigkeit der Ethikkommissionen.' In *Sozialrechtliche Probleme bei der Ausübung von Heilberufen*, edited by T. Tomandl. Vienna: Braumüller, 1996.

Berka, W. 'Präambel'. In *Mediengesetz*, edited by W. Berka et al. Vienna: LexisNexis/Orac, 2002.

Claassen, C.D. 'Art 17 AEUV'. In *Das Recht der Europäischen Union*, edited by E. Grabitz, M. Hilf & M. Nettesheim. Munich: Beck, 2023.

Dreier, H. 'Recht und Religion: Zur (Un-)Möglichkeit religiös-weltanschaulicher Neutralität des Staates'. In Religion und Gesellschaft. Sinnstiftungssysteme im Konflikt, edited by F. W. Graf & J.-U. Hartmann. Berlin & Boston: Walter de Gruyter GmbH, 2019.

Ehn, E. 'Das Arbeitsrecht in der Kirche aus Dienstgebersicht'. In *Arbeitsrecht und Kirche. Zur arbeitsrechtlichen und sozialrechtlichen Stellung von Klerikern, Ordensangehörigen und kirchlichen Mitarbeitern in Österreich*, edited by U. Runggaldier & B. Schinkele. Vienna & New York: Springer, 1996.

Gartner, B. 'Das neue österreichische Israelitengesetz: Eine historische Annäherung'. In *Neuere Entwicklungen im Religionsrecht europäischer Staaten*, edited by W. Rees et al. Berlin: Duncker & Humblot, 2013.

Gottas, F. 'Die Geschichte des Protestantismus in der Habsburgermonarchie'. In *Die Habsburgermonarchie. 1848–1918*, edited by A. Wandruszka & P. Urbanitsch. Vol 4. 2nd. Ed. Vienna: Verlag der Österreichischen Akademie der Wissenschaften, 1995.

Grabenwarter, C. 'Artikel 9 EMRK'; 'Artikel 14 StGG'; 'Artikel 16 StGG'; 'Artikel 63 Abs. 2 StV St. Germain'. In *Österreichisches Bundesverfassungsrecht*, edited by K. Korinek & M. Holoubek. Vienna & New York: Springer, 2003 and 2005.

Grabenwarter, C. 'Religion und Europäische Menschenrechtskonvention.' In *Religion und Internationales Recht*, edited by A. Zimmermann & U. Heinz. Berlin: Duncker & Humblot, 2006.

Grabenwarter, C., 'Wirtschaftliche Aktivitäten der Kirchen'. In *Das Recht der Non-Profit-Organisationen*, edited by T. Eilmansberger et al. Vienna: Linde-Verlag, 2006.

Grabenwarter, C. 'Religiöse Sendungen im Spannungsfeld zwischen Rundfunkfreiheit und Religionsfreiheit'. In *Staat im Wort. Festschrift Josef Isensee*, edited by O. Depenheuer et al. Heidelberg: Müller, 2007.

Hammer, S. 'Zur konfessionellen Bindung der Theologie aus Sicht der Wissenschaftsfreiheit'. In *Recht – Religion – Kultur. Festschrift für Richard Potz*, edited by B. Schinkele et al. Vienna: facultas.wuv, 2014.

Holoubek, M. 'Zur Begründung des Verhältnismäßigkeitgrundsatzes – verwaltungs-, verfassungs- und gemeinschaftsrechtliche Aspekte'. In *Grundfragen und aktuelle Probleme des öffentlichen Rechts*, eds. S. Griller et al. Vienna: Orac, 1995.

Holzleithner, E. 'Menschenrechte und Toleranz'. In *Recht – Religion – Kultur. Festschrift für Richard Potz*, edited by B. Schinkele et al. Vienna: facultas.wuv, 2014.

Jisa, W. 'Zur Diskriminierung wegen der ethnischen Zugehörigkeit in der schulischen (Aus-) Bildung und das Gleichbehandlungsgesetz'. In *Recht – Religion – Kultur. Festschrift für Richard Potz*, edited by B. Schinkele et al. Vienna: facultas.wuv, 2014.

Kalb, H. 'The Financing of Religious Communities in Austria'. In *The Financing of Religious Communities in the European Union*, edited by European Consortium of Church & State Research. Leuven et al.: Peeters, 2009.

Kalb, H. 'Religiös motivierte Beschneidung Minderjähriger – einige Anmerkungen', in *Interdisziplinäre Rechtswissenschaft – Schutzansprüche und Schutzaufgaben im Recht*, edited by E. Wagner & W. Bergthaler. Vienna: Verlag Österreich, 2013.

Kalb, H. 'Religionsstrafrecht – aktuelle Änderungen'. In *Recht – Religion – Kultur. Festschrift für Richard Potz*, edited by B. Schinkele et al. Vienna: facultas.wuv, 2014.

Kalb, H. 'Kommentar zu Art. 62-82 (Minderheitenschutz)'. In *Der Vertrag von St. Germain. Kommentar*, edited by H. Kalb, T. Olechowski & A. Ziegerhofer. Vienna: Manz, 2021.

Kalb, H. 'Sterben in Würde: Assistierter Suizid. Rechtliche Regelung'. In *Kanonist, Ordensmann und Gestalter*, edited by W. Ress, H. Kalb & C. Niemand. Berlin: Dunker & Humblodt, 2023.

Karakayali, S. Zur 'Islamisierung' der Einwanderungsdebatte. In *Die Rolle der Religion im Integrationsprozess,* edited by B. Ucar, Frankfurt/Main etc: Peter Lang, 2010.Klecatsky, H. R. 'Die Kirchenfreiheit in Österreich'. In *Kirche und Staat. Festschrift für Fritz Eckert*, edited by H. Schambeck. Berlin: Duncker & Humblot, 1976.

Klecatsky, H. R. 'Das Verhältnis von Kirche und Staat in der Republik Österreich'. In *Handbuch des katholischen Kirchenrechts*, edited by J. Listl, H. Müller & H. Schmitz. Regensburg: Pustet, 1983.

Klecatsky, H. R. 'Die Kirchen als Körperschaften des öffentlichen Rechts im Staatskirchenrecht der Bundesrepublik Deutschland und der Republik Österreich'. In *Arbeitleben und Rechtsordnung. Festschrift für Gerhard Schnorr*, edited by O. Martinek & G. Wachter. Vienna: Manz, 1988.

Koizar, W. 'Sozialrechtliche Stellung von Klerikern, Ordensangehörigen und kirchlichen Mitarbeitern'. In *Arbeitsrecht und Kirche. Zur arbeitsrechtlichen und sozialrechtlichen Stellung von Klerikern, Ordensangehörigen und kirchlichen Mitarbeitern in Österreich*, edited by U. Runggaldier & B. Schinkele. Vienna & New York: Springer, 1996.

Koja, F. 'Konkordat. Wissenschaftsfreiheit. Legalitätsprinzip'. In *60 Jahre österreichisches Konkordat*, edited by H. Paarhammer, F. Pototschnig & A. Rinnerthaler. Munich & Eichenau: Kovar, 1994.

Kolonovits, D. 'Meinungsfreiheit und Blasphemie in der jüngeren Rechtsprechung des EGMR'. In *Kontinuität und Wandel der EMRK. Studien zur Europäischen Menschenrechtskonvention*, edited by C. Grabenwarter & R. Thienel. Kehl, Straßburg & Arlington: Engel, 1998.

Korinek, K. 'Gedanken zur Bindung des Gesetzgebers an den Gleichheitssatz nach der Judikatur des Verfassungsgerichtshofes'. In *Im Dienst an Staat und Recht. Festschrift für Erwin Melichar*, edited by H. Schäffer. Vienna: Manz, 1983.

Korinek, K. 'Betrachtungen zur österreichischen Verfassungsgerichtsbarkeit'. In *Staatsrecht und Staatswissenschaften in Zeiten des Wandels*, eds. B.-C. Funk et al. Vienna & New York: Springer, 1992.

Kowatsch, A. 'Arbeitnehmer oder Unterhaltsempfänger?' In *Vom Ererbten und Anvertrauten. Die kirchliche Vermögensverwaltung auf dem Prüfstand*, edited by A. Kowatsch. St. Ottilien: EOS, 2022.

Krömer, P. & Brandner, M. in 'Art 91'. In *Praxiskommentar zum Datenschutzrecht – DSGVO und DSG*, edited by R. Knyrim. Vienna: Manz, 2023.

Kühnert, W. 'Die Rechtsstellung der Wiener Evangelisch-Theologischen Fakultät im Kraftfeld von Staat und Kirche'. In *Ex Aequo et Bono. Festschrift Willibald M. Plöchl*, edited by P. Leisching, F. Pototschnig & R. Potz. Innsbruck: Wagner, 1977.

Lehmkuhl, M.J. 2. Kapitel: Der sachliche und persönliche Anwendungsbereich des VbVG (§§ 1 und 2 VbVG). In *Handbuch Unternehmensstrafrecht*, edited by R. Soyer. Vienna: Manz, 2020.

Leisching, P. 'Die Römisch-Katholische Kirche in Cisleithanien'. In *Die Habsburgermonarchie. 1848–1918*, edited by A. Wandruszka & P. Urbanitsch. Vol 4. 2nd edn Vienna: Verlag der Österreichischen Akademie der Wissenschaften, 1995.

Leisching, P. 'Das Verhältnis von Kirche und Staat in der Republik Österreich'. In *Handbuch des katholischen Kirchenrechts*, edited by J. Listl & H. Schmitz. 2nd edn Regensburg: Pustet, 1999.

Lienbacher, G. 'Die rechtliche Anerkennung von Religionsgemeinschaften in Österreich'. In *Standpunkte im Kirchen- und Staatskirchenrecht*, edited by C. Grabenwarter & N. Lüdecke. Würzburg: Echter, 2002.

Lienbacher, G. 'Religiöse Rechte'. In *Handbuch der Grundrechte*, Band VII/1 Die Grundrechte in Österreich, edited by D. Merten & H.-J. Papier. Vienna: Manz, 2009.

Lienbacher, G. 'Gesetzliche Anerkennung als Religionsgesellschaft ohne Erwerb der Rechtspersönlichkeit nach Bekenntnisgemeinschaftengesetz?' In *In mandatis meditari. Festschrift Hans Paarhammer,* edited by S. Haering et al. Berlin: Duncker & Humblot, 2012.

Lienbacher, G. 'Raumordnungsrecht'. In *Besonderes Verwaltungsrecht*, edited by S. Bachmann. 14th ed. Vienna: Verlag Österreich, 2022.

Luf, G. 'Religionsunterricht – Ein Privileg der Kirchen?' In *Ex Aequp et Bono. Festschrift für Willibald M. Plöchl*, edited by P. Leisching, F. Pototschnig & R. Potz. Innsbruck: Wagner, 1977.

Luf, G. 'Die religiöse Freiheit und der Rechtscharakter der Menschenrechte. Überlegungen zur normativen Genese und Struktur der Religionsfreiheit'. In *Freiheit der Religion. Christentum und Islam unter dem Anspruch der Menschenrechte*, edited by J. Schwartländer. Mainz: Matthias-Grünewald-Verlag, 1993.

Luf, G. 'Zur Ethik der Ethikkommissionen. Tätigkeit und Rechtsgrundlagen der Ethikkommissionen in Österreich'. In *Zum Recht der Wirtschaft. Festschrift für Heinz Krejci*, edited by E. Bernat, E. Böhler & A. Weilinger. 2 vol. Vienna: Verlag Österreich, 2001.

Luf, G. '"Aufforderung zum Ungehorsam". Überlegungen zu den Aktionen der 'Pfarrer-Initiative'. In *Recht – Religion – Kultur. Festschrift Richard Potz*, edited by B. Schinkele et al. Vienna: facultas.wuv, 2014.

Mayer, H. 'Staatliche Warnungen vor 'Sekten' und Rechtsschutz aus verfassungsrechtlicher Sicht'. In *Staat und 'Sekten'. Staatliche Information und Rechtsschutz*, edited by H. Mayer. Vienna: Verlag Österreich, 2001.

Mayer-Maly, T. 'Betriebsverfassung und Religion'. In *Speculum Iuris at Ecclesiarum. Festschrift für Willibald M. Plöchl*, edited by H. Lentze & I. Gampl. Vienna: Herder, 1967.

Mayer-Maly, T. 'Loyalitätspflichten von Arbeitnehmern im Kirchendienst'. In *Gedenkschrift für Carl Holböck*, edited by F. Pototschnig & A. Rinnerthaler. Vienna: Verlag des Verbandes der Wissenschaftlichen Gesellschaften Österreichs, 1985.

Mazal, W. 'Zur Versicherungspflicht für kirchliche Dienstnehmer unter besonderer Berücksichtigung der Ständigen Diakone'. In *Arbeitsrecht und Kirche. Zur arbeitsrechtlichen und sozialrechtlichen Stellung von Klerikern, Ordensangehörigen und kirchlichen Mitarbeitern in Österreich*, edited by U. Runggaldier & B. Schinkele. Vienna & New York: Springer, 1996.

Mazal, W. 'Anmerkungen zur Kollektivvertragsfähigkeit kirchlicher juristischer Personen'. In *Recht – Religion – Kultur. Festschrift für Richard Potz*, edited by B. Schinkele et al. Vienna: facultas.wuv, 2014.

Merli, F. 'Die Zukunft des Staatsgrundgesetzes'. In 150 Jahre Staatsgrundgesetz über die allgemeinen Rechte der Staatsbürger, edited by F. Merli, M. Pöschl & E. Wiederin. Vienna: Manz, 2018.

Merli, F. 'Grenzen der Staatsinformation und staatlicher Propaganda'. In *Elektronische Medien im 'postfaktischen' Zeitalter – Dreizehntes Rundfunkforum*, edited by W. Berka, M. Holoubek & B. Leitl-Staudinger. Vienna: Manz, 2019.

Noll, J. 'Der Begriff 'Sekte' im Gesetz über die Einrichtung einer Bundesstelle für Sektenfragen'. In Staat und 'Sekten'. Staatliche Information und Rechtsschutz, edited by H. Mayer. Vienna: Verlag Österreich, 2001.

Paarhammer, H. 'Die vermögensrechtlichen Beziehungen zwischen Kirche und Staat auf der Grundlage des Konkordatsrechtes'. In *Kirchliches Finanzwesen in Österreich. Geld und Gut im Dienste der Seelsorge*, edited by H. Paarhammer. Thaur in Tirol: Österreichischer Kulturverlag, 1989.

Pabel, K. 'Beobachtungen zum Religionsgemeinschaftenrecht im österreichischen Staatskirchenrecht'. In *Die Zukunft der Verfassung – Die Verfassung der Zukunft? Festschrift für Karl Korinek*, edited by M. Holoubek, A. Martin & S. Schwarzer. Vienna & New York: Springer, 2010.

Pabel, K. 'Die religiöse Beschneidung von Jungen im Lichte der Grundrechte in Österreich'. In *Neuere Entwicklungen im Religionsrecht europäischer Staaten*, edited by W. Rees et al. Berlin: Duncker & Humblot, 2013.

Pabel, K. 'Das Grundrecht der Religionsfreiheit im Arbeitsrecht in der Rechtsprechung des EGMR'. In *Bildung, Wissenschaft, Politik – Instrumente zur Gestaltung der Gesellschaft – Christian Brünner zum 72. Geburtstag*, edited by W. Hauser et C. Brünner. Vienna et al: Böhlau, 2014.

Pöschl, M. 'Die Dogmatik des Staatsgrundgesetzes'. In *150 Jahre Staatsgrundgesetz über die allgemeinen Rechte der Staatsbürger*, edited by F. Merli, M. Pöschl & E. Wiederin. Vienna: Manz, 2018.

Potacs, M. 'Die Interpretation des Staatsgrundgesetzes'. In *150 Jahre Staatsgrundgesetz über die allgemeinen Rechte der Staatsbürger*, edited by F. Merli, M. Pöschl & E. Wiederin. Vienna: Manz, 2018.

Potz, A. 'Dienstverhinderung aus religiösen Gründen'. In *Recht – Religion – Kultur. Festschrift für Richard Potz*, edited by B. Schinkele et al. Vienna: facultas.wuv, 2014.

Potz, R. 'Öffentlichkeitsrecht – Verbandstätigkeit – Öffentlichkeitsauftrag'. In *Convivium uriusque iuris. Festschrift für Alexander Dordett*, edited by A. Scheuermann, R. Weiler & G. Winkler. Vienna: Wiener Dom Verlag, 1976.

Potz, R. 'Die inneren Angelegenheiten der anerkannten Kirchen und Religionsgesellschaften als Problem der Grundrechtsinterpretation'. In *Ex Aequo et Bono. Festschrift für Willibald M. Plöchl*, edited by P. Leisching, F. Pototschnig & R. Potz. Innsbruck: Wagner, 1977.

Potz, R. 'Nationalsozialismus und Staatskirchenrecht'. In *Nationalsozialismus und Recht. Rechtssetzung und Rechtswissenschaft in Österreich unter der Herrschaft des Nationalsozialismus*, edited by U. Davy et al. Vienna: Orac, 1990.

Potz, R. 'Citizens and believers in the Countries of the European Union: Austria'. In *Citizens and believers in the Countries of the European Union. A double membership to the test of secularization and globalization*, edited by European Consortium of Church & State Research. Milan: Giuffrè, 1999.

Potz, R. '30 Jahre österreichisches Orthodoxengesetz'. In *Kirchenrecht und Ökumene. Festgabe Panelaimon Rodopoulos* (Kanon XV), edited by C. G. Fürst, R. Potz & S. Troianos. Eichenau: Kovar, 1999.

Potz, R. 'Le confessioni religiose e la concezione federale dello Stato. L'esperienza dell'Austria'. In *Confessioni religiose e federalismo. Esperienze e prospettive*, edited by G. Feliciani. Bologna: Il mulino, 2000.

Potz, R. 'Zur öffentlich-rechtlichen Stellung der Kirchen und Religionsgesellschaften'. In *Die Anerkennung von Religionsgemeinschaften*, edited by R. Potz & R. Kohlhofer. Vienna: Verlag Österreich, 2002.

Potz, R. 'Der Islamische Religionsunterricht in Österreich'. In *Bürgerliche Freiheit und Christliche Verantwortung, Festschrift für Christoph Link*, edited by H. de Wall & M. Germann. Tübingen: Mohr Siebeck, 2003.

Potz, R. 'Covenantal and non-covenantal cooperation of state and religions in Austria'. In *Religion and Law in Dialogue: Covenantal and Non-covenantal Cooperation between State and Religion in Europe*, edited by European Consortium of Church & State Research. Leuven: Peeters, 2006.

Potz, R. 'Recht auf seelsorgliche Betreuung aus der Sicht der Patienten und der Religionsgemeinschaften'. In *Spiritualität, Religion und Kultur am Krankenbett*, edited by U. Körtner et al. Vienna & New York: Springer, 2009.

Potz, R. 'Österreichs Weg zum säkularen Staat im dritten Viertel des 20. Jahrhunderts'. In *Verdrängter Humanismus – verzögerte Aufklärung VI. Philosophie in Österreich 1951–2000. Auf der Suche nach authentischem Philosophieren*, edited by M. Benedikt et al. Vienna: wuv.facultas, 2010.

Potz, R. 'Das Ausschließlichkeitsrecht'. In *Vom praktischen Wert der Methode. Festschrift für Heinz Mayer*, edited by C. Jabloner et al. Vienna: Manz 2011.

Potz, R. 'Islamische Theologie an der Universität'. In *In mandatis meditari, Festschrift für Hans Paarhammer,* edited by S. Haering et al. Berlin: Duncker & Humblot, 2012.

Potz, R. 'Public Authorities and the Training of Religious Personnel in Austria'. In *Public Authorities and the Training of Religious Personnel in Europe,* edited by European Consortium of Church & State Research. Granada: Comares Editorial, 2015.

Potz, R. 'Der islamische Religionsunterricht in Österreich'. In *Islam, Recht und Diversität*, edited by S. Hinghofer-Szalkay & H. Kalb. Vienna: Verlag Österreich, 2018.

Potz, R. 'Neuer Wein in alte Schläuche? Aktuelle Entwicklungen im Religionsverfassungsrecht der Zweiten Republik'. In *Festschrift für Thomas Simon zum 65. Geburtstag. Land, Policey, Verfassung*, edited by G. Kohl, C. Neschwara, T. Olechowski, J. Pauser, I. Reiter-Zatloukal & M. Vec. Vienna: Verlag Österreich, 2020.

Potz, R. & B. Schinkele. 'Die kirchliche Trauung im staatlichen Recht Österreichs. Ein Beitrag zur Geschichte des Verhältnisses von Staat und Katholischer Kirche in den langen Fünfzigerjahren'. In *Österreich und der Heilige Stuhl im 19. und 20. Jahrhundert*, edited by H. Paarhammer & A. Rinnerthaler. Frankfurt am Main et al.: Peter Lang, 2001.

Potz, R. & B. Schinkele. 'State and Church in the Social Field in Austria'. In *Social Welfare, Religious Organizations and the State*, edited by European Consortium of Church & State Research. Milan: Guiffrè, 2003.

Potz, R. & B. Schinkele. 'Religion and Discrimination Law in Austria the European Union'. In *Religion and Discrimination Law in the European Union*, edited by European Consortium of Church & State Research. Trier 2012.

Potz, R. & B. Schinkele, 'Europarecht – Wie hast du's mit der Religion?' In *Religion in Europa heute. Sozialwissenschaftliche, rechtswissenschaftliche und hermeneutisch-religionsphilosophische Perspektiven*, edited by K. Appel et al. Göttingen: V&R unipress, 2012.

Potz, R. & B. Schinkele. 'Religion and Criminal Law in Austria'. In *Religion and Criminal Law*, edited by European Consortium of Church & State Research. Leuven: Peeters, 2013.

Potz, R. & B. Schinkele. 'The Mutual Roles of Religion and State in Austria'. In *The Mutual Roles of Religion and State in Europe*, edited by European Consortium for Church and State Research, Trier 2014.

Potz, R. & Schinkele, B. 'Religions- und Kunstfreiheit während der Corona-Pandemie. Überlegungen aus Anlass des VfGH-Erkenntnisses V 312/2021 vom 30. Juni 2022'. In *Kanonist, Ordensmann und Gestalter*, edited by W. Ress, H. Kalb & C. Niemand. Berlin: Dunker & Humblodt, 2023.

Pree, H. 'Gibt es ein dogmatisches Prinzip des österreichischen Staatskirchenrechts?' In *Im Dienst von Kirche und Staat. In memoriam Carl Holböck*, edited by F. Pototschnig & A. Rinnerthaler. Vienna: Verlag des Verbandes der Wissenschaftlichen Gesellschaften Österreichs, 1985.

Pree, H. 'Die Stellung des kirchlichen Laiendienstnehmers im CIC/1983'. In *Recht im Dienst des Menschen. Festschrift für Hugo Schwendenwein*, edited by K. Lüdicke, H. Paarhammer & D. A. Binder. Graz, Vienna & Cologne: Styria, 1986.

Primetshofer, B. 'Offene Fragen des österreichischen Staatskirchenrechts'. In *Festschrift für Fritz Eckert*, edited by H. Schambeck. Berlin: Duncker & Humblot, 1976.

Rees, W. 'Neuere Fragen um Schule und Religionsunterricht in Österreich'. In *Neuere Entwicklungen im Religionsrecht europäischer Staaten*, edited by W. Rees et al. Berlin: Duncker & Humblot, 2013.

Rees, W. 'Religions- und Meinungsfreiheit in Österreich mit einem Blick auf die Rechtsprechung'. In *Recht – Religion – Kultur. Festschrift für Richard Potz*, edited by B. Schinkele et al. Vienna: facultas.wuv, 2014.

Reiss, W. 'Religiös-kulturelle Betreuung im Strafvollzug. Herausforderungen für Staat, Anstalten, Religionsgemeinschaften und Forschung'. In Europa mit oder ohne Religion? II. Der Beitrag der Religion zum gegenwärtigen und künftigen Europa, edited by K. Appel & I. Guanzini. Göttingen: V&R unipress, 2016.

Reiss, W. 'The Management of Religious Diversity in the Austrian Armed Forces'. In Religion in Austria. Vol 3, edited by H. G. Hödl & L. Pokorny. Vienna: Praesens Verlag, 2016.

Rieger, J. & J. Schima. 'Kirche und Staat'. In *Rechtslexikon. Handbuch des österreichischen Rechts für die Praxis*, edited by F. Maultaschl, W. Schuppich & W. Stagel. Vienna: Hollinek, 1971.

Runggaldier, U. 'Das Arbeitsrecht in der Kirche: kollektivrechtliche Aspekte'. In *Arbeitsrecht und Kirche. Zur arbeitsrechtlichen und sozialrechtlichen Stellung von Klerikern, Ordensangehörigen und kirchlichen Mitarbeitern in Österreich*, edited by U. Runggaldier & B. Schinkele.Vienna & New York: Springer, 1996.

Scharfe, M. 'Des Amtsträgers Kleider: Dürfen Staatsbedienstete in Ausübung von Hoheitsgewalt religiöse Zeichen tragen?'. In *Islam, Recht und Diversität*, edited by S. Hinghofer-Szalkay & H. Kalb. Vienna: Verlag Österreich, 2018.

Schima, J. 'Zur Funktion der kirchlichen Autonomie nach Art. 15 StGG über die allgemeinen Rechte der Staatsbürger'. In *Convivium uriusque iuris. Festschrift für Alexander Dordett*, edited by A. Scheuermann, R. Weiler & G. Winkler. Vienna: Wiener Dom Verlag, 1976.

Schima, S. 'Neuerungen im österreichischen Anerkennungsrecht'. In *Neuere Entwicklungen im Religionsrecht europäischer Staaten*, edited by W. Rees et al. Berlin: Duncker & Humblot, 2013.

Schima, S. 'Die Aufhebung der Anerkennung von Religionsgemeinschaften. Anmerkungen zum neu erlassenen §11a des Bekenntnisgemeinschaftengesetzes'. In Recht – Religion – Kultur. Festschrift für Richard Potz, edited by B. Schinkele et al. Vienna: facultas.wuv, 2014.

Schima, S. 'Das im Islamgesetz 2015 verankerte Verbot der Auslandsfinanzierung. Anmerkungen vor dem Hintergrund der verfassungsgesetzlich gewährleisteten Religionsfreiheit'. In Islam, Recht und Diversität, edited by S. Hinghofer-Szalkay & H. Kalb. Vienna: Verlag Österreich, 2018.

Schinkele, B. 'Das Arbeitsrecht in der Kirche: Der verfassungsrechtliche und staatskirchenrechtliche Rahmen unter besonderer Berücksichtigung der katholischen Kirche'. In *Arbeitsrecht und Kirche. Zur arbeitsrechtlichen und sozialrechtlichen Stellung von Klerikern, Ordensangehörigen und kirchlichen Mitarbeitern in Österreich*, edited by U. Runggaldier & B. Schinkele. Vienna & New York: Springer, 1996.

Schinkele, B. 'Zur Rechtsstellung kirchlich bestellter Religionslehrer unter besonderer Berücksichtigung der katholischen Kirche'. In *Arbeitsrecht und Kirche. Zur arbeitsrechtlichen und sozialrechtlichen Stellung von Klerikern, Ordensangehörigen und kirchlichen Mitarbeitern in Österreich*, edited by U. Runggaldier & B. Schinkele. Vienna & New York: Springer, 1996.

Schinkele, B. 'Church Autonomy in Austria'. In *Church Autonomy*, edited by G. Robbers. Frankfurt/Main et al.: Peter Lang, 2001.

Schinkele, B. 'Die Rechtsstellung der Orientalisch-orthodoxen Kirchen in Österreich unter besonderer Berücksichtigung der Koptisch-orthodoxen Kirche'. In *Ius Canonicum in Oriente et Occidente. Festschrift für Carl Gerold Fürst*, edited by H. Zapp, A. Weiß & S. Korta. Frankfurt am Main: Peter Lang, 2003.

Schinkele, B. 'Religionsunterricht – ein Privileg der Kirchen und Religionsgesellschaften?' In *Historische und rechtliche Aspekte des Religionsunterrichts,* edited by A. Rinnerthaler. Frankfurt am Main et al.: Lang, 2004.

Schinkele, B. 'Vereinigungen von Gläubigen im Spannungsfeld von kirchlichem und staatlichem Recht. Überlegungen anlässlich des VfGH-Erkenntnisses Slg. 16395/2001'. In *Recht – Bürge der Freiheit. Festschrift für Johann Mühlsteiger*, edited by K. Breitsching & W. Rees. Berlin: Duncker & Humblot, 2006.

Schinkele, B. 'Religious Entities as Legal Persons – Austria'. In *Churches and Other Religious Organisations as Legal Persons*, edited by European Consortium of Church & State Research. Leuven: Peeters, 2007.

Schinkele, B. 'Verschleierung einer Angeklagten im Gerichtssaal? Überlegungen aus grundrechtlicher Sicht'. In *Islamophobie in Österreich*, edited by J. Bunzl & F. Hafez. Vienna & Innsbruck: Studienverlag, 2009.

Schinkele, B. 'Religionsfreiheit, Reichweite und Grenzen im Kontext religiöskultureller Praktiken – unter besonderer Berücksichtigung von Female Genital Mutilation und Zirkumzision'. In *Interkulturell kompetent. Ein Handbuch für Ärztinnen und Ärzte*, edited by M. Peintinger. Vienna: facultas.wuv, 2011.

Schinkele, B. 'The Application of the Freedom of Religion Principles of the European Convention on Human Rights in Austria'. In *Religious Freedom in the European Union: The Application of the European Convention on Human Rights in the European Union*, edited by European Consortium of Church & State Research. Leuven: Peeters, 2011.

Schinkele, B. 'Kirchenmitgliedschaft, Kirchenaustritt und europäisches Antidiskriminierungsrecht'. In *In mandatis meditari. Festschrift für Hans Paarhammer,* edited by S. Haering et al. Berlin: Duncker & Humblot, 2012.

Schinkele, B. 'Beichtgeheimnis und geistliche Amtsverschwiegenheit aus kirchen-, straf- und religionsrechtlicher Sicht'. In *Recht – Religion – Kultur. Festschrift für Richard Potz,* edited by B. Schinkele et al. Vienna: facultas.wuv, 2014.

Schinkele, B. 'Arbeitsrechtliche Fragestellungen abseits der "Kopftuch"-Debatte'. In Islam, Recht und Diversität, edited by S. Hinghofer-Szalkay & H. Kalb. Vienna: Verlag Österreich, 2018.

Schipka, P. 'Zwischen staatlicher Erwartungshaltung und Aufrechterhaltung kirchlicher Sendung: Institutionalisierte Kontakte zwischen Staat und Kirche in der Corona-Krise in der Republik Österreich'. In Religionsfreiheit in Seuchenzeiten, edited by S. Mückl. Berlin: Duncker & Humblodt, 2021.

Schnizer, H. 'Äußere Angelegenheiten der Kirche'. In *Katholisches Soziallexikon*, edited by A. Klose, W. Mantl & V. Zsifkovits. 2nd ed. Innsbruck et al: Tyrolia, 1980.

Schnizer, H. 'Kirchliches Vermögensrecht nach dem CIC 1983. Rechtsträger und Rechtsgeschäfte in Österreich'. In *Festschrift für Sebastian Ritter*, edited by H. Paarhammer. Thaur in Tirol: Österreichischer Kulturverlag, 1987.

Schrammel, W. 'Probleme des Tendenzschutzes in der österreichischen Betriebsverfassung'. In *Möglichkeiten und Grenzen der Rechtsordnung. Festschrift für Rudolf Strasser*, edited by W. Schwarz et al., Vienna: Manz, 1983.

Schrammel, W. 'Die Betriebsverfassung der gesetzlich anerkannten Kirchen und Religionsgesellschaften'. In *Recht – Religion – Kultur. Festschrift für Richard Potz*, edited by B. Schinkele et al. Vienna: facultas.wuv, 2014.

Schwarz, K. 'Die evangelischen Kirchen in Österreich von 1945 bis heute'. In *Evangelische Kirchen und Europa*, edited by M. Bünker. Vienna: Evangelischer Presseverband, 2006.

Schwarz, K. 'Historia docet: Freikirchen als Kläger über kultusrechtliche Beschränkungen der Religionsfreiheit'. In *Recht – Religion – Kultur. Festschrift für Richard Potz*, edited by B. Schinkele et al. Vienna: facultas.wuv, 2014.

Schwendenwein, H. 'Rechtsfragen der Vermögensverwaltung der Bischofskonferenzen. Alienationen und Akte der außerordentlichen Verwaltung'. In *Recht – Religion – Kultur. Festschrift für Richard Potz*, edited by B. Schinkele et al. Vienna: facultas.wuv, 2014.

Sökefeld, M. 'Sind Aleviten Muslime? Die alevitische Debatte über das Verhältnis von Alevitentum und Islam in Deutschland'. In *Aleviten in Deutschland. Identitätsprozesse einer Religionsgemeinschaft in der Diaspora*, edited by M. Sökefeld. Bielefeld: transcript-Verlag, 2008.

Stelzer, M. 'Korporative Aspekte der Religionsfreiheit in der Rechtsprechung des EGMR'. In *Religionsgemeinschaftenrecht und EGMR*, edited by R. Kohlhofer. Vienna: Verlag Österreich, 2009.

Thienel, R. 'Religionsfreiheit in Österreich'. In Religionsfreiheit in Mittel-und Osteuropa zwischen Tradition und Europäisierung, edited by G. Manssen & B. Banaszak. Frankfurt am Main et al.: Peter Lang, 2006.

Weilinger, A. & Miernicki, M. '§ 1 Vereinsgesetz'. In Vereinsgesetz (VereinsG), edited by A. Schopper & A. Weilinger. Vienna: Manz, 2019.

Windisch-Graetz, M. 'Gleichbehandlung in der Arbeitswelt ohne Unterschied der ethnischen Zugehörigkeit, der Religion oder Weltanschauung, des Alters oder der sexuellen Orientierung (Antidiskriminierung)'. In *Gleichbehandlungsgesetz. Kommentar*, edited by R. Rebhahn.Vienna & New York: Springer, 2005.

Wittreck, F. 'Religiöse Paralleljustiz im Rechtsstaat?'. In Ordnungen religiöser Pluralität. Wirklichkeit – Wahrnehmung – Gestaltung, edited by U. Willems, A. Reuter & D. Gerster. Frankfurt am Main & New York: Campus Verlag, 2016.

2. Articles in Journals

Apfalter, W. 'Is An Atheist Religion in Austria Legally Possible?'. *Journal of Law, Religion and State* 8 (2020): 93–123.

Aslan, E. 'Religiöse Erziehung der Muslime in Österreich'. *Österreichisches Archiv für Recht und Religion* 55 (2008): 1–13.

Berka, W. 'Die Europäische Menschenrechtskonvention und die Österreichische Grundrechtstradition'. *Österreichische Juristen-Zeitung* 34 (1979): 428–432.

Berka, W. 'Die Gesetzesvorbehalte der Europäischen Menschenrechtskonvention'. *Österreichische Zeitschrift für Öffentliches Recht* 37 (1986): 71–100.

Berkmann, B. J. 'Vom Pluralismus zum Laizismus? Die zweifach negative Religionsfreiheit in der jüngsten Rechtsprechung des Europäischen Gerichtshofs für Menschenrechte'. *Österreichisches Archiv für Recht und Religion* 59 (2000): 98–134.

Berkmann, B. J. 'Österreichische Caritas im europäischen Wettbewerb'. *Österreichisches Archiv für Recht und Religion* 55 (2008): 462–493.

Berkmann, B. J. 'Religiöses Recht vor dem Europäischen Gerichtshof für Menschenrechte'. *Österreichisches Archiv für Recht und Religion* 66 (2019): 7–60.

Birklbauer A. & Stiebellehner, Der besondere Schutz religiöser Sachen und Orte durch das Strafrecht – eine überkommene Regelung?. *Österreichisches Archiv für Recht und Religion* 64 (2017): 13–26.

Böckenförde, E.-W. 'Kreuze (Kruzifixe) in Gerichtssälen? Zum Verhältnis von staatlicher Selbstdarstellung und religiös weltanschaulicher Neutralität des Staates'. *Zeitschrift für Evangelisches Kirchenrecht* 20 (1975): 119–147.

Böhm, E. 'Kommentar zu BAG 10. 10. 2002, 2 AZR 472/01'. *Österreichisches Archiv für Recht und Religion* 51 (2004): 66–72.

Brünner, C., et al. 'Das Grundrecht auf Befreiung von der Wehrpflicht und die Zivildienstleistung in Österreich'. *Europäische Grundrechte Zeitschrift* 11 (1984): 485–501.

de Wall, H. 'Das Religionsrecht der EU – Grundstrukturen und Spannungen'. *Zeitschrift für evangelisches Kirchenrecht* 50 (2005): 383–402.

de Wall, H. 'Zur aktuellen Lage des Religionsrechts der Europäischen Union'. *Zeitschrift für evangelisches Kirchenrecht* 52 (2007): 310–324.

Erdoğan, Ö. 'Alevi Religious Education in Austria'. *Journal of Alevism Bektashism Studies* 15 (2017): 191–220.

Ferrari, S. 'Church and State in Europe. Common Pattern and Challenges'. *European Journal for Church and State Research* 2 (1995): 149–159.

Gampl, I. 'Die Rechtsstellung der Kirchen und ihrer Einrichtungen nach österreichischem Recht'. *Österreichisches Archiv für Kirchenrecht* 16 (1965): 3–30, 99–146.

Gampl, I. 'Staat und Evangelische Kirche in Österreich von der Reformation bis zur Gegenwart'. *Zeitschrift der Savigny-Stiftung für Rechtsgeschichte: Kanonistische Abteilung* 52 (1966): 299–331.

Gampl, I. '"Das religiöse Gefühl" als Schutzobjekt des Strafgesetzbuch-Entwurfs 1968'. *Juristische Blätter* 93 (1971): 109–114.
Gampl, I. 'Die inneren Angelegenheiten gem Art 15 StGG über die allgemeinen Rechte der Staatsbürger, RGBl Nr 142/1867'. *Zeitschrift für evangelisches Kirchenrecht* 16 (1971): 113–130.
Gampl, I. 'Veräußerung und Belastung von Kirchenvermögen in rechtsdogmatischer Sicht'. *Juristische Blätter* 107 (1985): 705–720.
Gartner, B. 'Aktuelle Herausforderungen für den Rechtsstaat einer plurireligiösen Gesellschaft'. *Österreichisches Archiv für Recht und Religion* 57 (2010): 37–65.
Gartner-Müller, B. 'Die Islamische Glaubensgemeinschaft und das Ausschließlichkeitsrecht der gesetzlich anerkannten Kirchen und Religionsgesellschaften'. *Österreichisches Archiv für Recht und Religion* 59 (2012): 251–283.
Gartner-Müller, B. 'Integration, Recht und Religion'. Österreichisches Archiv für Recht und Religion 64 (2017): 73–96.
Geroldinger, A. & Lukas, M. 'Kirchenglocken im Nachbarschaftsrecht. Überlegungen anlässlich der Entscheidung OGH 6 Ob 7/16x'. Österreichisches Archiv für Recht und Religion 64 (2017): 97–118.
Grabenwarter, C. 'Filmkunst im Spannungsfeld zwischen Freiheit der Meinungsäußerung und Religionsfreiheit'. *Zeitschrift für ausländisches öffentliches Recht und Völkerrecht* 55 (1995): 128–165.
Grabenwarter, C. 'Kirchen, Religionsgemeinschaften und andere'. *Journal für Rechtspolitik* 5 (1997): 265–277.
Grabenwarter, C. 'Staatsrechtliche Rahmenbedingungen katholischer Caritas'. *Österreichisches Archiv für Recht und Religion* 55 (2008): 373–398.
Grobner, A. 'Der Rechtsstatus der Friedhöfe in Österreich'. *Österreichisches Archiv für Kirchenrecht* 37 (1987/88): 265–289.
Gruber-Risak, M. 'Der Karfreitag (auch) als koalitionsrechtliches Problem. Grundrechtliche Überlegungen zur Aufhebung von "Karfreitagsregelungen" in Kollektivverträgen durch § 33a Abs 28 ARG'. Österreichisches Archiv für Recht und Religion 66 (2019): 322–338.Häberle, P. 'Gemeineuropäisches Verfassungsrecht'. *Europäische Grundrechte Zeitschrift* 18 (1991): 265–274.
Hagel, W. 'Teilkirchliche Aspekte zum Denkmalschutz in Österreich'. *Österreichisches Archiv für Kirchenrecht* 29 (1978): 396–425.
Hammer, S. 'Gott in der Verfassung? Zur Frage der Erwähnung der religiösen Dimension in der Präambel des Vertrages über eine Verfassung für Europa'. Österreichisches Archiv für Recht und Religion 49 (2002): 361–364.
Hammer, S. 'Zur Ungleichbehandlung von Religionsgemeinschaften'. *Österreichisches Archiv für Recht und Religion* 52 (2005): 209–226.
Hammer, S. 'Die Aleviten im österreichischen Religionsrecht – ein Kampf um Anerkennung. Der schwere Abschied vom Ausschließlichkeitsgrundsatz'. Österreichisches Archiv für Recht und Religion 65 (2018): 1–17.
Haunschmidt, A. 'Einige Fragen zur Alterspension für ehemalige Priester und Ordensleute der Katholischen Kirche'. Österreichisches Archiv für Recht und Religion 63 (2016): 248–274.
Heinig, H. M. 'Die Religion, die Kirchen und die europäische Grundrechtscharta'. *Zeitschrift für evangelisches Kirchenrecht 45* (2001): 440–464.

Heinig, H. M. 'Religiöse Pluralität und religionsrechtliche Diversität als Topoi in der Rechtsprechung des EGMR'. *Österreichisches Archiv für Recht und Religion* 60 (2013): 135–154.

Helfgott, N. 'Denkmalschutzgesetz und kirchliches Eigentum'. *Österreichisches Archiv für Kirchenrecht* 29 (1978): 426–445.

Hinghofer-Szalkay, S. 'Alleinvertretung des Islam im staatlichen Recht. Der Alleinvertretungsanspruch der IGGÖ zwischen Exklusivitätsprinzip, Zwangsgenossenschaft und Religionsfreiheit'. Österreichische Zeitschrift für öffentliches Recht 75 (2020): 773–799.Holzleithner, E. 'Kommentar zu EGMR 29. 4. 2002, Appl 2.346/02, Pretty vs Vereinigtes Königreich (Beihilfe zum Selbstmord)'. *Österreichisches Archiv für Recht und Religion* 50 (2003): 171–176.

Holzleithner, E. 'Das Diskriminierungsverbot aufgrund der sexuellen Orientierung: Reichweite und Grenzen'. *Österreichisches Archiv für Recht und Religion* 55 (2008): 251–265.

Höslinger, R. 'Das Ausschließlichkeitsrecht der Religionsgesellschaft'. *Österreichische Juristen-Zeitung* 2 (1947): 337–340.

Höslinger, R. 'Die gesetzliche Anerkennung einer Religionsgesellschaft'. *Österreichisches Archiv für Kirchenrecht* 4 (1953): 288–294.

Jandrokovic, M. 'Orthodoxer Religionsunterricht und ReligionslehrerInnenausbildung in Österreich'. Österreichsiches Archiv für Recht und Religion 63 (2016): 275–294.

Jisa, W. 'Zur Ausbildung der Religionslehrer in Österreich – eine gemeinsame Angelegenheit von Staat und Kirche?' *Österreichisches Archiv für Recht und Religion* 49 (2002): 377–393.

Jisa, W. 'Freikirchen in Österreich und Schule'. *Österreichisches Archiv für Recht und Religion* 60 (2013): 264–273.

Kalb, H. 'Durchsetzbarer Rechtsanspruch auf Anerkennung? Bemerkungen zum Verfassungsgerichtshoferkenntnis vom 12. 12. 1988, B 13/88, B 150/88'. *Österreichisches Archiv für Kirchenrecht* 39 (1990) 385–392, 40 (1991): 113–124.

Kalb, H. 'Kommentar zu OGH 12. 4. 1995, 9 Ob A 31/95'. *Das Recht der Arbeit* 46 (1996): 36–43.

Kalb, H. 'Kommentar zu OGH 22. 10. 1996, 10 Ob S 267/95'. *Das Recht der Arbeit* 47 (1997): 369–374.

Kalb, H. 'Kommentar zu VfGH 4. 3. 1999, B 565/97 (Theologische Lehranstalt, Prüfer)'. *Österreichisches Archiv für Recht und Religion* 47 (2000): 282–288.

Kalb, H. 'Die Katholisch-Theologische Universität Linz'. *Österreichisches Archiv für Recht und Religion* 47 (2000): 363–383.

Kalb, H. 'Kommentar zu VfGH 24. 6. 1999, B 1253/98 (Religionsbekenntnis im Meldezettel)'. *Österreichisches Archiv für Recht und Religion* 47 (2000): 404–410.

Kalb, H. 'Kommentar zu OGH 5. 9. 2000, 10 Ob S 121/00t (Weltpriester, Bundespflegegeld)'. *Österreichisches Archiv für Recht und Religion* 48 (2001): 272–281.

Kalb, H. 'Kommentar zu OGH, 5. 9. 2001, 9 Ob A 184/01a'. *Das Recht der Arbeit* 52 (2002): 470–475.

Kalb, H. 'Kommentar zu VwGH 21. 11. 2000, 99/11/0161 (Stellungspflicht, geistliches Amt)'. *Österreichisches Archiv für Recht und Religion* 49 (2002): 335–342.

Kalb, H. 'Kommentar zu BVerfG 2. 10. 2003, 1 BvR 536/03 (Vereinsverbot des 'Kalifatsstaates')'. *Österreichisches Archiv für Recht und Religion* 51 (2004): 469–483.

Kalb, H. 'Kommentar zu OGH 22. 6. 2011, 2 Ob 219/10k (Schadenminderungspflicht bei Verweigerung von Bluttransfusionen aus religiösen Gründen)'. *Juristische Blätter* 134 (2012): 251–256.

Kalb, H., R. Potz & B. Schinkele. 'Das Bundesgesetz über die Einrichtung einer Dokumentations- und Informationsstelle für Sektenfragen (EDISG)'. *Österreichisches Archiv für Recht und Religion* 46 (1999): 353–400.

Kalb, H., R. Potz & B. Schinkele, 'Österreichisches Religionsrecht in der jüngsten Straßburger Rechtsprechung'. *Österreichisches Archiv für Recht und Religion* 56 (2009): 400–432.

Kalb, H., R. Potz & B. Schinkele. 'Rechtsgeschäfte mit kirchlichen juristischen Personen'. *Österreichisches Archiv für Recht und Religion* 48 (2001): 353–418.

Kalb, H., R. Potz & B. Schinkele. 'Religions- und Weltanschauungsfreiheit im aktuellen österreichischen Verfassungsdiskurs'. *Österreichisches Archiv für Recht und Religion* 52 (2005): 1–37.

Kalb, H. & Wakolbinger, D. 'Das Kopftuch am Arbeitsplatz im Lichte der EuGH-Judikatur'. Journal für Arbeitsrecht und Sozialrecht 1 (2017): 154–176.

Klecatsky, H. R. 'Religionsfreiheit und Religionsdelikte'. *Österreichisches Archiv für Kirchenrecht* 21 (1970): 34–95.

Kletečka-Pulker, M. 'Seelsorger und Ethiker in Ethikkommissionen'. *Österreichisches Archiv für Recht und Religion* 47 (2000): 215–226.

Kneucker, R. 'Das neue Gleichbehandlungsrecht: Auswirkungen auf die Evangelische Kirche in Österreich'. *Österreichisches Archiv für Recht und Religion* 55 (2008): 238–250.

Kneucker, R. 'Verträge mit Kirchenleitungen'. *Österreichisches Archiv für Recht und Religion* 58 (2011): 293–309.

Kolb, E. 'Gegenwärtige Aufgaben der Kultusverwaltung in Österreich'. *Österreichisches Archiv für Kirchenrecht* 4 (1953): 38–52.

Koman, A. 'Mögliche Auswirkungen des Vergaberechts auf gemeinnützige Aktivitäten der Kirchen'. *Österreichisches Archiv für Recht und Religion* 50 (2003): 84–95.

Konrath, C. 'Vermittlung und Erinnerung. Anmerkungen zu den Präambeldiskussionen in der EU und in Österreich'. *Österreichisches Archiv für Recht und Religion* 51 (2004): 189–210.

Köstler, R. 'Religion und Religionsgenossenschaft'. *Juristische Blätter* 64 (1935): 339–343, 357–362, 378–382, 399–407.

Kowatsch, A. 'Staatliche Rechtsprechung in den inneren Angelegenheiten der Kirche? Anspruch und Grenzen des staatlichen Rechtsschutzmonopols. Ein Rechtsvergleich zwischen Österreich und Deutschland'. Archiv für katholisches Kirchenrecht 186 (2017-2019): 522–574.

Kowatsch, A. 'Gerichtliche Überprüfung von Konversionen als religionsrechtliche Herausforderung für den säkularen Staat'. Österreichisches Archiv für Recht und Religion 69 (2022): 1–48.

Kowatsch, A. 'Die freie Religionsausübung in Zeiten der Pandemie – ein religionsrechtlicher und kanonistischer Zwischenbericht'. Österreichisches Archiv für Recht und Religion 69 (2022): 225–297.

Krömer, P. 'Geistliches Amt in den Evangelischen Kirchen und Sozialversicherung'. *Österreichisches Archiv für Recht und Religion* 50 (2003): 123–148.

Krömer, P. 'Zur Problematik unterschiedlicher Rechtsvorschriften für Religionsgemeinschaften'. *Österreichisches Archiv für Recht und Religion* 57 (2010): 198–221.

Kronawetter, B. 'Zum Dienstverhältnis kirchlich bestellter Religionslehrer'. *Das Recht der Arbeit* 41 (1991): 198–201.

Kucsko-Stadlmayer, G. 'Die Rechtsprechung des österreichischen Verfassungsgerichtshofs auf dem Gebiet der Glaubensfreiheit'. *Europäische Grundrechte Zeitschrift* 26 (1999): 505–525.

Landau, M. 'Die Tätigkeit der Caritas vor dem Hintergrund ihres kirchlichen Anspruchs'. *Österreichisches Archiv für Recht und Religion* 55 (2008): 413–458.

Leisching, P. 'Haec Aedes Mysterium Adumbrat Ecclesiae. Kirchliches Recht zur Wahrung von Kunstwerken'. *Österreichisches Archiv für Kirchenrecht* 29 (1978): 340–351.

Leitner, S. 'Abgrenzung der sachlichen Zuständigkeit zwischen Bundes- und Landesverwaltungsgericht bei Beschwerden gegen Bescheide des Kultusministers'. *Österreichisches Archiv für Recht und Religion* 65 (2018): 18–30.

Lienbacher, G. 'Vereinsfreiheit und innere Angelegenheiten gesetzlich anerkannter Kirchen und Religionsgesellschaften. Zugleich eine Besprechung des Erkenntnisses des VfGH 11. 12. 2001, B 151/00'. *Zeitschrift für Verwaltung* 27 (2002): 647–654.

Luf, G. 'Grundrechte in Österreich. Gedanken zum Handbuch Berkas'. *Österreichisches Archiv für Recht und Religion* 47 (2000): 238–246.

Luf, G. 'Ethischer Pluralismus und staatliche Neutralität'. *Österreichisches Archiv für Recht und Religion* 50 (2003): 283–297.

Luf, G. 'Der säkulare Staat der Moderne als Herausforderung der politischen Theologie'. Religionen unterwegs 28 (1/2022): 4–11.

Luf, G., R. Potz & B. Schinkele. 'Gott in der Verfassung? Zur Frage der Erwähnung der religiösen Dimension in der Präambel des Vertrages über eine Verfassung für Europa'. *Österreichisches Archiv für Recht und Religion* 49 (2002): 353–360.

Luhmann, N. 'Die Gewissensfreiheit und das Gewissen'. *Archiv des öffentlichen Rechts* 90 (1965): 257–286.

Lumma, L. O. 'Staatliche Feiertage in Österreich: Anmerkungen aus katholisch-theologischer Perspektive'. Österreichisches Archiv für Recht und Religion 66 (2019): 258–268.

Margiotta Broglio, F. 'Gott in der Verfassung? Zur Frage der Erwähnung der religiösen Dimension in der Präambel des Vertrages über eine Verfassung für Europa'. *Österreichisches Archiv für Recht und Religion* 49 (2002): 365–367.

Mayr, K. 'Feiertage und Diskriminierung aufgrund der Religion im österreichischen Arbeitsrecht'. *ecolex* 15 (2004): 428–431.

Mazal, W. 'Religion und Weltanschauung. Zur Auslegung eines Tatbestands im GlBG'. Zeitschrift für Arbeits- und Sozialrecht 25 (2017): 140–146.

Mehmedi, I. 'Der lange Weg in die Freiheit: Das religiöse Selbstverständnis der Frei-Aleviten'. Österreichisches Archiv für Recht und Religion 69 (2022): 409–428.

Melichar, E. 'Die verfassungsrechtliche Stellung der gesetzlich anerkannten Religionsgesellschaften nach österreichischem Recht'. *Juristische Blätter* 79 (1957): 57–62, 91–96, 123–127.

Meyer-Teschendorf, K. G. 'Der Körperschaftsstatus der Kirchen. Zur Systemadäquanz des Art. 137 V WRV im pluralistischen Gemeinwesen des Grundgesetzes'. *Archiv des öffentlichen Rechts* 103 (1978): 289–333.

Mittermair, C. 'Religiöse Kindererziehung: Die Rolle der Eltern, der Pflegeltern, des KJHT und des Pflegschaftsgerichts'. Juristische Blätter 144 (2022): 212–225.

Mock, E. 'Der Eid als Problem der österreichischen Verfassungsordnung'. *Juristische Blätter* 99 (1977): 137–141.

Moser-Zoundjiekpon, B. 'Organisation von kulturellen Veranstaltungen in Einrichtungen der römisch-katholischen Kirche bzw durch solche'. *Österreichisches Archiv für Recht und Religion* 52 (2005): 393–423.

Muckel, S. 'Die Rechtsstellung der Kirchen und Religionsgemeinschaften nach dem Vertrag über eine Verfassung für Europa'. *Die Öffentliche Verwaltung* 59 (2005): 191–198.

Öhlinger, T. 'Die Grundrechte in Österreich. Ein systematischer Überblick'. *Europäische Grundrechte Zeitschrift* 9 (1982): 216–245.

Öhlinger, T. 'Gott in der Verfassung? Zur Frage der Erwähnung der religiösen Dimension in der Präambel des Vertrages über eine Verfassung für Europa'. *Österreichisches Archiv für Recht und Religion* 49 (2002): 368–371.

Pabel, K. 'Der Grundrechtsschutz für das Schächten'. *Europäische Grundrechte Zeitschrift* 29 (2002): 220–234.

Pabel, K. 'Religion im öffentlichen Schulwesen'. *Bildung und Religion. Schriften zum Bildungsrecht und zur Bildungspolitik* 10 (2006): 37–76.

Pabel, K. 'Verfassungsrechtliche Rahmenbedingungen des Religionsunterrichts in Österreich'. *Österreichisches Archiv für Recht und Religion* 59 (2012): 64–86.

Pernice, I. 'Religionsrechtliche Aspekte im europäischen Gemeinschaftsrecht'. *Juristen Zeitung* 32 (1977): 777–781.

Pernthaler, P. 'Gott in der Verfassung'. *Österreichisches Archiv für Recht und Religion* 47 (2000): 177–201.

Pernthaler, P. 'Gott in der Verfassung? Zur Frage der Erwähnung der religiösen Dimension in der Präambel des Vertrages über eine Verfassung für Europa'. *Österreichisches Archiv für Recht und Religion* 49 (2002): 374–376.

Pichler, H. 'Religionsfreiheit – Elternrechte – Kinderrechte'. *Österreichische Juristen-Zeitung* 52 (1997): 450–456.

Platzgummer, W. 'Herabwürdigung religiöser Lehren, Meinungsfreiheit und Freiheit der Kunst'. *Juristische Blätter* 117 (1995): 137–142.

Plöchl, W. M. 'Das neue österreichische Orthodoxengesetz'. *Österreichisches Archiv für Kirchenrecht* 20 (1969): 108–131.

Plöchl, W. M. 'Errichtung und Satzungen der bulgarisch-orthodoxen Kirchengemeinde zum heiligen Ivan Rilski und der russisch-orthodoxen Kirchengemeinde zum heiligen Nikolaus in Wien'. *Österreichisches Archiv für Kirchenrecht* 23 (1972): 195–211.

Pollack, D. 'Probleme der Definition von Religion'. Zeitschrift für Religion, Gesellschaft und Politik 1 (2017): 7–35.

Potz, A. 'Kommentar zu OGH 24. 2. 2009, 9 ObA 122/07t', *Österreichisches Archiv für Recht und Religion* 58 (2011): 210–223.

Potz, A. 'Das Karfreitagsdilemma: Ein Feiertag für alle oder niemanden?'. *ecolex* – Fachzeitschrift für Wirtschaftsrecht 28 (2017): 743–746.

Potz, A. 'Quo vadis Tendenzschutz?'. Das Recht der Arbeit 71 (2021): 13–23.

Potz, R. 'Das Religionsbekenntnis in der Volkszählung. Ein Beitrag zum Verhältnis von Kirche, Staat und Öffentlichkeit in Österreich'. *Österreichisches Archiv für Kirchenrecht* 39 (1990): 91–111.

Potz, R. 'Suum cuique – The Parity of the Recognized Churches and Religious Communities in Austria'. *European Journal for Church and State Research* 4 (1997): 187–204.

Potz, R. 'Europas Seele? Kirchen und Religionsgemeinschaften im europäischen Einigungsprozess'. *Österreichisches Archiv für Recht und Religion* 46 (1999): 6–13.

Potz, R. 'Das Datenschutzgesetz 2000 im religionsrechtlichen Kontext'. *Österreichisches Archiv für Recht und Religion* 47 (2000): 384–394.

Potz, R. 'Beeidigung eines Drusen nach der allgemeinen Eidesformel. Kommentar zu OGH 11. 11. 1999, 6 Ob 195/99s'. *Österreichisches Archiv für Recht und Religion* 47 (2000): 424–428.

Potz, R. 'Kommentar zu VfGH 11. 12. 2001, B 1510/00 (Untersagung, Initiativkreis)'. *Österreichisches Archiv für Recht und Religion* 49 (2002): 321–334.

Potz, R. 'Die Kirchen als Partner der Europäischen Union. Typen des Verhältnisses zwischen Kirche und Staat in den Mitgliedstaaten der Europäischen Union'. *Österreichisches Archiv für Recht und Religion* 50 (2003): 11–20.

Potz, R. 'Eintragung als Bekenntnisgemeinschaft, Vishwa Nirmala Dharma. Kommentar zu VwGH 15. 9. 2003, 2001/10/0139'. *Österreichisches Archiv für Recht und Religion* 51 (2004): 285–296.

Potz, R. 'Ist das Konkordat noch zeitgemäß?' *Österreichisches Archiv für Recht und Religion* 53 (2006): 64–86.

Potz, R. 'Aktuelle Fragen des österreichischen Religionsrechtes'. *Österreichisches Archiv für Recht und Religion* 56 (2009): 201–213.

Potz R. & B. Schinkele, 'Das Orthodoxengesetz 1967 und die serbisch-orthodoxe Kirchengemeinde zum Hl. Sava in Wien'. *Österreichisches Archiv für Kirchenrecht* 44 (1995–97): 197–224.

Potz, R. & B. Schinkele. 'Die 'Scientology-Kirche Österreich' – die Voraussetzungen für den Erwerb der Rechtspersönlichkeit als eingetragene religiöse Bekenntnisgemeinschaft'. *Österreichisches Archiv für Recht und Religion* 46 (1999): 206–251.

Potz, R. & B. Schinkele. 'Im Spannungsfeld von kirchlichem Selbstbestimmungsrecht und Universitätsautonomie: Das konkordatäre Zustimmungsrecht des Bischofs'. *Österreichisches Archiv für Recht und Religion* 49 (2002): 401–448.

Potz, R. & B. Schinkele. 'Kommentar zu EGMR 13. 2. 2003, Appl 41.340/98 ua, Refah partisi ua vs Türkei (Parteiverbot, Scharia, Demokratie)'. *Österreichisches Archiv für Recht und Religion* 51 (2004): 484–520.

Potz, R. & B. Schinkele. 'Gutachten zu den religionsrechtlichen Aspekten des Niederösterreichischen Kindergartengesetzes'. *Österreichisches Archiv für Recht und Religion* 57 (2010): 395–412

Potz, R. & B. Schinkele. 'Eintragung bzw gesetzliche Anerkennung alevitischer Gruppen in Österreich'. *Österreichisches Archiv für Recht und Religion* 58 (2011): 137–155.

Potz, R. & B. Schinkele. 'Das neue Israelitengesetz 2012'. *Österreichisches Archiv für Recht und Religion* 60 (2013): 303–335.

Potz R. & Schinkele, B. 'Zur Eintragung der Frei-Alevitischen Glaubensgemeinschaft in Österreich'. Österreichisches Archiv für Recht und Religion 69 (2022): 301–345.

Potz R. & E. Synek, 'Zur Novellierung des Bundesgesetzes über die äußeren Rechtsverhältnisse der griechisch-orthodoxen Kirche in Österreich'. *Österreichisches Archiv für Recht und Religion* 59 (2012): 391–404.

Potz, R. & J. Wallner, 'Antidiskriminierung und theologische Bildungseinrichtungen'. *Österreichisches Archiv für Recht und Religion* 55 (2008): 304–326.

Pree, H. 'Die vermögensrechtliche Lage ausgeschiedener Religionsen nach kanonischem Recht und staatlichem Recht unter Berücksichtigung der 29. ASVG-Novelle'. *Österreichisches Archiv für Kirchenrecht* 24 (1973): 303–327.

Pree, H. 'Die Hintergründe der vermögensrechtlichen Sonderbehandlung von Klerikern und Ordensleuten im österreichischen bürgerlichen Recht'. *Österreichisches Archiv für Kirchenrecht* 26 (1975): 290–323.

Pree, H. 'Kirchliche Lehraufsicht und österreichisches Bundesverfassungsrecht'. *Österreichisches Archiv für Kirchenrecht* 29 (1978): 82–115.

Primetshofer, B. 'Zur Frage der staatlichen Wirkung kirchlicher Ehen'. *Österreichisches Archiv für Kirchenrecht* 12 (1961): 131–148.

Primetshofer, B. 'Die Bestellung akademischer Lehrer an katholisch-theologischen Fakultäten Österreichs'. *Österreichisches Archiv für Kirchenrecht* 39 (1990): 153–161.

Primetshofer, B. 'Church and State in Austria in 1995–1996'. *European Journal for Church and State Research* 3 (1996): 83–91.

Primetshofer, B. 'Church and State in Austria in 1996–1997'. *European Journal for Church and State Research* 4 (1997): 121–131.

Reingrabner, G. 'Das Protestantengesetz – 'Unerledigte Wünsche Streit' von damals'. *Österreichisches Archiv für Recht und Religion* 58 (2011): 249–292.

Rinnerthaler, A. 'Von Glöckel bis Rintelen – Kontroversen um die religiösen Übungen in der Ersten Republik und im Ständestaat'. *Österreichisches Archiv für Recht und Religion* 50 (2003): 372–404.

Runggaldier, U. 'Kommentar zu OGH 5. 9. 2001, 9 Ob A 184/01a (Kirchenautonomie, Mitarbeitervertretung)'. *Österreichisches Archiv für Recht und Religion* 49 (2002): 488–505.

Schacherreiter, J. 'Kommentar zu OGH 22. 6. 2011, 2 Ob 219/10k (Schadenminderungspflicht bei Verweigerung von Bluttransfusionen aus religiösen Gründen)'. *Österreichisches Archiv für Recht und Religion* 60 (2013): 207–223.

Schima, J. 'Die gemeinsamen Angelegenheiten von Kirche und Staat'. *Österreichische Juristen-Zeitung* 20 (1965): 523–541, 565–571.

Schima, J. 'Ende des kirchlichen Ausschließlichkeitsrechts'. *Österreichische Juristen-Zeitung* 37 (1982): 141–147, 169–173.

Schima, J. 'Das Islamgesetz und die Grenzen der Verfassungsgerichtsbarkeit'. *Österreichische Juristen-Zeitung* 44 (1989): 545–555.

Schima, S. 'Kommentar zu VfGH 6. 10. 1999, B 15/99 (Gefängnisseelsorge)'. *Österreichisches Archiv für Recht und Religion* 47 (2000): 266–268.

Schima, S. 'Die religionsrechtlichen Aspekte des Ersten Bundesrechtsbereinigungsgesetzes 1999'. *Österreichisches Archiv für Recht und Religion* 48 (2001): 200–219, 49 (2002): 190–229, 449–463.

Schima, S. 'Die wichtigsten religionsrechtlichen Regelungen des Bundesrechts und des Landesrechts, Jahrgang 2005'. *Österreichisches Archiv für Recht und Religion* 53 (2006): 272–317.

Schima, S. 'Das IslamG im Kontext des österreichischen Religionsrechts'. *Österreichisches Archiv für Recht und Religion* 59 (2012): 225–250.

Schima, S. 'Taufe, Schahada, Beschneidung oder auch gar nix? Zugehörigkeit zu einer Religionsgemeinschaft'. Zeitschrift für Familien- und Erbrecht 16 (2021): 167–172.

Schima, S. 'Die wichtigsten religionsrechtlichen Regelungen des Bundesrechts und des Landesrechts im Jahr 2017'. Österreichisches Archiv für Recht und Religion 70 (2023) [in press].

Schinkele, B. 'Zur Weltanschauungsfreiheit in Österreich'. *Österreichisches Archiv für Kirchenrecht* 39 (1990): 50–80.

Schinkele, B. 'Kommentar zu OGH 9. 9. 1999, 8 Ob A 230/99b (§867 ABGB)'. *Österreichisches Archiv für Recht und Religion* 47 (2000): 289–294.

Schinkele, B. 'Kommentar zu VwGH 30. 4. 1999, 98/16/0317 (Gemeinnützigkeit)'. *Österreichisches Archiv für Recht und Religion* 47 (2000): 411–418.

Schinkele, B. 'Zur öffentlich-rechtlichen Stellung von Religionsgemeinschaften'. *Juridikum* 13 (2001): 123–130.

Schinkele, B. 'Kommentar zu VfGH 3. 3. 2001, B 1713/98; 14. 3. 2001, B 98/99; VfGH 14. 3. 2001, G 68/99 (Anerkennungsvoraussetzungen BekGG)'. *Österreichisches Archiv für Recht und Religion* 48 (2001): 239–261.

Schinkele, B. 'Religiöse Bekenntnisgemeinschaften und verfassungsrechtlicher Vertrauensschutz'. *Juristische Blätter* 124 (2002): 498–509.

Schinkele, B. 'Kommentar zu EGMR 18. 2. 1999, Appl 24645/94, Buscarini & della Balda vs San Marino (Religiöser Eid)'. *Österreichisches Archiv für Recht und Religion* 49 (2002): 293–295.

Schinkele, B. 'Kommentar zu EGMR 6. 4. 2000, Appl 34369/97, Thlimmenos vs Griechenland (Diskriminierung, Wirtschaftsprüfer)'. *Österreichisches Archiv für Recht und Religion* 49 (2002): 305–309.

Schinkele, B. 'Kommentar zu EGMR 15. 2. 2001, Appl 42393/98, Dahlab vs Schweiz (Islamisches Kopftuch, Lehrerin)'. *Österreichisches Archiv für Recht und Religion* 49 (2002): 310–320.

Schinkele, B. 'Die Kirchen als Arbeitgeber. Herausforderungen im Zusammenhang mit dem Tendenzschutz, dem Gebot der Nichtdiskriminierung und der Anerkennung von Schul- und Berufsausbildungen'. *Österreichisches Archiv für Recht und Religion* 50 (2003): 56–75.

Schinkele, B. Gewissensgebot und Normativität des positiven Rechts. Überlegungen unter besonderer Berücksichtigung des so genannten 'Kirchenasyls'. *Österreichisches Archiv für Recht und Religion* 50 (2003): 448–480.
Schinkele, B. 'Church and State in Austria in 2003'. *European Journal for Church and State Research* 11 (2004): 45–58.
Schinkele, B. 'Kommentar zu BVerfG 24. 9. 2003, 2 BvR 1436/02 (islamisches Kopftuch, Lehrerin)'. *Österreichisches Archiv für Recht und Religion* 51 (2004): 61–64.
Schinkele, B. 'Zum 'Streit' um das islamische Kopftuch. Kommentar zu BVerfG 24. 9. 2003 – 2 BvR 1436/02 (unter Berücksichtigung von BAG 10. 10. 2002, 2 AZR 472/01, BVerfG 30. 7. 2003, 1 BvR 792/03)'. *Recht der Wirtschaft* 22 (2004): 30–37.
Schinkele, B. 'Die Rechtsstellung der Orientalisch-orthodoxen Kirchen in Österreich nach dem Orientalisch-orthodoxen Kirchengesetz 2003 unter besonderer Berücksichtigung der Koptisch-orthodoxen Kirche'. *Österreichisches Archiv für Recht und Religion* 51 (2004): 221–243.
Schinkele, B. 'Kommentar zu VfGH 3. 10. 2003, B 1408/02 (Religionsbekenntnis in Personenstandsurkunde, Jehovas Zeugen)'. *Österreichisches Archiv für Recht und Religion* 51 (2004): 269–274.
Schinkele, B. 'Kommentar zu VfGH 10. 10. 2003, B 1768/02 (Ausländerbeschäftigung, Jehovas Zeugen)'. *Österreichisches Archiv für Recht und Religion* 51 (2004): 275–281.
Schinkele, B. 'Kommentar zu VwGH 18. 3. 2003, 2002/11/0256 (Befreiung vom Zivildienst, Jehovas Zeugen)'. *Österreichisches Archiv für Recht und Religion* 51 (2004): 282–284.
Schinkele, B. 'Kirchliches Arbeitsrecht in der aktuellen Rechtsprechung des Europäischen Gerichtshofs für Menschenrechte'. *Österreichisches Archiv für Recht und Religion* 55 (2008): 155–173.
Schinkele, B. 'Religionsfreiheit und europäisches Antidiskriminierungsrecht – Einige grundsätzliche Überlegungen'. *Österreichisches Archiv für Recht und Religion* 55 (2008): 179–211.
Schinkele, B. 'Staat – Kirche – Schule und das neue Gleichbehandlungsrecht'. *Österreichisches Archiv für Recht und Religion* 55 (2008): 179–211.
Schinkele, B. Die öffentlich-rechtliche Stellung von Religionsgemeinschaften – eine aktuelle Herausforderung. *Österreichisches Archiv für Recht und Religion* 56 (2009): 358–374.
Schinkele, B. 'Zum Tendenzschutz von gesetzlich anerkannten Kirchen und Religionsgesellschaften – Überlegungen aus Anlass des OGH-Beschlusses 8. 1. 2009, 9 ObA 156/08v'. *Recht der Wirtschaft* 27 (2009): 678–685.
Schinkele, B. 'Beschneidung von nicht einwilligungsfähigen Knaben'. *Recht der Medizin* 19 (2012): 277–283.
Schinkele, B. 'Aktuelle Fragen des österreichischen Anerkennungsrechts am Beispiel evangelischer Freikirchen und alevitischer Gruppierungen'. *Religionen unterwegs* 19 (2013): 17–23.
Schinkele, B. 'Positive und negative Religionsfreiheit – zwei Seiten einer Medaille? Zugleich eine Besprechung des EGMR-Urteils Grzelak gegen Polen'. *Österreichisches Archiv für Recht und Religion* 60 (2013): 23–45.

Schinkele, B. 'Gesetzliche Anerkennung der 'Freikirchen in Österreich' aus religionsrechtlicher Sicht'. *Österreichisches Archiv für Recht und Religion* 60 (2013): 357–363.

Schinkele, B. 'Von der Religionsbeschimpfung zur 'Hassrede' – einige Überlegungen'. Österreichisches Archiv für Recht und Religion 64 (2017): 497–515.

Schinkele, B. 'Ist die „Kirche des Fliegenden Spaghettimonsters' eine Religionsgemeinschaft bzw ihre "Lehre" eine Religion?'. Österreichisches Archiv für Recht und Religion 67 (2020): 1–45.

Schmied, M. 'Die Islamische Religionspädagogische Akademie (IRPA)'. *Österreichisches Archiv für Recht und Religion* 46 (1999): 434–443.

Schrammel, W. 'Diskriminierungsverbot, Privatautonomie und Religionsfreiheit'. *Österreichisches Archiv für Recht und Religion* 55 (2008): 219–227.

Schwarz, E. & K. Schwarz. 'Die Evangelische Religionspädagogische Akademie (ERPA)'. *Österreichisches Archiv für Recht und Religion* 48 (2001): 1–14.

Schwarz, K. 'Der 'Anschluss' 1938 und seine unmittelbaren staatskirchenrechtlichen Folgen für die Evangelische Kirche'. *Österreichisches Archiv für Kirchenrecht* 38 (1989): 268–284.

Schwarz, K. 'Befreite Kirchen im freien Staat. Zur Religionspolitik der Republik Österreich in den 50er-Jahren'. *Österreichisches Archiv für Kirchenrecht* 44 (1995–97): 289–314.

Schwarz, K. 'Der RU in der Schule – eine 'gemeinsame Angelegenheit' von Staat und Kirche zur Gewährleistung religiöser Interessen in der Gesellschaft'. *Schulfach Religion* 21 (2002): 225–242.

Schwarz, K. 'Religionsfreiheit und Religionsgemeinschaften in den rechtlichen-Strukturen eines künftigen Europa'. *Österreichisches Archiv für Recht und Religion* 50 (2003): 43–55.

Schwarz, K. 'Eine kultusrechtliche Quadratur des Kreises?Anmerkungen zur gesetzlichen Anerkennung der Herrnhuter Brüderkirche im Jahre 1880'. *Österreichisches Archiv für Recht und Religion* 50 (2003): 481–496.

Schwarz, K. 'Zwischen Subvention, Mitgliedsbeitrag und Kultursteuer: Wege der Kirchenfinanzierung in Österreich'. *Österreichisches Archiv für Recht und Religion* 51 (2004): 244–260.

Schwarz, K. 'Polizeiseelsorge – berufsfeldbezogene Supervision vor dem Hintergrund der Religionsfreiheit'. *Österreichisches Archiv für Recht und Religion* 55 (2008): 30–46.

Schwarz, K. 'Das Anerkennungsrecht aus der Sicht der Kultusbehörde'. *Österreichisches Archiv für Recht und Religion* 57 (2010): 228–236

Schwarz, K. 'Von der Kirchenhoheit zur Kirchenfreiheit'. *Österreichisches Archiv für Recht und Religion* 58 (2011): 233–248.

Schwarz, K. 'Freikirchen' in Österreich und 'Staatskirchenrecht' – eine österreichische Problemgeschichte. *Österreichisches Archiv für Recht und Religion* 60 (2013): 347–356.

Synek, E. 'Kommentar zu EGMR 13. 12. 2001, Appl 45.701/99, Metropolitane Kirche von Bessarabien u.a. /. Moldawien (religiöse Neutralität)'. *Österreichisches Archiv für Recht und Religion* 50 (2003): 156–170.

Synek, E. 'Zur staatlichen Anerkennung orthodoxer Kirchengemeinden in Österreich. Einige grundsätzliche Überlegungen anlässlich der staatlichen Anerkennung der Antiochenisch-Orthodoxen Kirchengemeinde zu den Heiligen Petrus und Paulus in Wien'. Österreichisches Archiv für Recht und Religion 66 (2019): 165–184.

Thurnhart, R. 'Privatrechtlicher Vertrauensschutz und §867 ABGB'. *Österreichisches Archiv für Recht und Religion* 48 (2001): 419–454.

Tichy, H. 'Religiöse Gemeinschaften nach dem Vereinsgesetz 2002'. *Österreichisches Archiv für Recht und Religion* 51 (2004): 379–397.

Tichy, H. 'Die Abgrenzung zwischen religiöser und ethnischer Diskriminierung nach den EU-Gleichbehandlungsrichtlinien'. *Österreichisches Archiv für Recht und Religion* 55 (2008): 266–278.

Torfs, R. 'Die rechtliche Sonderstellung von Kirchen und religiösen Gemeinschaften im europäischen Kontext'. *Österreichisches Archiv für Recht und Religion* 46 (1999): 14–45.

Torfs, R. 'Warum das EU-Recht für Kirchenjuristen immer wichtiger wird'. *Österreichisches Archiv für Recht und Religion* 50 (2003): 21–42.

Trauner, K.-R. 'Wandel von Staat und Kirche am Fallbeispiel Militärseelsorge'. *Österreichisches Archiv für Recht und Religion* 59 (2012): 174–198.

Trofaier-Leskovar, V. 'Die "Kirche des Fliegenden Spaghettimonsters"'. Ein religionsrechtliches Verfahren wird zu einer 'unendlichen Geschichte'. Österreichisches Archiv für Recht und Religion 67 (2020): 84–99.

Ulrich, S. 'Kopftuchverbote – Neutralitätspolitik von Unternehmen auf dem Prüfstand'. Österreichisches Archiv für Recht und Religion 64 (2017): 560–571.

Wallner, J. 'Strafrecht und Kunstfreiheit im Kontext der religiös-weltanschaulichen Sphäre. Überlegungen anhand eines Anlassfalls'. *Österreichisches Archiv für Recht und Religion* 49 (2002): 239–259.

Wallner, J. 'Beschneidung von nicht einwilligungsfähigen Knaben'. *Recht der Medizin* 19 (2012): 277–283.

Weninger, M. 'Einige der wesentlichen religionsrechtlichen und kirchenpolitischen Aspekte des EU-Verfassungsvertrages'. *Österreichisches Archiv für Recht und Religion* 50 (2003): 96–102.

Wibiral, N. 'Liturgie und Denkmalpflege nach dem Zweiten Vaticanum'. *Österreichisches Archiv für Kirchenrecht* 29 (1978): 352–395.

Wieser, B. 'Wohnsitznahme und Zugehörigkeit zur evangelischen Kirche – zugleich zur Rechtspersönlichkeit der Schwedischen Evangelischen Gemeinde AB in Österreich'. Österreichisches Archiv für Recht und Religion 63 (2016): 343–366.

Wieshaider, W. 'Kommentar zu VfGH 4. 12. 1999, B 1518/98, B 1519/98 (Freie Versammlung, Totengedenken)'. *Österreichisches Archiv für Recht und Religion* 47 (2000): 268–281.

Wieshaider, W. 'Auswirkungen der Novelle 1999 zum Denkmalschutzgesetz auf die Religionsgemeinschaften'. *Österreichisches Archiv für Recht und Religion* 47 (2000): 395–403.

Wieshaider, W. 'Stellungnahmen von religiösen und weltanschaulichen Gemeinschaften zum Entwurf einer Grundrechtscharta der Europäischen Union'. *Österreichisches Archiv für Recht und Religion* 48 (2001): 78–91.

Wieshaider, W. 'Kommentar zu VwGH 23. 2. 2001, 98/06/0240 (Kleinkapelle, Baubewilligung)'. *Österreichisches Archiv für Recht und Religion* 48 (2001): 262–271.

Wieshaider, W. 'Auswirkungen der Novelle 1999 zum Denkmalschutzgesetz auf die Religionsgemeinschaften'. *Österreichisches Archiv für Recht und Religion* 49 (2002): 395–403.

Wieshaider, W. 'Profane Regeln für sakrale Bauten. Religionsrechtliche Aspekte des Raumordnungs- und Baurechts'. *Baurechtliche Blätter* 4 (2003): 138–148.

Wieshaider, W. 'Iterum: Schächten: Rund ums neue österreichische Tierschutzgesetz'. *Österreichisches Archiv für Recht und Religion* 52 (2005): 227–262.

Wieshaider, W. 'Das staatliche Feiertagsrecht als vergessene Umsetzungsmaterie der Richtlinie 2000/78/EG'. *Österreichisches Archiv für Recht und Religion* 55 (2008): 279–289.

Wieshaider, W. 'Der Begriff religiöser Einrichtungen im Kulturgüterrückgaberecht'. Österreichisches Archiv für Recht und Religion 64 (2017): 662–675.

Wieshaider, W. 'Jagdgründe fürs Schächten'. Österreichisches Archiv für Recht und Religion 68 (2021): 244–274.

Windisch-Graetz, M. 'Antidiskriminierungsrecht und Selbstbestimmungsrecht der Kirchen'. *Österreichisches Archiv für Recht und Religion* 55 (2008): 228–237.

Windisch-Graetz, M. 'Freistellung bei Entgeltfortzahlung aus religiösen Gründen'. Zeitschrift für Arbeits- und Sozialrecht 52 (2017): 147–151.

Winter, F. '40 Jahre Buddhistische Religionsgesellschaft in Österreich'. Religionen unterwegs 29 (1/2023): 32-34.

Zellenberg, U. E. 'Effektiver Sonntagsschutz oder Staatszielbestimmungen mit Placebowirkung?' *Österreichisches Archiv für Recht und Religion* 49 (2002): 260–278.

Selected Bibliography

Index

The numbers here refer to paragraph numbers.

Index

www.ingramcontent.com/pod-product-compliance
Lightning Source LLC
Chambersburg PA
CBHW070242030525
26096CB00033B/1224